European Churches and Chinese Temples as Neuro-Theatrical Sites

Cognition, Poetics, and the Arts

The **Cognition, Poetics, and the Arts** series fosters high-quality interdisciplinary research at the intersection of the cognitive sciences and the arts that focuses on cognitive approaches to literatures, arts, and cultures from around the world with three major objectives: (1) to develop theories and methodologies that further our understanding of the arts as central and complex operations of human minding; (2) to investigate the ways models of minding and artistic creation and reception that have been developed and revised in relation to each other throughout history and in different cultural contexts; and (3) to develop theoretical and methodological understandings of how the arts illuminate and contribute to the cognitive sciences.

Series Editors
Alexander Bergs, University of Osnabrück, Germany
Margaret H. Freeman, Myrifield Institute for Cognition and the Arts, USA
Peter Schneck, University of Osnabrück, Germany

Volumes in the Series:
Emily Dickinson's Poetic Art: A Cognitive Reading, by Margaret H. Freeman
Rhythm in Modernist Poetry: An Essay in Cognitive Versification Studies, by Eva Lilja
European Churches and Chinese Temples as Neuro-Theatrical Sites, by Mark Pizzato
Cognition in the Poem: Processes of Subjectivity in Comparative Poetics, by Victor Bermúdez (forthcoming)
Thinking through Poems: Composition, Emotion, and Decision-Making in Romantic-Era Women's Novels, by Yasemin Hacioglu (forthcoming)

European Churches and Chinese Temples as Neuro-Theatrical Sites

Mark Pizzato

BLOOMSBURY ACADEMIC
NEW YORK • LONDON • OXFORD • NEW DELHI • SYDNEY

BLOOMSBURY ACADEMIC
Bloomsbury Publishing Inc, 1359 Broadway, New York, NY 10018, USA
Bloomsbury Publishing Plc, 50 Bedford Square, London, WC1B 3DP, UK
Bloomsbury Publishing Ireland, 29 Earlsfort Terrace, Dublin 2, D02 AY28, Ireland

BLOOMSBURY, BLOOMSBURY ACADEMIC and the Diana logo are trademarks of
Bloomsbury Publishing Plc

First published in the United States of America 2024
Paperback edition published 2026

Copyright © Mark Pizzato, 2024

For legal purposes Acknowledgments on p. xii constitute
an extension of this copyright page.

Cover design by Tjaša Krivec and Eleanor Rose
Cover image © Mark Pizzato

Online resources to accompany this book are available at
www.bloomsburyonlineresources.com/european-churches-and-chinese-
temples-as-neuro-theatrical-sites. If you experience any problems,
please contact Bloomsbury at: onlineresources@bloomsbury.com

All rights reserved. No part of this publication may be: i) reproduced or transmitted in any form, electronic or mechanical, including photocopying, recording or by means of any information storage or retrieval system without prior permission in writing from the publishers; or ii) used or reproduced in any way for the training, development or operation of artificial intelligence (AI) technologies, including generative AI technologies. The rights holders expressly reserve this publication from the text and data mining exception as per Article 4(3) of the Digital Single Market Directive (EU) 2019/790.

Bloomsbury Publishing Inc does not have any control over, or responsibility for, any
third-party websites referred to or in this book. All internet addresses given in this
book were correct at the time of going to press. The author and publisher regret
any inconvenience caused if addresses have changed or sites have ceased to
exist, but can accept no responsibility for any such changes.

Whilst every effort has been made to locate copyright holders the publishers would be
grateful to hear from any person(s) not here acknowledged.

Library of Congress Cataloging-in-Publication Data
Names: Pizzato, Mark, 1960– author.
Title: European churches and Chinese temples as neuro-theatrical sites / Mark Pizzato.
Description: New York : Bloomsbury Academic, 2024. |
Series: Cognition, poetics, and the arts | Includes bibliographical references and index.
Identifiers: LCCN 2023043353 (print) | LCCN 2023043354 (ebook) |
ISBN 9798765109113 (hardback) | ISBN 9798765109106 (paperback) |
ISBN 9798765109120 (ebook) | ISBN 9798765109137 (pdf)
Subjects: LCSH: Church buildings–Europe–Psychological aspects. | Temples–China–
Psychological aspects. | Experience (Religion) | Performance–Religious aspects.
Classification: LCC NA5450 .P49 2024 (print) | LCC NA5450 (ebook) |
DDC 726.5094—dc23/eng/20231206
LC record available at https://lccn.loc.gov/2023043353
LC ebook record available at https://lccn.loc.gov/2023043354

ISBN:	HB:	979-8-7651-0911-3
	PB:	979-8-7651-0910-6
	ePDF:	979-8-7651-0913-7
	eBook:	979-8-7651-0912-0

Series: Cognition, Poetics, and the Arts

Typeset by RefineCatch Ltd, Bungay, Suffolk

For product safety related questions contact productsafety@bloomsbury.com.

To find out more about our authors and books, visit www.bloomsbury.com
and sign up for our newsletters.

*Dedicated to Amanda
(Zhou Aihua)
who gave me initial access to China,
introduced me to many temples,
and continues to enlighten me
with her beauty and joy
(wo feichang ai ni)*

Contents

List of Diagrams	viii
List of Tables	ix
List of Illustrations	x
Acknowledgments	xii
Introduction	1
1 Evolving Neuro-Theatrical Elements	39
2 Monumental Developments in Patriarchal, Maternal, and Trickster Designs	103
3 Places and Spaces with Super-Natural Translations	175
4 Conclusions	243
Works Cited	277
Index	299

Diagrams

1.1	Typical Ground Plans of European Churches and Chinese Temples	58
1.2	Levels of Animal Legacies within the Human Brain	69
1.3	Ancient Theatre Theories of Emotions and Catharsis	84
1.4	Moral Emotions in Psychology, Linguistics, Philosophy, and Neuro-Theatre	86
1.5	Sources and Solutions to Human Suffering	89
1.6	Family Extensions of the Brain's Inner Theatre (IT) toward a Cosmic Theatre	98

Tables

1.1	Transformations of Animal Drives into Human Emotions and Cultural Values	40
1.2	Inner Theatre Elements	51
1.3	Brain Hemisphere Functions	56
1.4	Neuroscience Research on Ecstatic Experiences	66
1.5	Western and Eastern Cognition with Church/Temple Extensions	78
1.6	Ideal Affects and Self Models	81
1.7	Moral Foundations Theory	87
1.8	European (and Jerusalem) Sites Selected as Representative	99
1.9	Chinese Sites Selected as Representative	100

Illustrations

Below is a list of photographs reproduced in the book, duplicated from a larger bank of images found in the accompanying online resources: www.bloomsburyonlineresources.com/european-churches-and-chinese-temples-as-neuro-theatrical-sites. The numbering system throughout the book corresponds to the online images as photographs not printed here are also referenced within the text.

All photos and videos were created by the author. He apologizes for any unfocused ones.

2.10	Fresco of people with upraised arms, under Basilica of Saints John and Paul	110
2.45	Interior of Saint Constantina	119
2.50	Interior of Saint Agnes Outside the Walls with *matroneum* and mosaic	120
2.67	Incense burner and Mao bust, with other deities, Tianning Temple	123
2.86	Tianning pagoda, Budai shrine, and dragon pillar, viewed from Triratna Hall	126
2.122	View of temple from Tianning pagoda	128
2.133	Guardian statues near entrance of Wanfo Dong Cave	130
2.186	Laughing Budai-Maitreya at Thousand Buddha Mountain	133
2.193	Giant Leshan Maitreya cliff carving	134
2.209	Apse view of chancel screen and Three Kings reliquary, Cologne Cathedral	137
2.213	Tympanum with Last Judgment and hell-mouth, Strasbourg Cathedral	139
2.229	Copenhagen's Church of Our Savior	140
2.268	Cathedral of Syracuse	146
2.282	Iconostasis in Uspenski Orthodox Cathedral	148
2.316	Interior of Saint Stephen in the Round	151
2.347	Dome mosaic of Ravenna's Arian Baptistery	157
2.350	Lateran Baptistery interior	159

2.386	Coin play and incense bow in Jing'an Temple	161
2.410	Monk and family with offerings for burning in Baohua Temple	163
2.415	Donglin Temple entry gate	165
2.438	Multi-headed, multi-armed Avalokiteshvara in Yunxiang Temple	166
3.94	Visitor touches Peter's statue in Saint Peter's Basilica	188
3.126	Cliff-carved Buddhas and sutra trip, Feilai Feng	195
3.185	800-year-old Wei Tuo statue, Lingyin Temple	198
3.201	Manjushri and arhats, 500 Arhats Hall, Lingyin Temple	199
3.212	Amitabha flower-burning rite, Lingyin Temple	200
3.236	Lay women and monks near Medicine Buddha, Lingyin Temple	202
3.342	Daoist Blessing Star Guardian God in Yongfu Buddhist Temple	207
3.365	Three Guanyin figures in Taoguang Buddhist Temple	208
3.529	Guanyin scene and Samantabhadra in corner, Middle Tianzhu Temple	212
3.592	Kings of the East and South, with feet on *asuras*, Upper Tianzhu Temple	215
3.674	Visitor bowing below arhat wall, Upper Tianzhu Temple	217
3.744	Hall of Prayer for Good Harvests, Temple of Heaven	221
3.848	Gatehouse roof figures, Temple of Heaven	223
3.926	Circular Mound to Lingxing Gates and Imperial Vault, Temple of Heaven	226
3.1045	Initial stairway, trees, and guard lions, Sanyuan Palace	230
3.1140	True Man Sun on a water buffalo, Sanyuan Palace	233
3.1162	Finnish Lutheran Cathedral	235
3.1288	Lutheran Rock Church interior	237
3.1340	Ground plan and reflection of Kamppi Chapel of Silence in its window	238

Acknowledgments

Earlier versions of Diagrams 1.2, 1.3, and 1.4, and Tables 1.1, 1.2, 1.3, and 1.6 were published in my previous books, *Beast-People Onscreen and in Your Brain* (2016) and *Mapping Global Theatre Histories* (2019).

Thanks to the editors of this series and to the Bloomsbury staff, especially Amy Martin, Hali Han, and Lisa Carden, for their work on our project—and to the anonymous reader who sent fourteen pages of additional notes. Thanks to colleagues in the "Origins" reading group at UNC-Charlotte, who commented on an early draft of this book: Bill Chu, Travis Jones, Ron Lunsford, Joanne Maguire, Jon Marks, and Trevor Pearce. Thanks to David Bashor, whose discussions with me about biology, neuroscience, and the humanities continue to inspire, years after his death. Thanks also to David, Bill, and Mirsad Hadzikadic for the hours of helpful discussions (with various guests) in our podcast, "Conversations about Buddha, Jesus, and Mohammed." Thanks to cognitive psychologist Bernard Baars for meeting with me two decades ago and replying to my later emails, when I started applying his theatre metaphors in my books. And thanks to cultural psychologist Jeanne Tsai for her friendly encouragement when meeting with me and hearing about this project at the Society for Affective Science conference in Boston in 2019.

Thanks to my students who gave me many insights through the honors course that I taught, across several semesters, related to this research. Thanks as well to the librarians at UNC-Charlotte, especially Patricia Quinn and Sue Pardue, who helped me get the books I needed and keep them beyond their normal due dates. And thanks to UNC-Charlotte for funding parts of my research travel across a decade and my Reassignment of Duties Leave in spring 2023 with time to complete this book.

Thanks to the Buddhist monk, Kosho Finch, who answered my questions in various Zoom meetings. Thanks to Aihua Zhou, who helped me with Chinese translations and temple visits. Thanks also to Richard Schechner for encouraging our group to visit Tianning Temple, when we were in Changzhou through the generosity of the Shanghai Theatre Academy (STA) after it held the Performance Studies International conference in 2014. Special thanks to Lu Jun and Shen Daniel, who started my Chinese odyssey by bringing me to lecture at STA in 2012, and Huang Yiming of STA, who helped me visit temples and (for many years) answered my questions about Daoism and Buddhism, introducing me to others with insights (including Master Cheren).

I am also grateful for insights from David Mozina, Janna Shed, and Alexandra Kaloyanides, regarding those religions—plus Kent Brintnall, Eric Hoenes del Pinal, Sean McCloud, James Tabor, Barbara Thiede, and Will Sherman about Christianity, Judaism, and Islam. Dale Grote helped with a biblical Greek/Latin translation. UNC-Charlotte architecture professors Zhongjie Lin, Brook Muller, Eric Sauda, and Peter

Wong gave me valuable suggestions as well. Professor Lin even took me on a tour of Suzhou temples, which I hope to write about in a subsequent book. So, thanks again to all of them. And finally, thanks to my father, John Frank (Gianfranco) Pizzato, who passed away in 2022, but helped me to connect with churches and temples, at home and with foreign trips, when my inner theatre was forming in fundamental ways.

Introduction

How do religious buildings interact with our brain's inner theatricality, as outer theatrical sites, staging a sense of "self" (ideal ego or soul) in relation to Otherness? What do they reflect of prior brains and their cultural networks, bearing a common human heritage, expressed in different traditions, which show "inner theatre" possibilities? This book considers such questions through a representative sample of European and Chinese churches/temples, with about 2,000 photos and videos on the Bloomsbury website, while considering their religious traditions and mimetic rivalries. It draws on theatre theories, architecture, art history, philosophy, anthropology, religious studies, psychology, and neuroscience. It thus compares patriarchal, maternal, and animal-trickster paradigms of individualist/collectivist, analytical/dialectical, and arousing/calming dimensions *reflected* in religious buildings. These also *affect* our inner theatres of reality representations, memories, fantasies, and dreams. Many quotes are used to evoke a dialog between disciplines, through comparisons of church and temple visits and the reader's related experiences.

Such reflections involve animal-human drives of competition and cooperation,[1] expressed to varying degrees in churches and temples, through "nature" and "nurture" in gene-culture coevolution. This includes primary and social (more complex) emotions of survival, reproduction, territoriality, nurturing care, alliance-hierarchy, and play—in distinctively human, theatrical domains of mimetic belonging and mythic seeking. Admittedly, I use Western theatrical and scientific lenses to compare European and Chinese examples.[2] (If readers do not accept the science of evolution, I hope they will still consider the animal-human comparisons.) Yet I also draw on ancient Indian aesthetics, plus cross-cultural psychological experiments, to consider how Western and Eastern traditions have shaped neural networks differently, as reflected in religious buildings. This indicates crucial directions for secular politics too: more melodramatic, as good versus evil, dominating nature with transcendent ideals, or tragicomic, as *yin-yang* balancing, natural harmony and non-attachment with interdependent values—both of which involve dangers and benefits.

---

[1] See Narvaez 220–2, on symbiotic, self-organizing cooperation in evolution, not just competition, regarding cultural practices in child-raising and moral development.
[2] Cf. Blowers on the development of Chinese psychology, influenced by yet critical of Western.

I encourage the reader, even if not interested in all the neuroscience, social science, or philosophical details here and in Chapter 1, to consider the photo and video examples in subsequent chapters, along with related experiences, through these ten questions. Observe how religious buildings reflect your inner staging of self and Otherness, while comparing their traditions. This will increase your mindfulness of how theatrical sites affect neural, social, and cultural networks, in linear/holistic, individualist/collectivist, melodramatic competitive (individual and between group) or tragicomic cooperative ways.

1. What surrounds the building and how do people approach it or use related buildings around it?
2. Looking from various angles, what are its major shapes, spaces, and materials, with edges and symmetries (or asymmetries), more rectilinear or curved, vertical or horizontal, enclosed or open, especially regarding sky and earth, humans and animals, or water, fire, and blood?
3. How do these aspects appear from outside the building and then enclose you or elevate your eyes, perhaps in multiple ways as you move into and through it—and what is the threshold (limen) as you enter each area?
4. What appears to be the focal point or holiest area of the building?
5. Along with sight, how are hearing, smell, touch, balance, proprioception, and vicarious taste involved?
6. Which feelings do they evoke, regarding approach/avoidance, pleasure/pain, and arousal/calmness?
7. Which images do you see, outside and inside, in sculptures, paintings, or other media?
8. How do they relate to personal associations or religious stories?
9. Which actions do you perform outside and inside the building, as expected rituals or not?
10. Which actions or rituals, personal or collective, do you witness?

Throughout this book, I use the term "brain spirits" to mean brain activity (mapped by neuroscience) experienced subjectively as mind/psyche (studied by psychology), extending to social and cultural interactions (anthropology) with metaphysical implications (philosophy and religious studies). This involves signals in one's body and brain, between persons, and among groups, as bio-cultural motivational "drives," yet also the focus of conscious "attention," extending from body-brains. As each of us approaches a church or temple, personal associations appear in our heads. We enter the religious space bearing a unique world of experiences, beliefs, and meanings that interact with present sensations—in the perpetual restaging of self and Other with potential afterlife and cosmic projections. The outer theatre of the religious building, with its exterior/interior architecture, artworks, spaces, and rites, not only reflects, but also affects the *inner theatre* of the visitor's mind, as spectator and actor, rewiring brain circuits of meaning and purpose. Whether non-material spirits exist or not, the interplay of inner theatre perceptions, memories, and imaginings with a religious building—including other brain-bodies in it and their traces from the past—creates spirited material effects. Thus, theatre terms will be used here as "building blocks" to interpret religious experiences in churches and temples across cultures, akin to embodied "image schemata" and "I-you" interactions (Taves 65–7). This also relates to cognitive linguistic "blends" and "mental spaces" applied in theatre and performance studies (A. Cook 227).

In everyday life, each of us performs, even when alone, with ideas of how others might view us. But believers also perform in a *cosmic* theatre, with ancestral spirits and gods (or God) potentially watching and interacting with them. Even in our secular age, this is akin to political identifications with group frameworks for meaning and purpose in one's life. Yet they may involve social-media conspiracy theories, evoking "melodramatic" conflicts (often trauma-inspired) of good versus evil, with heroes, victims, and villains in a "paranoid style" (Melley). European churches and Chinese temples reflect meta-theatrical projections from many prior generations, affecting the inner theatre of current visitors, with awe, consolation, and hope for many. But such projections also involve a dangerous melodramatic potential: the social drama of psychological "splitting" between the idealized in-group and denigrated out-group (Watts 92–3). And yet, each visitor's inner theatre, with unique memorial frameworks, while alone or in collective rites, may interact with beneficial, complex, tragicomic reflections in a religious monument and its performance spaces. This book explores eighty-one examples of such neuro-theatrical sites (including caves and giant statues), selected from 670 that I visited over the course of a decade. It interprets and compares their material cultures, with monumental "scripts," spatial "settings," and imagistic "scenes," along with performance areas, as outer theatrical sites, regarding the inner theatre of self/Other brain spirits, which extend animal-human drives as personal emotions and collective values.

Personal Notes

My background is more Western than Eastern. I was raised Roman Catholic (in a suburb of San Diego, California) and went to Catholic grade schools. The local church, Our Lady of Grace, became very important to me, as an altar boy assisting the priest or attending daily Masses with my father, especially after my mother died when I was almost ten, feeling closer to her in church than elsewhere. My mother's older sister (Helen Hammack Hogan), a chronicler of family lore and ancestry, told me that she saw a vision of my mother after her death and heard her calm, reassuring voice, "I will always be with you." I often hoped to have such a spiritual experience, but did not. To this day, a half century later, I cannot say whether my mother's spirit actually appeared to my aunt. But the experience was real to her inner theatre, probably influenced by her Catholicism and by stories of Jesus appearing to his followers, saying something similar after his death (Matt. 28.20). As anthropologists explain, using neuroscience, "cultural models of the mind and ... personal orientations ... shape people's phenomenological experiences and ... reports of spiritual presence events" (Luhrmann et al. 1). Thus, "gods and spirits become social relationships in human lives" (Luhrmann, *How* 158).

My inner theatre connections to religious buildings were also kindled, as an adolescent, by tourist trips with my father to Europe, East Asia, and Mexico, including pilgrimage sites. Through such experiences, I became increasingly interested in Eastern religions, especially Buddhism, and in "ritual studies" regarding literature, theatre, and postmodern theories. Likewise, my early work as a playwright and screenwriter often explored matters of faith and metaphysics. My subsequent books analyzed sacrifices and supernatural figures in rituals, plays, films, and television episodes, mostly Western, yet with examples of non-Western works, such as Aztec rites and a Japanese noh play. This book gathers research from various fields, applied with theatre terms to the qualitative data of my tourist-pilgrim experiences, as I share details and imagery from religious sites I visited, chosen as representative for their historical and thematic significance.

In college, I learned that Buddhism focuses on the problem of suffering (or dissatisfaction) in human life. We suffer more when attached to things and people, even to ideas about ourselves or others through love and hate (Bowen et al. 390). Christianity, however, celebrates suffering and sacrifice, from the pain of our disobedient primordial parents, banished out of Paradise, to obedient Abraham, willing to sacrifice his son, to Jesus as God's son, showing his love by becoming one of us and suffering for our sins. Catholic and Orthodox Christians add many martyrs with mimetic crucifixions and other agonies, or stigmatic wounds on saints, inspired by Christ's passion. Indeed, Christianity began not only with Christ's cross, but also with periodic persecutions in the second and third centuries when believers were tortured and executed, by crucifixion, burning at the stake, or wild animals in the arena, for not sacrificing publicly to the Roman emperor and gods. Early Christian stories portrayed martyrs (from a term meaning "witness") as being "in mystical communion with God" through physical suffering, which was also "a test of loyalty to God," purifying believers and healing spiritual wounds of sin, while teaching "humility and gratitude" (King 295). Some Christians would *seek* this painful punishment as a guarantee of heavenly rewards (Ziegler and Saler 49–52). Yet the longer tradition of Buddhism offers many insights and skills for humans to become godlike by *not suffering* with repeated errors. This involves multiple lifetimes, instead of just one with a final judgment of reward or punishment, and less pressure to convert others to save them from that eternal threat. Jataka tales of the Buddha's prior lives include sacrificial scenes of suicidal, body-part, and child offerings, sometimes represented at pilgrimage sites and cave temples in India and China. But they exemplify virtuous non-attachment to self, body, and possessions (Bell 116), rather than valorizing passion, blood, and pain as transcendent payment for original and subsequent sins.

From 2012 to 2014, I traveled to China five times, and then returned in 2019, visiting 138 temples. I traveled to Europe multiple times, too, visiting hundreds of churches, with a mix of emic and etic, subjective and objective viewpoints. Prior to that, over many years, my beliefs shifted toward Buddhism by reading about it and meeting Buddhists who impressed me with their calmness and wisdom. Now I see myself as "Catholic-Buddhist" (like I am Italian-American and German-American) because the Roman Catholic tradition in my parents' families and my upbringing continues to be an influence. My perspective in presenting a comparison of temples and churches is that of a curious tourist, yet also a developing Buddhist who was raised Catholic. Sometimes, camera in hand, I bowed, knelt, and prayed, genuinely moved, yet also performing properly for potential "observers" (Taves 86). Afterwards, I continued to contemplate the history, architecture, art, folk ideas, and philosophical traditions in the sacred sites I visited.

Since 2020, my hindsight has changed about the values and dangers of democratic, capitalist, individualist freedoms. *Independent* rights and states hindered the potential for collective control of the Covid-19 pandemic in Western cultures, compared with greater initial successes in East Asia, although cruel demands for *interdependent* sacrifices were enforced in China and then suddenly reversed in 2022. In the United States, collectivist concerns have arisen through "Me Too" and "Black Lives Matter" movements, especially via social media, with iconic celebrities and statues brought down. This iconoclasm, with related movements in other countries, shows the overlap of religious and secular identities, beliefs, and morals, through righteous rage, with the potential for change. Writing in a pandemic context, I reflected on my experiences with religious buildings in prior years—while gatherings at such places created health dangers, especially with choirs and Communion practices.[3] Yet online alternatives emerged, such as virtual rites and pilgrimage sites. Tragically, however, "Holy Land" conflicts in 2023 also made parts of this book more pertinent.

Self and Otherness with Mirrored Emotions

As philosopher Daniel Dennett reminds us (*Consciousness*), there is no "Cartesian Theater" in the brain, with a fixed self or soul, watching perceptions and ideas from a central point (Descartes's *cogito* in the pineal gland). Yet there are performative aspects in the complex body–brain mechanisms that produce the theatre of mind. Subjective feelings, images, and ideas of an egoistic self emerge as an integrated consciousness with various potential states: reality perceptions, memories, fantasies, dreams, and mystical alternatives. Indeed, our brain's prediction/recognition of reality, with novelty-filtering through degrees of top-down abstraction and bottom-up precision, is a "*controlled hallucination*," according to cognitive science (A. Clark 16, 39–40).

---

[3] In my home city of Charlotte, North Carolina, in October 2020, the United House of Prayer for All People had a weeklong gathering of more than a thousand people that resulted in over 140 cases of Covid and twelve deaths from the virus. In 2020, there were also super-spreader events with choirs singing unmasked at a Baptist church in Hendersonville, NC, and the Protestant cathedral in Berlin, Germany. In spring 2020, Greek Orthodox authorities insisted that their thousand-year-old Communion rite would not spread Covid, using a long spoon to give consecrated wine, mixed with leavened bread, from a common chalice to multiple mouths. According to Rev. Georgios Milkas, a theologian in Thessaloniki: "there is not a shred of suspicion of transmitting this virus, this disease, as in the holy chalice there is the Son and the Word of God" ("Communion"). The Orthodox custom of kissing icons in churches also continued through fall 2020—when Thessaloniki became the worst pandemic region in Greece and a bishop died from the disease ("In Greece").

In the metaphors used by psychologist Bernard Baars for his Global Workspace Theory, an inner "staging" of consciousness, with the "spotlight" of attention, is produced by unconscious networks of "operators" and "audience," with "players" as conscious contents on the "stage" of working memory (*In* 41–8). Such an inner theatre involves dynamic, reentrant, core clusters of brain circuits, cooperating and competing to produce each moment of self-awareness (Edelman; Edelman and Tononi). Likewise, philosopher Nidesh Lawtoo describes, through modernist literature, a "phantom of the ego," involving a "mimetic unconscious" (*Phantom*).[4] The self becomes an illusory, yet experiential whole, with various social personas, as full-body masks performed in everyday life, which also shape the inner stagings. Thus, a mimetic phantom ego develops from the baby's initial sensory interplay with larger humans—mimicking facial expressions less than an hour after birth, attending to others' goals by six months, and following gazes by nine months—to numerous mirroring episodes throughout life, which prune the brain's wiring (Pizzato, *Beast-People* 84–5).

Feelings of self may be unique to each mind, according to scientists in our individualistic Western culture, as the subjective interpretations of homeostatic (inner balanced) body–brain signals. Yet emotions are also shared through allostatic (outward anticipatory) perceptions of others' actions, gestures, and facial expressions. Thus, "communication of the human internal theatre" evolved in and between our ancestors, extending survival and reproduction drives toward shared, psycho-somatic meanings through art (Agnati et al. 430–1; Rolls 475). With mirror neurons and "emotional contagion" (Hatfield et al.), the self is permeable: simulating others' actions and feelings in the viewer's inner theatre, as the brain automatically sends signals of mimicry, usually inhibited by other circuits. Projections onto others, through the brain's cultural predictions, and "ejections" from others continually interact (Candea), with subconscious *stagehands* signaling between bodies. The degree of permeability varies, with performance temperaments and situations, including "Openness to Experience," as one of the "Big Five" personality types defined by psychologists. This increases the likelihood of a "chill response" through greater sensitivity "to art and beauty," related to evolved emotions of "nurturing" (Brattico 312). Yet such "transliminal" permeability of inner/outer theatres is a potential for each us, as mimetic phantoms, through sensorimotor emotional mirroring—even during the "presentation" of self in everyday life (Watts; Goffman).

Experiments reveal a multisensory "Mirror Mechanism" within each brain-body, which signals the mimicking of actions/emotions, *simulating* them through the inner theatre when observing: (1) the actions of others seen or heard, (2) an object that is typically grasped and manipulated, and (3) others' disgust, pain, or touch (Gallese 186–8). The intensity of this inner simulation, with its "ensuing perceptual contents," also depends on "one's previous experiences, memories, and expertise" (194). It involves the

---

[4] Cf. Stump on philosophical arguments for a "true self," as moral, higher-order volition or as narrative memory, both of which she finds inadequate, while still developing the idea, regarding Christian beliefs in the afterlife and resurrected body.

"double theatrical nature of our body [as it] . . . stages subjectivity by means of a series of postures, feelings, expressions, and behaviors. At the same time, the body projects itself in the world and makes it its own stage where corporeality is actor and beholder" (182).

In the late 1800s, Friedrich Nietzsche theorized how the collective *chorus* in the orchestra of Greek theatre, as visionary singing-dancing beholder, projected a transfiguration of the masked *actor* onstage, from Dionysian passions to Apollonian ideals, as characteristics of ancient and modern cultures. This book uses further theatre metaphors to explore how mirror-neuron simulation, through emotions, memories, and Theory of Mind (imagining others' views), involves various neural and social networks. These include, especially at religious sites: choral stagehands, audience, staging of consciousness, actor, character as persona-mask, stage manager, director, operator, costumer, scriptwriter/critic, and mime-improviser/scene-designer.[5]

Mirroring relations between mother and child, with shared facial expressions and emotions, are key to the development of inner-theatre neural circuits, especially through right-hemisphere "mentalizing" or imagining the other's views (Ammaniti and Gallese 116–17). But according to psychoanalytic phenomenology, the alienated self in each of us (through fantasy desires and misrecognition by others) projects an "armor" of ego defenses against potential permeability, around "fragmented" bodily experiences, from the "drama" of the "mirror stage," at age 6 to 18 months, onward (Lacan 78–9). This relates to Terror Management Theory (from the anthropology of Ernest Becker) with empirical research on adults' defensive psychological buffers of "worldview beliefs and self-esteem" against death anxieties, especially through religious ideals of immortality (Vail et al. 264). Yet the phantom ego of a mimetic self is still vulnerable, according to critical affect theory (from Silvan Tomkins), with the "*in-between-ness*" of visceral, edge-of-consciousness "resonances that circulate about, between, and sometimes stick to bodies and worlds" through an "accretion of force-relations" (Seigworth and Gregg 1). Ordinary self-other relations, as a basis for metaphysical soul-Other rituals and beliefs, depend on embodied mimetic and narrative simulations. These involve the inner/outer theatre of sensorimotor emotional empathy: "not dissolving oneself within another, but recognizing another as someone similar to ourselves, who is however not us" (Ebisch and Gallese). And yet, mystical, romantic, or schizophrenic alternatives occur as well.

Bounded or Porous Selves in Individualist/Collectivist Cultures

In modern, Western, secular cultures, a more "bounded" or "buffered" ideal of self is promoted, but in other cultures, a "porous" sense of self is acknowledged, as interdependent identity (C. Taylor 37–9). Degrees of bounded (individualist) or porous (collectivist) identities frame and fuel the outer/inner interplay, as "cultural kindling"

---

[5] "Mime" is meant in the ancient sense of a fully mimetic performer, not just mute pantomime. Yet I also associate the inner *mime* with right-cortical, non-verbal, alternative communications.

through high or low arousal, along with the personality trait of "absorption" in sensory phenomena, especially in spiritual experiences of hearing, seeing, and communicating with divine presences, as anthropologists have explored (Cassaniti and Luhrmann; Luhrmann, *How*; Luhrmann et al.). Alan Fiske, who critiqued the individualist-collectivist dichotomy two decades ago, acknowledged even then how a meta-analysis of many experiments showed that "college students from Chinese cultures (People's Republic [PR] of China, Taiwan, and Hong Kong) are somewhat less individualistic" than North American (NA) students, while those "from Taiwan and PR China ... are appreciably more collectivistic than NA students" (79). Further research shows that Chinese cultures, in various ways, promote more "embeddedness and hierarchy" than Western ones, through the Confucian tradition, with small and big (personal and group) "face" saving or losing, plus "high-context" communication constraints, while valuing modesty more than self-enhancement, *guanxi* (family, town, or school connections), social harmony, and holistic thinking (P. Smith 700–05). Thus, cross-cultural comparisons in anthropology and psychology benefit from multiple viewpoints—with a *lateral* approach, from identity through analogy and contrast to alterity, *and frontal* approach, from identity through objectivity and subjectivity to reflexivity (Candea). Both are employed here.

Scientists apply the terms "individualist" and "collectivist" across many countries, especially with "ideal affects" of high arousal and positive valence (pleasure) in Western cultures, contrasting with East Asian. Evidence shows that the US is a "dopamine nation" of addictive, happiness-seeking ideals (Lembke 34–5). Yet affective scientists find other "emotion models" internationally, including Latin Americans in the US, mixing in- and inter-dependent identities through high-arousal positive (HAP) ideals and "convivial collectivism" (Senft et al.) For decades now, cultural psychologists have gathered data about individualist-collectivist differences in Eurasia and the US. They find that "people from the Aristotelian cultural tradition ('the West') tend to endorse an independent self-construal consisting of inner attributes that make an individual distinct from others" (Yik 210). Those from "the Confucian cultural tradition ('the East') tend to endorse interdependent self-construal" (211). The latter is shown by a belief that "the self cannot be separated from the social context." It is "embedded in layers of relationships." People should "regulate their emotions and thoughts to fit the agendas of others." The ideal is "to maintain harmony with others and to fulfill one's social duties" through a balance of high and low arousal, pleasurable and painful emotions.

There are many variations in the continuing development of such individualist, independent, bounded identity or collectivist, interdependent, porous identity traditions. For example, researchers find that more "bounded" *urban* or "porous" *rural* identities shape Christian experiences in China, but with the mind "held to be permeable to spiritual personae" by both church communities (Ng 95). I would add that groups themselves may be more bounded or porous in maintaining harmony or accepting diversity, while competing or cooperating with other groups—as reflected in religious buildings, spaces, and artworks. Such "tightness" or "looseness" in cultures has also been explored by cultural neuroscientists "in the production of moral judgments," regarding the serotonin transporter gene, with adherence to norms or deviance toleration corresponding to greater or lesser ecological threats in different nations (Chiao 137–8). This relates to research on the cultural learning of emotion recognition by the brain's amygdala, in the temporal lobes, especially of fear expressions on others' faces, with heightened perceptions of one's own ethnic group, in the US or Japan (138). One might apply such cultural emotion-recognition correlations to high/low arousal preferences in pain/pleasure expressions of church and temple artworks, along with their architectural designs, as considered here with examples from Europe and China. They also relate to cultural psychology experiments comparing linear-analytic or holistic-dialectical thinking/emotions in Western and East Asian countries (see Chapter 1).

Maternal, Patriarchal, and Trickster Dimensions

Porous experiences of spirituality can happen anywhere. They may draw on a person's original contacts with the Other in the mother's womb through sound, touch, taste, and movement.[6] They may also draw on primal experiences of sight and smell against the caregiver's body through preverbal musical and later symbolic interactions. Mother-infant caregiving is fundamental to the "socialization of emotions." Studies find that negative emotion words are used more by Chinese mothers in dialog with the child, "focused on proper behavior" about shared events, while American mothers use "an emotionally explanatory style," regarding antecedents to emotions (Yik 214–15). Other researchers find that Chinese mothers and children use more verbs, especially in relational play with mechanical toys, compared to object labeling with picture books, while American mothers and children use more nouns during play (Tardif et al.).

The socialization of emotions through negative/positive words, focusing on behavior/explanation through verbs/nouns, relates to various cultural psychology experiments considered later in this book. It involves patriarchal frameworks beyond the dyadic relations of maternal caregiver and child[7]—with the developing brain structured in different cultural ways (through mother, father, and other influences)

---

[6] According to researchers, "maternal stress is known to affect fetal and infant development" (Lehrner and Yehuda 145). Pregnant mothers exposed to the stress of terrorist attacks on September 11, 2001, had babies with "heightened glucocorticoid sensitivity, a vulnerability factor for later development of PTSD." Parental experiences, even before pregnancy, can "strongly influence," the child's developing "emotional sensitivity and regulation," through the inherited epigenetics of chemical markers affecting gene expression. This may have evolved as adaptive in stressful environments, but also became maladaptive through the big-brain prematurity of human birth, with higher-order consciousness and mortal anxieties, yet with spiritual experiences and sanctuaries as potential ways of rebalancing emotions.

[7] In cross-cultural research, Broesch et al. found dyadic, mother-child relations as primary, with affective mirroring, despite the diversity of caregiving traditions, involving multiple parental figures, in Fiji, Vanuatu, Bolivia, Peru, and Central African Republic. Children "less than 5 years old spend the majority of their observed time in the presence of one female adult" (208). Cf. Hrdy for more on multiple (allo)parenting traditions.

stressing relational behavior or explanatory labeling, for example. Such Symbolic law/language frameworks of proper behavior and abstract explanation, through Imaginary play and Real losses (Lacan), via mothers in primary caregiving roles and a secondary caregiver as "father," are reflected in religious buildings as emotion theatres.[8] They involve clerical rites and scriptural teachings, which cultivate animal-human drives (remnant instincts open to reprograming) and personal desires (with lost objects and substitute fantasies) as brain spirits.

The terms "patriarchal" and "maternal" (or Symbolic and Imaginary) are used here as psycho-social structures, gendered in various ways through religious traditions and their buildings—not as determining all parental identities, historically or today. Indeed, there are two fathers, divine and human, in the Christian "Holy Family." There is a popular transgender, yet child-granting deity, Avalokiteshvara/Guanyin, in Chinese Buddhism (Mai), along with another, Mahasthamaprapta, who is male, but sometimes appears as the female Shih Chih (see Chapter 2 on Donglin Temple). While not depicted as a father figure, the historical Buddha tells a story, in the *Lotus Sutra*, about a father saving his children from a burning house by luring them outside with toys, when they were too attached to playing inside, as an allegory for his teachings. Also, "Mahayana Buddhism often personifies wisdom as a goddess [Prajnaparamita] and refers to her as 'the mother of all Buddhas'" (Mitchell 115). The wisdom bodhisattva, Manjushri, also gets that title, though typically appearing as male. According to the *Lankavatara Sutra*, within every sentient being, there is a Buddha-nature as "womb," *Tathagata-garbha*: the Nirvana of emptiness,[9] yet "storehouse-consciousness," like the deep ocean below the waves (105). Thus, the relation of humans to divine authority or compassion/wisdom is more complex in Buddhism than the masculine Father God or feminine Madonna/Sophia of Catholic and Orthodox Christianity (or clergy called "Father"). But it still involves aspects of gender and family, especially for laypeople.

Religious buildings show collective expressions of affect cultivation, with patriarchal or maternal deity offerings and communion across many generations. This inner/outer theatre grooming of personal to group mindsets confirms authorized ways that spiritual porosity may occur as positive ecstasy, rather than evil "possession" or disordered "madness." And yet, authorized affect cultivation has also taken tragic turns in the perverse "grooming" of young victims by sexual predators, even in religious contexts, confusing physical pleasure, hierarchical power, and divine ecstasy. Historically, in positive and negative ways, the power of ecstatic human-divine connection in many believers and their sacred spaces fueled, or at times disrupted and

---

[8] I use a few Lacanian terms that I see as insightful correlations, but not the full French Freud. I also use the terms "drive" and "unconscious" in a biological and neuroscientific sense, related to, but different from psychoanalytic theory. On further relations between these disciplines, through a "Lacan-influenced neuro-psychoanalytic metapsychology of affect," see Johnston and Malabou (193).

[9] "Buddhist emptiness... isn't the absence of 'something,' but the absence of 'intrinsic nature'" (Ricard and Thuan 95).

even revolutionized, patriarchal/maternal traditions, as a supportive or *trickster* element, within and between brain-bodies, as well as collective cultural systems.

Tricksters transform identities as key figures in many indigenous colonized cultures and in the Greco-Roman roots of Christianity, which involved the theatre and wine god, Dionysus/Bacchus. They appear at the edges of churches, or within them, crossing between worlds and challenging established orders, as gargoyle beasts, mischievous cherubs, threatening devils, and subdued dragons. Some authority figures have trickster aspects, becoming crucial to the animal-human-divine conduit: the Holy Spirit dove, angels with bird wings, and Jesus as rebel against the Roman Empire, through an Immaculate Virgin Mother. In Buddhist temples, there are various transformative, between-world figures: flying/dancing apsaras (shape-changing, sage-seducing, celestial nymphs), Avalokiteshvara-Guanyin as male and female (sometimes with multiple heads and arms to see, hear, and aid devotees), Maitreya in laughing pot-belly or heroic ruler forms, and dragons as protective forces of nature and empire (unlike Christian dragons). Chinese folk religion and Daoism involve many positive/negative tricksters, such as the Eight Immortals. They are deified human sages, "misfits and eccentrics" who exemplify individualism in a collectivist culture, including the drunken Han Zhong Li, Lü Dong Bin, and Lan Cai He, or Zhang Guo Lao who rides his donkey backwards and folds it up to put it in his pocket (Ni 184–98). These European and Chinese figures reflect the brain's major networks with patriarchal, maternal, personal-memorial, and supportive/trickster dimensions—explored through sacred sites in the chapters ahead.

Cultural Views of the Phantom Ego and Other

The brain's phantom ego has been deconstructed by mapping experiments, which find many mini-agents, more than 90 percent non-conscious, producing the conscious feeling of agency with an integrated subjective ego-self (Grigg 209–10). Some scientists declare that all of "reality" as we perceive it, not just the self, is a fiction produced by our brains, like symbolic "icons" on a computer screen (Hoffman).[10] Others connect

---

[10] Donald Hoffman has developed an Interface Theory of Perception, involving "icons" on the "desktop" of consciousness, as a "Multimodal User Interface"—without considering further theatrical dimensions of this or the older religious sense of "icons." Hoffman includes a "Fitness Beats Truth" theorem, drawing from evolutionary psychology, about consciousness always fictionalizing our reality perceptions for survival and reproduction purposes—although the "fiction" has to be taken *seriously* to avoid harm. Hoffman's theory of "conscious realism" only involves sensory perceptions as fiction, not mathematics and logic, while focusing its metaphors on our contemporary experience of computer media (also referencing videogames). And yet, Hoffman briefly proposes a "scientific theology," which involves "conscious agents" at various hierarchical levels of what neuroscientists measure as "unconscious processing," related to other life forms (194, 200). Such conscious agents combine to form more complex ones and eventually "infinite agents, with infinite potential for experiences, decisions, and actions ... like the religious notion of God ... [but with a] precise mathematical description" (200).

"selflessness" to the neuroscience of "spiritual transcendence," involving deactivation of networks for a psychophysical sense of self, in the right parietal lobe (Johnstone and Cohen). Another neuroscientist insists that the "person" exists as an oscillating integration of neural networks, *in process* toward a spiritual goal, with contrasting needs of agency and community, especially through "eschatological personalism" in Western monotheism (P. McNamara, *Religion*).

According to some cognitive scientists and humanists, the brain is "enmeshed with ... non-neural bodily and environmental factors" (Anderson et al. 2). Hence, cognition is "distributed" in four ways: embodied, embedded, extended, and enacted (3). These relate to inner/outer theatre explorations beyond the Western stress on an individual self, especially with ties between 4E cognition and Buddhism (Varela et al.). One might add "evolving" and "emotional" cognition: biologically and culturally, collectively and individually, through remnant instincts as drives. Such cognitive motivations are experienced as personal feelings and shared emotions—through "beliefs," desires, and fantasies, "between reflexes and reasoned behavior" (Adolphs 6–10). Thus, researchers have found "culturally different patterns of emotions," regarding autonomy or relatedness (Mesquita et al. 395; De Leersnyder et al.).

Many people today, especially in Westernized cultures, value the autonomous sense of an *independent* self, with individual rights, akin to the Christian ideal of a transcendent soul, triumphing over mortality, as exemplified by the martyr's sacrifice (Ziegler and Saler 48–9). This contrasts with the multiple or cyclical souls and more *interdependent* identities in various Asian traditions, stressing Confucian family obligations, Daoist natural harmony, or the Buddha-nature of pure, subtle, storehouse consciousness in each person, interrelated through karmic law and dependent origination. The "Other" of the brain's inner theatre may thus be projected differently, as a metaphysical extension of the self's framework from personal to social to divine. It is anthropomorphized (and zoomorphized) as the Father, Son, and Holy Spirit in Christianity—with no such Creator-God, but many compassionate higher beings in Buddhism and with a less personalized, yet maternal Way of nature in Daoism (cf. Wildman et al. 155).

Even for non-religious people today, there are trans-physical frames of "performing cultural Otherness" in New Age practices, involving "experiential spirituality" in many theatrical spaces (Dox xix–xxi). Traditional spirituality in churches and temples is also akin to collective performances of idealized or scapegoated, virtual and viral selves in mass and social media, especially with online rites and pilgrimages since the pandemic. What do we experience in common with others, present and past, through the animal ancestry and human structures of our brains, shaped in different ways by more bounded-self (independent identity) or porous-self (interdependent) cultures, regarding a metaphysical Other? This book explores how the monumental designs of European churches and Chinese temples, as outer theatrical spaces, *reflect* animal-human drives and neural circuits evolving through various historical tastes in the cultural pruning of the brain's inner theatre—while *evoking* affective interactions today.

Neural, Social, and Cosmic Theatres

The outer/inner interplay of self, presented in social scenes of everyday life, involves various forms of Otherness in the theatre of the mind. Cognitive consciousness occurs on the "stage" of working memory, in a limited "spotlight" (one to four separate items), through unconscious "scene setters" (Baars, *On* 101). This involves cooperating and competing neural circuits, especially between the cortex and thalamus, as the inner voice of thought performs with sensory imagery, in relation to conceptual, deep goal, and outer contextual "frames," plus long-term memories as "audience," shaping conscious "scenes" (*In* and *On*). Baars also uses the theatre terms "director" (as unconscious executive functions in the frontal cortex) and "actors" (as complex multimodal sensory systems, competing for stage space). But I apply them a bit differently, using the social neuroscience of Matthew Lieberman and italicizing such terms as metaphors for correlative neural networks. According to Baars in 2019, "all of our unified models of mental functioning today are theater models; it is essentially all we have" (*On* 100). In my view, this would include Hoffman's iconology of the mind's computer screen.

Self-Other thoughts, images, and feelings of consciousness involve an inner *actor* (with deeper self-knowledge) playing a *character* (the persona presented to others), regarding one's "mentalizing" or Theory of Mind about others' views, as an inner *director*—while the outer context of others' views also influence the inner *actor* network. Thus, there is no "true self" as a central, stable spectator within the brain. The self is continually re-presented, as if on a mirroring yet shifting inner screen, regarding imagined views of others in various contexts, while interacting with them or even when alone.

Memories are constructed or "reconsolidated" in the brain, each time one remembers them (or dreams), drawing on the inner *audience* of experience traces, intuitive values, and implicit desires. We also use memory to imagine the future, as "a spatial structure within which scenarios could be constructed," through the hippocampal *audience* in the temporal lobes (Fernyhough 129). It processes initial associations for unconscious memories and generates "relivable scenarios" as conscious "autobiographical memories" with spatial and temporal "*scene construction*" (130). Mostly unconscious cognitive elements shape past-to-present perceptions and future expectations at the *stage edges* of consciousness. Yet the spotlight of attention may shift toward the inner *audience* of long-term memories—as with "mind-wandering," a form of thinking similar to dreaming (Solms 229). Both mind-wandering and dreams involve "problem-solving," in relation to the deliberate imagining of future actions through the hippocampus, "injecting the quality of perspectival 'mine-ness' into normally unconscious cortical memory processes" (230).

Each explicit declarative (conscious) memory "requires the hippocampus," in order to "replay the patterns to the cortex over and over," thus reconsolidating experience traces into episodic images and narrative meanings, through neurogenesis, "the growth and insertion of new neurons" (Eagleman 216–18). The brain's memory-learning system reveals "forms of plasticity [that] interact with one another . . . [through] layers operating in concert" (221), as an interactive *audience*, mostly in the dark (unconscious) but sometimes partly conscious. At another scale of cooperative/competitive performances, religious buildings reflect the collective consolidation of memories and dreams across many minds, with existential problem-solving through a cosmic theatre of watchers and actors, perhaps also a divine director. This involves each visitor's (and many historical actors') inner theatre of mostly unconscious *audience* circuits, framing the conscious present, recalled past, and predicted future—regarding emotional mysteries of moral judgment, birth, and death.

As an altered state of consciousness, dreams offer fantasy scenes akin to hallucinogenic trance, spirit possession, or ritual chanting and meditation, "mediated" by religious traditions and observers (Taves 74–86, 164–5). During sleep, desires and fears are at play in the brain regarding daily and long-term experiences, as the dream-self watches or acts, eventually shifting to a waking-self who barely remembers the show. (We all dream, but some people remember more afterward or experience a "lucid" dream self.) Dreamer and dream alterations of self-consciousness, as *actor* and *character* with *audience*, involve an internal sense of the Other, too, as social or metaphysical *director*. They also involve a moral, self-monitoring *stage manager* and supportive, bodily network of *stagehands*, which can sometimes be devilishly disruptive, through animal-human drives and emotions at the edges of the *stage*.

Ancestral spirits, gods, angels, and devils reflect such inner theatre elements, through collective myths, rituals, and sacred sites. Even in earthly dimensions, the visitor to a church or temple enters a theatrical space, performing as a character when re-cognized by other people, whether as community member, visiting pilgrim, or just a tourist. But the visitor is also a spectator of the religious building and its displays, while becoming an actor within its architectural scenes. Viewing the artworks in a church or temple evokes inner-theatre images and stories. Yet for believers, performing in the ritual space also involves an awe-full cosmic theatre. God(s), angels, ancestors, or other spirits may be watching and acting in return, as divine director(s), supernatural stage managers, memorial audience, or trickster stagehands, through believers' inner theatres.

(Melo)Dramatic or Contemplative (Tragicomic) EAE

During a formal service, ministers, their helpers, the congregation, and supportive workers (as directors, stage managers, participant viewers, and stagehands) maintain the ritual scene, props, and performance. There may be a greater degree of belief in the metaphysical "reality" of a church or temple service than with the "as-if" imaginings of playful artistic productions. But religion and theatre share a "performative ground" with varying degrees of investment or observation, depending on the context and people present (Mason). Religious buildings also present the *historical* Other by showing physicalized beliefs of the past, even without rituals being performed. Not only are the brain spirits of prior visitors indicated, with their offering props remaining, but also of major donors, authorities, artists, and artisans, as supportive audience, directors, performers, and stagehands—in the current visitor's experience of awe-inspiring architecture and artworks.

As this book explores, Christian imagery often stresses an individual heroic self, through mythic figures aligned with the divine Other in a cosmic battle against devilish Otherness, encouraging *(melo)dramatic* investments of the church visitor's inner theatre. Buddhist imagery, ritual chanting, and meditation skills involve the *tragicomic* questioning of ego illusions, cravings, attachments, and aversions, through the contemplative observation of collective interdependence. Yet heroic figures and dramatic rites also appear in Chinese Buddhist temples, such as the Four Heavenly Kings dancing on demigod asuras in the initial shrine or the burning of "spirit money" and cardboard houses in the courtyard to aid departed ancestors. Thus, according to some scholars, "the Buddhist imaginaire must be conceived of 'on the mode of the debt and the gift rather than that of belief, as act rather than thought'" (Faure, quoted in Tarocco 630). Yet it also involves holding down rival energies (asuras) to rebalance with them, to teach, not destroy them—through chanting, meditation, merit donation, and "'gift-giving, as something that breaks the economic circle, moving beyond into pure loss or expenditure.'"

In Christianity, along with dramatic individualism, there is a *contemplative* tradition that values meditative spaces, including monastic chapels with minimal or no imagery, especially with Cistercian dictates from St. Bernard in the twelfth century (Barrie 143–4). But even in medieval abbeys, dedicated to communal prayer and work, while structured by church rites several times a day: "Personal power in the form of individual spiritual fulfillment, regardless of the abbots' control over one's material life, lay at the heart of the monastic life" (Kilde 63–4). Historically and today, dramatic awe or contemplative serenity may be evoked, through degrees of "*energizing* and *calming qualities*," in the various theatrical contexts of sacred architecture, as a "transformative agent" (Barrie 218–21).

From 2007 to 2008, through online surveys in English and Spanish, 2,982 volunteers were asked to remember "Extraordinary Architectural Experiences" (EAEs) that fundamentally altered their normal state of being (Bermudez, "Amazing"). Most of them recalled religious buildings that evoked arousal and quiescence, using the survey terms: "strong body reactions" and yet "introspective/silent states," through "a higher level of awareness" and "abandonment to the moment." Reports also involved lower ratings for "Analytical/Intellectual" experiences, which suggested to researchers that the architecture evoked "other ways of knowing, feeling, and sensing beyond left-brain, neo-cortex, or discursive operations." This occurred, according to the reported memories, through a statistical correlation between EAE "Intensity" and "Sudden Arousal/Surprise" ("Empirical" 375). Yet such EAEs went "beyond a 'surprising' situation," with a paradigm shift that broke through "existing preconceptions, ideas, and constructs," often involving the travel context of immersion and "distancing" in an "alien environment," or "a taxing and committed 'pilgrimage,'" described in respondents' remembered accounts ("Profound" 23–4).

A subsequent brain scan study with questionnaires of a dozen professional architects used *photos*, moving from exterior to interior, of five of the ten most frequently remembered buildings in the EAE study, including three churches: the Pantheon, Chartres Cathedral, and the Chapel of Ronchamp (Bermudez et al. 123–5). In comparison with five "ordinary" buildings as controls (houses, offices, or shopping malls), the EAE "contemplative" sites evoked distinct reports and neural patterns: more attentive, receptive, absorbing experiences with "diminished internal dialogue" and *less* activity in the medial prefrontal cortex (MPFC), along with related areas, as the Default Mode Network of social and self-referential rumination.[11] This deactivation of the MPFC *actor* rumination network is akin to the effect of therapeutic "mindfulness" meditation in other studies (Watkins 103). Nine of the twelve architects reported being "emotionally moved, transported and connected to the settings," while two reported a dramatic "loss of the sense of self" through unity with the buildings' spaces, mentioning "atmosphere," "wholeness," and "totality" (Bermudez et al. 130–2).

Brain scans of the architects confirmed that externally induced meditation with churches (or photos of them) matches the neural effects of mindfulness in the Buddhist tradition: decrease of midline narrative-self circuits and increase of inferior parietal lobe, body image, saliency, "Open Monitoring," and "non-evaluative aesthetic" networks (Bermudez et al. 132–3). This may involve child-parent, anxious, avoidant, or secure "attachment" legacies—with mindfulness balancing "a midline observing-narrating-witnessing self-circuitry and a lateralized sensing-perceiving-experiencing self-circuitry," as internal attunement, "honoring their differences" (Parker et al. 227). Perhaps the shell of one's lateralized *character* circuitry (along with parietal-lobe *costume-body definer/designer* networks) is to some degree hollowed out by the EAE of religious buildings, with midline MPFC *actor* deactivation. This evokes a smaller self, yet *extended* self-Other, connecting one's sensory body, through quiescent or arousing awe, to divine images and sacred spaces. According to our developing hypothesis, this may occur in a more contemplative tragicomic or competitive (melo)dramatic way, in the different traditions of Chinese temples and European churches.

Rasas of Expansive, In(ter)dependent Awe

Awe is a typical emotion experienced by first-time visitors to a monumental religious site, evoked by its theatrical grandeur, beauty, strangeness, and perhaps age. Moving through the initial gateway into a Chinese temple courtyard, or from the smaller space of a European church's narthex to the "suddenly much larger space" of the nave, may activate the brain's frontal cortex, midbrain, amygdala (fear center), and cerebellum (balance mechanism) with a sense of "expansion" (Eberhard, *Brain* 100, 112). Hence, the inner theatre's *restaging* of a "small self," in relation to the Otherness of such vast,

---

[11] Cf. Hamilton et al. on "depressive rumination" and the Default Mode Network, so called because it was noticed by neuroscientists as a pattern of activity when the brain was in a default state between tasks—and then found to be involved with social relationships, including memories and "feelings of guilt" regarding "social values" (83). See also Li et al.

exotic, mysterious places, represents communal, historical, and divine beliefs through "collective identity" (Piff et al. 883–4).

The awe-full restaging of a smaller yet extended self toward collective identity relates to the ancient Indian theory of *rasas*, nine emotional "juices" (or flavors and aftertastes), including awe, sensed by the viewer or reader of an artwork. Religious awe may also evoke the *rasas* of fear and courage, plus a taste of love and joy, en route to peace. Theoretically, *rasa* tasting in a church or temple would involve the visitor's inner *audience* of temporal lobe networks, including the amygdala, which processes emotions, thus detecting the *rasa*'s "intensity of flavour" (Mee, "Dancing"). Like in theatre, emotions in a religious building, with its artworks, reverberate as poetic language (*dhvani*), through "echoes" beyond word meanings, with the "latent impressions" of emotional experiences in the visitor's subconscious mind, especially through the story's "catalysts" and the actor's "manifestations"—although at a "psychical distance" (Chandra 100–04, 136). Yet this would also depend on how much the visitor knows about and believes in the religious scenes.

Rasa savoring evokes a "generalizing process of emotions, in which a spectator can at the same time participate in enduring feelings ... and still preserve the necessary distance for understanding" (Virtanen 64). This includes a fluid "melting" (smaller self), then "enlargement and folding," and then "expansion" of consciousness (extended self). Such "profoundly felt," yet paradoxically "removed" savoring, as an extended "generality" without personal relishing, is "free of all ego-driven considerations," leading to the ninth *rasa* of peaceful "detachment" or *shanta* (Chandra 104, 136–42). The observer's tasting of "ego-less emotion," via "total absorption," evokes an "expansion" of self and imagination, through pleasure, moral instruction, and joyful bliss, as "recognition" (139, 146–7, 167). This can also happen with today's screen media, "asking partakers to ingest, relish, internalize, and personalize the event" (Mee, "Rasa"). A more tragicomic than melodramatic *rasa*-tasting might be cultivated, with compassion (not objectification) at a distance, as considered with religious buildings in the chapters ahead. Such *rasas* become "desireless emotions" and thus "passion with equanimity," in a meditative choice as deconstructed actor and "Empty Spectator of the dance—the ceaseless play of forms, arising interdependently, dissolving, re-assembling," rather than a "bit-player" following "kārmic scripts" (George 32, 58–9, 65).[12]

Various psychological studies of awe show that subjects writing about an experience of natural beauty, or seeing videos of tornadoes, hurricanes, and slow-motion waterdroplets colliding, have a "diminished sense of self" regarding something "vast and powerful" (Piff et al. 884). This evokes gratitude, empathy, generosity, ethical decision-making, and prosocial values—or "helping behavior" when subjects stand in a grove of "towering trees" (885–95).[13] Awe also reduces ego aggression, through narrative recall

---

[12] I value George's epistemology of Buddhist performances via *rasa* theory. But I disagree with his valorizing of performance over theatre as "always ... shadowed by the text" and with his formula "Theatre = illusion + emotion = attachment = suffering" (17, 81).

[13] See also Stellar et al. on compassion, gratitude, and awe as "self-transcendent" emotions.

or video watching of a natural panorama (Yang et al.). With its sense of vastness "altering mental frames," awe may involve a sense of threat (with cultural variations), beauty, admiration for exceptional abilities, elevation through virtue, and supernatural spirituality (Chirico and Yaden 223–4; Keltner and Haidt). The "self-transcendent" quality of awe includes a spectrum of intensity with a mystical extreme, from "reduced self-boundaries and self-salience" to expansive feelings of "complete oneness with other people and environment" (Chirico and Yaden 227; Yaden et al., "Varieties" 145). Thus, awe may shift the *independent* model of self in the Western tradition toward a more *interdependent*, cooperative identity, regarding both in- and out-group members, or "kin and as-if kin" (Hrdy 12–14), especially for the faithful who frequent a church's rituals and perform charitable works beyond it.

Other studies of awe, with the watching of television commercials, writing of personal experiences, or reading about views of Paris from the Eifel Tower, find that it increases "the perception of available time," along with the "willingness to volunteer time to help others, preference for experiences rather than material objects, and life satisfaction" (Rudd et al.; Shiota et al. 366). Awe may have the "adaptive function" in human cultural evolution of facilitating the "intake of new information" and stabilizing "social hierarchies," with leaders using "awe-inspiring displays to elicit buy-in from their communities" (Shiota et al. 363–4). There are thus "communal connotations" of awe, related to religious rituals in many cultures, "targeted at staving off large-scale natural disasters" (Ejova 164–5). Yet the e-motion (energy in motion) of awe may be disruptive, too, bordering on an "altered state of consciousness" that challenges one's sense of "time, space, and self"—leading to "transformation," as with the legendary "conversion of Saint Paul" (Chirico and Yaden 222, 227).

The Christian ideal of union with an alpha-male God, "Maker of heaven and earth, and of all that is seen and unseen" (Nicene Creed), through church-evoked awe, might inflate the inner staging of a righteous self, united with the faithful against other groups, persons, or forces as evil threats. This melodramatic temptation may be re-presented in theatrical rites of sacrifice led by priests or preachers, including "Communion" with Christ's Body and Blood. As a current theologian puts it, "the divine hostility to suffering ... [involves] the normative attack on death in the resurrection of Jesus" (Lloyd 278–9). In the Chinese tradition of filial duty (with family name first), the inner staging of a more *interdependent* self is evoked, with tragicomic ideals of high/low-arousal, negative/positive affect balancing. Yet temples' awe-inspiring statues, with ritual offerings to gods, bodhisattvas, and departed family members, may reinforce submission to patriarchal orders and situational control, through fear of vengeful, dishonored spirits. Submission to God and patriarchal authorities is also a key component of the Christian tradition, but with a more *independent* self (or soul), developing from ancient to early modern, Romantic, and postmodern ideals, in relation to the "Big Gods" of monotheism, colonialism, and capitalism (Norenzayan; Wright).

Psychologists have studied the "dark side" of sublime awe, regarding a "punitive, powerful God" (Gordon et al. 310–11). Amie Gordon and her colleagues note that the etymology of "awe" in English derives from "fear, dread, or terror," and that the Chinese logographic term for it is "a combination of respect and fear" (311). Across a half dozen experiments with hundreds of participants, recalling personal moments of awe or seeing photos and videos of positive natural scenes and negative ones with tornados, a substantial number of experiences (one-tenth to one-quarter) were "tinged with fear and threat" (324). These "threat-based awe" experiences involved personal uncertainty about "situational control," with physical indications of sympathetic *arousal* in the autonomic nervous system of participants, through heartbeat and sweat measurements. Unlike positive experiences of awe, producing parasympathetic calm (and joyful elevation of an extended self), the negative aspects resulted in less "well-being" through a feeling of "powerlessness."

However, Gordon and her colleagues admit that their "samples were from the United States, where more positive forms of awe may prevail" (325). Other studies by cultural psychologists suggest that such findings involve Western ideals of an independent, powerful self in control of situations (like the soul identifying with God). This was found in comparison with the traditional East Asian acceptance of interdependent contextual relations, with a non-intrinsic compassionate self, valuing low-arousal, cyclic, negative and positive emotions. As applied here, a neuro-theatrical approach to church/temple, threat-based, yet sublime awe involves observational tasting of fear, courage, love, joy, and peace in various *rasa* recipes of pain and pleasure, arousal and calmness identifications. Such mindful, comparative savoring of religious awe (and how it evokes group allegiance) may increase cathartic awareness, not only of its tragicomic benefits, but also its melodramatic, righteous, submission-demanding dangers and heroic-flaw temptations.

Upright or Relational, Patriarchal or Maternal

All of us use the left and right hemispheres of our brains, including frontal, parietal, temporal, and occipital lobes, all the time. But they specialize differently, as considered further in Chapter 1. I apply theatre metaphors to the left and right cortices, and to specific network hubs in the prefrontal and parietal lobes, along with the temporal lobes (within the two hemispheres) and subcortical circuits, while also acknowledging the occipital lobe's role in vision. The left hemisphere's objectifying, analytical, "instrumental" functions filter the right's more sensitive, dialectical, "holistic" alternatives, across the corpus callosum between them (Teasdale 55–62). Thus, the inner theatre's "framework for conscious experience" involves a "*narrative interpreter*" in the left frontal cortex, as "observing self," along with an "inarticulate *self*" in the right (Baars, *On* 107). These characteristics are reflected and potentially evoked by aspects of religious buildings, which show more independent or interdependent ideals, with melodramatic threatening awe or tragicomic contemplative communion. Such reflections also involve "upright" or "relational" values, which philosopher Adriana Cavarero associates with masculine and feminine, patriarchal and maternal dimensions, as "two different models of subjectivity, two theaters for questioning the human condition" (10).

This book explores how rectilinear, upright-vertical, monumental designs or curved, horizontal, domestic "inclinations" reflect patriarchal, regal, judgmental ideals or maternal, natural, nurturing relations[14]—across various Catholic and Buddhist spaces, along with Protestant, Orthodox, Islamic, and Daoist examples. This design dynamic does not rest on an essentialist binary of either feminine or masculine. It involves a *spectrum* of sacred structures and potential experiences, with *degrees* of maternal inclination and patriarchal uprightness—plus playful or rebellious creativity, in melodramatic or tragicomic directions. Both the negative and positive aspects of these family paradigms (maternal, patriarchal, and child/trickster) are explored through neuroscience research, while acknowledging related terms from Lacanian theory: Imaginary, Symbolic, and Real. I leave it to the reader to make comparisons, if desired, with Jungian theory or other structuralist approaches. Each religious building is considered through its own cultural tradition, as a gathering place for believers, an attraction for tourists, and a "house" for one or more supernatural figures: God, gods, ancestral spirits, arhats, or bodhisattvas. It reflects a combined *projection* of inner Others by authorities, artists, workers, and visitors—with desires from the past meeting those of the present, as embodied brains enter and perform in the church or temple.

Degrees of inclined relationality (with love and grief/joy as *rasas*) or upright rectitude (with fear and courage) may correspond to cultural differences between matriarchal and patriarchal societies around the globe. The former still exist, but the latter have become dominant, according to another feminist philosopher, who offers detailed anthropological evidence. "Matriarchal realms are first, relationship societies.... They are fundamentally different from patriarchal empires or states, which arise as a result of conquest" (Goettner-Abendroth, *Matriarchal* 423). And yet, the primary maternal emotion/behavior of mammalian care may be related to patriarchal hierarchy, as with the collective fetishizing and religious feeding of an elite male leader's memory, tomb, and spirit. Three and five thousand years ago, in ancient China and Egypt (later influencing Europe), a "spectacular phase of mass killing," which turned "violence into kinship," created a *patrimonial* system, with "all the king's subjects ... working to care for the king" (Graeber and Wengrow 402). At least in this paradigm of statecraft, domestic care is turned into its apparent opposite: the "mechanical labour" of seasonal tomb-building and "daily servicing of the ruler's body"—with most human activity "directed upwards" to the priests and king, assisting in their task of "feeding and caring for the gods" (408).

In the Christian tradition, Cavarero values collective caring kinship through the Madonna with Child image, as a popular counterpoint to patriarchal rectitude. "Some stereotypes, such as that propagated by the iconography of the Virgin Mary, have a great critical potentiality that risks remaining concealed precisely because they are too

---

[14] Cavarero's feminist theory of "inclinations," as a critique of patriarchal "rectitude," offers Leonardo da Vinci's portrait, *The Virgin and Child with St. Anne*, as an example. Its "asymmetry," modulated by the inclination of Mary and the child Jesus toward each other, instead of regally facing the viewer for adoration, shows "the movement of a relationality that reflects the everyday experience of the maternal rather than the monumentality of the sacred" (99). Cf. Gilligan, whom Cavarero cites for her "feminine ethics of care" against the "masculine predisposition to form abstract judgments" (102–03).

exposed" (14). This book uncovers the *rebalancing* power of relational, maternal elements, regarding upright, patriarchal ideals and supportive/trickster edges, in the architecture and performance spaces, as well as imagery, of religious buildings—reflecting many centuries of individual and collective, outer and inner, brain-spirit theatricality.

The chapters ahead explore such dynamics in various ways:

1. monumental *dimensions* as more vertical or horizontal, dominant or balanced, protective or playful, with sacred sites reflecting historical conflicts as well
2. spatial *designs* as more rectilinear or round, focused or dispersed, mechanically enclosed or naturally open, shaping performances with patriarchal authority or maternal care, while also involving trickster edges
3. potential *emotions* evoked in naïve tourists or knowledgeable believers, interacting with the spaces, figures, and sensual elements

Personal and collective performances will be mentioned, as ritualized or improvised, when observed during my visits. The main concern is how religious architectures reflect the cultural programing of brain networks in the past and evoke each visitor's neuro-performances today, in the shared interplay of inner and outer theatres, even without participatory rites. This may also suggest trajectories of future cultural programing, West and East, in secular as well as religious realms. But we must be careful to consider multiple "patterned practices … defining preferences, predispositions, and expectations for actors"—not just "a single pattern [with] … internal homogeneity," nor with objectifying Orientalist projections, as neuro-anthropologists warn against (Roepstorff et al. 1059; Downey and Lende 35).

The focus here is on Catholic churches in Europe (tied to holy territories in Jerusalem) and Buddhist temples in China. But pre-Christian, Orthodox, Protestant, Muslim, Confucian, and Daoist sites are also considered—to sketch a spectrum of Eurasian cultures, as different expressions of the brain's inner theatre networks. This comparative, inner/outer theatre approach offers insights for scholars at a distance and for visitors to churches, temples, and mosques, observing how they reflect the best and worst in human cultures, through awe-inspiring performance spaces. Religious buildings, with designs, artworks, and rites, groom our animal-human drives and emotions toward varying degrees of melodramatic (good versus evil) or tragicomic (complex victim/hero) identifications. Such sanctuaries evoke group rivalry and scapegoating, yet also self-sacrifice and generosity, through personal desires for meaning and purpose in this life and beyond.

Comparative Contexts

Protestant forms of Christianity stress the personal reading of the Bible for truth, with God's grace as the way to heaven. Catholicism offers various rituals conducted by clergy to help the believer with forgiveness of sins and spiritual growth through good works, along with the Bible and God's grace. Both focus on the significance of *individual* human souls in a cosmic conflict of good and evil, of warring angels and devils, with one side ultimately victorious over the other. Especially with the Post-Reformation development of a modern Western sense of self, "experienced directly via self-reflection," concerns shifted from the shared problem of Original Sin, with salvation through church rituals, to "the individual whose salvation can only be restored through direct communion with Jesus, the divine in human form" (Johnstone and Cohen 121).

Today, cultural psychologists find a greater emphasis on such "individual autonomy" in Protestants, compared with "social solidarity" among Catholics (Cohen and Neuberg 862). For example, US Protestants "are more prone to the fundamental attribution error," stressing others' dispositions over their situations, than US Catholics, "because of Protestants' greater beliefs in a personal soul" (864). Yet all religions encourage cooperation, especially with "moralizing, punishing gods" (859). They are "adaptive" at the group level, with synchronized rituals and "costly signals" of sacrifice for in-group cooperative trust, sometimes through out-group competitive enmity (859).

Aiming at a balance of forces, Chinese Daoism helps persons to live longer and understand their fate, in relation to divine ancestors, afterlife judges, and hellish punishments, through a more *interdependent* sense of identity than in the West. Confucian propriety stresses ritual behaviors for harmony in this world, with each person having a fixed role (*fen*) in the family, society, and cosmic order. Although they differ with a focus on natural or social order, both value interdependent identity: "as a share of the whole, such as the Tao, and not a distinct set of rights belonging to the individual" (Munro 18). This deemphasizes the individual's personal qualities, with Neo-Confucian, Daoist, and Buddhist theories of each mind as being part of the whole, as One Mind (19).

The ancient Chinese tradition of "cyclic progression" in the five phases (water, fire, wood, metal, and earth) and *yin-yang*, which "tend naturally in the direction of rhythmic balance and harmony," influenced Daoism and Buddhism with a holistic, interdependent, organismic universe of *kan-ying*, "sympathetic resonance" (Sharf 78–83). This contrasts with the European Christian tradition of linear progress in history, dominion over nature, and independent individual (undivided) souls. Yet Confucianism focuses on the *yang* of masculine actions with filial duties, while Daoism emphasizes the *yin* of feminine, peaceful, natural, and mother-child ideals, related to Buddhist "compassion" (Ching 95–6). There is also a tension between "wrestling with nature," in the longevity goal of Daoist alchemy, and "harmony with nature," in the primordial, maternal Way of Daoist philosophy (224), especially when scholars acknowledge the continuities between religious and philosophical Daoist traditions (Prothero 311–12).

From the eighth century onward, Neo-Confucians connected social rites with rationalist metaphysics and practical realism, theorizing the "destiny of individuals" in relation to the "purpose of nature as a whole [which] is the nourishment and perpetuation of creativity and life." But philosophical Daoists and Chan Buddhists viewed reality as illusory—and the whole, whether Dao or One Mind, as not having a purpose (Munro 17). More like Neo-Confucians, Christians saw reality as God-given and each individual as having the purpose of union with God, through faith, hope, and love, or the Orthodox sense of deification (*theosis*, merging with divine energy, not essence). This also involved Catholic missionary and Protestant evangelical drives of converting others and their territories as part of God's purpose in the world. Such religious colonizing spread from the Holy Land, Roman Empire, and later European powers to Asia, Africa, and the New World, building numerous churches, yet with pilgrims also returning through sacred nostalgia. Thus, the individual ego (as *cogito* or *conquistador*) connects with the divine Creator in the Christian tradition. But ideas of self and Other, reality and purpose, are questioned more in Buddhism and Daoism, with contingency, resonance, and interdependence emphasized.

Extending Chinese interdependence through multiple lifetimes and levels of being, across clan identities and good/evil conflicts, Buddhism advocates an individual path to nirvana, yet compassion toward others, even those who commit evil, balanced with equanimity about change and error. Evil arises from "defilements," which are ultimately insubstantial and "imagined by the deluded mind" (Harvey 116). This may be countered by an awareness of emptiness as "the antidote to all views," in a "positive appreciation of ... harmonious organic unity" (120). In twelfth-century Buddhist philosophies of "empty learning," unlike Confucian practical learning, "true individuality merged with, rather than was submerged in, holistic unity" (de Bary 341). Christianity stressed historically revealed truths in sacred texts, with good conquering evil and "specific points of doctrine as factual assertions" against others (Ching 132). But Buddhism viewed myths and "divergent doctrinal formulations" as secondary to salvation, with major schools emphasizing Emptiness or Consciousness "to reconcile a difficult range of often contradictory teachings attributed to the Buddha." Interpretations of the sayings of Jesus, as biblical or apocryphal, created more conflicts between competitive Christian sects.

As Buddhism spread from India to China, it mixed with preexisting Daoist, Confucian, and ancestor worship traditions for two thousand years. Thus, "syncretism, multiplicity, and diversity were the norm rather than the exception through history" (Mai 174–5). Eastern Christianity also spread to China, as early as the seventh century. But all of these religions were repressed as China modernized. Temples were destroyed through Christian influences during the Taiping Rebellion (1851–64) and through nationalist movements in the early twentieth century (Schipper 17–18). Most of the remaining temples were destroyed or turned into factories, police stations, army barracks, government offices, and schools—with the rise of Maoist Communism. Further destruction and religious persecution occurred during the 1966–76 Cultural Revolution (Fisher 513–14). However, various forms of religion have reemerged in recent decades. Many temples have been rebuilt, through believer's donations for spiritual "merit" (Bruntz 74), plus the Communist government's support and control. This was partly an attempt to address the popular perception of a morality crisis in China, but also to officially "sing an economic opera" of capitalism on the stage of cultural revival (Shive 251).

Five religions have been legal in China since 1982—Buddhism, Daoism, Catholicism, Protestantism, and Islam—with the Communist Party "educating clergy to be loyal to the state" (Bruntz 73). Yet some religions, such as Tibetan Buddhism and Falun Gong, are restricted or repressed as political threats to Party rulers. Thus, there are "red market" (official), "black market" (outlawed), and "gray market" religions with "ambiguous legal status" (Yang). Even in red-market, state-sanctioned religions, "clerics and laypeople must often fight to control temple sites when their goals of religious revival do not coincide with the money-making schemes of local officials or hired developers" (Fisher 514). Many temples "have been turned into tourist sites," with Buddhism "caught between the state and the market," and some monasteries are managed "like conventional, for-profit companies" (D. S. Yü 104).

Daoism and Buddhism do not require exclusive professions of faith like Christianity or Islam—and there is no rite of initiation for lay people (Ching 223; Shahar, "Violence" 183–5). A person might seek ritual help or medicine from a Daoist priest, regarding spiritual forces and physical longevity, which involve the proper balance of various aspects of *qi* (or *chi*). The same person may meditate and chant near a small Buddhist statue at home. This "polytropic" person might bow with lit incense, burn spirit money, light candles, and leave a food offering in similar ways at a Buddhist or Daoist temple— for progress in multiple lives or longevity in this one and to appease family ghosts. The same person may also follow Confucian principles of proper thinking and acting in this world, for harmony in the current social order. "A person with a particularly difficult problem will go to a Daoist temple, then a Buddhist temple, then a spirit medium, and then even a Catholic church or a Muslim mosque" (Chau, "Efficacy" 80). A Daoist priest may perform both Daoist and Buddhist rites within his lineage, "to protect or heal the living" and "ferry the deceased through the trials of purgatory" to the next rebirth, wearing a different vestment and using a different text for each tradition (Mozina 48). Chinese folk religion also influences urban Buddhism, with *feng-shui*, ancestor worship, and auspicious date beliefs (and rites) creating a "harmonious and vital interactive relationship" between textual and popular Buddhism (Yao and Badham 111–13). This involves the desire for both spiritual and material benefits, while the "political separation between religion and communism has become very blurred" (114).

Historically, there have been periodic rivalries between Chinese religions for favoritism from the emperor, with various persecutions, including the laicizing of monks and destruction of temples, yet not to the degree of Europe's sectarian violence. "Much like the Western monotheistic faiths, Chinese religions tend to adopt one another's holy places. But whereas in Jerusalem and in Constantinople (Istanbul) this has led to warfare, in China, divergent religious establishments often coexist harmoniously" (Shahar, "Violence" 186). In European churches and their communities, especially since the medieval Gothic period, "*harmonia* or a fitting order established by God is a central theme" (Sheldrake 53). Yet this also points to "a higher sense of beauty" (54)—with the mimetic rivalry of cities, nations, and church towers competing for divine authority, between Christian denominations and against their Abrahamic cousins.

Traditionally, Confucian temples and family ancestral halls "were only open to a precisely defined group of people ... [while emphasizing] civil virtues and social rules" (Schinz 401). But Daoist and Buddhist temples were open to all, with many providing "general public services." Currently, Daoism tends to serve people with "ceremonies pertaining to marriage, children, and the prosperous future of the family," while Buddhism specializes in funerals (402). Both have involved "social organizations, such as guilds, merchant associations, provincial clubs, and others, [which] combined their meeting halls and charitable institutions with temples to their respective patron saints." Yet there is also a museum-like aspect to urban Buddhist temples, which often have "an exhibition hall to showcase the monastery's historical objects" (Robson, "Faith" 127). Confucian temples are mostly museums today, but with attendants who help visitors with individual rites. The veneration of Confucius has lessened since the twentieth century with a modern school system replacing temple-oriented institutions (Ching 195).

Buddhist or Daoist rituals may be arranged by a family, with lay people attending and monks or nuns leading (as I have observed at a distance). Sometimes these rites involve local village gods, subsumed into the city temple's pantheon with urban territorial expansion (Goossaert, "Territorial" 60). The sponsorship of such rites brings merit to one's family and ancestors, for "worldly benefits" as well as "personal salvation"— and thus has been a "lucrative market" for Buddhist monasteries across many centuries (Poceski 55–6). Entry fees are also charged at major temples. Despite the Buddhist doctrine of non-attachment, lay Chinese often purchase religious props for personal performances in them. Thus, "materializing ... [karmic] merit and venerating sacred objects" are central to Chinese Buddhism and its buildings (Tarocco 628).

Some European churches charge tourists for entering or for taking photos, but most are accessible without a fee, even at popular times of the year. Monumental churches, as tourist and pilgrim attractions, often have religious goods for sale at a counter near the entrance. They sometimes display museum-like signs with their artworks and may have an exhibition hall for religious treasures. Most Catholic churches are open daily for personal prayers and communal rites, whereas Protestant churches are typically closed during weekdays, unless open for tourists. The Catholic tradition values church architecture, art, and spaces as having *substantial* (or trans-substantial) sacredness, in the House of God, while Protestants tend to value church community more as *situational*, in the House of the People of God (Crosbie, "Hermeneutics" 48; Jones 2: 103–5).

Unlike Christians required to attend church every Sunday, followers do not need to attend weekly services if Daoist (with many gods and afterlife realms) or Buddhist (with bodhisattvas helping devotees, but no God as creator/judge). Yet several Buddhists I talked with in China said they usually go to the temple at the beginning and middle of each month. I saw many people drop money into donation boxes at the various statues, more so than in Catholic churches. There are also retreats for Buddhist lay groups, who study and chant with the monks, along with private performances, such as family funeral rites, with monks serving "the laity in several priest-like ways" (Harvey 217). Thus, there is often a "close lay-monastic relationship ... unlike [with] most Christian 'monks.'"

Temple-monasteries have abbots, but unlike the pyramids of priests, bishops, and patriarchs in Catholic and Orthodox Christianity, there has been, in Chinese Buddhism, "no national hierarchy in recent centuries" (Harvey 237). Most monasteries act as "independent institutions," although some are "branch monasteries of larger ones." Earlier as well, during the Ming dynasty (1368–1644), Buddhism involved

> little institutions dispersed randomly across the country, without hierarchy, internal organization, or any regulatory body other than what the state supplied. With the exception of limited ties among sister monasteries and linked pilgrimage sites, Buddhist institutions did not participate in a larger institutional framework at any level. Unlike European Christianity, Ming Buddhism was not woven into the net of secular power.
>
> Brook 29

And yet today, there is a state bureaucracy that monitors and "subjugates all Buddhist affairs to local authorities" (Wu and Tong 19–20).

Most Buddhist temples in China, especially in large cities, are typically monasteries where a community of monks or nuns perform as contemplatives, while also helping visitors with acts of devotion. Buddhist clergy are usually not married, abstaining (like many Buddhist laity) from meat and alcohol, as well as sex. In the fifth century, Daoist priests began adopting such celibate and monastic practices (Bauer 174). But asceticism, part of Buddhism from the start, "never became an integral part" of Daoism. Clergy in the Daoist Zhengyi tradition may be married and leave the temple, after working there for part of the day, to join their families or work part-time elsewhere. In both Buddhism and Daoism, clerical orders may be temporary positions, not a lifelong commitment as with Catholic priests, monks, and nuns, who vow to be celibate for life. So do Orthodox bishops, monks, and nuns, although priests may be married, like Protestant pastors. Hence, the religious buildings considered here have various theatrical contexts, with different types of clergy as actors, characters, directors, and stage managers.

Evolutionary Gains and Losses (with Devilish Directions)

It may seem odd, with research on temples and churches, to use neuroscience and evolutionary theory. Dualist traditions in Eastern and Western religions view the mind as soul-like, distinct from the body, migrating after death to another lifetime or a supernatural realm, unlike a brain-based view of the mind. Buddhism and Christianity also involve human progress toward perfection, through degrees of enlightenment or union with God. Darwinist evolution means *adaptive success* within a given environment *and flexibility* to change with it, not progress toward a divine state of being. And yet, I refer to the animal-human heritage of our brain's inner theatre networks to investigate how temples and churches are *bio-cultural* expressions of our shared humanity. This "bottom-up" view will appeal, I hope, to readers who believe in a transmigratory mind or soul, evolving toward perfection, as well as readers who do not. I also consider a "top-down" view of emotions as socially and psychologically "constructed," according to recent research in affective science. We are all embodied beings, dependent on our brain matter and related to animals—even if *they* do not build temples and churches, with ideas of a "more perfect" species or union with the divine. We are indeed culturally transformed animals, whether through a divine Creator, as Author and Audience of our mortal lives, or not.

Perhaps we seek "perfection," through advanced brains, minds, and technologies, because of our human ancestors' adaptive success and yet extreme flexibility, conforming to many habitats, but radically changing them, while dreaming of better realms. This enabled much "progress" by our species, especially in recent centuries, yet it also produced great destructiveness of natural environments. Our species' evolution, beyond instinctual ties to a given habitat, produced globally successful minds. But evolution (with or without a creator God) also produced the primal *alienation* of humans, unlike other animals. We bear a drive for psycho-spiritual belonging, meaning, and purpose, beyond mortality, even at the cost of physical survival, which religions have shaped in divine and devilish directions, through their sacred spaces.

The devilish directions include territorial and reproductive conflicts of "God's chosen people" or a restored "Caliphate," and related secular attempts at perfection on earth through a "master race." These led to crusades, inquisitions, pogroms, euthanasia laws, genocides, and terrorist acts across the centuries. Good versus evil battles "in every religious tradition" offer a justification for violence as "cosmic war," elevating socio-political conflicts "into the high proscenium of religious drama" (Juergensmeyer 282), with the "martyrdom of fallen heroes and demonization" of enemies (de Vries 517). But Christianity may be exceptional in this regard.

> Whereas most religious systems in history, including Buddhism, rabbinic Judaism, and Islam, have attributed an ambiguity, even (in Asia) a ritual flexibility to maleficent supernatural forces, Christianity's explicit attention to the absolute evil of the Satanic host preoccupies its earliest scriptures and pervades its historical negotiations with non-Christian cultures.
>
> Frankfurter 529–30

And yet, religions often encourage compassionate charity, showing the best as well as worst in "human nature" with its remnant instincts, moral intuitions, and righteous orders continuing to evolve in many "en-brained," bio-cultural varieties (Downey and Lende 32).

While respecting the varieties of religious designs, I want to explore what different cultural traditions have in common, too, as ways of "programming" human consciousness—both in the anthropological sense of Clifford Geertz (Bassil-Morozow 11) and in the neuroscience analogy of our brains as "wetware" computers, "rewired" through experiences. What do we *share* in our brain structures and evolutionary heritage that emerges in the distinctive religious buildings of China and Europe, especially regarding good and evil forces in the world? Keys to this question can be found in our animal-human drives or "innate dispositions" (Ziegler and Saler 46), primary to social emotions, and "higher order" consciousness, shaped in particular ways by each culture—through personal, familial, and spiritual experiences.

Animals seek pleasure and avoid pain through a primary *survival* goal and a seasonal *reproductive* drive, involving territories, hierarchies, nurturing, and playfulness in social mammals. Humans, however, have lost much of the instinctual patterning of drives, emotions, and behaviors that regulate other animals. We became flexible in adapting to and altering environments around the globe—living together in numbers far greater than any other primate. Yet with such flexibility came a greater uncertainty of human reactions, especially with past and future projections of loss and mortality. We became *wilder* than wild animals, as individuals and groups, needing moral norms to constrain our behaviors. For example, unlike most mammals, humans are sexually active throughout the year, except as restricted by religious and civil rules. With our vastly larger groups, we evolved the interplay of cooperative and competitive emotions, complex behaviors, and cultural norms to refocus our primal drives, "for more cohesive patterns of social organization" (J. Turner 2). Yet we exhibit reckless emotions and behaviors at times, beyond the coordinated inner and interpersonal signals that we inherited and moral values that we learn.

Our species' mix of highly cooperative and competitive drives can lead to group influences that objectify others. Anthropologist Scott Atran points to an experiment finding that a college student's perceptions, even of the length of one line compared with other lines, can be altered by other students' false reactions (219–20). Atran relates such group effects to the "essentialism bias" of human beings as they categorize and scapegoat out-group members, to "dominate others by seeing them as belonging to a different species" (306). This "universal and innate propensity" helped our ancestors to survive, fostering in-group cooperation, but also out-group enmity, increasing the "risk of conflict" (306–07). Thus, humans "are their own worst predators" (307).

Atran's research on Indonesian madrasas (Muslim schools) found that students who think all humans are born evil were "about eleven times more likely to believe it was their duty to kill non-Muslims" (308). Atran also states that women typically score higher on measures of group cooperation than men, except during competition with other groups when men score higher (325).[15] Also, men "kill more than women do in competitive situations," including those that involve "small bands of buddies." Transcendent group and ideological emotions are thus involved in warfare: "of status and pride, ... dread and awe, ... to dominate, and to avenge" (333). This relates to the patriarchal networks of our inner theatres and to the threat displays of our primate relatives, especially of males during competitive mating rites or in situations of natural awe. Hence, religious buildings reflect a distinctively human, hyper-theatrical display of cooperative and competitive drives, evolved from our animal ancestors: reproduction and care, yet also survival, alliance-hierarchy, and territoriality, with angelic and devilish twists in us, through extended playfulness, mimetic belonging, and mythic seeking.

---

[15] See Fine 143–9, on various experiments about social circumstances influencing higher levels of testosterone "with competition" and lower "with nurturance" in both men and women.

Animal-Human Drives in Religious Buildings

Historically, cultures around the globe have extended the instinctual drives, evolved constraints, and self/other-deceptions inherited from animal ancestors, through sacred ideals of judgment, community, and sacrificial beliefs. *Survival and reproduction* drives, with pain/pleasure signals, become: (1) the soul's survival with eternal or multi-life punishments and rewards, (2) immortal ties to ancestors sometimes seen as ghosts or gods, and (3) suffering turned into ecstatic joy or calm wisdom, exemplified by martyrs being sacrificed or bodhisattvas accepting change with equanimity. Mammalian *care* becomes idealized in the Virgin Mary as Madonna with Child (for Catholics), or Jesus as personal Lord and Savior (for many Protestants), or Guanyin as Bodhisattva of Compassion and Child-Birth (for Chinese Buddhists). While Jesus offers his nurturing body and blood, in bread and wine, Mary and Guanyin are associated with miraculous milk, water, or "sweet dew" (Reis-Habito 66). And yet, building on care, primate group *hierarchies* extend, through bio-cultural evolution, to human religious orders of being and political structures of orthodoxy, which demand moral devotion, as explored through churches and temples in the chapters ahead.

Territoriality in animals, for biological sustenance and safety, extends to human religions also, with sacred spaces, food offerings, ritual objects, and peaceful "sanctuaries." Yet this animal-human drive, in a cosmic framework, sometimes evokes a fighting instinct for the "holy land" or against invasive satanic threats. This gives believers a transcendent sense of belonging and purpose, even beyond biological survival and reproduction, with the sacrifice of self or offspring. A church or temple is thus a special kind of territory, a piece of holy land deriving from the cultural contexts of past hierarchies, often built upon the site of dominated or subsumed cults. It engages the visitor's survival and reproduction drives in current spiritual forms with pleasure/pain, arousal/calmness, and various emotions, through moral norms and self/Other beliefs or deceptions. Unlike European churches, however, the traditional siting of a Chinese temple "must respond to the local flow of *qi*, and structures therefore tend to complement, rather than dominate, their natural surroundings ... [through] interdependent sequences of space" (Cannon 204–05).

Play is another element of our evolutionary heritage, extending from physical to metaphysical forms in churches and temples. Humans have evolved an extended juvenility, or "neoteny," related to our extreme flexibility in behavior, with enlarged brains and our long period of learning, as "altricial" (underdeveloped at birth) social carnivores (Alcorta 249–50). Chimpanzees mature around age three, but human brains continue to grow, with "wires" (axons) not fully "insulated" (wrapped with myelin) until the mid-twenties. Physically, human adults appear to be immature apes, with a large, round skull, and flat, broad, hairless face, including large eyes, small teeth, and "the smooth, vertical dome of the forehead," plus our "relative ease of bipedality" (Brin 257). We extend play into adulthood, as silly and serious, joyful or "dark" (Schechner, *Performance*), with numerous theatrical media. Inner/outer hyper-theatricality is a distinctive aspect of our species, reflected in the transcendent playfulness of temples and churches. This involves angelic, cherubic, and devilish dimensions of animal-human drives, through mimetic belonging and mythic meaning-making.

Among other species of primates, only bonobos have been observed playing as adults. Yet young mammals play in many species. With extra energy and clumsiness at times, they rehearse fighting, fleeing, or hunting skills, gaining confidence and trust when playing together. Experiments with rats find that social play, along with positive maternal care, helps them to recover rapidly from adversity, such as the fearful smell of a predator (Siviy). Other experiments show that rat brains, while asleep, rehearse the same networks through "hippocampal replay" that were active in exploring a maze while awake (Bendor and Wilson). This suggests that humans use *playful dreams* to consolidate memories, especially regarding survival tasks. The joy of PLAY and the wonder of dreams extend to theatrical media, involving various other *primary emotions*: SEEKING, FEAR, PANIC/GRIEF, RAGE, LUST, CARE, disgust, and surprise—in safe spaces, through "as if" doses of mimicry.[16] Yet humans also SEEK immortal meaning and purpose through group (grooming/gossip) belonging, as these primary emotions extend to social feelings through mimetic and narrative, symbolic and metaphysical frameworks.

Religious buildings often evoke solemnity, not silliness. Personal sacrifices are demanded for elite membership, as "costly signals" of full commitment (against free-riders), exchanging material for spiritual values. This involves martyrdom as a traditional Catholic ideal, paralleled by believers who handle venomous snakes and drink poison, as performances of faith, in some American Protestant churches (Bulbulia and Sosis; Iannaccone). In Asian traditions, Buddhist monks have burned their fingers to show non-attachment or immolated themselves in political protests. Japanese kamikaze pilots in the Second World War used Zen Buddhist techniques and Islamic extremists have more recently become suicide bombers, although such practices involved great harm to others, beyond religious restraints.

Even with ordinary visitors to a church, temple, or mosque, some measure of respect is required as a sacrificial signal, especially regarding bodily display. I recall, for example, seeing a young woman, who had waited with her family in line for an hour to enter Saint Peter's Basilica in the Vatican, being prevented entry near the door because

---

[16] Following neuroscientist Jaak Panksepp, I use capital letters here for "primary-process emotions" that he researched in rats and cats, as correlative to "affective systems" in humans (Panksepp and Biven xi), involving "whole brain functions, not only the feelings" (Solms 105). But I also list two others specified by Antonio Damasio, who further defines background emotions "such as well-being or malaise, calm or tension," social emotions "such as embarrassment, jealousy, guilt, or pride," feelings of feelings, and "as-if body loop" feelings (*Feeling* 51, 281–8). See also Damasio, *Looking* 117–18: "the body-sensing areas constitute a sort of theatre where not only the 'actual' body states can be 'performed,' but varied assortments of 'false' body states can be enacted as well, for example as-if-body states, filtered body states, and so on." In Chapter 1, I consider the work of Lisa Feldman Barrett, drawing on James Russell's psychological construction model of emotions and challenging Panksepp's theory of primary, animal-human emotions. The reader might also compare such categories and lists of emotions to Silvan Tomkin's "primary affects": Positive (Interest-Excitement and Enjoyment-Joy), Resetting (Surprise-Startle), and Negative (Distress-Anguish, Fear-Terror, Shame-Humiliation, Contempt-Disgust, and Anger-Rage).

her skirt was too short. Likewise, my wife was told by a uniformed guard in the Basilica of Saint Francis in Assisi to cover her bare shoulders with her scarf. At the doorways of mosques that I have visited in Istanbul, scarves were loaned to women visitors for a similar reason. And yet, the images in churches and temples (though not in mosques) involve playful, dreamlike, and sometimes erotic figures, as well as an ordering—a summoning and putting in place—of dangerous, dark play by devilish spirits, animal figures, or rebellious humans.

In medieval Europe, a half millennium after the fall of the Roman Empire, formal theatre reemerged through churches. Monks acted as biblical characters during meditative songs around the altar. Lay people performed religious dramas between the Gothic arches in churches and in church squares, playing angels and devils as well as human characters (Pizzato, *Inner* and *Mapping*). In the Baroque era, Jesuit priests used theatre to teach religious ideals with elaborate special effects (O'Malley 43). Even more fundamentally, throughout their histories, Catholic Masses and Protestant Communion services have reenacted the offering of bread and wine by Jesus at the Last Supper. With different interpretations of the rite's substantial or symbolic meaning, the priest or minister *played the role* of Jesus for watching believers (Dix).

Traditionally, Chinese Buddhist temples held festivals with monks performing plays about the Buddha's mythic and historical lives (George 162). Today, Daoists priests and nuns perform temple rites (as I witnessed in Shanghai) to lead a ghost over a bridge to a better afterlife realm or to exorcize demons from someone's home. Chinese Buddhists also bathe a statue of "baby Buddha" (annually) or burn incense, spirit money, and other paper offerings (daily) to help departed family members, as is also done in Daoist temples. Musical performances are likewise crucial to many temple and church rituals, along with the play of sunlight in an open yard or through stained glass, plus the theatricality of candle flames, incense smoke and its scents, or other sensual elements, evoking various emotions and dreams of divine immanence or transcendence. Thus, religious buildings extend the creativity yet danger of play, dreams, and mimetic emotions from the primal drives of our animal-to-human evolution, toward supernatural frameworks of meaning. Specific examples of this will be explored in the pages ahead, with a focus on *patriarchal, maternal, and playful (childish/devilish) dimensions*, related not only to Family Extensions in various cultures, but also our brain's inner theatre structures and evolutionary drives.

Neuro-Precedents

Theorists in architecture and aesthetics have drawn on neuroscience to develop a more complete view of relations between such fields. John Eberhard, founding president of the Academy of Neuroscience for Architecture, uses the analogy of a "cathedral" (borrowed from archeologist Steven Mithen) to describe the evolution of the human brain with "naves" and "chapels" of general and specialized intelligence, along with further details from neuroscience as a new knowledge base for architects (*Architecture* 22–4). Ann Sussman and Justin Hollander develop four main principles of "cognitive architecture": Edges Matter (with humans as a "wall-hugging" species), Patterns Matter (with our visually oriented brains), Shapes Carry Weight (with the human preference for bilateral symmetry), and Storytelling is Key (as a distinctive role in our species' "place-making"). Such principles inform the current study, regarding *which* edges, patterns, shapes, and stories matter in specific religious buildings, especially through Family Extensions: patriarchal, maternal, and trickster.

Harry Francis Mallgrave relates mirror neurons in the brain (firing both when an action is performed and observed) to empathic theories of architecture, according to which we "animate architectural events" through our own bodily experience of gravity ("What" 22–4).[17] In his book, *The Architect's Brain*, Mallgrave charts various neuro-architectural expressions in Western culture: (Neoclassical) humanist and enlightened; (Romantic) sensational, transcendental, animate, empathetic, and gestalt; and (Modern) neurological and phenomenal—involving principles of anatomy, ambiguity, metaphor, and hapticity (touch). Mallgrave's terms are insightful for the current study, including his view of the eighteenth-century Baroque as a "picturesque" style, exemplifying the "sensational" brain, which correlates to the *playful* supportive/trickster *stagehand* in my view. It also relates to an earlier period of church history, as Mallgrave suggests. The medieval Gothic, "with its variety of forms and lack of symmetry, is picturesque" (47)— but through different values given to edges, patterns, shapes, and stories. Such cultural styles of "architecture seeking transcendence" (Bermudez, Introduction 8) are compared here regarding outer theatricality,[18] created through ideals of the past interacting with a visitor's inner theatre, especially with compassionate or threat-based awe.

While acknowledging such "embodied" approaches to architecture, neuroscientist Michael Arbib stresses the "disembodied" rationality of human language and culture (91). Humans experience a building through both "cues afforded by the spatial structure" and "signage, appealing to the symbolic aspect of their cognition." However, architect Juhani Pallasmaa reminds his colleagues that all the senses are involved in spatial designs, not just vision but also hearing, touch, smell, taste, muscle and bone movement, and bodily identification/projection ("Architecture" and *Eyes*). In this book, I consider both the *disembodied*, abstract, symbolic dimensions of religious buildings and the *embodied*, holistic interplay of imagery and space performing with the visitor's senses. The latter includes bodily movement/projection, hearing, touch, and smell (e.g. incense), evoking pleasurable and painful emotions (or tasteful *rasas*), potential identifications, and theological ideals.

Regarding artistic imagery and the emerging field of neuro-aesthetics, V. S. Ramachandran has defined nine "laws," based on evolution and brain science: grouping, peak shift, contrast, isolation, problem solving, abhorrence of coincidence, orderliness,

---

[17] See also Pérez-Gómez who describes the neuro-phenomenology of architecture as "a heteropoietic system, capable of harmoniously complimenting the metabolic process of human consciousness" (225).
[18] See also Rufford, on theatrical mimesis, performativity, scenography, and dramatic space in architecture.

symmetry, and metaphor, as considered in my previous book (*Beast-People* 37–40). For example, the peak shift effect, with seagull chicks pecking even more at a yellow stick with red lines than at the mother's yellow beak, which has a red dot as instinctual trigger for them to get food, relates to abstraction in art and to *rasa* as the purified "essence" of aesthetic emotion (Ramachandran 210–11; Ramachandran and Hirstein 17–18). This peak shift has been observed in rats, too, when they are trained to respond to rectangles for food and become more attracted to 3:2 than 4:3 figures because of the greater "rectangularity" (Renoult 283). Ramachandran speculates that specific neurons in the human brain may respond to a "sensuous, rotund feminine form as opposed to angular masculine form," especially with such a *rasa* in art (Ramachandran and Hirstein 18). This relates, in my view, to rectilinear and curved, patriarchal and maternal *rasas*, in the peak shifts of religious buildings. Likewise, liturgical design specialist Richard Vosko argues that "rectilinear" pews will "prompt the participants to focus on the leader or action at one end of the room," as a "spatial setting that is confining and exclusive" (133–4). But when "seated in a circle or semi-circle participants are encouraged to engage with each other and the leader of the group" (134).

Physiologist Semir Zeki offers several cross-cultural principles of art—constancy, ambiguity, and abstraction—while relating distinctive styles of Western artists to vision processing circuits in the brain ("Art"; *Inner*; and *Splendors*). Alex Coburn and his colleagues extend such neuro-aesthetic explorations toward architecture, with a further consideration of neural systems involved: sensory-motor, emotion-valuation, and knowledge-meaning. They analyze the "immersive and multisensory nature of buildings" with potential "effects" of various types on "behavior, health and well-being" (1522). I will explore immersive and multisensory aspects of religious buildings, reflecting/evoking animal-human drives of primary, social, and (im)moral emotions. These relate to knowledge-meaning as abstract, constant, or ambiguous—through patriarchal, maternal, and supportive/trickster paradigms of inner/outer theatre networks in Western and East Asian traditions.

Various neuroscientists, who map the brain while relating it to theatre and culture, have been helpful in my quest, especially Bernard Baars and Iain McGilchrist. I also draw on the social neuroscience of Matthew Lieberman and the affective neuroscience of Jaak Panksepp, along with neuroscientific studies of world religions, led by Patrick McNamara. The mapping of brain areas active in *spiritual experiences* is considered, through the "neurotheology" experiments of V. S. Ramachandran, Michael Persinger, and Andrew Newberg. Affective, social, and cultural psychology research by Lisa Feldman Barrett, Jonathan Haidt, Richard Nisbett, and Jeanne Tsai is used as well. Thus, the current book is unique in its connections, examples, and theories about cross-cultural meeting points in the human brain, reflected in (and shaped by) diverse religious buildings.

The Plan

Chapter 1 investigates the major networks of the brain's inner theatre, using theatrical and filmic terms, as well as neuroscience research, regarding the inner/outer interplay of minds, performances, and spaces, through animal-human emotions and family paradigms. Artistic terms are applied cross-culturally—not to assume universality, but to discover common structures, while remaining open to differences. Drawing on the ancient Greek theory of *catharsis* (as clarifying, not just purging emotions) and ancient Indian theory of *rasas* (aesthetic emotional flavors) offers a connection between Western and Asian traditions. The chapter also uses modern theatre theories, along with neuroscience, psychology, philosophy, anthropology, and religious studies.

The chapter considers neuro-theological research on brain areas active with spirituality: from a sensed presence of Otherness to ecstatic mystical union, regarding Catholic prayer, Protestant "speaking in tongues," and Buddhist meditation. Relating such spiritual experiences to religious buildings and artworks, the chapter offers a "Family Extensions" model of design dimensions, involving patriarchal, maternal, and trickster figures in European and Chinese traditions. These family dimensions, extending from animal drives and human desires toward imagined (or pre-existing) divinities in a cosmic realm, are evoked in personal yet collective ways, from past to current brains, with the visitor's potential "*rasa*-catharsis," through specific designs in religious spaces.

Especially with East Asian comparisons, such a *rasa*-catharsis may evoke what philosopher Teresa Brennan calls "discernment" of how an apparently "self-contained Western identity" is also "permeable," as a "construction [that] depends on projecting outside of ourselves unwanted affects" (11–12). The inner *stagehands* of animal-human drives within and between brains (through mirror-neuron emotion-contagion signaling) are sometimes projected as devilish tricksters at the edges of religious sanctuaries, threatening the mythic-mimetic phantom egos of patriarchal and maternal ideals. This has produced historical conflicts between groups and individuals at holy sites, as hierarchic territories of reproductive survival.

My model, akin to recent trends in the Bio-Cultural Study of Religion (BCSR), involves a visitor's *projections* from personal experiences and particular inner theatre structures. This relates to the theory of the human brain's "hypersensitive agency detection device" (Shults, "Science" 73, 82), a tendency to see agency everywhere, affected by what is *reflected* in the church or temple. Like the BCSR, my model explores religious traditions with "anthropomorphic" projections/detections of god-birthing, and "sociographic" morals as god-bearing, in relation to mimetic scapegoating at sacrificial sites (81–5). However, I also explore them through the maternal, patriarchal, and trickster dimensions of different cultural orientations, regarding animal-human drives in inner/outer theatre networks, as "brain spirits."

Of course, there is not enough space here to consider all the varieties of sacred architecture from all parts of Europe and China. Yet the transcendent aspirations, group identifications, and political dangers reflected in my church and temple examples offer insights about current conflicts within Europe (between secularists, Christians, and Muslims), within China (between communists, capitalists, and certain religious groups), and with related ideologies and terrorist perceptions in the United States (or Israel). The various comparisons of religious buildings will be set up in Chapter 1, regarding experiments in cognitive psychology and neuroscience that show more *in*dependent, left-cortical characteristics in Europeans or Euro-Americans and more *inter*dependent, left- and right-cortical orientations in East Asians or Asian Americans. There is also a different sense of *time* in the myths of ancient China and other cultures, as "circular," like cyclical Buddhist lifetimes, in contrast to the Western "linear" sequence of Christian myths and lives (Yang and An 76). Yet a linear axis from south to north, public to private, *yang* to *yin*, and past to future in traditional house or palace designs also structures Chinese Buddhist temples, aligned with patriarchal family values. Yet again, ancestral tablets are honored toward the back of the building as a cyclical, maternal nurturing, future past for the living (Meyer 74, 85–90).

In religious buildings, sequential, focused, rectilinear designs and patriarchal figures relate to the brain's left-hemispheric, judgmental but hopeful, individualistic, courageously aggressive, objectifying networks (McGilchrist 446–8). And yet, drawing the visitor, through religious awe, toward an ecstatic *loss and rebirth* of self, curved, contextual, and womblike designs, with maternal figures, relate to right-hemispheric, nurturing, communal, danger-wary, subjective networks of the inner theatre. As psychiatrist Daniel Siegel points out, the right hemisphere mediates many basic emotions, including "withdrawal states" and facial expressions, while the left processes "social display rules" and "approach states" (*Developing* 151–3).[19] This relates to the holistic, "context-rich" perception of music and images through the right hemisphere or "linguistic symbols in a linear, logical, detail-oriented mode" through the left. Such emotive, yet ordered, perceptions are stirred in religious buildings, through awe as threat-based withdrawal *and* elevating approach, to lift the soul in beneficial or sacrificial ways.

Regarding indoor architecture more generally, a brain-mapping study found that curvilinear elements were judged by participants as more "beautiful" than rectilinear ones (in 100 photos, proportionally balanced in ceiling height and spatial openness)— activating the anterior cingulate cortex (ACC), which responds to "the reward properties and emotional salience of objects" (Vartanian et al. 10446). This relates to the inner *stage manager* in my model, which includes the dorsal (upper) ACC. Yet the functional characteristics of right and left hemispheres, and central frontal networks such as the ACC, also involve deeper emotional circuits and survival/reproduction drives, with more anger, jealousy, and gloating circuitry on the left side of the brain and various other feelings on the right.

Following Baars and others, I use theatre terms for key aspects of brain circuitry and shared performances, not as universals, but as metaphors for neural and cultural networks. "Comparative phenomenology does not universalize; it shows us how deeply cultural expectations shape intimate human experience" (Cassaniti and Luhrmann 342). Thus, the various strands of research considered in this book may help us to see our commonalities as human beings *through* cultural differences. Animal-human

---

[19] Brain hemisphere mapping is done mostly on right-handed people because left-handers can have the opposite functions, especially with withdrawal and approach emotions (Brookshire and Casasanto).

drives and inner theatre structures are radically open to cultural programing and neural rewiring—in our evolving identities as hyper-cooperative and hyper-competitive "baby gods," reflected in different religious buildings.

Chapter 2 explores *monumental developments* in European churches (and holy sites of Jerusalem) with comparisons to Chinese temples, regarding altar areas, reliquaries, crypts/caves, spires/pagodas, columns, screens, domes or curved eaves, courtyards, pools, and graves/memorials. It starts with the early evidence of prehistoric maternal-oriented temples in Malta and then considers ancient, more patriarchal, Greco-Roman paradigms. This chapter explores domestic, judicial, and funeral foundations for religious buildings in Europe, developing from ancient Rome in relation to the holy city of Jerusalem, and in China vis-à-vis India, as an expanding "sacred geography" (Robson, "Buddhist"). It considers ground plans and key figures of current examples, as reflecting more bounded or porous, independent or interdependent, heroic or harmonizing identifications. Such dynamics involve animal-human drives that all people have in common, transformed into culturally specific, metaphysical values, with patriarchal, maternal, and supportive/trickster dimensions. They appear in the sacred (purified) spaces of different religious traditions, with enduring or progressive styles. These also reflect past conflicts and the continuing evolution of democratic, communist, and capitalist ideals today—through self and other sacrifices to make mythic meanings beyond our mortal lives.

Chapter 3 compares how church and temple *spaces* perform around the visitor at significant historical and mythical sites, translating prior events and relics. Such spatial performances involve more rectilinear or curved, vertical or horizontal, sequential or contextual, focused or dispersed, and enclosed or open designs, along with the use of materials dominating nature or blending with it. These differences express the dominance of left-cortical[20] *scriptwriter/critic* networks—or more balance between those and right-cortical *mime-improviser/scene-designer* circuits—regarding temporal-lobe *audiences* and subcortical *stagehands*, with trickster aspects. Subcortical *stagehand* networks also make brain-body connections with the sensorimotor cortex at the top, through central thalamic, hypothalamic (autonomic nervous system), mid to hind-brain, and brainstem areas, plus the cerebellum, for the inner theatre's staging of self and Other. Thus, my model relates to the anthropology of spatial performances, regarding the cerebellum's role in evolving belief systems: "social sensory-motor skills, aspects of imitation, and production of complex sequences of behavior" (Fuentes 107).

Across the world's diverse cultures, basic human questions appear through sacred sites, as expressed in the title of a painting by Paul Gauguin in 1897: "Where do we come from? What are we? Where are we going?" Gaugin's painting might be criticized for depicting indigenous Tahitians as orientalist fetishes through modernist, Western, colonizing eyes. Yet its questions resonate across many cultures. The chapters ahead consider such questions through the potential emotions and actions evoked by religious buildings, with historical layers, design elements, and artistic styles. Depending

---

[20] Cf. Demaree et al. on left-frontal "dominance" emotions and right "submissive."

on the visitor, this may involve sublime awe, hopeful joy, moral righteousness, mournful guilt, or perspective-changing awareness. Each person's choices within religious buildings (and with this book's photos/videos), observing, engaging, or questioning such monumental spaces, may perpetuate or alter traditions of communal grooming, transcendent meaning, and mortal purpose, yet also group conflict, scapegoating, and self-sacrifice.

The concluding chapter summarizes how the initial hypotheses in Chapter 1 are confirmed or complicated by the qualitative data of re-membered experiences with churches and temples, detailed in other chapters, as auto-ethnography. Of course, various visitors have different experiences in the same religious building. Hence, the data of photographs and videos are shared with you, the reader, for further confirmations or complications.

This book considers the "ideal affects" of emotion models in Western and East Asian cultures, as they shape perceptions, decisions, and interactions, with different religions influencing brain networks, as cultural psychologists and neuroscientists have found (Tsai and Clobert 300; Tsai et al. 415; Han 70). It explores evolving animal-human drives and emotion signals, along with core affects (arousal/calm, pleasure/pain), plus family paradigms, extended in different cultural ways, as competitive and cooperative ideals, through church and temple details, with potential *rasa*-cathartic effects. It shares photos and videos for readers to consider whether European churches, with ancient temple precedents, reflect and evoke more left-cortical *scriptwriter/critic* melodramatic networks, through rectilinear, enclosed, focused, mechanical (bounded) designs. It also asks readers to contemplate whether Chinese temples, by comparison, reflect those aspects in more balance with right-cortical *mime-improviser/designer* tragicomic networks, through holistic, dialectical, harmonious, natural (porous) orientations. These characteristics involve other theatrical elements, too, such as prosody, kinetics, and narrative metaphors with music, ritual, and images, which I hope to explore in a subsequent volume.

How do West and East meet in our common evolutionary ancestry, animal-human drives, and neuro-theatrical networks, with sacred designs reflecting differences also, through family and individualist/collectivist paradigms? How do such commonalities yet differences set up today's secular values, with perceptions of good and evil—as sacrifices are demanded for collective meaning and *purpose* beyond mortality (sometimes through rivalry)? Exploring these questions may help us to find a kinship with others across religious traditions, by better understanding their perspectives, as attractive, threatening, or awe-inspiring.

1

Evolving Neuro-Theatrical Elements

Each of us has a particular sense of self in relation to the Other (natural or supernatural), from moment to moment, performing inside the brain—with an "inner voice," imagery, and emotions—while alone or interacting with others outside, in social and architectural contexts. Whether we believe in metaphysical beings or not, numerous experiences of others, especially in early life, shape the collective Other within the brain, which provides a mirror for the self, changing throughout one's lifetime. Those who believe in God or spirits, through religious definitions, perceive further imaginary and symbolic reflections of self in such aspects of the "big Other." Believers' self-Other reflections are not just within the brain, or in everyday social hierarchies, but also projected toward an immortal cosmic theatre, involving historical traditions and communities. What insights are offered from science, philosophy, and performance theory about "brain spirits," as animal-human emotions/motivations across the millennia, developing into metaphysical ideals of supernatural Others, with temples and churches honoring Him, Her, It, or Them?

Survival, Reproduction, and More

As mentioned in the Introduction, we inherit from our animal ancestors the drives of survival (with basic needs such as food, water, and sleep), reproduction (involving eroticism and aging), territoriality (including safety), mammalian nurturing care (needing and giving it), alliance/hierarchy (with cooperation and competition), playfulness (in waking and dream life), and primate belonging (especially through grooming/gossip as bodily purity and social conformity).[1] Humans have extended these biological drives, with the latter building on the former, far beyond remnant instincts, into many cultural realms. Other animals may not experience the same emotions that we do, certainly not with our cultural terms. But their instinctual behaviors show a common heritage of evolution, extending into four dimensions in our species: genetic, epigenetic (with survival/reproduction), social, and symbolic (Jablonka and Lamb). As highly social mammals, those four dimensions are felt and expressed through our seven motivational drives, plus an overarching aspiration for symbolic meaning and narrative purpose in our self-reflective, mortal lives (Table 1.1).

---

[1] I credit biologist David Bashor for inspiring my model of animal-human drives, with these terms, through our many discussions, prior to his death in 2015.

Table 1.1 Transformations of Animal Drives into Human Emotions and Cultural Values (with negative aspects)

Animal Drives	Primary Emotions	Human Cultural Extensions	Complex Social Emotions	Religious Ideals
seeking "immortality"	hope/grief	fantasies of past & future	meaning/mourning	gratitude & purpose
belonging-grooming	trust/disgust (alienation)	communal purity via gossip	liking/shame & guilt	good/evil rites
play	joy-surprise/mischief	games, sports, arts, media	freedom/rebellion	spirit powers
alliance-hierarchy	**fairness/rivalry**	**laws & rulers**	**honor-awe/envy**	**moral devotion**
nurturing-care	*empathy/panic*	*self-sacrifice*	*kin & reciprocal altruism*	*charity & compassion*
territoriality	**security/rage**	**border trade/war**	**nostalgia/vengeance**	**sacred site & sanctuary**
reproduction	love/lust	cooperative legacies	*friendship/greed*	beliefs & community
survival	desire/fear	ego & group pride/conflict	courage/anxiety	*soul's reward/punishment*

Competition and cooperation (as more **subcortical trickster**, *right-cortical maternal*, or left-cortical patriarchal networks) in humans:

- evolving from bipedal form, bigger cortex, premature birth, alloparenting, extended youth, abstract language, & self-awareness
- projected toward the Creator and higher species of gods, angels, devils, & bodhisattvas
- via pleasure/pain signals of arousal or calmness extending toward ecstasy as holy/addictive

Bio-cultural *survival* involves an ego that fears the body's aging and eventual demise, yet may also imagine a soul transcending mortality. Ironically, the human awareness of death sometimes twists, through self-esteem and worldview defensiveness, into addiction and sacrifice, which increase its likelihood, according to Terror Management Theory (Schimel et al.). Religions provide many examples of this, with myths about holy figures, rituals of transcendence, and miracles from immortals helping their devotees, yet sacrificial paradigms and demands. Thus, religious buildings evoke transcendent survival desires, but also fears of afterlife judgment, with ego and group continuation beyond death, through pride and conflict, courage and anxiety, toward perpetual reward or punishment.

The biological drive of *reproduction* becomes radically transformed through the imaginary and symbolic realms of various human cultures. Unlike other primates (except bonobos), humans have a sexual instinct that operates frequently for pleasure and social connection, not just the functional timing of reproduction. Sexual desire can evoke generous love, with beautiful fantasies and cooperative legacies through complex friendships, especially when sublimated as the reproduction of religious beliefs and rites, involving churches and temples. However, reproductive desires may turn into egoistic lust and greed, with objectifying control through the voyeur's passion, the pedophile's obsession, and the rapist's violence. Even pain can become pleasurable through uncanny twists of sexuality and this sometimes appears in religious imagery, with the transcendent ecstasy of a suffering martyr. European churches, more than Chinese temples, display a tension between physical beauty and spiritual value, with various period styles involving degrees of voyeuristic, sadomasochistic eroticism in artistic scenes, sculpted ideals, and fetishized, bejeweled relics. Yet such artifacts became miraculous power sources and pilgrim attractions, inspiring larger buildings and taller spires in reproductive, mimetic rivalry.

Territoriality and Alliance-Hierarchy

The *territorial* drive becomes magnified from primary emotions of security or defensive rage, through cross-border trade or wars, to complex emotions of personal nostalgia or group victimization and vengeance, often involving religious sanctuaries. Chimpanzees patrol their territories, killing intruders and sometimes warring with other groups (as the Netflix docuseries, *Chimp Empire*, shows). But humans compete over vast territories in much larger numbers and not just for material sustenance or reproductive safety. We also compete due to mythic traditions involving ancestral lands—or a "Manifest Destiny" to conquer new territory, as with God's "chosen people" in Euro-American, colonizing, Christian terms. The common drive for belonging and a purpose in life can be tied up with violent territorial disputes, especially regarding "holy" lands. Consider the example of Jerusalem, with nearby areas of Israel/Palestine, sacred to Judaism, Christianity, and Islam. Much blood was shed on various sides during Jewish diasporas and returns to the "Promised Land" (including the biblical, God-directed extermination of Canaanites and others), Christian crusades for hundreds of years, and Islamic occupations or displacements. Repeated, vengeful suffering and death involved righteous, melodramatic competition with the claims of others, while Yahweh, God, or Allah was believed to be watching.

The vexed sacredness of Jerusalem was crucial to distinctive developments in European churches. Yet ideological battlegrounds with artistic inspirations can also be found at Chinese sites. Ancient stories, beliefs, and natural features contributed to the value of certain places, across contending subcultures and various periods, toward the eventual Daoist or Buddhist temple. In medieval China, Buddhism was initially viewed as a foreign invader, with its celibate monks as anti-Confucian, anti-filial, anti-imperial, and economically unproductive threats (Poceski 45). By the end of the sixth century, however, Buddhism "established durable roots throughout the whole territory of China" (46), encouraging beliefs about afterlife realms and multiple lifetimes. Rivalries between indigenous Daoism and imported Buddhism led to the mimetic copying of sacred texts and divine figures. An early fifth-century text in the Daoist canon narrates how the sage Laozi rode west on his blue ox to India, a millennium before, and was reborn as the Buddha (Mollier 8). There were also "warrior monks" in the history of Buddhism, who "perpetuated state religious violence" (Wellman 41).

Attacks erupted against Buddhist clergy and their temples, especially in the fifth, sixth, eighth, ninth, and tenth centuries, or against Daoist in the sixth, under emperors allied with the other side. During the Taiping Rebellion (1850–64), "many Buddhist monasteries were damaged or destroyed" (Poceski 58). In the nineteenth to twentieth centuries, both Daoism and Buddhism suffered oppression under the "anti-traditionalist policies" of the late Manchu Qing dynasty and subsequent Nationalist Republican regime, defrocking clerics and monks (Chau, Introduction 4, 12; Nedostup). Maoist Communism increased the oppression, especially during the Cultural Revolution (1966–76) with the "proscription of all forms of religious belief and expression" (Poceski 60). Most temples were destroyed or turned into factories. But afterward, many were rebuilt as cultural heritage sites, sometimes with Daoist figures in Buddhist temples and vice-versa.

Despite the destruction of tens of thousands of temples in the fifth and ninth centuries, the rivalries between Confucians, Daoists, Buddhists, and secularists at various points in Chinese history involved less personal violence than Europe's many religious conflicts, including the long history of antisemitism climaxing in the Holocaust. Even the realm-expanding Mongol emperors, who ruled China in the thirteenth century, valued Buddhism and accepted multiple religions. Yet Europeans launched at least eight medieval Crusades to recapture the Holy Land, with Catholics brutalizing Orthodox Christians and "pagans," as well as Muslims. From the twelfth to nineteenth centuries, there were French, Roman, Spanish, and Portuguese Inquisitions against "heretics" in Europe and the New World colonies. From the fifteenth to eighteenth centuries, Catholics and Protestants executed at least 40,000 "witches." In the seventeenth century, wars between Catholics and Protestants killed about a third of Europe's population (Wellman 26). Such conflicts are reflected in many European churches, built on ruins or incorporating remains of prior temples and mosques, or with histories of iconic/aniconic battles in and between Orthodox, Catholic, and Protestant denominations.

Religious buildings also express the *alliance-hierarchy* drive in humans, shown in primate troops with dozens of individuals, but extended by our species into the power politics of tremendously larger groups. This involves fairness and rivalry with laws and rulers, plus honor, awe, and envy, especially at religious sites. Imperial histories in Western and Eastern Eurasia are rife with political patriarchs increasing their power through coalitions and violent conflicts. Many patriarchs in ancient Rome, China, and elsewhere were eventually viewed as gods, consolidating their power from prior fathers or creating a new dynasty. In medieval Europe, they claimed a "divine right" to rule, with one Almighty God believed to be watching and validating the human hierarchy, as alpha male, through His (and further) bloodshed. For example, the "Holy Crusades," involving Catholic ideologies of a "just war" with survival, reproduction, and territorial drives against religious rivals, included massacres of Jews and Orthodox Christians. It also involved carrying the heads of defeated Muslims on spears, boiling pagan adults in pots, and grilling children on spits, then eating them, according to a medieval report (Kimball 426–8).

This book explores how European churches, when compared with Chinese temples, reflect a Western bias toward left-cortical, competitive, melodramatic territoriality and hierarchy, extending globally through colonialism and capitalism. Yet China, in the last century, has also increased its competitiveness, while importing "communist," capitalist, industrial, and "hi-tech" ideals from the West, with a potential imbalance of left and right cortical characteristics, against the traditions shown in temples. Even more competitively, at the time of this book's writing, Russia, situated geographically between Europe and China, with their examples of democratic and autocratic, individualist and collectivist capitalism, drew on territorial, hierarchic traditions of colonial imperialism and medieval brutality in invading Ukraine, supported by the Russian Orthodox Patriarchate and mass/social media propaganda theatres.

Play

Extending competitive drives in positive ways, too, the hyper-theatricality of our embodied brain derives from the normal prematurity of human birth, with a radical openness to reprograming and rewiring by the cultural environment. This involves the extended youthfulness (neoteny) of our species, as mentioned in the Introduction. Our hyper-theatricality appears in the prolongation of a *play* instinct well into adulthood through various cooperative and competitive media today: sports, fantasy role-playing games, live theatre, film, television, virtual reality, web networks, etc. Play can function as a "rehearsal" (related to dreams) in practicing physical and social skills, including teamwork, for more serious, territorial and hierarchical battles later in life. The rough and tumble physicality of play appears in various species of young mammals, with violent yet restrained energies and joyful expressions—as can be seen at "dog parks." But play in humans can also be a way, especially with satire and protest, to reframe, question, or subvert social norms and situations, even regarding traditional beliefs about the divine order of things and the Spectator watching from above.

Joyful, rough-and-tumble play is a crucial emotional activity for young mammals of many species, practicing competitive and cooperative skills that are "aggressive, predatory and sexual, performed in a modified or exaggerated form," starting with specific signals of a fictive context (Vanderschuren et al. 86). In humans, this involves subcortical/limbic areas (nucleus accumbens, striatum, habenula, hypothalamus, and thalamus), plus the amygdala and prefrontal cortex, through opioid, dopamine, endocannabinoid, and noradrenaline systems. Rats deprived of play "have trouble adjusting their behavior" in new contexts. Studies also show that play-deprived, socially isolated, adolescent rats suffer greater levels of anxiety and depression, later in life as well. With mammals such as rats, various primate species, and humans, play apparently evolved for joyful stress-relief, with sensorimotor, emotional, social, and cognitive learning, as juveniles practiced adult behavior skills, especially through opioid pleasure and oxytocin bonding networks, within and between brains (Pellis and Pellis).

In humans, starting about age four, play is a key element for self and other reflections, as a developing "mentalization" skill, a Theory of Mind about others' views, in the child's inner theatre (Leuzinger-Bohleber 68–9). Survival/territorial/hierarchical and reproductive/nurturing drives, with fighting and mating skills in e-motional play theatres, have also been extended, in numerous human cultures, toward super-natural, destructive and creative realms. These involve higher-order species of deities, as evil, good, and tragicomic Others, reflecting back upon the human realm through myths, images, rituals, and beliefs. Unlike other primates, humans make such communal religious extensions through multiple nests of inner theatre mentalizing, imagining up to the "fifth-order intentionality" of others' minds within others' minds and so on, toward supernatural minds (Dunbar, *How* 166–8).

Our playfulness continues far into adulthood, sometimes becoming mischievous or rebellious toward the dominant order. Yet it is also subversively creative, especially when combined with the reproductive power of sexuality, as a "Dionysian" trickster fueling "Apollonian" beauty, in Nietzsche's terms for artistic drives. Religious and secular cultures try to control such tricksters, but moral limits also change with time. Such changing or clashing morals may trigger political conflict, violence, and oppression. Within a moral framework, however, our survival, reproduction, and play drives are sublimated toward non-biological legacies, with ideals of a person, image, or name living on—in the minds and monuments of future generations. Churches and temples are examples of this, with statues, paintings, mosaics, altars, relics, tablets, and buildings reproducing aspects of famous persons who died, yet live on, by image and name—even if there was no son or daughter to continue the genetic recipe.

Religious sublimation of the survival and reproduction drives often demands sacrifices, as "costly signaling" or "credibility-enhancing displays," for communal membership and divine rewards (Norenzayan 98–103). Yet so does the secular ideal of "no pain, no gain," in personal devotion to health, physical attractiveness, business success, or popular fame, especially through the current gods of mass and social media. Such ideals may involve the play drive with primary emotions of joy and mischief; cultural extensions in sports, artworks, and stage/screen media; complex social emotions such as freedom and rebellion; or spiritual powers in and beyond religious contexts (Table 1.1). Consumer capitalism and our expanding media cultivate transcendent, perhaps illusory ideals of self and community that also make sacrificial demands (Mavelli), as in the longer history of religious rites, sites, and buildings.

Often muted by respectful awe in religious buildings, playfulness emerges at significant edges—in architectural styles, artistic imagery, and performance spaces. By exploring this and other animal-human drives, we can see how distinctive traditions of religious buildings, East and West, reflect common aspects of the human staging of self and Other. They extend our survival, reproduction, territoriality, care, hierarchy, play, and belonging (grooming/gossip/purity) drives, through the acute need to find meaning and purpose in life, yet also beyond it.

From Nurturing Care to Belonging and Meaning/Purpose

Religious and secular sacrifices involve our animal drive for social *belonging* and our distinctive human need for *meaning* in life, which drives us beyond physical satisfaction. These drives come partly from mammalian herd and pack instincts, for safety or predation (with right or left hemisphere networks), as well as mother-infant bonding and *nurturing care*, creating transitional play spaces. Thus, the drive for belonging and need for meaning reflect our human evolution beyond the instincts of other animals, through the external womb of culture, especially as prematurely born apes dependent on multiple caregivers as other mothers (Hrdy). Emotion, image, and language networks develop in each child's inner theatre, toward symbolic abstractions of "mental time-travel" and perspective taking with embedded "recursion" (Corballis). This may involve a modeling of physical and social relationships in metaphysical frames— toward a sense of narrative *purpose* as well.

In Lacanian terms, we suffer from a Real "lack of being," unlike other animals, as an alienated "want to be" in being human (manque-à-être). This involves various desires and fantasies (with each person's unconscious "chains" of signifiers, especially through childhood experiences), as we seek Symbolic and Imaginary meaning for our lives, with a specific purpose in relation to others, as they mirror the value of self. The chapters ahead explore patriarchal and maternal ideals of Symbolic and Imaginary, outer and inner theatre dimensions, with angelic/devilish, childlike/monstrous, animal-human figures of the Real at their edges, as semiotic *chora* (Kristeva)— regarding left-cortical *scriptwriter/critic*, right-cortical *mime/designer*, and limbic *audience* with subcortical supportive/trickster *stagehand* networks.

Infant mammals, such as rat pups, show panicked distress calls when the mother is gone (and pain with lower opioid levels in their brains), SEEKING her briefly, and then show depressive GRIEF, as a withdrawal behavior to avoid predators (Panksepp and Biven 100, 295–8). These are key approach and withdrawal behaviors, with apparent primary emotions in our primate relatives, too, a "core affect system ... [of] separation distress that binds adult members of kin and social groups together" (Teasdale 23). In humans, though, it is not just physical separation, as for primates with jungle dangers. Meaning and purpose matter also: "the *perception* of isolation and disconnection . . . triggers fear and agitation," sometimes in a crowd or with people we know. "On the other hand, we can feel at one and connected with all beings even when, physically, we are completely alone." How do we gain that existential or spiritual framework?

When the rat mother returns, her licking of the pup improves its biochemical ability (through cortisol receptors) to function well during stressful situations later in life. This relates to the primate drive of *grooming*, building on mammalian *care*. Monkeys and apes spread hair and touch skin, picking and eating insects from each other's fur, for up to twenty percent of their waking hours, fueling their sense of belonging and reciprocation. Primate grooming increases cleanliness, food sharing (beyond insects), and possibilities for sex between mutual groomers, through endorphin pleasure and oxytocin bonding. Such extended connections may occur, with human friendliness as well, through (1) direct exchange, (2) "good feeling" and the good deed returned, or (3) good feeling plus the attribution of goodness to the giver (Bonnie and de Waal 223). The latter involves "gratefulness" from the receiver and thus a feeling of "debt" with an obligation to return the favor. Social exchanges with good feeling, gratitude, and attributions of goodness/debt are vital for supportive bonds between adults of various hierarchical standings, especially when extended in a divine direction, as reflected in churches and temples.

According to evolutionary psychologist Robin Dunbar, our *Homo erectus* ancestors developed "vocal grooming" in the form of *gossip* as groups grew increasingly larger about two million years ago (*Grooming* 115). This freed their hands for gestures and greater tool use, although touch continued to be vital for social bonds. Such mimetic bonding through vocal grooming also involved laughter, which other apes perform today, along with choral singing and dancing (*How* 102). These probably evolved in humans about 500,000 years ago, and then religious feasting and storytelling about 200,000. We now use about 65 percent of our verbal interactions for social topics, maintaining alliances through gossip ("Gossip" 105). Yet we also "trash" and "troll" others, whom we dislike or "unfriend" online, as impure regarding our group ideals. This becomes fodder for theatrical art and entertainment—or for beliefs in God "watching" to make us act morally (Bering 7, 191–2).

Through grooming/gossip, as personal purity and social conformity, a distinctively human "super-natural" drive evolved, regarding mortality, loss of loved ones, and ego/group identity: *seeking "immortal" meaning and purpose*, with feasting/sacrifice, gestural language, verbal storytelling, and mythic rites at sacred sites. This points to the end, yet also involves the beginning of each human life. With the bigger brains and upright bodies of our hominin ancestors, we evolved a normal prematurity of birth, with brains radically open to cultural influences. We each experience about half the proportional womb-time of other primates and thus extreme dependency on others as babies, affected by symbolic networks within and between human brains. Eventually, we extend trust, even to total strangers, through meta-physical signs of alliance (religious or not). Yet we are still vulnerable to alienation, with our physical and emotional needs, from childhood losses to later traumas, through communal grooming and gossip, sometimes with teasing, bullying, or other apparent evils.

Key aspects of animal-human, neuro-performance relations are shown in Table 1.1, with the survival drive based *more* in subcortical homeostatic body-brain connections, reproduction/care in right-cortical maternal circuits, and territoriality/hierarchy in left-cortical patriarchal networks. Mammalian play, primate social grooming, and human immortality-seeking arise in neural ties between those (and limbic) networks, building on the other drives. The most distinctively human drive extends from primal hope and grief in animal seeking to social emotions of meaning/mourning, narrative past and future fantasies, and religious ideals of gratitude and purpose.[2] In animals, the primal seeking drive is aimed instinctually at food, water, and safety, with panic for infant mammals when the mother is missing. Yet in humans, existential seeking involves mimetic and mythic dimensions: self-esteem value and world-view meaningfulness as "shields against the fear of extinction," shown by social psychology experiments with mortality reminders (Solomon et al. 189).

Mimetic, Mythic Play and a Trojan Horse

Human play, beyond that of other mammals, relates to the shift from an episodic animal awareness to the "mimetic" stage of our hominin ancestors, about two million years ago, with "playacting, body language, precise imitation," and tonal prosody through the larger frontal lobes of *Homo erectus*, according to psychologist Merlin Donald (261). Such developments, including rhythmic rituals, skill rehearsals, and advanced tool-making, may show the origins of "religion" in social relations and childhood imagination, extending to the supernatural with group survival benefits (Rossano 11, 110–16, 137–9). Developments 1.5 million years ago likewise involved "shifting patterns of caretaking, increased quality of diets, and an expansion of social coordination and communication" (Fuentes 143).

Thus, "cooperative breeding and hunting... by the time *Homo erectus* emerged" led to "control of fire and the practice of cooking" as a "precondition" for the gene-culture coevolution of "human moral order," with a central site for shared food and "a fairness ethic" (Gintis 24, 33). This involved anti-hierarchical egalitarianism, or *"reversed dominance hierarchy,"* as observed with hunter-gatherers today (according to Christopher Boehm), with collective warnings and punishments for would-be alphas (Gintis 33–4). Competitive scavenging through "coordinated collective action," driving away predators from their kill with "accurate overhead [rock] throwing" by *Homo erectus*, and with later forager weapons for big game, also set up in-group executions and out-group "warfare" (30–1), extending our ancestors' alliance-hierarchy and territoriality drives.

In Table 1.1, social grooming via human *gossip* relates to a further "mythic" stage, with *Homo sapiens* about a half million years ago. It included oral storytelling and left

---

[2] As anthropologists Michael Winkelman and John R. Baker put it: "The evolutionary drive for transcendence may derive from the desire to overcome the emotions of grief and loss" (132).

cortical language circuits in anatomically modern humans (Donald 260–2). This stage also involved early religious developments of in-group morality and out-group rivalry, through mimetic-mythic grooming, gossip, and belonging.

The distinctly human drive of immortal meaning and purpose seeking, which emerged in new ways with storytelling during the mythic stage, relates to the next as well, the "theoretic" stage. By 40,000 years ago, the "externalization of memory" began, through symbolic devices, such as Paleolithic cave paintings and figurines (or engraved lines on red ochre stones, at least 80,000 years ago in southern Africa).[3] Thus, Robert Bellah uses Donald's stages of human culture to explore possible details in the prehistoric evolution of religion, from practice to belief and sacred objects (118–35).

Today we experience all four stages—episodic, mimetic, mythic, and theoretic—in our infant to adult development, retaining them as inner/outer theatre levels. Mass, social, and spirit media devices "liberate consciousness from the limitations of the brain's biological memory systems" (Donald 305). Yet their external memory fields may also play the role of a "Trojan Horse," which "invades the innermost personal spaces of the mind. It can play our cognitive instrument, directing our minds toward predetermined end states along a set course" (316). Religious buildings, as symbolic devices with external memory fields, may play outer/inner, Trojan Horse tricks as well.

Together, the animal-human drives in Table 1.1 are somewhat akin to psychologist Abraham Maslow's "hierarchy" of needs, building on one another: physiology, safety, belonging/love, esteem, and self-actualization.[4] Spiritual "self-transcendence" was added at the top, in Maslow's journals, according to architects Robert Birch and Brian Sinclair, who argue for restoring that quality in current urban design (80–1). In my model, such needs, as emotional-motivational drives, involve the inner/outer theatre layers of animal heritage, brain circuitry, social networks, and symbolic complexity. They extend from primary emotions, through cultural behaviors, to social emotions and religious ideals (left to right in the table). The "higher" levels build on *and include* the older animal drives, with positive and negative aspects in the human (or divine) realm. Even among mammalian drives, play "hovers, as it were, between all the other instinctual emotions—trying them out and learning their limits" (Solms 119). Play, with its "as if" quality, may thus be a bridge from animal to human consciousness: "a biological precursor of thinking in general (i.e. of all virtual versus real action) and the whole of cultural life" (120, 234). It involves the expression and yet limiting of "free energy" (228–34) in neural and social, inner and outer theatres, related to trickster figures in many religious traditions.

The extent of panic, grief, anxiety, depression, and alienation shown by humans far outstrips the pragmatic instincts of other mammals. Our highly reflective, hyper-theatrical brains may be given to us by evolution alone, or karmic law, or a creator God.

---

[3] Recently, similar cross-hatch marks were found in a deep cave in South Africa where another species with much smaller brains, *Homo naledi*, buried their dead, 250,000 to 300,000 years ago. But the evidence is controversial.
[4] See Topa and Narvaez 194, on the influence of "Blackfoot understandings about self-actualization," after Maslow visited their reservation in Canada in 1938.

Either way, belief systems have material effects in believers' brains. Numerous rituals and myths around the world extend inner-theatre and social networks toward imagining super-natural mechanisms and beings. Different cultures have altered the remnant instincts of survival, reproduction, territoriality, care, hierarchy, play, and belonging/grooming/gossip through the human need for meaning in life, as the "storytelling animal" (Gottschall). Today, as in prior eras, many humans imagine a divine viewpoint, with a superior species of one or many, nurturing yet judging Spectators, watching and interacting with us, in a cosmic theatre involving our daily lives, especially at sacred sites, as external memory fields (with Trojan Horses).

Seeking Spirits through Liking, Wanting, and Bonding

From bodily perceptions to feelings and ideas, we experience animal-human drives through the distinctly human need for *meaning* with language and *purpose* with narratives, involving pain/pleasure signals. Yet these natural drives and super-natural needs are radically reshaped by each culture. A pang of hunger or thirst becomes a longing for a certain product to eat or drink, with the "affordances" and lures of the cultural environment (Gibson). Although modern societies may be more or less religious, they are consumerist across the globe, with the spirits of mass and social media increasing our greedy fantasies.

In each of us, current pain or remembered pleasure triggers a felt *desire* as a signal from the body that nutrients and possessions are needed for survival, focusing on a specific object, in a shift from right to left cortical, competitive activity. This involves the primary emotion of "SEEKING" or expectation-reward, in the dopamine (enthusiastic anticipation) and opioid (pleasure) systems. These systems also connect with the oxytocin system of *trust*, related to primate grooming and human gossip, through group bonding, along with personal mating and nurturing activities.[5]

Pleasure arises in the embodied brain through the anticipation of reward, even before getting it (Solms and Turnbull 115). Such anticipation, pleasure, and in-group trust systems are evoked by traditional religious buildings, through "social contract thinking" about how God or gods "should be appeased" in the reciprocal altruism of offerings (for physical or spiritual rewards), plus communal "kinship" with ancestral ties and "coalition psychology" (Kirkpatrick 253–4, 263, 267).

However, the left-cortical (*scriptwriter*) dopamine network of "wanting" is distinct from the opioid/oxytocin system of "liking," in both senses of that term, pleasure and bonding. Liking involves the ventromedial prefrontal cortex (VMPFC) and insula (Berridge; Hurlbut 184–5), as inner *stage manager* and *audience* networks.[6] This

---

[5] Trust tends to have a longer activation in women than men, perhaps due to their evolutionary role in child raising (Panksepp 145).
[6] The orbital frontal cortex, adjacent to the VMPFC, also functions in the "discrimination of rewarding and punishing stimuli, in order to influence feelings, visceral responses, and decision-making" (Schroeder and Matheson 27).

distinction between liking and wanting is exemplified by addicts who dislike or even hate their drug, yet crave it as a scripted "habit." There is thus a tragic feedback loop of expectation-reward: illusory pleasure at the *ritual* of using a drug, through the memory of loving it the first time, and then disappointment at less opioid/oxytocin pleasure (liking), yet increased dopaminergic wanting. Addictive craving arises with habitual reinforcement of dopaminergic partial pleasure, anticipating reward—yet the impossibility of returning to the original high.

Christian responses to sinful craving involve ritual confession to a priest in the Catholic tradition, with prescriptive penance and God's mercy given, or exorcism in more extreme cases, administered by evangelical Protestant laypeople as well. But in Daoism and Buddhism, craving is viewed as an imbalance in natural energies or as ignorance causing suffering. This is remedied by purifying desire and awareness, rather than conquering devilish temptations. Yet there are exorcism rites, too, in Daoism and tantric Buddhism.

One might see positive aspects of liking (opioid/oxytocin pleasure/bonding) and wanting (dopamine reward/craving) in the theatricality of religious buildings. Research suggests that "oxytocin can promote a reduced focus on the self [and] ... it may stimulate a heightened spiritual disposition, including a sense of connection with the world or with a higher power" (Johnstone and Cohen 136-7). This may relate to dopamine reward systems involved in addictions (137), as evidenced by the loss of religious belief and behavior in Parkinson's disease patients with dopaminergic neuron damage (Yaden et al., "Neuroscience" 293). If a believer experiences emotional pleasure through the architecture, art, and music of a religious building—especially during a participatory rite—opioid/oxytocin *liking/loving* is probably evoked in that person's inner theatre of self vis-à-vis communal others and the metaphysical Other. Studies show that "liking" increases with imitation, in looking or sounding "like" others in a group, which may include ritual gestures and singing. As biologist Kevin Laland puts it, citing psychologist Cecelia Heyes, there is a "'virtuous circle' of subconscious imitation and prosocial attitudes" (278). Thus, in human evolution, cultural "group selection" may have favored "the development of enhanced imitative capabilities," especially with religious practices and spaces. "Synchronous action that triggers endorphin [opioid] release" evokes an association with a "positive reward" through collective rhythms and music, which promote "social bonding" (278-9)—as groups compete for cooperative fitness in bio-cultural environments, which they also alter.

With religious sites, this may lead to the dopaminergic *wanting* of spiritual communion in subsequent visits and rites. Each "hit" of self-transcendent pleasure, as bio-cultural salience through the temporal-lobe *audience*, might trigger a feedback loop—like an opiate drug, but with milder, endogenous opioids in the brain (Solms and Turnbull 121, 130-2). This would increase fantasy attachments to divine ideals, evoking primal memories of infantile bliss or loss—like the rat pup connected to, but then missing its mother. The church or temple experience might involve existential PANIC/GRIEF and SEEKING, yet with increased opioid pleasure and oxytocin bonding levels at the (m)Other's return, through sacred nurturing. Thus, family traits extend to divine icons and ritual bonds, needed again and again, as with addictive drugs, but perhaps in

Table 1.2 Inner Theatre Elements (added to social neuroscience findings)

Theatre Element	Cognitive/Affective Function	Neurological Network & Hub
character	outer performing self (awareness in the mirror test)	lateral prefrontal cortex (LPFC) (Lieberman)
actor	private knowledge of self (adjectives applied to oneself, yet reflecting the influence of others)	medial prefrontal cortex (MPFC) & precuneus (Lieberman)
director	sense of other's viewpoint (mentalizing system or Theory of Mind)	dorsomedial prefrontal cortex (DMPFC), temporoparietal junction (TPJ), temporal poles (TP), posterior cingulate cortex (PCC), & precuneus (PC) —plus the limbic septal area with *empathy* (Lieberman)
stage manager	moral evaluation of actions with social & physical reward/pain	ventromedial prefrontal cortex (VMPFC), dorsal anterior cingulate cortex (dACC), & ventral striatum (Lieberman)
light/sound operator	control of impulses & attitudes (delayed gratification & emotion regulation) or changing prior beliefs & perspectives (as with mindfulness meditation)	ventrolateral prefrontal cortex (VLPFC) (Lieberman) —with left/right VLPFC or LPFC activity for the *cognitive reappraisal* of emotions (left talking about, right re-imagining aversive, sad, or erotic photos/films) (Lieberman; Beauregard et al.)
stage (or film editor)	working (short-term) memory, rational attention, time chunking, & inhibiting of self-interest	dorsolateral prefrontal cortex (DLPFC) (Zacks)
audience	memories, emotions, & intuitions, shaping percepts/concepts onstage	limbic (temporal-lobe) hippocampus, amygdala, & insula, plus angular gyrus (Baars & others)
scriptwriter/critic	objectifying, abstract, audio-verbal, individualist, rationally consistent	left hemisphere of the neocortex, especially PFC (McGilchrist)
mime-improviser/scene-designer	subjective, contextual, visuo-spatial, collectivist, tonal openness to the new	right hemisphere of the neocortex with stronger ties to limbic, subcortical, & brainstem areas (McGilchrist)
costume-body definer & designer	binary self vs. other distinction, while mapping body & spaces around self	left & right parietal lobes & TPJ (Newberg et al. & others)
stagehands	core affects & primary emotions (animal-human drives) with sensorimotor ties & coordination	subcortical & brainstem (brain-body) ties, with hypothalamus, thalamus, sensorimotor cortex, & cerebellum (Baars; Solms & Turnbull)

a healthier way. Whatever their degree of intensity, addictive danger, or spiritual sustenance, such primary emotions are mostly unconscious, yet bodily expressed (Damasio, *Self* 175), through neurotransmitter networks with endogenous, drug-like chemicals. Thus, emotions become conscious, *staged* in the brain's inner theatre, as pleasurable or painful, arousing or calming feelings, intuitions, and ideas—through church and temple reflections. But the liking, wanting, and bonding emotions may also be cultivated toward melodramatic, good versus evil, Trojan Horse tricks (projected stereotypes, scapegoating, corrupt leadership, and sacrifices) or a more tragicomic awareness of the external memory field's gifts yet flaws, as cure and curse.

Inner Theatre Networks

Table 1.2 offers theatrical and filmmaking metaphors that I ascribe to neural network functions, in what cognitive scientist Bernard Baars calls the "staging of consciousness." I also draw on the various research findings of neuroscientists Matthew Lieberman, Iain McGilchrist, Andrew Newberg, and Jeffrey Zacks. Notice the multiple hubs involved with each network, which is not just a modular brain area. For instance, the inner "audience" of implicit, declarative, and autobiographical memory circuits "hiss or applaud" (inhibit or excite) various unconscious signals, forming "coalitions to bring other messages to the stage" (Baars, *In* 43–7).[7] This relates to bio-cultural salience in religious buildings, involving the temporal lobes' insula, amygdala, and hippocampus as *audience* members (intuitive, emotional, episodic memories)[8] and the VMPFC as *stage manager* (behavior monitoring with reward/pain).

Similar to the theatricality of cognitive consciousness in Baars's Global Workspace Theory, with a "spotlight" of attention on the "stage" of working memory, Michael Graziano and colleagues have developed "Attention Schema Theory" (AST). It describes information-consciousness or "i-consciousness" as constructed by the brain, along with "source monitoring," which gives us the higher-order illusion of "mysterious consciousness" (m-consciousness), culturally developed as "soul, ka, qi, and spirit" (Graziano et al. 155, 158). This has encouraged my use of the term "brain spirits," though I apply it also to the remnant instincts of animal-human drives, as emotional motivations and contagions, with personal/group attention effects and attributions.

According to AST, "awareness serves as the control model for attention," which models the "attentional state of others," also attributing m-consciousness to them, like the body schema of one's own body modeling others' bodies (Graziano et al. 164). "We live in a sea of perceived consciousness that we paint onto ourselves, others, and even inanimate objects and empty spaces." As anthropologist Stewart Guthrie points out, we

---

[7] Cf. Fields, regarding brain waves and consciousness.
[8] See Fields 290–1. "The temporal lobes, hippocampus, and parahippocampus are engaged in remembering the past, imagining the future, and recognizing places and scenes.... The salience network activates the anterior insula and dorsal anterior cingulate cortex."

also attribute human-like consciousness to natural elements through "systematic anthropomorphism" in religious traditions. Cognitive psychologist Justin Barrett calls this our "hypersensitive agency detection device" (773), which extends to divine attributions of m-consciousness in religious buildings.

Experiments by Graziano and his colleagues show that we model other people's attention "as a fluid-like substance that is generated inside of an agent and flows out toward targets" (Graziano et al. 165). They locate our self-attention schema and awareness of others in temporoparietal junction (TPJ) and prefrontal cortex (PFC) networks, including the dorsolateral and dorsomedial PFC (166–8). In another article, Graziano considers how the right TPJ is active during the "social perception of others," as well as the spatial perception of self (Graziano and Kastner 106). Deactivation of the right TPJ produces out-of-body experiences, confirming the brain's spatial modeling of conscious awareness.[9] Such evidence about the TPJ relates to my use of *audience* and *costume-body definer/designer* metaphors for temporal and parietal lobe networks— regarding spiritual out-of-body experiences or attributions.

Various inner theatre elements come into play with the staging of self in relation to Otherness. Pyramidal neurons in the dorsolateral prefrontal cortex (DLPFC), the upper outside areas of the forehead, play a key role in the top-down integration of self-consciousness. They are much smaller with fewer connecting spines in schizophrenics, who experience too much bottom-up signaling (Dehaene 256). A network with hubs in the DLPFC for working memory, rational attention, time "chunking", and inhibition of self-interest is thus like the *stage itself*—or like a *film editor*, cutting and splicing scenes, according to neuroscientist Jeffrey Zacks (206–27). The DLPFC *stage/editor*, in its "censorship of emotional processing," is also vital, along with the VMPFC *stage manager* and subcortical basal ganglia *stagehands*, in the preconscious "inhibition" of empathy. This involves a mirror neuron system mimicking e-motions when viewing another person's actions, gestures, facial expressions, or even a painting with such things displayed (Freedberg 172). "It is precisely the constraints on this [mirroring] engagement that are ... cognitive, regulatory and productive of self-awareness."

The moral inhibiting of self, with "delayed gratification" (Nelson 189), involves an inner *director* network centered in the dorsomedial (upper inner) prefrontal cortex (DMPFC), with one's sense of the other person's or divine Other's viewpoint. It also involves the *stage manager* in the ventromedial (lower inner) prefrontal cortex (VMPFC), monitoring one's actions through social and physical reward or pain. This self-inhibiting network includes the orbital frontal cortex, anterior cingulate, and basal ganglia (subcortical *stagehands*) "assigning affective value" with dopamine circuitry (Badgaiyan 127–9). As in live theatre, with the stage manager calling the show, the VMPFC calls upon the ventrolateral prefrontal cortex (VLPFC) *light/sound operator*, especially on the right side (larger by late adolescence), to control impulses and

---

[9] Graziano and Kastner also explore awareness as "a construct of the social machinery of the brain," involving the "synchronized activity of neurons," as well as an inner modeling of others' minds using the TPJ, right MPFC, and superior temporal sulcus, plus mirror neuron networks (98, 100, 103).

attitudes, or change beliefs and perspectives, as the "hub of the *brain's braking system*" (Lieberman 208–15). This is shown with cognitive "reappraisal," "self-regulation," and mindfulness meditation experiments (Beauregard et al. 166–80). Such networks relate also to the inner *actor* and *character*: a medial prefrontal cortex (MPFC) *actor* circuit for "self-knowing," when asked which adjectives apply to oneself,[10] and a lateral prefrontal cortex (LPFC) *character* network with "self-recognition," as the performing self or persona,[11] when looking in a mirror (Lieberman 185).

The brain's floating, multilevel, multimodal platform of these various self-Other networks, shifting in each moment of attention, even with more private, MPFC *actor* circuits, becomes a permeable "Trojan horse self" with traces of others' influences throughout one's life (Lieberman 11, 235). This is evidenced by hypnosis and advertising experiments with MPFC activation better predicting future choices than the subjects' self-reported awareness (194–200). Thus, religious ideals, reflected in churches and temples, become deeply imbedded in the inner *actor*, while the *character* performs outwardly for others present, through intuitive memorial *audience* circuits, predicting outer audience reactions. For believers, this may also involve a divine *director* mirroring that inner network, along with *stage manager* restraints and supportive/trickster *stagehands*. Examples in Chapters 3 and 4 show various reflections of such inner theatre networks in the monumental spaces of Chinese temples and European churches, as external memory fields, especially regarding tragicomic or melodramatic, Trojan Horse influences.

Left and Right, Predator and Prey/Mate, Focused or Open

The interplay between a left-cortical, more objectifying, linear-thinking *scriptwriter/ critic* and right-cortical, subjective, contextual *mime-improviser/scene-designer* shapes the inner staging of ego-self vis-à-vis holistic Self and Other.[12] The left hemisphere "interpreter," according to neuroscientist Michael Gazzaniga, "builds a narrative in each of us about why we do things" (227–8). This includes "script-sharing" with other people, in the top-down control of actions (A. Clark 286; Roepstorff and Frith). Right hemisphere networks, on the other hand, create a nonverbal, contextual, visceral, and "more integrated somatosensory representation of the body" (Siegel, *Developing* 182). This involves feelings, music, metaphor, and prosody, as with "religiosity" (Trimble 127, 158, 178). Through its ties to perceptions and actions on the body's left side, the right hemisphere's stronger limbic/subcortical emotional connections may also appear with

---

[10] McGilchrist associates the "verbalising, self-scrutinising and discursive self" with the MPFC "in both hemispheres" (*Matter* 117).
[11] Cf. Bassil-Morozow 111, on the Jungian sense of "persona" in relation to film tricksters.
[12] See McGilchrist, *Matter* 876, on the Jungian "ego" as more left-hemispheric, with objective "conscious will," while the Jungian integrated Self is more right-hemispheric, as social, empathic, continuous, and holistic, "with 'depth' of existence over time," through "spiritual growth." See also Narvaez 118, on the right hemisphere (PFC) facilitating "subjective experience."

the Western tradition of wearing a wedding ring—traceable to the ancient Roman "belief that a nerve ran from the third finger of the left hand direct to the heart" (Knott 139). Also, in many mammal species, including humans, various primates, walruses, and flying foxes, mothers hold or keep offspring mostly on the left side, probably due to the "social processing" role of the right hemisphere (Giljov et al.). Often, baby Jesus appears on the left side of Mary, whether she inclines toward him or holds him with stiff enthroned rectitude. But in patriarchal, melodramatic, objectifying Last Judgment scenes, evil souls appear to the left (Latin *sinister*) of an enthroned Christ, as he sends them down to a monstrous hell mouth with many devils, while good souls rise heavenward on his right (tied to the left-cortical *scriptwriter/critic*).

Table 1.3 lists specific, complementary, yet sometimes cross-inhibiting, right and left hemisphere functions, mapping Iain McGilchrist's meta-analysis of neuroscience research across several decades (*Master*).[13] I add the theatre terms, plus Lacan's psychoanalytic phenomenology of "Imaginary" and "Symbolic" orders, involving maternal and patriarchal dimensions of mimetic experiences and socio-linguistic networks. These develop in the child's gradual separation from somatosensory mirroring contact with the (m)Other through the Father's Name/No. The Symbolic order of words/rules redefines Imaginary memories/fantasies—correlating to left and right cortical functions, in my view. Desires and drives also involve the Real order, as a primal lack yet eruption of being—correlating with limbic and subcortical networks. Thus, the continual rewiring of patriarchal Symbolic left-cortical and maternal Imaginary right-cortical networks (in the Real of brain matter) develops through various parental figures and role models, with different cultural paradigms.

Regarding religious beliefs and moral issues, notice in Table 1.3 that left-hemispheric (including left-cortical) *scriptwriter/critic* networks perpetuate familiar, rule-based, orthodox, Symbolic, patriarchal positions. These are in tension with right-hemispheric *improviser/designer* networks, which are more flexibly aware of new details and discrepancies as the "Devil's Advocate" (a term that McGilchrist cites from Ramachandran and Blakeslee). The belief-based left hemisphere usually works with, yet may also conflict with the care-oriented right, regarding religious judgment or compassion, while the right has stronger ties to subcortical (supportive/trickster *stagehand*) networks of bottom-up body signals. And yet, researchers have found more "approach" or "dominance" emotions, such as anger, with left-frontal activity and more "withdrawal" or "submission," disgust and fear, in right-frontal (Demaree et al.), which relates to territorial and hierarchical drives explored here with religious buildings. Other studies have found more "anti-social" competitive emotions in the left hemisphere versus "social" cooperative in the right (Hecht), relating also to our exploration of melodramatic and tragicomic *rasas* in churches and temples.

---

[13] See also Trimble 91, for a similar but shorter list, summarizing research from the 1950s to 1970s and published in 2007, two years before McGilchrist's *Master*.

Table 1.3 Brain Hemisphere Functions (outlined from McGilchrist, *Master*, with Lacanian terms and inner theatre elements added in bold)

LEFT HEMISPHERE (**Symbolic patriarchal**) **includes left-cortical scriptwriter/critic** *predator (focused, objectifying, tool-using)*	RIGHT HEMISPHERE (**Imaginary maternal**) **right-cortical mime-improviser/scene-designer** *prey or mate (broad awareness, life/death/ sex-oriented)*
belief, competitiveness, conscious agency	care, cooperation, unconscious socio-environmental influences
abstract/analytical thinking [inhibiting →]	emotional/sensory intuition (with limbic/subcortical ties)
familiar, rule-based, orthodox ideas	"anomaly-detector" & Devil's Advocate awareness of new
examining parts in a linear, categorical way	comprehending the whole in a cyclical, contextual way
rectilinear, unidirectional, fixed, & mechanical	round, circular, flowing, & natural appreciations (446–8)
sequential, cause & effect, literal language	deductive, parallel, paradoxical, & poetic associations
manipulation of known, static, isolated, general	care of individual, evolving, interconnected, incarnate beings
self-referential (thing/machine-oriented)	other-engaged (toward living-world), empathic
self-certainty, yet toward virtual, unrealistic	responsibility, shame, & guilt, but more realistic
optimistic, yet with projection & anger	melancholic, yet sensitive to tears & alert to change
denotation (with confabulation to repress)	connotation, appreciating ambiguous meanings, ironic humor
concerned with social or willed emotions	primary-process, bonding, & unconscious emotions
affinity to major keys & basic rhythms	minor keys, complex syncopation, & harmonic progression
identifies simple, easily categorized shapes	identifies complex, varied figures
produces schematic representations	depth in time/space (self-image & Theory of Other's Mind)
focused attention, grasping (right hand)	sustained attention, exploratory (left-side facial expressions)
looks at other's mouth (detached from body)	looks at eyes during conversations
more dopamine (pleasure seeking) networks	more noradrenaline (excitatory) networks
parasympathetic (quiescent) nervous system	sympathetic (arousal) nervous system ties
schizophrenia, MPD, ASD, anorexia, BPD	depression with anxiety
"Western strategies skewed toward left ..."	"East Asian cultures use ... both hemispheres more evenly" (458)
uses categories, focuses on individual components	attends to broad fields, relations, changes, family resemblances
analytic, one-dimensional, rule-based responses	less formal logic, more intuitive, with contextual, global causes
seeks one correct answer over its binary opposite	seeks contradictory views for dialectical synthesis & compromise
prefers "half a loaf is better than no bread"	prefers "too humble is half proud" (455–7)
independent self-regard, over-estimating abilities	*interdependent* self-criticism, in social web, valuing harmony

Right hemisphere ties to subcortical networks, especially with sympathetic arousal in "aesthetic processing," include the right insula (part of the temporal-lobe *audience*) and distinctive von Economo neurons with "rapidly conducting axons" (Agnati et al. 438). These neurons are 30 percent more numerous in the right insula than the left, contributing to "rapid intuition" in self-awareness and decision making (437). Thus, subcortical hubs at the *stagehand* threshold of consciousness—the superior colliculi distilling bodily senses, the midbrain locomotor region organizing bodily movements, and the periaqueductal gray producing affects—may generate "the primal SELF, the very source of our sentient being" (Solms 139), in relation to right-cortical *improviser/ designer* and left-cortical *scriptwriter/critic* networks.

According to McGilchrist, in various animal species, including birds, the *predatory* focus of the left hemisphere formed the evolutionary basis for this asymmetry, counterbalanced by the *prey-wary and mating* functions of the right, with its stronger ties to limbic/subcortical emotions (*Master* 25–8). In humans, this evolved in a bio-cultural direction, with the left hemisphere examining parts in a linear, categorical way, while the right comprehends the whole in a cyclical, contextual way. Both are involved in image processing, especially the right hemisphere. Applying McGilchrist's research to interactions with religious sites, the functions of the left-cortical *scriptwriter/critic* relate more to "rectilinear" spaces with focused, enclosed, and "abstract" patterns (*Master* 241, 372, 414, 446–8), especially with judgmental, Symbolic, patriarchal figures of upright "rectitude" (Cavarero 6).

The functions of the right-cortical *improviser/designer* relate more to curved spaces in religious buildings with multilateral, dispersed, open, embedded, and lifelike aspects, especially with compassionate, maternal figures of "inclination" (Cavarero). McGilchrist suggests this, too, with an "understanding of the divine" that relies on "indirect and metaphorical expression, not direct and literal," as the "right hemisphere is better at accepting uncertainty and limits to knowledge," through *Gestalt* forms of "I-Thou, not just an I-It relationship" (*Matter* 1211). This involves "stilling the inner voice, as in prayer and meditation," while valuing "empathy" and the "consensual rather than individualistic self," through right-hemispheric "vulnerability." McGilchrist locates the "objective self, and the self as an expression of will," in the left hemisphere, but the empathetic, relational, "continuous sense of self" in the right, including the experiential self, "recruited by mindfulness" (117).

Thus, the left-hemispheric, rectilinear, and abstract aspects of theatricality stressed by European churches may reflect how "Westerners tend to view the world analytically, focusing on the attributes of distinct, salient objects" (*Matter* 1265). On the other hand, Chinese temples may reflect how "East Asian cultures, preferring holistic thinking," attend to "'both focal and contextual information'" (McGilchrist 1265, quoting Masuda and Nisbett). As cultural psychologists explain, this corresponds to ancient Chinese traditions of medicine with "the coordination of natural forces (*chi*) throughout the body," topography with *feng-shui* orientations, and philosophy with *yin-yang* balancing (Masuda and Nisbett 933).

Both left and right cortical functions, with their cultural extensions, are in tension with subhuman tricksters at the shadowy edges of sacred spaces. These appear as evil threats to rule-based systems in the left cortex or as erotic lures in the right, involving subcortical, otherwise supportive, animal-human drives as *stagehands* (of brain-body homeostasis and social allostasis). They arise from the "theater of the body" as emotion signals, which are mostly offstage, but sometimes at the edges: moods, intuitions, and feelings, shaping the "theater of the conscious mind" (Damasio, *Feeling* 8, 37). This relates to liking, wanting, and bonding in religious buildings, especially with communal rites, as the VMPFC *stage manager* and subcortical *stagehands* assess reward pleasures, with the temporal-lobe *audience* clamoring for more. Thus, personal cues in the environment evoke positive (or negative) experience traces and fantasy desires, sometimes with conscious memories.

Regarding positive awe in church spaces, an experiment showed the left precuneus was activated, along with the left middle frontal gyrus, as brain "structures associated with visuospatial attention and exploration," when participants preferred "rooms with high ceilings" (Coburn et al. 1524). This may correlate with the visitor's inner *actor* (MPFC plus precuneus) and *scriptwriter/critic* (left cortex), as stressed by the Western independent model of self, reflected in the vast, yet focused interior of enclosed cruciform churches, with a rectilinear nave and high ceiling over the altar at the eastern-sunrise end, symbolic of the soul's resurrection. In contrast, the East Asian sense of interdependency may be reflected in the contextual (more right-cortical *improviser/designer*) spaces of Chinese temples, with yards open to nature and dispersed, one or two-story shrines, behind a southern entry gate, receiving more of the cyclic sunlight across the whole day (Diagram 1.1).

In(ter)dependent Victory or Compassion

Table 1.3 also indicates characteristic differences in the inner theatre networks of a more *in*dependent or *inter*dependent sense of self. The left hemisphere, with its "narrow" spotlight of attention, focuses on manipulation of known, static, isolated objects—while the right's "flexibility" includes care for evolving, interconnected, incarnate beings (*Master* 27–9, 112–15, 174). Adding inner theatre terms, the left-cortical *scriptwriter/critic* objectifies and categorizes other people, manipulating them

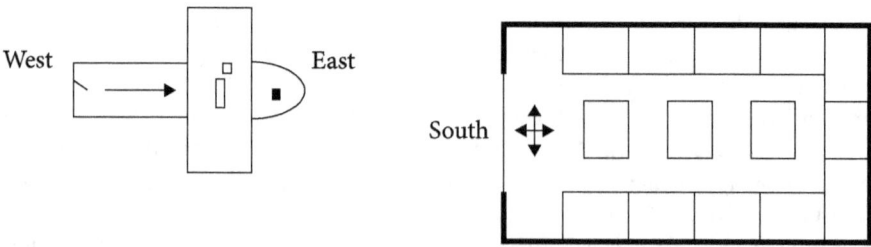

Diagram 1.1 Typical Ground Plans of European Churches and Chinese Temples.

mentally, while stressing one's own individuality (90, 113, 195, 402). The right-cortical *mime-improviser/scene-designer* perceives complex relationships with others through concern about emotions, personality details, and contexts (49–50). The left hemisphere is more thing-oriented and self-referential; the right is more empathic and other-engaged (57, 88, 147). Thus, the *scriptwriter/critic* offers a strong inner voice in the staging of self, yet such optimism may involve left-cortical networks of projected prejudices or righteous rage toward others (6, 84–5, 425, 440). The *mime/designer* tends toward melancholy with its wider awareness and greater sensitivity to others (85, 380). Too much compassion can be overwhelming, but the right hemisphere is also more alert to change than the left, thus staging a flexible self (37–41).

The focus on an isolated vertical cross, piercing its horizontal plane, atop many Protestant churches and on saints as heroic role models in Catholic or Orthodox churches relates to the left-cortical staging of a strong self, with heavenly optimism, even as martyr or crucified Christ, with melodramatic victory over sin and death. Yet right-cortical empathy with such suffering figures might also be evoked, as a tragicomic, *rasa*-cathartic, holistic awareness. In Buddhist and Daoist temples, the emphasis on compassionate bodhisattvas and *yin-yang* balancing gods relates to the contextual, flexible, Other-engaged self of right-cortical networks, through left-cortical ideals of detached equanimity and ancestral authority.

According to McGilchrist, the left hemisphere (*scriptwriter/critic*) focuses on literal, denotative meanings; yet it may confabulate to repress alternatives, building a stronger platform for an independent self (*Master* 81, 127, 174). The right (*mime-improviser/scene-designer*) is open to the connotation of words, playing with metaphor, appreciating ambiguity, and relishing ironic humor—with a more interdependent self (49–51, 80–2, 99). The left hemisphere is concerned with "more superficial, social emotions," when competitive, consciously represented, "willed, or forced" (62–3). The right has stronger ties to limbic (*audience*) and subcortical (*stagehand*) networks, involving emotional receptivity and expression, primary bonds with others, and unconscious drives (28, 58–71). This left/right dichotomy even relates to music: the left hemisphere is more attuned to upbeat, major keys and basic rhythms, the right to minor chords, complex syncopation, and harmonic progression (73–5). Applying McGilchrist's meta-analysis to sacred imagery, as well as music, the left's *scriptwriter/critic* identifies with simple, easily categorized shapes (Symbolic order), while producing schematic representations and time sequences (52, 77, 257). The right's *mime-improviser/scene-designer* engages with complex, varied figures, while considering "depth" in space and time, including one's self-image (Imaginary dimension) in relation to other people's inner theatres (77–9, 88–9).

The last six pairs in Table 1.3 show McGilchrist's review of left and right hemisphere research regarding Western and Eastern cultures. Western strategies are "steeply skewed toward the left hemisphere," and more so in certain historical periods, while "East Asian cultures use strategies of both hemispheres more evenly," as shown by various experiments in cultural psychology and neuroscience (*Master* 455–8). McGilchrist explains the Western symptoms of left-hemispheric bias: (1) using categories that focus on individual components, (2) analyzing with one-dimensional, rule-based responses, and (3) seeking one correct answer over its binary opposite. East Asians, on average, show more balance between hemispheres: (1) attending to broad fields, relations, and family resemblances, (2) using less formal logic, with more intuitive responses, while perceiving contextual, global causes, and (3) valuing contradictory views for dialectical holism. Regarding the third comparison, McGilchrist mentions an experiment showing that Americans preferred non-contradictory proverbs such as "half a loaf is better than no bread" to similar, yet paradoxical phrases like "too humble is half proud," but Chinese preferred the latter (455). Summarizing his findings, McGilchrist says that Westerners have a left-hemispheric bias with *independent* self-regard, over-estimating their control abilities, while East Asians show more right as well as left hemisphere functions with *interdependent* self-criticism, in a social web that values balanced harmony. This appears also in "Oriental art," which emphasizes "the field" and de-emphasizes "individual objects, including people, by comparison with Western art."

Cross-cultural studies are sometimes attacked for their Orientalist essentialism[14] or "ethnocentric imperialism," but a "new comparativism" has emerged recently in anthropology (Weisman and Luhrmann 134–5). This book attempts comparisons both frontally, moving from objects encountered to subjective auto-ethnography to reflections, and laterally, with similarities and differences between objective-subjective effects (Candea). It considers how Western and East Asian biases in "specific phenomena" reflect potentials for all brains and cultures, with benefits and dangers. Individual rights, modern sciences, and many current technologies have developed in Western cultures, perhaps through a left-cortical bias, but they also have a global appeal. Asian cultures, like indigenous cultures in Africa, the Americas, and the Pacific, have stressed relatedness longer, through respect for nature, which may be even more valuable today. Rather than the ancient Greek motto, "Know Thy Self," theirs might be "Know Thy Relations." For example, a study showed Native American and Aboriginal Australian students as individualistic, yet less competitive than non-Indigenous ones, maybe through a matriarchal egalitarian heritage and "healthy right hemisphere development," unlike people raised in Western, Christian, "egocentric, self-protective… [and] anthropocentric" traditions (Topa and Narvaez 22, 62, 114–15).

There are potential drawbacks to an emphasis on traditions, rituals, and family ties: lack of progress, social pressures, and nepotism (as with Chinese *guanxi*). There are also drawbacks to Western individualism. Yet China has changed rapidly in the last century to catch up with the West, rebalancing the right- and left-cortical orientations of collectivism and individualism (Fung and Cheng 315). It has swung from imperial rule with European colonial influences (and exploitations) to collectivist autocratic communism, forced modernization, and the Cultural Revolution. Since the 1980s, the PRC has moved toward individualist entrepreneurship with managed capitalism (and more women becoming highly educated), while supporting revivals of Confucianism, Daoism, and Buddhism. These religious revivals were encouraged by the Communist

---

[14] For an oversimplified critique of various studies on individualism and collectivism in cultural neuroscience, as "essentialist," binary, Eurocentric, and Orientalist, see Mateo et al.

Party, through government controls and marketing pressures, as addressing a "moral crisis," with popular films and TV shows also increasing tourist interests, especially in Buddhism (Zhe 33–4).

Such shifts between individualism and collectivism, involving the bias or balance of left and right cortical networks, have occurred in Western and Chinese traditions, as reflected in the historical developments of churches and temples. Indeed, McGilchrist maps in detail, as a literature scholar, psychiatrist, and neuroscientist, the cultural evidence of more right-hemisphere processing in ancient Greece to more left in Rome, to a "rightward shift" with Renaissance art, but to the left again during the Reformation and Enlightenment "attack on religion," to the right with Romanticism, and then a "leftward shift" with modernism (*Master* 258, 440). There are dangers in both individualist (more left-hemisphere) and collectivist developments, especially with projected threats being demonized—through melodramatic, ego and group rivalries, across many generations with sacrificial demands. Yet there are also tragicomic alternatives with different modes of awe and awareness.

Inner Audience Awe and Related Spirits

The brain's *audience* of memory circuits has its network hubs in the temporal lobes, at the sides of the head, each of which include the hippocampus, amygdala, and insula. Short-term, "working memory," as the *stage* (or *film editor*) for self/other consciousness, has its network hubs in the DLPFC, left verbal and right spatial, in relation to the somatosensory cortex (with *stagehand* ties), as attention shifts. But the indexing and accessing of long-term, episodic, "autobiographical memories," as the *audience* of experience traces (influencing in the dark or getting the spotlight of consciousness), occurs through the hippocampus, with emotional salience and intuitional flavor from the amygdala and insula, in the temporal lobes. "Implicit memories" for subconscious emotions, rewards, habits, and skills involve the basal ganglia and cerebellum, at the core and bottom of the brain. (I also use the metaphor of *stagehands* for such implicit emotion-action networks.) The inner *audience* includes the angular gyrus (AG), just above and behind the temporal lobes. The AG is involved with metaphors, number processing (left AG), visuospatial attention, movement awareness (intended versus consequential), memory retrieval, unusual cases of synesthesia, and experimentally induced out-of-body experiences with the right AG stimulated, or ghostly presences with the left AG, as part of the temporoparietal junction (Ramachandran and Hubbard; Seghier). Synesthesia in the inner *audience* networks of exceptional brains, such as seeing colors while hearing music, may also relate to the aesthetic experience of awe for many brains in religious buildings, through the more common form of "heuraesthesia," the multimodal overlap of sensory perceptions, including balance and movement, while viewing artworks (Mignerot; Londero et al.).

A study showed that threat-based awe correlates to activity (regional gray matter volume) in the insula, known as a hub for empathy, fear, anger, sadness, and disgust networks, and part of the temporal-lobe *audience* in my model—while positive awe correlates with activity in the precuneus, involving "self-reflections" (Guan et al. 7), part of the inner *actor*. Patients with temporal-lobe epilepsy, with excessive firing of *audience* networks, have awe-full, mystical experiences, with feelings "on fire" (Ramachandran and Blakeslee 179). They perceive ordinary things and trivial events as being rich with "cosmic significance," creating an ecstasy of "divine presence" as if in "direct communication with God." They also exhibit "hypergraphia," writing excessively about mystical revelations.

Various prophets and mystics possibly had seizures involving their temporal lobes: St. Paul, Muhammad, Margery Kempe, Joan of Arc, St. Catherine of Genoa, St. Teresa of Ávila, St. Catherine of Ricci, Emanuel Swedenborg, Shaker founder Ann Lee, and Mormon founder Joseph Smith (Nelson 251; Trimble 143). Neuroscientist V. S. Ramachandran finds in temporal-lobe epileptics a "selective enhancement" of bodily reactions, measured in sweat responses, to "religious words and images" (Ramachandran and Blakeslee 186–7). He describes the temporal lobe as a potential "God module," revealing a bio-culturally evolved mechanism for religious experience in all of us, related to sexual ecstasy (188). Likewise, neurologist Rhawn Joseph calls the temporal lobe a "transmitter to God." In the extreme case of temporal-lobe epileptics, the conscious self may be staged as supernatural, with the inner *audience* applauding furiously, as ordinary things gain an intense survival value and reproductive pleasure, sublimated into transcendent, spiritual meanings—with arousing/quiescent, terrifying yet joyous awe.

Such experiences require validation from community members and hierarchical authorities, as external audience, to give further salience to the mystic's ecstasy. Communal confirmation might continue after the mystic's death, especially if prayers and relics bring about miracles, related to the saintly corpse as holy territory. If not confirmed by religious bonds, transcendent salience in epileptics, or others with a *porous* identity, might be considered an illness to be cured, instead of a sacred, painful pleasure as ecstatic *jouissance*. In all of us, there is a similar potential to feel the self radically transformed, dying and reborn, through threat-based, yet sublime awe, as with exemplary figures in churches and temples—via the temporal-lobe *audience* energizing an altered form of consciousness on the inner stage.

Since the 1980s Michael Persinger has conducted experiments (recently replicated by Tinoca and Ortiz) showing that the right temporal lobe, with the amygdala as fear center and insula/hippocampus as memory hub, can be stimulated to create, in most people, a sense of a spiritual presence in the lab as a "God Experience" (*Neuropsychological* 11–12; "Neuropsychiatry" 516–17).[15] This suggests that the Otherness of divine beings,

---

[15] Other studies did not replicate Persinger's findings, which led to a debate about "suggestibility" in them (Larsson et al.). Another study used a "sham" helmet to produce a "placebo" effect, especially with believers (Simmonds-Moore). But cf. Nelson 253: "Cases collected from neuroscientists around the world indicate that [epileptic] seizures with spiritual content tend to originate from right-sided limbic structures." Nelson points to lab experiments with LSD showing that its mystical effects involve increased activity of the anterior cingulate, along with the temporal lobe, which he also relates to serotonin-1 and serotonin-2 receptors in research on fear as well as mysticism (244–6).

experienced by the inner theatre of self, involves right to left cortex communications, or *improviser/designer* to *scriptwriter/critic* networks, along with the temporal-lobe *audience* of emotional memory circuits. According to another neuroscientist, Michael Trimble, commenting on Persinger's research, "the sense of self is an emergent property of language, thus implicating the left hemisphere, and ... there is likely to be an equivalent homologue for this in the right hemisphere" (167). Thus, "right hemisphere intrusions to consciousness are experienced as paranormal events and may lead to sudden moments of enlightenment or even religious conversions," also involving "the prefrontal areas" and the "gradual modification of stored memories" in the temporal lobes. Such experiences have influenced, yet threatened religions and their buildings across many centuries.

Prosody in language, as well as music, including "pitch, tone, melody, cadence, timbre, stress, accent, and pauses," primarily involves right hemisphere networks as "limbic-dominated affect-laden" expressions (Trimble 200). Trimble ties such studies, plus evidence from temporal-lobe epilepsy and other brain disorders with hyper-religious symptoms, to the power of poetry, music, and "religious art," moving us emotionally through the "right hemisphere of our wonder full human brains." Yet this also reveals foundational *cracks* (tragic flaws) in our inner theatres, with core affects as body-brain signals. We start our lives in profound dependency and vulnerability, as young mammals, with a "primitive vocal system, one attuned to the experience of distress and the cries of danger and separation." Thus, animal vocalizations are organized in the subcortical midbrain, especially in the periaqueductal grey (PAG). This area also triggers laughter in humans when electrically stimulated, and various sounds made by animals, "in the ancient depths of the brain" (Corballis 37). Animals have instinctual programs for such deeply emotional expressions in natural niches. But humans, in socially varied, symbolic environments, with recursive time-traveling, other mind-reading, and meaning-seeking brains (15–16), experience misfires through remnant instincts. Trickster urges erupt against *moral frames*, with resonant limbic memories and fantasies, from the maternal (Devil's Advocate) right cortex to patriarchal left, evoking theatrical, super-natural extensions, represented in religious buildings.

The brain-mapping research of Andrew Newberg and his colleagues finds specific, left and right cortical areas involved, along with the temporal lobes, in mythic beliefs and spiritual experiences (Newberg et al. 63, 170–17, 196). They locate a "causal operator" and "abstractive operator," both in the left cortex, related to myth making, yet also science (49), which are key aspects of the *scriptwriter/critic*. Likewise, a "binary operator" in the left inferior parietal lobe is active with ideas of good and evil, as abstractions of survival boons and threats in the natural or cultural environment (59–64, 196). Yet the right parietal lobe's "holistic operator" gives "depth and authority" to intuitive spiritual images and emotions (65, 69), corresponding to the *costume-body designer* (with the left as *costume-body definer*).

In our developing hypothesis, the staging of self vis-à-vis Other involves patriarchal orders of good versus evil in the left hemisphere's binary, causal, and abstractive operators. They are reflected more in the dominant (mechanical over natural) monuments, rectilinear designs, and enclosed focused (bounded self) spaces of European churches. However, the left-cortical *scriptwriter/critic* and right-cortical holistic *mime-improviser/scene-designer* work together to produce religious myths and moral beliefs across the globe. A mix of hemispheric functions is expressed in Chinese temples with multiple shrines in open yards, emphasizing natural harmony, *yang–yin* balance, and cyclical lives with collectivist (porous) identities. Thus, various Eurasian traditions of sacred buildings reflect, and potentially evoke, animal-human drives as "brain spirits." These extend differently from primary to social emotions, through communal monuments, performance designs, divine figures, and religious values, in the wanting and liking/bonding of meaning and purpose, with tragicomic or melodramatic, mimetic-mythic mirroring.

Mirror Neurons, Mystical Melting, and Spillover Effects

Language production and reception hubs in the left cortex, known as Broca's and Wernicke's areas (in the inferior frontal and posterior temporal regions), involve mirror neuron systems for interpreting "symbolic gestures," tied to such systems in the right, more mimetic-oriented cortex, "linking meaning with symbols whether these are words, gestures, images, sounds, or objects" (Corballis 60–4; Xu et al. 20664). Mirror neurons were discovered first in monkeys—with the same brain cells firing when a salient action is performed or watched. But only in humans do they fire with "intransitive" as well as transitive verb-scenes, through "canonical neurons" (Corballis 62; Iacoboni 6–7, 14). These are activated when viewing a typical object and context for an action, such as graspable food or a teacup scene, as when performing it—or reading about it—simulating that action in the viewer's inner theatre. Humans also have intuition neurons (von Economo neurons) and auditory mirror neurons, adding to the empathy evoked by "architectural forms, such as a twisted Romanesque column," or when viewing or hearing other artworks, "automatically simulating the emotional expression, the movement or even the implied movement within the representation" (Freedberg and Gallese 197). This involves both the artwork's "representational content" and the artist's "creative gestures" (198). Especially with figural art, the viewer's brain simulates emotions and bodily states, including touch, "seen in or implied by the painting or sculpture, 'as if' the body [in the artwork] were present" (201).

In a religious building, the visitor's mirror neuron system increases empathy by simulating the self-performance of actions seen/heard with artworks or with ritual props, sounds, and spaces. This evokes shared emotions, especially in the inner theaters of those who know the story or participated before. Experiments show that mirror neuron areas are activated *more* in dancers who watch videos of a dance style or movement types from their own "motor repertoire" than from others (Calvo-Merino et al., "Action" and "Seeing"). Thus, the left-cortical symbolic and right-cortical imaginary staging of self, with regard to the metaphysical Other, includes the temporal-lobe *audience* of personal memory networks. These draw on primal experiences of child-mother "attunement," especially in the right hemisphere (Cozolino 192), with the potential for right temporal-lobe, spiritual presences or "God experiences," as in Persinger's lab.

Subcortical *stagehands* are also involved in the varieties of religious experience. Psychologist Fraser Watts finds that meditation techniques, drawn from Eastern religions and developed by Western scientists, may produce "low autonomic arousal but heightened cortical arousal," with decreased activity in "the more linear and articulate 'propositional' subsystem ... [compared with] the more intuitive and holistic 'implicational' subsystem" (97–8). I would relate this to less activity in the left-cortical *scriptwriter/critic*, with linear, articulate, propositional functions, compared with the right-cortical *improviser/designer*, as intuitive, holistic, and implicational, involving subcortical *stagehands* in the parasympathetic (low arousal) autonomic nervous system. Paradoxically, the "rebalancing" shift from parasympathetic *stagehand* activity aligned with the left hemisphere to sympathetic with the right might create a mix of both low and high arousal, through meditative chanting or prayer in temples and churches (or glossolalia in a right to left shift).

Newberg's team mapped the brains of Tibetan Buddhists during meditation and Franciscan nuns at prayer (Table 1.4). With both, they found increased activity in the "attention association area" of the prefrontal cortex (Newberg et al. 29–31). But they found *decreased* activity in the left (posterior superior) parietal lobe, the "orientation area" creating one's spatial sense of self, as a "limited, physically defined body" (4, 28). With the Buddhist meditators "melting into nothingness" or the Catholic nuns "melting into Christ," the inner theatre's staging of self dissolves (119–23) with less activity in that left parietal *costume-body definer*. The right parietal orientation area is also deactivated, staging the loss of the self's "spatial context," as *costume-body designer*, while the attention area is focused on nothingness or the image of Jesus (119, 122). Thus, the narrative *scriptwriter/critic* and imaginary *mime/designer* of self may shift, with its dissolution, toward oneness with the metaphysical Other. This may involve a paradoxical mix of brain-body, autonomic nervous systems that are usually opposed. Sympathetic (arousal) and parasympathetic (calmness) are both activated with ritual intensity and yet peacefulness, in a "spillover" effect between these systems (d'Aquili and Newberg 25–6), through the limbic *audience* and subcortical *stagehands* of the inner theatre—as with threat-based and positive awe combined.

Such a spillover effect in mystical self-to-Other transcendence relates to religious buildings as arousing and calming, dramatic and contemplative mirrors. Yet it can be a threat to organized orthodoxies. Indeed, it draws on bottom-up, inner theatre networks for sexual ecstasy, sublimating the erotic reproductive drive (Newberg et al. 125–6). Anthropologist Michael J. Winkelman sees a similar "rebound" effect as crucial to the evolution of religion: from sympathetic arousal to parasympathetic bliss in shamanic all-night dancing, with animism and "soul flight," or out-of-body experiences, through the brain's opioid and dopamine systems ("Shamanic" 129–31). This may involve high arousal, sympathetic, serotonin and noradrenalin circuits in the right hemisphere, combined with low arousal, parasympathetic, dopamine systems in the left—disinhibiting prefrontal cortex filters with bottom-up slow (theta and alpha) waves of

Table 1.4 Neuroscience Research on Ecstatic Experiences

Left Cortex "Operators" & Areas	Right Cortex "Operators" & Areas
causal operator	holistic operator (right parietal lobe)
abstractive operator (left parietal lobe)	emotional value operator
—forming general concepts and links (as in myth-making & science)	—give depth and authority to intuition in agreement with causes/effects of left parietal
binary operator (left inferior parietal lobe)	

orientation association areas:
left posterior superior parietal lobe	right posterior superior parietal lobe
—self in space	—space around self

(mediation and prayer decrease activity in these areas, producing a sense of self dissolving)

attention association area in prefrontal lobe: concentration on a goal which increases with meditation/prayer

hyper-quiescent and hyper-aroused "spillover" of parasympathetic and sympathetic nervous systems (involving hypothalamus, limbic system, pituitary, and adrenal glands) experienced as *mystical union with divine Other* with Catholic nuns in prayer & Buddhist monks meditating

OR "speaking in tongues" with increased midbrain, thalamus, and temporal lobe activity yet decrease of prefrontal attention association area, also increase of left orientation area, as *Holy Spirit speaking through one's self* with Christian Pentecostals in praise-singing glossolalia

Informed by Andrew Newberg, Eugene d'Aquili, and Vincent Rause, *Why God Won't Go Away*, and Andrew Newberg and Mark Robert Waldman, *Why We Believe What We Believe*

---

subcortical-limbic, sensory and emotional signals ("Shamanism" 360–3). Such brain waves may flood the frontal lobes with altered and newly integrated consciousness, through rhythmic music, chanting, and dancing, as with ultra-running or psychedelics, creating mystical experiences (363–70).

Neuroscientists find, with electro-encephalographic measurements of brain activity, that shamanic trance involves a *shift* from left to right cortical, frontal-parietal to temporal-parietal networks, as the inner theatre changes from ordinary, analytic, causal to altered, intuitive, holistic states of consciousness (Shapiro and Scott 155). Such a trance includes "altered perception of time, body and self; communion with spiritual entities, such as a wolf alter-ego; and synesthetic experiences." Thus, animism, totemism, and shamanism may have fueled the development of various religions, evoking mystical awe in believers, as ancestor worship and deity devotion became more hierarchical (Winkelman, "Evolutionary" 58 and "Supernatural" 103–04). This involved mirror neurons, emotion contagion, and altered states of consciousness, extending collective inner/outer theatres toward higher brain-spirit realms, as with awe-inspiring edifices and statues today.

Religious historian Louise Sundararajan applies the psychological model of threat-based awe to "negative theology," theorizing the mystic's "self annihilation" in a "dark night of the soul" when sublime ecstasy cannot be assimilated, but becomes a "dramatic transformation" into transcendent joyful wonder (179–80, 184). In my view, this might involve a spillover mixture of temporal-lobe *audience* networks, especially the right amygdala, which processes fear and panic, and the left amygdala, involving pleasant/unpleasant emotions, while right and left, posterior and anterior insula circuits combine brain-body arousal and calmness (Chouchou et al.; Lanteaume et al.; Trimble 53). Adding to our hypothesis, the *dramatic* potential of threat-based awe, with a mystical melting of self into the divine Other, is stressed in cruciform churches with vast interior spaces focusing on the sacrificial altar, through crucifixion and martyrdom imagery. More *contemplative* awe, melting into nothingness, is reflected in Chinese temples, open to the sky, with dispersed shrines, smoking incense sticks, and serene faces on many of the divine figures. But a spillover effect of both types of awe, with various arousing and quiescent emotions, might occur in any church or temple.

As summarized in Table 1.4, brain research on the mystical experience of Pentecostal glossolalia, a babbling speech that believers interpret as "speaking in tongues" while possessed by the Holy Spirit, finds a paradoxical (trickster) mix of arousal and calmness (Newberg and Waldman 191–209). This involves the temporal-lobe *audience*, plus thalamus and midbrain *stagehands*, like Buddhist meditation and traditional Catholic prayer. But unlike meditation and prayer, brain scans during glossolalia show less activity in the frontal lobe "attention area" and a slight increase in the left-parietal "orientation area" (1, 205)—for a different *staging* of an empty self, with a more active *costume-body definer* perceived as the big Other. Instead of dissolving into nothingness or Christ, the babbling believer has "a realistic sense that the Holy Spirit is communicating through the self" (209). Other studies find that right hemisphere activity increases during glossolalia, which also relates to the *improviser/designer* network as holistic, spontaneous, and prosodic Devil's Advocate in the musical babbling of Holy Spirit tongues (Philipchalk and Mueller; Walter; Watts 74). Such mystical examples connect SEEKING in the animal-human body-brain to spirit realms and religious spaces, through *positive* trickster experiences, involving maternal nurturing and patriarchal ordering, which may include hearing God's voice as well. They relate especially to the Cenacle in Jerusalem (Chapter 3), as legendary site of the biblical Pentecost when the Holy Spirit appeared as tongues of fire on the apostles, who then spoke in other tongues. Yet such permeability also reflects the *negative* potential of demonic possession (Luhrmann, *When* xxiv, 24–5, 334n31).

Research shows that glossolalia may be "regressive" in a healthy way, with "positive personality benefits," through playful Pentecostal or more serious mainline Charismatic interpretations (Watts 74–5). An evangelical Christian who speaks in tongues, sounding like an infant's preverbal language, with head back and hands raised in praise-worship, like a child reaching toward an adult, is more likely to be rated as "anxious" on the attachment theory grid (rather than "secure," "avoidant," or "ambiguous") with a recent "anxiety crisis" (Kirkpatrick 60–2, 106, 140–1). The believer's brain, with "internal working models," responds to the parental ideal of a *nurturing*, body-permeating Holy Spirit through particular personal experiences, programed in childhood and extended in later years toward the divine, as compensation for what was experienced or missed, with God as a "substitute attachment figure" (64, 101–45). Such inner theatre networks of self and Other include an "exploration system" in the brain, along with attachment and caregiving systems (30–1). This may include the "self-conscious cultivation" of pretend play with God as a hyper-real figure, at church or elsewhere, "using props," like a child with an "imaginary friend" (Luhrmann, "Hyperreal" 378–9). Thus, mirroring, inner/outer theatre emotions of dramatic or contemplative awe, anxiety, care, seeking, and joyful play may be evoked, while alone or with others, in a new or familiar church, temple, or Pentecostal sanctuary. Historically, this involves a shift in Western Christianity from colonial Father to Victorian Son to modern/postmodern Spirit (Prothero 87). But how did such playful, ecstatic brain spirits arise in our species, eventually creating distinctive religious buildings, in Europe and China, with moral yet transcendent frames?

Evolving Selves

Diagram 1.2 shows the evolutionary levels of our brain's architecture, with theatrical elements of self in relation to Other (or soul/ego to God), developing from animal ancestors toward hyper-reflective, metaphysical aspirations. In the womb, our developing brain has structures akin to other vertebrates, including fish: hindbrain, midbrain, and forebrain.[16] But gradually the latter mushrooms into the distinctive, multiple folds of cortical layers. After birth, vertebrate subcortical *stagehand* and mammalian limbic *audience* circuits are active at the edges of our conscious awareness. They are crucial during meditation, prayer, and speaking in tongues, for the calmness, arousal, or ecstatic spillover effects of polyvagal, autonomic nervous system ties to the body.

Such bottom-up, low/high arousal, pleasure/pain networks collaborate with dispositional "puppeteers" (as further *stagehands*) in subcortical association areas, plus temporal, parietal, and frontal cortices (Damasio, *Self* 151, 162–3, 201). They produce perceptions, ideas, and actions through the "image spaces" of upper brainstem, occipital (visual), temporal (auditory), sensorimotor, and prefrontal association areas—as self/Other consciousness is "staged" by deep goal and conceptual contexts (Baars, *In*). Note that my theatrical model, extending neuroscientists' metaphors, does *not* match the triune theory of a neo-mammalian, paleo-mammalian, and reptilian (or "lizard") brain, defined by Paul MacLean in the 1960s and popularized by Carl Sagan in *The Dragons of Eden*. Yet the expression of bottom-up drives and emotions, through subcortical *stagehands* and limbic (temporal-lobe) *audience* circuits, are reflected in the supportive or trickster dragons, plus animal-

---

[16] Cf. Shubin on the inherited fish structures of the human body.

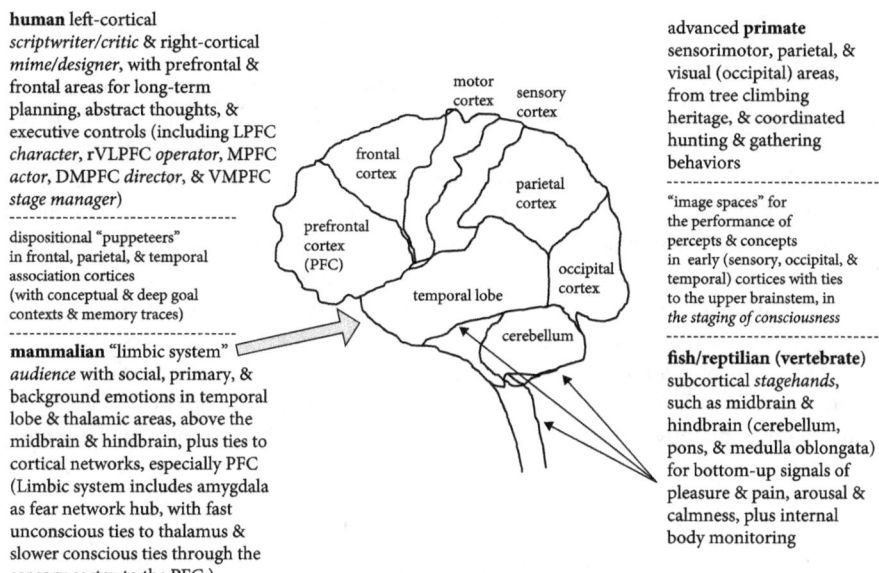

Diagram 1.2 Levels of Animal Legacies within the Human Brain.

humanoid figures, of Chinese temples and European churches. Our fish-mammalian inheritance might also be glimpsed with Nanhai Guanyin standing on a fish (as protector of South Sea sailors and fishermen) or the ichthys and lamb symbols of Jesus in churches.

Parietal areas, above the temporal lobes at the sides of the head, evolved in our primate and human ancestors, from branch-balanced lives to bipedal, hunter-gatherer groups of increasing sizes. Along with bodily coordination (through ties to the cerebellum), this evolution included the complex coordination of primary and social emotions, through mimetic and verbal languages, in the staging of self and other *spaces*, within and around the body. In the parietal lobes, the "left orientation area creates the brain's spatial sense of self, while the right side creates the physical space in which that self can exist" (Newberg et al. 28, 120). Such spatial identifications relate to Newberg's findings on meditation and prayer: decreased activity (deafferentation) in the left and right parietal "orientation" areas of self and peripersonal space. This deactivation of *costume-body definer* and (body-scene) *designer* creates a dissolving of self into the expansive Other, especially with contemplative non-attachment and interdependency, as emphasized in Chinese Buddhist temples, through meditative offerings and chanting. It might be evoked with prayer, too, in European churches' contemplative areas. It is also a potential with dramatic awe in vast enclosed church spaces, diminishing yet extending the self/soul, through the arousal/calmness spillover of threatening yet positive awe. Pentecostal (or Charismatic) praise-singing evokes ecstasy within the spatial self, however, as left parietal orientation activity increases in glossolalia. Thus, selves become porous brain spirits in different ways.

Ecstatic spiritual experiences in a temple, church, or elsewhere, like the ghostly presences evoked in Persinger's lab, involve the inner *audience* of mammalian, temporal lobe, emotional memory networks as well. Such an intense self-Other merging, with the melting of ego into nothingness or Christ, or with one's own voice becoming an instrument of the Holy Spirit for mysterious speech, also involves the distinctively human, prefrontal cortex as "attention association area" (Newberg et al. 29–31, 120). Thus, the self is *not* staged in just one brain area, as Cartesian *cogito*. The brain's "miniagents and microagents" create multiple narrative drafts of its performances, in an inner selective environment, evolved from animal ancestors (Dennett, *Consciousness* 458; *Darwin's* 374–81). And yet, there is a functional "dynamic core" of brain networks, clustering while in process, like an orchestra of instrumentalists playing independently but coming together, which provides the illusion of an integrated self—although with a potential for "splinter cores" (Edelman and Tononi 106, 139–44, 189).

Ramachandran describes various aspects of the self as zombie-like *selves* in different areas of the brain (Ramachandran and Blakeslee 82–4). There is a malleable, "embodied self" in the parietal and frontal lobes (247)—related to mystical melting in meditation or prayer, with decreased parietal activity, as mapped by Newberg. There is also a "passionate self" centered in the amygdala and a "visceral, vegetative self" tied to gut reactions through the insula, with these limbic areas contributing to a distinctive personality through the VMPFC (Ramachandran and Blakeslee 248) as *audience* and *stage manager*. This involves an "executive self," too, with body image and action commands in the sensorimotor cortex, plus an illusion of unity and free will through the vigilant self in the anterior cingulate (249–53). And there is an autobiographical "mnemonic self" centered in the temporal lobe's hippocampus, which forms long-term memories (250). Thus, various inner-theatre selves, as brain spirits, are reflected in religious ideals of souls, gods, and buildings.

Souls with One or Many Divine Mirrors and Heaven/Hell Realms

European Christian cultures have increased the phantom-ego armor of an individual (undivided) self through the religious ideal of an immortal *soul*, mirrored by one almighty God, creator of the world and ruling from Heaven, who made humans, male and female, "in our image, in our likeness, so that they may rule . . . over the livestock and all the wild animals" (*New International Version*, Genesis 1.26). The Western soul-self developed historically from the ancient Platonic dualism of "spirit and flesh" to the Renaissance Cartesian *res cogitans*, or thinking thing, as "individualistic ego" (Trimble 26–7, 54). Evidence of individualism appears in early Christianity with the notion of "inner conviction" as more important for morality than outer behavior, which offended other ancient Romans (Luhrmann, "Mind" 13). Western individualism developed further through a medieval shift toward "the inner" in the tenth and twelfth centuries and an "inner loneliness" during the Protestant Reformation "to purify the relationship between human and God" (12–13). The ideal of an individuated ego, integrating soul with the deity, also appears in Carl Jung's modern archetypal theory: "the Self as the image of God in the psyche" (Watts 21).

Chinese Daoism, however, maintains the ancient sense of multiple souls and gods, which also existed in Egypt, Greece, and Rome, prior to Christian dominance. In Daoism, each person has at least two souls, a *yang* (masculine, active) *hun* that leaves the body at death and a *yin* (feminine, passive) *po* that stays with it (Y.-S. Yü, "'O Soul'"). The *hun* (cloud spirit) can also leave the body during sleep (Baldrian-Hussein 522). But traditions differ as to how many *hun* and *po* each person has, as finer celestial spirits and baser animal or bone souls (Harrell 522–3). The *hun/po* typology of spirits in the brain-body goes back at least to the Warring States Period (475–221 BCE), in ancient Chinese traditions prior to Daoism.

There are also many gods in Daoism with various images. Temples often display prominent statues of the Three Great Emperor-Officials (of Heaven, Earth, and Water) or the Three Pure Ones (each with his own heaven). The latter represent the "original pure state of the three internal energies," spiritual *shen*, vital *qi*, and generative emotional *ching* (Wong 148). Along with the three heavenly realms that they rule, there are others in Daoism, plus a purgatorial hell, Diyu, with various levels and courts.

Buddhism has a similar notion of temporary hells, or *Narakas*, where a being might be sent, in multiple cycles of rebirth, through *karma*. It is represented by King Yan in China (like Yama in India), who judges the deceased in Daoism as well, with his assistants, Ox-Head and Horse-Face. There are Buddhist heavens of gods and demi-gods above the human, animal, ghost, and hell realms. Above these sense-desire realms are also pure form and formless realms, at higher levels of rebirth (Harvey 36). Yet the heavens offer distractions of pleasure and the animal/ghost/hell realms of suffering, with the human realm having both. For those who are temporarily in hell, there are various tortures, such as being burned, cut up, or eaten, until the next rebirth (33–4). Some Chinese temples and parks feature simulations of underworld, Daoist and Buddhist, hell realms (Ni 47–8).

Even more akin to neuroscience than the multiple souls of Daoism, Buddhism has a doctrine of *anatman* or "non-self." The human experience of an abiding, permanent self is believed to be an illusion. Tibetan Buddhism and some other branches also define multiple minds (or consciousnesses) within each person. But in all types of Buddhism, unlike neuroscience, a person's mental processes—the *avacya* as "inexpressible self" (not personal self) or "spiritual vector" in conscious vows and unconscious predispositions—continues beyond the body's death with rebirth into another lifetime (Buswell and Lopez 708–09; Leighton 18). The goal of Buddhism is to escape such cycles by attaining Nirvana (not a place, but ego "blowout") with enlightenment beyond the heavens and thus ultimate "immortality" (no life-death-rebirth). In Buddhist temples there are many images of saint-like "arhats" (Chinese: luohans), who exemplify various enlightenment journeys, and god-like "bodhisattvas," who delay their full enlightenment through compassion, returning to help suffering beings by sharing the miraculous powers of spiritual merit.

Significant differences developed historically between Protestant churches focusing on scriptures, preaching, and music with almost no religious figures; Catholic and Orthodox churches with numerous images of saints, yet still a focus on one God; Daoist temples with many gods; and Buddhist temples with many bodhisattvas and arhats. But such reflections in religious buildings also show common aspects of the brain's inner theatre: staging self (or non-self) in the mirror of a big Other. We inherit a "protoself" from animal ancestors, signaling "the state of the living body," which influences our higher-order "apparent self [that] emerges as the feeling of a feeling" (Damasio, *Feeling* 22, 30). Such feelings arise from our subcortical *stagehands* and temporal-lobe *audience*, with needs, perceptions, and memories, as the "core self" and "autobiographical self" evoking a reflective, narrative staging of "extended consciousness" (16–17) through survival/reproduction drives and bio-cultural projections of the Other.

King, Family, and Feet

Anthropologists have theorized that prehistoric humans, like current hunter-gatherers, imagined "metapersons" as rulers over them, with animal spirits, ancestors, and deities in "cosmic polities" (Graeber and Sahlins 2). Adding 4E terms for such fluid consciousness, metapersons *extend* the brain's *embodied* cognition, *embedded* and *enacted* in family and clan groups, while expressing a greater hierarchical drive. "There are kingly beings in heaven even when there are no chiefs on earth." Even with egalitarian cultures, "God is an expression of the lack of power in human society," regarding the forces of nature and mortality (57). Yet the eventual transfer of divine power to kings "did not follow a single or a simple trajectory," with various experiments performed: seasonal rulers, ritual regicides, and sovereigns "confined in space" (459–61). Such developments involved many choices across different cultures, producing deity-king-priest alignments and their buildings.

Prehistoric egalitarian cultures also experimented with agriculture, "'play farming' on a grand scale," while continuing to hunt and gather wild foods (Graeber and Wengrow 293). Gradually, many cultures shifted toward hierarchical social structures, with settlements, cities, and states, featuring warriors, priests, and kings, which dominated natural environments across the globe during the last twelve thousand years. This involved changes from matriarchal, matrilineal, or matrilocal to patriarchal cultures (Goettner-Abendroth, *Matriarchal*). Indeed, males may have appropriated the symbolic make-up, blood-ritual, moon-cycle, reproductive power of "female cosmetic coalitions," from women's separate menstruation huts to men's solar-focused temples or Christian churches with a bloody Jesus and bread/wine rite, as animal-human-divine sacrifice (Knight; Power; Watts et al.). Thus, mammalian maternal care developed as human patriarchal violence, especially through the Western heritage of Roman law. This is reflected in the word "family," related to the Latin *famulus* (house slave) and *paterfamilias* (patriarch), while "dominate" relates to *domus* (household) and *dominium* (emperor's or citizen's power over property, including slaves), as anthropologists point out (Graeber and Wengrow 510).

In China, patriarchal collectivist rectitude developed a foot-binding tradition for girls, starting at age five to seven, perpetuated by mothers across many generations of family domination. The girl's small, pointed, broken-bone, blood and pus leaking, infection-smelly, "golden lotus" feet (*jinlian*) were fetishized as attractive in their special shoes—through shared *costume-body designer/definer* networks. "The trauma radically changed her sense of the body in space and her sense of being" (Wang P. 6). Bound feet showed "discipline," marriage value, "character," and family "face" (reputation), plus "control over reproductive functions," thus conflating maternal care with pain as *teng* through Neo-Confucian ideals (Blake, "Foot-Binding" 681–4, 691; Wang P. 19). Related also to Buddhist ideals, with the story of lotus flowers appearing under a deer-girl's hoof-steps (or the infant Buddha's footsteps), this domestic rite included prayers to the Tiny-Footed Maiden goddess and Guanyin (Ko, *Cinderella's* 114, 283n14; *Every* 32, 64–6; Wang P. 11–12). Foot-binding lasted for a thousand years, eventually involving nearly all social classes and up to 50 percent of Han women by the nineteenth century. It ended in the early twentieth through the work of Christian missionaries and Chinese intellectuals, including feminists. Yet the valuing of boys over girls, for education and work, continued during the twentieth-century one-child policy and after. Centuries of foot-binding, increasingly popular even with Qing period bans by Manchu emperors, show the potential harm in collectivist harmony, reflected in temple ideals of family debt/duty and cooperative sacrificial care, especially when balancing on little girls' feet.

The next chapter will consider evidence for prehistoric "temples" with matricentral inclinations on the Mediterranean islands of Malta. It will then focus on historical developments of Greco-Roman-Christian religious monuments, from ancient to modern, compared with sites in China. Both European and Chinese traditions reflect familial frameworks, with blood, fire, and other elemental rites, plus heaven and hell as cosmic political theatres, integrating to some degree the multiple selves or souls in each person and community.

The evolving hypothesis is that European churches display left-cortical *patriarchal* characteristics through dramatic ideals: monuments dominating their sites with rectilinear, focused, enclosed designs and father/son figures stressing individualist single-soul identifications of binary, good versus evil, melodramatic, competitive conquests—although with maternal elements, too, as tragicomic inclinations. Chinese temples display right-cortical *maternal* characteristics (along with left-cortical patriarchal), through more contemplative, cooperative ideals: monuments tied to nature with curved, dispersed, open designs, emphasizing collectivist multiple-soul identities in harmonious tragicomic balance. Yet both involve *trickster* elements, crossing realms or challenging such ideals as moral frameworks—regarding patriarchal figures of dominance and maternal of care, especially at Catholic and Buddhist sites, with sacrificial demands.

Plus . . . Moral Scripts, Scapegoats, and Sanctuaries

Psychologist Frans de Waal offers an anecdote about his home country of the Netherlands, which has many churches but not many churchgoers: children sometimes ask why the pointed buildings have a "plus sign" on top (*Bonobo* 220–1). Whether that symbol on a church is seen as a plus or a cross, it still points the viewer upward toward the sky with an indication of divine oversight, perhaps in both senses. Thus, the feelings the symbol evokes in each person may vary greatly, such as curiosity, awe, gratitude, nurturing love from a self-sacrificing God, moral pressure from a judgmental Father, or a meaningless plus.

Many children and adults today, in Europe but also elsewhere in our postmodern, hi-tech, consumer-oriented world, develop passionate attachments to transitional objects on *screens*, more than religious icons from the past on church walls and spires. Yet the imaginary windows and symbolic frames of TV (as nurturing "boob tube"), laptop, and cellphone devices, with the popular audience playing a godlike role, are akin to the theatrical *agon* of religious imagery and myths. The "postmodern sacred" may be less earnest about its fantasy beliefs (McAvan), extending Dionysian trickster spirits against Apollonian traditional values. But today's mass and social media continue to express the animal-human heritage and family dynamics of our brain's inner theatre, with emotional drives fueling or disrupting patriarchal ideals. This interplay exemplifies a danger, as well as pleasure, in any devotion to binary, good versus evil ideals. The typical melodramatic formula of screen fictions and games, like religious projections of saints and angels against devils, promotes stereotypes of superheroes, villains, victims, and scapegoats, with righteous acts of fighting evil, through revenge and reciprocal violence. Some devotees not only rehearse such scripts in virtual spaces, but also perform them—in real life and death scenes, as law enforcers, soldiers, school shooters, or terrorists.

Psychologists and sociologists use the theatre term "scripts" for learned patterns of behavior, absorbed from earlier experiences, unconsciously priming our actions in "social dramas," both individually and collectively (Alexander). Such "procedural scripts and semantic schemas" also relate to religious rituals, which create communal "identity markers" through "doctrinal" norms of "high-frequency" participation—or through less frequent, yet more intense, "imagistic" rites (Whitehouse and McQuinn 602–03). With further neuro-theatrical terms, we can parse such psychosocial script absorption, regarding the brain networks that create various degrees of moral Apollonian or perverse Dionysian actions.

In a church or temple visit, as in everyday life, temporal-lobe *audience* networks recognize patterns from prior experiences and personal models (including parents, peers, and media stars), while appraising current situations. Inner *audience* circuits cheer or boo other brain signals in the staging of consciousness, exciting or inhibiting their synaptic connections, which also "chat" and "chant" while building to a "cheer" (Baars, *On* 602–03). The left-cortical *scriptwriter/critic* gives the illusion of fully choosing one's actions, scripting and interpreting them in each active and reflective moment (while drawing on prior scripts). But the brain-body is primed toward its ideas, perceptions, and actions through many unconscious, internal and external influences.

The right-cortical *mime-improviser/scene-designer* filters subcortical *stagehand* drives and emotions toward imaginative, subjective, intuitive appraisals. These are filtered even further by cognitive, objective, analytical, left-cortical *scriptwriter/critic* ideas. The interplay may also involve trickster feelings, images, and ideas, with acts of playful mischief, from subversive *stagehands*, through maternal (more right-cortical) care and empathy modes, against patriarchal (more left-cortical) norms of order and judgment. Such subcortical *stagehand* drives are supportive of patriarchal norms most of the time, internally and collectively, even when offering creative alternatives and Devil's Advocate impulses. Yet trickster *stagehands* sometimes disrupt social norms with passionate counter-scripts, altering the patriarchal *scriptwriter/critic*'s controls through *mime-improviser* gestures and *scene-designer* plans, in personal and political theatres, involving religious and secular morality.

Such "social dramas" include a breach, a continued crisis rising to a climax, and then redress with reintegration, but also the potential for further conflict cycles (V. Turner). They hinge upon repeated yet revised scripts of *sacrifice*, with mimetic envy, rivalry, and scapegoating (Girard), evoking *sacredness* in religious or secular terms, through the threat of *sacrilege*, often projected onto other persons and groups. Psychologically, each of us must sacrifice our infantile pleasures as we grow up (with prematurely born, culturally programmable brains), through specific scripts of actor-character identities, developing in family, peer, and social networks. Even rebellion against parental or social norms involves sacrifices. Delayed gratification offers hope, from real needs to imagined goals and symbolic rewards. Yet in our life's drama and inner theatre, personal sacrifices create unconscious scripts of *desire* for lost pleasures and objects. Such desires circulate, through *fantasies*, around idealized people and products, as emotionally meaningful and thus "sacred," even in popular culture.

To maintain sacred ideals, personal and group impurities are sometimes projected onto *scapegoats*, as strangers who threaten from within and are thus sacrificed or expelled, through the animal-human drive of cleanliness/grooming/gossip. The ancient Greeks held a springtime ritual for such scapegoating. During the *Thargelia* festival, two ugly or deformed men were picked as *pharmakoi*, beaten, and then exiled or executed. This relates to the term "scapegoat" in the King James Version of the Hebrew Bible, tied to the Dionysian satyr as "goat idol" and to the demon Azazel (De La Torre and Hernández 59–60). One can also see scapegoating in today's political rhetoric, inspiring violence against immigrants, minorities, or others viewed as abnormal, disgusting, and evil threats.

If one is scapegoated, one must accept moral guilt, as a breach of collective trust, even if undeserved, and then repent and be reintegrated—or rebel and be exiled, perhaps finding a new group identity elsewhere. Hypocritically, scapegoating usually involves projecting the inner trickster, and its potential evils *within* the person or group, onto others, blaming *them* as morally disgusting, sacrilegious, and dangerous, through the patriarchal *scriptwriter/critic*, especially with the *binary* circuits of its (left parietal) *costume-body definer*. Recruited for this also, in each person's prefrontal cortex, with group ideologies of good versus evil, are the inner *stage manager's* moral behavior monitoring, the *character's* appearance awareness, the *actor's* self-knowledge, and the *director's* theory of Other minds (social and divine), watching it all—plus temporal-lobe *audience* intuitions and subcortical *stagehand* passions.

The trickster (or Jungian shadow) exists in *each* of us, through our animal-human drives and pleasure-seeking, ego-filling desires. It must be acknowledged, modulated, and expressed to some degree, through various inner-theatre networks. Yet its danger lies not just in eruptive misrule, but also in social drama projections of melodramatic good versus evil, with righteous moral emotions attacking people perceived (in real life) as devilish threats. Thus, group purification through scapegoating may enact evil and destruction—exemplified by the many persecutions, witch trials, and "ethnic cleansing" events of religious and secular cultures.

De Waal's research on primates suggests how moral emotions have evolved in humans toward religious ideals, tragic flaws, and melodramatic scapegoats, with or without divine intervention. From the emotional contagion and motor mimicry of *herd mammals* to sympathetic concern, sense of fairness, shared goals, and self-sacrifice shown by *primates* to active consolation, reconciliation, perspective taking, and targeted helping of *apes*, many aspects of maternal care extend beyond the mother-infant bond to social support between group members, especially with bonobos (*Bonobo*; *Primates*; "Putting"; "Russian"; Preston and de Waal).[17] Such values in humans, however, through abstraction, meta-consciousness, and collective myths, may extend to group goals of righteous vengeance and imperial expansion. Chimps show some of this, not only with hierarchic rivalries, but also territorial patrols, which focus violent tensions within the group upon an unlucky outsider, even a former member, found at the border, as a scapegoat who gets beaten to death, sometimes torn apart and eaten (de Waal, *Our* 204–09; Wrangham and Peterson 5–12). Yet humans have vastly expanded such sacrificial scapegoating, through religious and nationalist ideals, with inquisitions, wars, terrorist acts, and genocides.

When we enter the "sanctuary" of a church, temple, or mosque as a purified space (perhaps with water washing rites), the feeling of communal safety and nurturing may be shadowed by fear of evil spirits, even in fellow human beings. The monumental site might also evoke fear of the divine patriarch's judgment or hope that his rage will turn upon those perceived as evil, through our own passion for mimetic, reciprocal vengeance. One might feel anger, too, *against* the alpha-male Creator or Meta-Spectator, concerning humans in the world or specific scenes in one's life. Indeed, various animal-drive emotions, with primate moral elements, may arise in the inner theatre when one visits a religious building: SEEKING spiritual security and meaning beyond mortality (with hope for targeted help), CARE for body or soul (plus consolation), and PLAYful joy through sacred awe (with reconciliation and new perspective-taking). Yet there might also be GRIEF and PANIC at life's unfair sacrifices, FEAR of the world's evil, LUSTful temptations to violate moral rules (even when inspired by beauty), or RAGE at the divine ruler and specific people.

---

[17] Cf. Topa and Narvaez 208, on "what Darwin called 'the moral sense,' a collection of traits that other animals have," which evolved into human "pleasure being with others, concern with fitting into the social group, empathy, [and] habit development."

Such primary emotions are shown in Table 1.1 (without Panksepp's capital letters), regarding animal-human drives and related cultural extensions, social emotions, and religious values, positive and negative, which might be reflected at a sacred site. Patriarchal designs and imagery may evoke feelings of territoriality and hierarchy in the visitor, through social emotions and religious values: nostalgia, honor, awe, and moral devotion. Supportive/trickster edges reflect survival affects through holy/sinful desires, ego pride/conflict, courage/anxiety, and divine reward/punishment—or playful joy/mischief and freedom/rebellion with spirit powers. Maternal reproductive and nurturing-care drives might be evoked, too, from love and empathy to collective kinship with altruistic charity and compassion. These emotions and values relate to moral elements in our primate heritage: shared goals, fairness, consolation, reconciliation, perspective-taking, targeted helping, and self-sacrifice as cooperative group behaviors. However, religious monuments may also reflect (and evoke) apparently "moral," melodramatic, good versus evil scripts of sacrificial scapegoating, especially with analytical, objectifying, left-cortical aspects of Western churches.

Analytical or/and Dialectical

Research by cultural psychologists correlate with McGilchrist's findings about Western and East Asian cognition (Table 1.3). As I summarize in Table 1.5, experiments show that Americans tend to focus more on foreground objects in pictures, whereas Japanese attend (with a wider spotlight of consciousness) to the overall scene, including "inert, background objects" (Nisbett 90). When given an abstract sculpture with an arbitrary name, Americans tend to associate the name with the shape of the sculpture, Japanese with its material. Such differences occur as early as age two. In other studies, Americans tend to interpret abstract animated figures on a video screen as having internal causal factors for their movement, like shape and weight, but Asians tend to see them as affected by contexts, like gravity and friction. "Tend to" is important to remember with all of these experiments. There is a spectrum of responses within each cultural group, but looked at collectively and averaged, these are the comparisons.

Another experiment shows that Americans believe more in fixed personality types and consistent trends, while Koreans believe in situational influences and changing fortunes (Nisbett 119–20). Americans often infer a false rule in random association tests; Chinese do so less often. When given various images of an object (a rod) at different angles inside a field (a box), Americans are better than Chinese at judging the object's position without influence from the field, because they are less context-oriented (96). This perceptual finding correlates with neuroscience experiments showing that Westerners have greater neural activity in "object processing" areas than East Asians, especially in elderly brains, due to an "expertise effect" shaped by culture (Domínguez et al. 57–8).

According to surveys, European Americans associate health with feeling "in control" more than Asians and Asian Americans (Nisbett 96). Asians feel less in control of their lives than Westerners, but instead of trying to control situations, they are more likely to adjust (97). Likewise, through their collectivist traditions, Asians are more likely than

Table 1.5 Western and Eastern Cognition with Church/Temple Extensions.

Westerners, use more individualist, abstract-rule-based, categorical, analytical, linear thinking (more left-hemisphere functions)	East Asians use more collectivist, material-relational, holistic-contextual, dialectical, cyclical thinking (with more right-hemisphere processes, less inhibited by left)
• Americans focus more on foreground objects in pictures & shapes of sculptures (with arbitrary names) • Americans interpret abstract moving figures on a video screen as having more internal causal factors like shape & weight (also grouping pictures by category > activity) • Americans believe more in fixed personality types & consistent trends • Americans often infer a false rule in random association tests • Americans are better at judging the position of an object (rod) without influence from field (box) *according to surveys*: • Feeling "in control" of their lives is associated with health by European Americans more than Asians or Asian Americans	• Japanese attend more to background scenes & the sculpture's materiality, even at age two • gravity & friction (also grouping pictures by activity more than category, such as cow with grass, not chicken) • Koreans believe more in situational influences and changing fortunes • Chinese less often • Chinese are more contextually oriented (box > rod) • Asians feel less in control of their lives than Westerners & instead of trying to control situations, they are more likely to adjust • Asians feel more well-being than Americans when they are part of a controlling group However, Nisbett's research shows that an individual Asian American or Hong Kong resident (influenced by British culture) *may be primed in either direction* with Eastern or Western cues, such as a dragon or Mickey Mouse, calligraphy or a cowboy, or with personal memories—toward collectivist, holistic or individualist, self-motivated perceptions.
My theoretical interpretations (with cultural neuroscience):	
Western cultures have shaped the human brain more toward left-hemisphere, egoistic, analytical, local cause-and-effect functions, stressing individual freedom, related to American "free market" ideals involving "less government."	East Asian cultures involve more right-hemisphere networks, along with left, for communal, relational/dialectical, holistic processes, emphasizing group harmony and individuals submitting to interdependent organization.
REFLECTIONS and EVOCATIONS in European (Catholic, Orthodox, & Protestant) churches: *rectilinear, cruciform* shapes with *enclosed* narthex, nave, transept, and apse for the *focused* approach (of persons or a procession) along the main aisle toward the lectern and altar—*as more individualistic, abstract rule based, and linear*	Chinese (Daoist & Buddhist) temples: *embedded rectangles with curled* roof corners and *open* design behind an outer wall (based on an imperial palace) in a series of *multi-directional, dispersed* central and side halls around a courtyard—*as more holistic, relational-contextual, and cyclical*

These areas function as a melodramatic/tragicomic stage space for *the priest or minister (as lead performer)* to preach from the Book and reenact Jesus's Last Supper, including a communion rite for the congregation. (Catholic churches also have a sanctuary "tabernacle" for the transubstantiated communion bread, as dwelling place of God, plus other areas with statues & paintings of saints, for personal prayer.) There is an obligation to attend the collective event every Sunday. [Some churches were converted to Protestantism and some damaged during the sixteenth-century Reformation.]	People buy incense, light it in a *communal* fire, hold it to the head, bow three times in each of the four cardinal directions, leave the incense stick in the *collective* burner, and then go to various halls on the sides. They may also visit the central elevated hall, to kneel before *various* statues (of gods or bodhisattvas) and bow to the floor three times—or join *a group of monks or nuns* chanting prayers, who play drums and other instruments, in a hall or courtyard, tied to the natural environment within the yard and perhaps along a hillside. [Temples were closed and many damaged during the communist Cultural Revolution (1966–76).]

Americans to express well-being when they are part of a group controlling them (97–8). And yet, Nisbett's research shows that an individual Asian-American or Hong Kong resident (influenced by British culture) can be primed for such tests and surveys in either the Eastern or Western direction: through cultural cues such as a Chinese dragon or Mickey Mouse, calligraphy or a cowboy, or with personal memories (118–19). These bicultural subjects show the potential for *both* contextual and individualistic (more right- or left-cortical) perceptions. Gender variations have also been found: "females of both [Eastern and Western] cultures tend to be more holistic than males," but more so among Western participants (99–100).[18]

Such research has continued across several decades, especially regarding East Asian, collectivist, "dialectical" thinking versus Western, individualist, analytical cognition.[19] Cultural psychologists define several elements in dialectical cognition: expectation of change, tolerance of contradiction, and perception of interconnectedness, leading to family-based (instead of abstract, rule-based) associations with field-dependent attention and contextual attribution of causality (Spencer-Rodgers et al. 4–5). East Asian interdependent, dialectical thinking is Confucian (social, filial loyalty), Buddhist (karmic, "middle way"), and Daoist (mental/ritual harmony with nature), through continual "yin-yang balancing," as an "either/and" interplay (6–7; Lau and Cheng 589; Li 44–6). This differs from "synthesis" in the Hegelian sense of sublation, which resolves the thesis-antithesis of Aristotelian either/or oppositions (46).[20] Retaining compatible but removing conflicting elements of a paradox, Hegelian dialecticism "is only temporarily both/and,

---

[18] This finding of a more holistic orientation in females may relate to brain mapping studies that show females using bilateral and right cortical areas more, while males use left-cortical areas, in verbal phonetic and virtual reality maze tasks (Roughgarden 230–1).

[19] Researchers find mixed variations, with collectivist yet low dialectical cultures in some countries, such as Mexico, Spain, and Morocco (Spencer-Rodgers et al. 13; Wong and Liu 548), which may share analytical, yet interdependent, Iberian-Islamic influences.

[20] According to Karsten Harries, the early nineteenth-century philosopher G. W. F. Hegel viewed human mind and spirit (*Geist*) as godlike, laboring "to impose order on matter," by transforming the natural world "in their own image,... their own spirit" (220–1). For Hegel, unlike his predecessor Immanuel Kant, "nature cannot really be considered beautiful" (220).

and is ultimately either/or." However, Eastern "philosophical and religious traditions emphasize balanced emotional experience, ... both negative and positive ... [as] healthy, ... when expressed to moderate degrees" (Ryff 397). Both kinds of emotions, along with paradoxical ideas, are "intertwined such that each is embedded within the other."

Buddhism cultivates dialectical, dependent-origination, "middle-way" cognition, in contrast to Christianity. Researchers find that Buddhists "do not influence their positive and negative emotions, whereas Christians use an influence strategy of emotion regulation" (Wilken and Miyamoto 536–7). Christians increase positive feelings over negative, rather than "balancing" them as in Buddhist mindfulness meditation, recently adopted by Western psychotherapy. This relates to European church imagery of competitive, melodramatic, holy figures conquering evil, as emotion/action regulation, with man-made designs dominating the landscape (and man created in the image of God with dominion over nature in Genesis). By comparison, Chinese temples show protector deities in warrior poses, but balance them with serene, regal or meditative models of divinity, in dispersed halls across open-air courtyards, more attuned to the natural context. And yet, the ancient culture of Jesus may have been more dialectical than later Christendom, as reflected in Semitic languages, where "all seeming opposites are really connected" in a larger field—with people feeling "less 'individual,' less separate from nature and others than today" (Douglas-Klotz 16–22).

Ideal Affects of Individualism and Collectivism

Across many studies, psychologist Jeanne Tsai and her colleagues have found that Europeans and Euro-Americans prefer "ideal affects" that are high-arousal positive (HAP), while East Asians and Asian-Americans prefer low-arousal positive (LAP), even accepting more negative (LAN). Such ideal affects are different from actual experiences of emotions, which also involve personal "temperament," such as "extraverted" (outgoing vs. solitary) or "neurotic" (sensitive vs. resilient) in the Five Factor or "Big Five" personality model that many psychologists use. And yet, "ideal affect shapes what people consciously and unconsciously do to feel good, as well as what decisions they make, how they think about health and well-being, and how they perceive and respond to others" (Tsai and Clobert 300).

For example, a study showed computer-generated faces with various positive expressions to Chinese females, who had lived in the US for less than five years (Park et al.). Compared with European-American female viewers, the Chinese women found "excited (versus calm) faces to be less rewarding," with less activity in their brains' pleasure areas, the bilateral ventral striatum and left caudate (Tsai and Clobert 310). In that comparison, Chinese brains also showed greater activity in "regions associated with identity and self-relevance (i.e., medial prefrontal cortex) when viewing calm Asian faces"—thus involving inner *actor* networks of affect identifications, but with the cultural ideal of LAP as an actual bias.

Cultural psychologists find such Western versus East Asian characteristics in various contexts, including popular media, peer interactions, and mother-child communications.

Table 1.6 Ideal Affects and Self Models

Europeans and European Americans	East Asians and Asian Americans
prefer high-arousal positive (HAP)	prefer low-arousal positive (LAP) & accept more low-arousal negative (LAN)
independent model of self	*interdependent* model of self
acting on the environment & influencing others	changing beliefs, desires, & preferences to be consistent with others while assessing what others want
Jesus as an energizing power with a passionate quality	Buddha as cool, dispassionate, & calm
Heaven with lightning, thunder, & roaring waters (in Revelation)	Nirvana as hidden & peaceful
Christian Bible & ritual practices with more HAP emotions	Buddhist sutras & ritual practices with more LAP

Religions, too, idealize affects differently, regarding models of self, afterlife goals, and sacred rites (Table 1.6). Tsai cites religion scholar Huston Smith, who summarizes Jesus as "an 'energizing power'" with a "passionate quality," while the Buddha "is described as 'cool,' 'dispassionate,' and 'calm'" (245–7). She also finds that Christian texts and ritual practices stress HAP emotions, but Buddhist ones emphasize LAP. Heaven involves lightning, thunder, and roaring waters in the Book of Revelation, yet Nirvana is hidden and peaceful in Buddhist sutras. Christian worship includes "*enthusiastic*" practices, but Buddhist services primarily involve meditation, along with sermons and chanting, especially in the Western context (246). In a study searching for HAP terms, including "*rejoice, proud, glory, exalt,* and *desire*," and LAP words, such as "*serene, placid, calm, peace,* and *harmony*," which were encouraged or discouraged (or neutral) in context, Tsai and her colleagues found that "Christian classical texts endorsed HAP more than did Buddhist classical texts, despite similarities in the frequency of HAP words" (Tsai et al. 417). The Buddhist classical texts (Dhammapada, Lotus Sutra, Diamond Sutra, and Heart Sutra) endorsed LAP terms more, but with a statistically non-significant difference. Another study of current Christian and Buddhist self-help books showed a significant difference in these HAP and LAP directions (418–19).

Using online questionnaires with hundreds of European-American (EA) and Asian-American (AA) college students, Tsai found that "non-participants" in religion valued ideal HAP the most, then Christians, and then Buddhists the least (Tsai et al. 413–15). She found the reverse for ideal LAP, with Buddhists valuing it the most, then Christians, and then non-participants—and such results "held for both AA and EA" (415). She also assessed their temperaments, finding that Christians were more extraverted and Buddhists less neurotic (introverted) than the others, but AA participants were more neurotic than EA. As she concludes, "results support the prediction that religion influences ideal affect."

Tsai explains such findings with a theory (developed from Nisbett and others) that Western cultures have more "independent models of the self, influencing others— changing one's environment to be consistent with one's beliefs, desires, and preferences"

(Tsai and Clobert 303). This involves acting on the environment with "increases in physiological arousal" and HAP states "like excitement, energy, and enthusiasm" as dominant ideals. East Asian cultures, in contrast, have more "interdependent models of the self, adjusting to others—changing one's beliefs, desires, and preferences to be consistent with those of others." This includes assessing what others want, with "decreases in action" and arousal, through ideal LAP states "like calm, peacefulness, and serenity"—akin to the ultimate Indian *rasa* as a string for the other eight as jewels.

With ethnic varieties on the Western-Eastern spectrum, experiments found that "European Americans and Chinese Americans wanted to feel positive more and negative less (across all levels of arousal) than Hong Kong and Beijing Chinese" (Tsai and Clobert 300). The valuing of LAN and HAN by East Asians was because negative emotions "might elicit less envy from others and make people more sensitive to other people's pain." On the other hand, even within such groups, "the more individuals valued independent over interdependent values, the more they wanted to feel positive vs. negative states." Thus, in my inner theatre model, evidence from cultural psychology points to the programing of inner *scriptwriter/critic* and *mime/designer* networks with more *balance* between left and right hemispheres in the East Asian *yang–yin* orientation. It also points to more *dominance* by left-cortical, egoistic, optimistic, objectifying functions over right-cortical, holistic, melancholic, contextual in the Western analytical (versus dialectical) tradition, as listed in Table 1.3. Recent brain mapping studies confirm "a greater contextual bias in East Asians and a more object-focused bias in Westerners" when given visual tasks (Goh and Park 107).

Degrees of object-focused independent identity in Western cultures and contextual interdependent in Eastern also relate to moral standards. As philosopher Jesse Prinz puts it, "Westerners derive greater well-being from self-satisfaction, positive emotions, and personal enjoyment; Easterners care more about fulfilling obligations, working toward goals, and doing good things for others" (*Emotional* 292). For Western "individualist cultures," this involves an "ethics of autonomy," while collectivist cultures, "such as those in the Far East, may place comparatively more emphasis on community norms, including those that have to do with rank" (304). Yet collectivist cultures are not always freely harmonious. "Conformity is valued ... [and] behaviour is very strictly regulated ... prescribing everything from etiquette and attire, to posture and facial expression" (Prinz, *Beyond* 195). For example, studies show higher degrees of "vigilance" toward in-group members, "anticipating more unethical behaviors" from peers, in China than in the US—and in more collectivist, rice-growing areas of southern China than in wheat-growing areas of northern China (S. S. Liu et al. 14538).

Counter-currents to the Western individualist and Chinese collectivist paradigm can be found in their corresponding histories. Individualism arose in ancient Greek philosophy, developing through Greco-Roman theatre and law, and then through Christian beliefs in "free will" with a transcendent soul and "personalist" Creator God who connects with human history (Bloom 293; P. McNamara, *Religion*). Yet a comparatively more "holistic vision dominated Europe from the decline of Epicureanism until well into the Renaissance" (Munro 23). Western individualism only became "mainstream" near the end of the eighteenth century, especially with the German Romantics who stressed personal uniqueness, introspection, and solitude (3). Also, monastic communities in Europe have long explored collectivist ideals of spiritual balance.

On the other side of Eurasia, Confucian, Daoist, and Buddhist traditions included self control, life prolonging, and individual enlightenment as aims. But those were in a "part-whole" relationship, rather than the many-one, particular-universal framework of European traditions (Hansen 37). Family ties of blood and *qi* demanded loyal obligations to progenitors and "to heaven or nature, rather than in direct relation to God as creator of . . . an individual soul" (Bloom 294). A form of individualism ruptured Chinese collective consciousness in the third century, with a Neo-Daoist emphasis on "Pure Conversation" and natural feelings (*qíng*), against the prior Han Confucian stress on social ritual (*li*) and conformity (Y.-S. Yü, "Individualism" 140–2). Buddhism across the centuries involved introspective meditation for some, yet in a more monastic than eremitic tradition, not for the "appeasement of self" as in Daoism, but for the "perception of its nonexistence" (Bauer 182), while giving merit to others.

Regarding these countertrends in Europe and China, experiments with bicultural subjects demonstrate how each of us might shift toward independent or interdependent awareness—through Western or Eastern teachings and imagery. But which emotions are redesigned in such a shift? How are ideological programs re-scripted through the self-Other relations of various inner theatre elements, in church and temple spaces? How might such outer theatre sites relate to the benefits of self-less tragicomic "melting," in sacrificial ecstasy or compassionate wisdom (with HAN/HAP and LAN/LAP spillover effects)—or to the dangers of dopaminergic reward/craving and oxytocin care/bonding, with the potential melodramatic (HAP over HAN) scapegoating of others as impure?

Rasa-Catharsis of Moral Emotions

Located between Europe and China, ancient India developed a theatre tradition involving aesthetic "juices" or "flavors" (*rasas*) of certain emotions (*bhavas*), evoked in spectators by the play onstage. Credited to Bharata and perhaps other authors, between 200 BCE and 200 CE, the *Natya-Shastra* specifies eight *rasas* with related *bhavas*: sadness, fear, love, anger, awe, courage, disgust, and humor.[21] In traditional Chinese literature, a similar list of primary emotions can be found (Pollock 199). An Indian commentary on the *Natya-Shastra*, the *Abhinavabharati* (c. 1000 CE) by Abhinavagupta, adds a ninth *rasa*, "peace" (*shanta*), showing the influence of Buddhism: an aesthetic refinement of emotions, through resonance and distancing, not just for pleasure, but also enlightenment. In the Hindu context, this involves union with Brahman (Over-Soul) through *tanmayibhavana* (universal communion) with calmness beyond sensual attachments. "The aim of *rasa* is self-forgetfulness," from mundane experience to otherworldly "transcendence" (Rodríguez 52–3). And yet, an alternate, high-arousal tradition stresses *bhakti* as devotional immersion through reading or viewing religious

---

[21] For various theories of *rasas* and *bhavas* in Hindu religions, see McDaniel.

> Ancient Greek theory of *catharsis* as cleansing certain emotions, according to Aristotle's *Poetics* (with Panksepp's animal-human emotions in CAPS)
> tragic sympathy/GRIEF/CARE & FEAR/PANIC (evoking love & hate/anger) in the audience, as they admire the hero's courageous SEEKING, with the play's growing conflicts through plot twists & recognition moments, toward its climax & final catastrophe—revealing the hero's tragic flaw (*hamartia* or "error in judgment")
>
> Eight ancient Indian *bhavas* (emotions) & their *rasas* (flavors evoked by art) according to Bharata's *Natya-Shastra*
>
> - *shoka* & *karuna*: sadness/GRIEF/compassion/pity (as in Aristotle's theory)
> - *bhaya* & *bhayanaka*: FEAR/shame (as in Aristotle's theory)
> - *rati* & *shringara*: erotic/romantic desire, love, and happiness (mentioned by Aristotle, related to LUST & CARE)
> - *hasa* & *hasya*: humor (joyful PLAY, basic to all theatre, in Aristotle's notion of *mimesis*)
> - *krodha* & *raudra*: anger (or RAGE/hate, briefly mentioned by Aristotle)
> - *utsaha* & *vira*: courage or heroic vigor (with obstacles to the hero's SEEKING)
> - *vismaya* & *adbhuta*: awe/surprise (suggested by Aristotle with the audience's admiration for the tragic hero)
> - *jugupsa* & *bibhatsa*: disgust (suggested by Aristotle's notion of the hero's tragic flaw or *hamartia*)
>
> And the 9th *rasa* of peace (*shanta*), as the goal of mindful attentiveness to such feelings [union with *Brahman* (the Over-soul), through *tanmayibhavana* (universal communion), as influenced by Buddhism, with calmness as the goal of enlightenment, beyond sensual attachments, according to Abhinavagupta's *Abhinavabharati*]

Diagram 1.3 Ancient Theatre Theories of Emotions and Catharsis.

artworks: a "fusion ... with the divine form" akin to "possession rituals" in Indian folk traditions (60).

In a previous book, I related *rasas* to the modern theatre theories of Antonin Artaud (immersive "cruelty") and Bertolt Brecht (critical "alienation"), along with Aristotle's ancient theory of catharsis (clarifying tragic sympathy and fear), regarding current neuroscience, our continuing bio-cultural evolution, and various film examples (*Beast-People*). Diagram 1.3 compares the two cathartic feelings and nine *rasas*, in relation to neuroscientist Jaak Panksepp's research on animal-human emotions. Ancient Greek catharsis, from *kathairô*, "to wash," was associated with ritual purification, performed by priestly *katharai*, as suggested by Aristotle's *Politics*: "sacred music ... [with] tunes that violently arouse the soul … [as if in] medicinal treatment," akin to theatrical catharsis in his *Poetics*. According to remnant scripts, violent acts rarely appeared onstage, but were heard offstage or described by a witness, with after-effects shown. Yet bloody animal sacrifices were involved in the Dionysian religious context of theatre. Tragedies were featured during the festival, with three on each of three days, but there were also mythic satires (satyr plays) and comedies. In other shamanic performances and seasonal rites of mimetic violence, catharsis was related to *katharma*, the evil object, sacrificial animal, or scapegoated person that was purged, from the body or from society (Girard 94–6, 286).[22]

In this book, I apply *rasa*-catharsis theory to religious sites. This involves a modern sense, too, of *tragicomic* cruelty, alienation, and awareness, in the emotional savoring and cognitive cleansing of inner theatre networks, with right and left cortical shifts. I also consider the danger of cathartic backfire, with *melodramatic* ideals of good versus evil, in heroic battles against perceived villains, making them scapegoated victims, in the bloody histories of territorial hierarchies at religious sites. Churches and temples have the potential to arouse immersive, contagious, painful/pleasurable emotions, with melodramatic dangers. But they may also transform such tastes with calm, distanced, tragicomic observations—especially through cross-cultural comparisons.

Diagram 1.4 shows social psychologist Jonathan Haidt's self-other "families" of emotions regarding his "Moral Foundations" theory, linguist George Lakoff's findings on conservative versus liberal metaphors (Strict Father or Nurturant Parent), and philosopher Jesse Prinz's moral emotion blends—as related to my model, drawing on brain-mapping research by Iain McGilchrist and others. Table 1.7 adds Haidt's Moral Foundations theory, which includes the relationship between instinctual animal behaviors and human emotions like my model. Of course, such models do not include all of the brain's complexity, particularly with social emotions such as guilt and shame, which involve activation in specific left and right cortical areas (Hecht 4–5; Michl et al. 152–5). Many emotion networks extend from subcortical *stagehands* and limbic *audience* toward the right-cortical, maternal (Nurturant Parent) *mime-improviser/ designer*, in the more subjective, holistic-oriented hemisphere (McGilchrist, *Master* 33). But anger and related emotions are more active on the left-cortical, patriarchal (Strict Father), objectifying side, through dopamine anticipation-reward circuits (61) and the left-parietal "binary operator" (Newberg et al. 196).[23] This may involve moral-rationalized, melodramatic pleasures of righteous "good" fighting perceived "evils," such as lustful, rebellious tricksters or impure scapegoats.

---

[22] Cf. Lawtoo, *Violence*, especially 103–10, on catharsis as affective, medical embodiment and purging through sacred music, according to Aristotle's *Politics*, yet involving "distance" with theatre or reading in his *Poetics*. Lawtoo also explores René Girard's emphasis on theatrical catharsis as purging, with the actor as *katharma* and *pharmakon* (poison/cure/scapegoat).

[23] Cf. J. B. Taylor on the four "characters" of our brain: left thinking, left emotional, right emotional, and right thinking.

Jonathan Haidt's emotion "families" in his essay, "The Moral Emotions" (Psychology)
embarrassment, shame, and guilt—as the "self-conscious" family
compassion (related to sympathy and CARE)—as the "other-suffering" family
contempt, anger (RAGE), and disgust—as the "other-condemning" family
gratitude and elevation (admiration, awe)—as the "other-praising" family

Jonathan Haidt's Moral Foundations Theory (*Righteous*), from conservative to liberal (Table 1.7)
loyalty, authority, sanctity, liberty, fairness, care

George Lakoff's *Moral Politics model of rhetorical metaphors* (Linguistics)
Strict Father (conservative) & Nurturant Parent (liberal)

Jesse Prinz's blends of Moral Emotions in *Beyond Human Nature* (Philosophy)
positive: pride, happiness, admiration, gratitude, and elevation
negative: guilt (fear + sadness) as counterpart to anger at others
  shame (from embarrassment) as counterpart to disgust at others
  self/other-contempt (guilt/anger + shame/disgust)

Mark Pizzato's neuro-theatrical model (**nine *rasas*** & related emotions regarding inner theatre elements)

more left-cortical *scriptwriter/critic*	more right-cortical *mime-improviser/scene-designer*
[dominance/control OR **peace** . . . rebalancing:]	
hope/confidence (ego & social bonds)	tragic sympathy/**sadness**/GRIEF/PANIC (at loss)
anger[1]/RAGE & pride	FEAR & guilt
disgust[2]	romantic **love**/CARE or LUST/shame
awe as admiration/respect[3]/jealousy	awe as surprise/gratitude/empathy (self-transcendence)
SEEKING/anticipation/**courage**	trust/despair (primal alienation/abjection)
revenge & gloating (schadenfreude)[4]	fairness[5] & **humor/joy** in open-minded PLAY[6]
individualist/competitive "anti-social"	collectivist/cooperative "pro-social emotions" (Hecht)[7]

 with subcortical supportive/trickster *stagehands* & temporal-lobe memorial *audience* networks

---

[1] Siep et al.
[2] Holtmann et al. Cf. Gan et al., on core disgust with threat detection as left and social-communicative disgust as right.
[3] See Nakatani et al. on left anterior temporal lobe activity with "respect" even more than "admiration" (of behavior).
[4] See Hecht, on anger, jealousy, and gloating (schadenfreude) as left hemisphere emotions.
[5] See Hecht, on sadness, fear, guilt, gratitude, empathy, trust, and fairness as right hemisphere emotions.
[6] See Marinkovic et al. on right prefrontal "reprocessing" of verbal jokes with "distant unexpected creative coherence" (113). See also Ammaniti and Gallese 118–19, on right cortical and subcortical, mirror-neuron joy shared between mother and child.
[7] See also Demaree et al. on left-frontal "dominance" versus right-frontal "submission" emotions.

Diagram 1.4 Moral Emotions in Psychology, Linguistics, Philosophy, and Neuro-Theatre (with Panksepp's animal-human emotions in CAPS and ancient Indian *rasas* in bold).

Table 1.7 Moral Foundations Theory (adapted from Haidt and Joseph's "Intuitive Ethics" [2004] plus Haidt's *Righteous Mind* [2012, p. 125])

Ape [or Animal] Behavior	Human Emotions	Moral Binary (Good/Evil)
being loyal to group bonds	group pride, rage at traitors	loyalty/betrayal
respecting hierarchical authorities	respect, fear [& awe]	authority/subversion
maintaining cleanliness	disgust [& shame]	sanctity/degradation
[fighting for freedom]	[courage & rage]	liberty/oppression
supporting fairness	anger, gratitude, guilt	fairness/cheating
minimizing suffering	compassion	care/harm

"Across 4 studies using multiple methods, liberals consistently showed greater endorsement and use of the Harm/care and Fairness/reciprocity foundations compared to the other 3 foundations, whereas conservatives endorsed and used the 5 foundations more equally," with those studies not including liberty/oppression as a possible moral foundation.

(Graham, Haidt, and Nosek, 2009, p. 1029)

According to Prinz's "Sentimentalist theory," moral judgments are based on emotions (*Beyond* 321). As in Haidt's categories of self-conscious, other-condemning, and other-praising emotions (Diagram 1.4), Prinz explores relations between moral emotions, but without mentioning compassion as other-suffering. Positive moral emotions may involve pride, happiness, admiration, gratitude, and elevation, through pleasure networks in the brain (308), plus oxytocin trust with allegiance to a group hierarchy, I would add. On the negative side, *guilt* relates to a person being harmed, as the "counterpart of anger," when turned on oneself (307). It involves "a blend of fear and sadness," not observable in other ape species (321). *Shame*, however, drawing on embarrassment, relates to "crimes against nature," or against God, or the body being sullied, and as "the counterpart of disgust" turned against oneself (307). For theists, "the emotion that enforces . . . divinity norms is disgust. We must remain pure before God." Yet there is also a moral emotion regarding crimes against community, as a hybrid of crimes against nature and persons, namely *contempt*, a "blend of disgust and anger." Such emotions may be evoked in a religious building, but they may also be redesigned through *rasa*-cathartic awareness.

Christianity portrays God as the divine spectator of our human drama with all these emotions in play. Through the believer's moral reflection, with ritual confession to a priest in church (in the Catholic and Orthodox traditions), guilt is expressed for personal offenses, shame at bodily impurities or trickster drives, and yet forgiveness given from God. There might also be disgust and anger, yet tragic sympathy and fear at others' violations of communal norms—or the other-condemning melodramatic projection of contempt at scapegoats and out-groups. Chinese folk religion (with Confucianism) stresses debt to ancestors and (with Daoism) fear of malevolent spirits or bodily imbalances. Afterlife punishment or reward involves collectivist dimensions of personal guilt, natural shame, and communal contempt (with alienation/abjection) or admiration, gratitude, and elevation. But Buddhism questions the egoism that may be involved with such moral emotions and their attachments, as temple chanting rites offer counterpoints to incense and spirit-money burning as attempts at guilt/shame reconciliation with ancestors and others.

Building on the filial piety tradition in Confucianism, medieval Chinese Buddhism developed popular tales of sexual guilt in mothers, who were reborn in painful Dantean hells, pleading for help, and then saved by family-indebted, yet heroic sons, through donations they gave to monasteries and the merits of monks' rites (Cole 5–11). This sounds like Catholic indulgences, purchased by laypeople across the centuries for priests' rites and saints' merits, to reduce purgatorial pain. But Buddhist monks are traditionally forbidden to farm, unlike Catholic clergy in monasteries, and thus are more dependent on local support, like urban priests with ritual collection plates and church donation boxes.

The chapters ahead will consider how self-directed disgust and anger, with moral emotions of shame and guilt about lust and craving, have been refocused, not only as family debt and spirit reconciliation, but also as heroic sacrifice and scapegoat contempt, through egoistic group liking and bonding—in the historical spaces of religious monuments. Such reflections involve spiritual, yet material economies, which continue to evoke melodramatic brain spirits through good versus evil imagery. Hopefully, our interdisciplinary approach will help you gain new perspectives about these psycho-social dimensions, through cathartic awareness of various *rasa* flavors, more melodramatic or tragicomic, competitive or cooperative, in church and temple experiences.

Original Sin, Debt/Duty, or Delusion

In Christian theology, the *original sin* of our first parents, with a trickster snake as competitive, rebellious, fallen angel, explains suffering as punishment for the persistent bodily temptations of primal pleasures against patriarchal norms (Diagram 1.5). Yet God's self-sacrifice as Jesus (along with that of many martyrs) gives a new value to suffering, as the heroic triumph of spirit over flesh, enabling the believer's inner-theatre transcendence beyond subcortical tricksters. This also involves maternal nurturing, especially by Mary and other saints, in Catholic and Orthodox churches (or by a personal relation to Jesus in Protestant). There is patriarchal judgment, too, rewarding good souls eternally, with an afterlife paradise of spiritual pleasures, and punishing sinful ones, who succumbed to the pleasures of the flesh. Thus, original and further, venial or cardinal sins put believers in need of God's sacrificial grace. This leads to debt/duty, with ritual grooming/gossip of in- versus out-groups, and perpetual gratitude for divine favor, which can never be equally returned. "So that, although we do not give thanks for our sins, we do give thanks for . . . God's forgiveness of them. . . . But for Christians, human beings are essentially debtors—not only to God, but to fellow human beings as well" (Roberts 71–3).

Bio-Cultural Evolution—the drives of **competition and cooperation** (in all animals) involve environmental survival, sexual reproduction, territoriality, nurturing-care, alliance-hierarchy, communal belonging, and (in humans) extended playfulness. Yet the need for meaning and purpose, through *reflective self-awareness*, with **arousal/calm and pleasure/pain** signals, has been **translated into these religious ideas:**

Christianity—the "**original sin**" of ancestral parents causes human suffering. So the solution is **redemptive sacrifice and salvation**, with God offering himself (his Son), plus saints as further examples. Believers (in **debt** to God for his suffering and forgiveness) freely choose bread/Body and wine/Blood communion, good works, and/or scriptural grace (to varying degrees in Catholic, Orthodox, and Protestant churches), leading to heavenly bliss in **God's love** or eternal damnation without it.

Confucianism or Daoism (via Chinese folk religion)—the **original debt/duty** to ancestral spirits and transcendent beings, through super-natural **interdependency**, requires ritual behavior and sacrifices. But if social or natural forces are **out of balance**, chaos and suffering develop. So the solution is **filial loyalty and humaneness through propriety (Confucianism)** or **a longer flourishing life through harmony with nature's Way**, also involving elixirs, exorcisms, and afterlife judgments with various heaven/hell realms **(Daoism)**.

Buddhism—the **original delusion** of desires, fantasies, and attachments increases human suffering. So the solution is **non-attached equanimity**, realizing non-self, inevitable change, and **interdependency** (dependent origination) with **ethical compassion**. This involves progress or regress across multiple karmic lifetimes (manifesting **debt/duty**) and heaven/earth/hell realms, toward or away from **Truth/ Nirvana as awakening**, with help along the way from arhats and bodhisattvas as models of enlightenment.

Islam—the **original delusion** of independent self-sufficiency, with ingratitude, pride, and arrogance, causes suffering. So the solution is full **submission** (as **debt/ duty**) to **Allah** for communal **order**, with the profession of faith, prayers to Mecca five times a day, charity, ritual fasting, and a once-in-a-lifetime pilgrimage to Mecca, rewarded with paradise (while others are punished) at the end of life.

Diagram 1.5 Sources and Solutions to Human Suffering (with the higher-order awareness of loss and mortality).

In Chinese folk religion, the *original debt/duty* to one's ancestors, along with respect for divinities, means repeated sacrifices of incense and spirit money—or suffering the consequences. They are burned in temple courtyards, along with cardboard goods, sent as smoke to the spirit realm. Donations of food, drink, and human currency are also placed at temple statues and given for renovations. (European churches likewise encourage monetary offerings with signs of devotion, from coin boxes and lit candles by statues to donation baskets at services or side chapels funded by wealthy families.) The Chinese sense of metaphysical debt/duty relates to the Confucian fear of social chaos—with orderly ethics and rites, cultivating *ren* (humaneness) and *li* (propriety), as the solution (Prothero 113). Thus, Confucianism stresses filial loyalty and proper rituals for social harmony, somewhat like Islam with submission and five-times-daily prayers to Allah, but that goes beyond family, addressing the *original delusion* of individual self-sufficiency (31–2).

Daoism emphasizes natural flourishing, as the response to metaphysical debt/duty and interconnectedness, extending one's life through harmony with the Dao as nature's "Way." Evil as disharmony causes illness and suffering in human life, through the wickedness of demons or sins of one's ancestors up to ten generations. The solution is a rebalancing of *yin* and *yang* through sacrificial offerings, talismans sent to the spirit realm by burning them, and exorcism rites, but not a cosmic conquering of evil, or devils by angels, as in medieval Christianity. "The goal of exorcism in Magical Taoism is not to destroy the ghost but to prevent it from doing mischief in the future. This can take the form of educating, placating, or rehabilitation" (Wong 111–12). And yet, hierarchical "obligations" and "martial" imagery are involved in the key texts of religious lineages, talisman writing, and mental visualizations used by Daoist masters to interact ritually with deities or demons, while purifying "primordial qi" through imagined body cutting, burning, and ash clearing (Mozina 169–70, 184–95, 210), as inner theatre, spiritual sensations.[24]

In Buddhism, the temptation of egoistic pleasure-seeking, with inevitable disappointment, loss, and suffering, is viewed as an *original delusion*, not as evil to be conquered. Sins in one's past or in past lives lead to karmic problems in current and future lifetimes, possibly in animal or spirit realms. This can be partly remedied through collective confession rites in Buddhist temples, with Confucian and Daoist parallels extending back thousands of years (Konior). The "common expiation" for Buddhist monks involves shame, fear of consequences, disgust about the body, desire for enlightenment, equanimity toward enemies as well as loved ones, gratitude to the Buddha, and emptiness "to realize the illusory nature of sin" (96). More comprehensively, the problem of evil and suffering is addressed by Buddhist sutra chanting, Dharma teachings, and meditation, with monks and nuns gathering merit for all. This involves accepting change, detachment from ordinary desires, and awareness of an empty non-intrinsic self—yet also compassion for all sentient beings, even evil ones, with

---

[24] For a consideration of *qi* (or Japanese *ki*) through Eastern and Western philosophy, physiology, and psychology, see Yuasa.

patriarchal wisdom and maternal care. Thus, Buddhist exorcism rites are performed not only for the victim of possession, but also to improve the demon's karmic destiny (George 76). Sometimes this involves "comic banter and satirical reference," persuading the victim to "become a spectator ... [by] rupturing any identification of actor and role," through an "alienation effect" akin to Brecht's theatre theory, with a disruption of emotional involvement for analytical distance (82).

Such ideals are like and unlike the Christian doctrine of "free will," with the choice of turning toward God and away from sin, through divine grace and human charity. God allows evil, as the absence of his love, to give humans that choice—although Catholic/Orthodox and Protestant interpretations differ about the need for good works. Buddhism "sees the basic root of suffering as spiritual ignorance, rather than sin, which is a wilful turning away from a creator God" (Harvey 56). It has "a doctrine of something like 'original sinlessness.' While the mind is seen as containing many unskillful tendencies with deep roots, 'below' these roots it is pure." Likewise, Daoism does not focus on death as punishment for original sin, in the Christian sense, but rather on "various psychic estrangements that signal corruption of the natural mind" (Kitts 353). These differences are reflected in church and temple examples ahead, with objectifying melodramatic dominance over sinful nature, through guilt-anger projections, or contextual tragicomic catharsis of (desire-delusion) *rasas*, such as shame-disgust and sympathy-fear in natural cycles, yet also continuation of ancestral debt and other Trojan Horse tricks.

Tricksters, Miracles, and Cathartic Backfire

Religion scholar Stephen Prothero compares Christianity, Islam, Confucianism, Daoism, and Buddhism as having different problem-solving goals: salvation, submission, propriety, flourishing, and awakening. I would add that the problems of suffering, with original sin, debt/duty, and delusion in such religious traditions, relate to the fundamental cruelties and tricks of "Mother Nature"—and yet the potential for tragicomic *rasa*-catharsis in sacred spaces. With human genes and organisms competing in their environments, the pleasures of beauty and sexuality become, in time, the pains of parenting and/or aging. Seasonal orders of survival and communal development may also be disrupted by natural disasters and social conflicts, such as the Covid-19 pandemic with its global economic effects. Religions have framed such trickster forces, in nature or humans, as coming from gods, ancestral spirits, or demons that might be appeased, rebalanced, or conquered through rites of sacrifice, purification, confession, and exorcism (related to theatrical catharsis). Thus, supernatural forces and rites order human behavior, belonging, meaning, and purpose within religious spaces. This enables the survival and reproduction of our prematurely born, hyper-playful, and highly flexible species, in very different environments around the world—alienated from instinctual orders, needing parental limits, yet also challenging them, through rebellious generations of cultural creativity.

In various religious traditions, trickster challenges against patriarchal morals involve female, youthful, and daring aspects: Eve biting the forbidden fruit in Christian mythology, feminine *yin* as the shadowy negative energy in Daoism, and beautiful daughters of Mara tempting the Buddha as he meditated, along with a demon army trying to distract him. And yet, unlike the purely evil demons of the Christian tradition, the Maras are beneficial tricksters. According to the two-thousand-year-old *Vimalakirti Sutra*, "the Maras ... are all bodhisattvas dwelling in the inconceivable liberation, who are playing the devil in order to develop living beings through their skill in liberative technique" (Thurman 54). Mara is thus more akin to the Hebrew meaning of "the *satan*" in the Book of Numbers and Job. In "mainstream Judaism to this day," this figure is an adversary to humans, yet a trickster allied with Yahweh: "one of the angels sent by God for the specific purpose of blocking or obstructing human activity" (Pagels 39).

Youthful female beauty is often idealized in trickster ways through religious art. For example, Mary appears as a young woman with the adult Jesus, unchanged for thirty years through her "immaculate" holiness. Yet she also reflects pleasure-pain transformations, from Annunciation and Nativity joy to mourning the death of her son in Pietà scenes (evoking comic-tragic *rasas*). Other beautiful artworks frame and decorate miracle-working, pain-pleasure relics from the corpses of saints, believed to heal the living, as holy tricksters and tricks in European churches. Relics are likewise revered in Buddhist temples, sometimes as whole-body mummies "fused with images in sacred space" (Ritzinger and Bingenheimer 38 n.5). But usually Buddhist relics are smaller pieces hidden within a stupa.

Like Jesus, the historical Buddha reportedly gave physical healing to devout followers (Harvey 26). Yet the Buddha regarded miracles as dangerous, potentially evoking self-glorification and attachment. Like Jesus tempted by Satan, he rejected Mara's offer to turn the Himalayas into gold. And yet, the Buddha prescribed how his cremated remains should be treasured in a burial stupa after his death, promising welfare and happiness to those who honored it with flowers, scents, or whitewash (27).

In Catholic imagery, such devotional fetishism and hopes for miracles may involve some degree of masochistic voyeurism—with decorated reliquaries related to beautifully painted scenes of tortured martyrs and Christ on the cross. Catholic artworks thus became fearful, sublime attractions of spiritual power, sometimes with realistic, fleshy, and dramatic details, especially through Renaissance and Baroque enticements. Basic circles and squares became, in Baroque church designs, "ellipses and elongated forms" bending perspectives with "visual mazes" (Kilde 109). The wealth of details, plus depictions of wealth, involved a tension between invitation and exclusivity for "the faithful as gazers upon the sacred narrative." By comparison, iconic, regal, natural, and peaceful forms expressed devotional hopes more consistently in Orthodox Christianity, Daoism, and Buddhism, although also with competing socio-political agendas in their different traditions.

Religious buildings often involve sacred sites of territorial conflict. Evocative artworks are covered or destroyed when a rival group converts a church to a mosque (as with Hagia Sophia in Constantinople, also looted by Catholic Crusaders), a Catholic church to Protestant (in parts of the Netherlands, France, Switzerland, Germany,

England, Scotland, and Denmark), or a temple to a Communist warehouse (in China). Such iconoclasm, by religious or atheistic groups, may occur through ostensibly righteous ideals of *purifying* the space from the perceived evil of idol worship. But this *projection* onto others' religious artworks, of one's own trickster temptations toward sin and delusion, is the opposite of *rasa*-cathartic empathy with self-aware distancing. In prior books, I called the scapegoating of others, to purify one's group, "cathartic backfire," because it involves self- and other-damaging rage, which may be evoked by plays and movies with melodramatic, good versus evil ideals (Pizzato, *Inner Theatres* and *Beast-People*). It is also a possibility with religious buildings, which induce immersive awe and communal bonding. Yet churches and temples may offer an antidote, too, especially through reflective comparisons: the *rasa*-cathartic awareness of a tragic flaw in humans, which appears when mimetic rivalry leads to melodramatic violence, as we seek meaningful group identities.

Identifying *Rasa* Emotions: Top-Down and Bottom-Up

Ancient Indian *rasa* theories, from the writings of Abhinavagupta and Bharata, one to two thousand years ago, involve various types of plays, not just tragedy, with mixtures of primary and secondary feelings in each show, like the tasty flavors in a well-made dish. The *rasas*, as tastes of the show, evoke inner-theatre elements of the spectator's brain that participate with the emotions, self/other-relations, and choices onstage, yet at a certain distance, through a fluid melting, enlargement, folding, and expansion of consciousness (Virtanen 64). This may involve shifts between right and left cortical activity, between Artaudian immersion with the inner *mime/designer* and Brechtian observation by the *scriptwriter/critic*, plus "mentalizing" by the inner *director* taking the perspective of others (Pizzato, *Beast-People* 195–8). Through the spectator's mimetic mirror-neuron system and contagious emotions, right-cortical imaginary and left-cortical symbolic identifications resonate with those of the players and characters onstage. Yet, plot twists and performance gestures, or choices in watching, might activate VLPFC *operator* circuits, right and left, reappraising emotions (Table 1.2)—as a savoring of *rasas*. This could alter the left hemisphere filtering (inhibiting) of right, making that more flexible.

Aristotelian catharsis as the reflective purifying of emotions (with pity and fear featured, but love/hate and anger mentioned) implies left hemisphere *control* over the right's emotional ties. However, the juice-savoring metaphor of Indian *rasa* theory suggests a *rebalancing* of right and left hemisphere networks, along with bodily memories, through intimacy and distance, as when a "connoisseur" uses knowledge in "ways of sampling in order to fully appreciate a wine" (Schechner, "Rasaesthetics" 31–3). This may also involve ties to the "second brain" of gut feelings (37). Regarding church and temple spaces with their moral emotion imagery, various inner theatre elements might be rebalanced at *rasa*-cathartic moments in the visitor's experience, with self/Other stagings rescripted and redesigned.

My term "*rasa*-cathartic" combines *rasa* and catharsis theories while acknowledging their distinct traditions—with connections to the modern theatre theories of Artaud (immersive, ritual "cruelty") and Brecht (critical, political "distancing effects"). Specifically, the moral emotions of embarrassment, shame, and guilt might be stirred, with past events that the visitor's brain brings to the church or temple through an inner *audience* of memory patterns, evoked by current experiences of symbolic spaces, artistic images, people, and rituals. Such "self-conscious" emotions in Haidt's list (Diagram 1.4), would also involve the inner *character* (imagining one's appearance to others), *actor* (private knowledge of self), *stage itself* or *film editor* (shaping self in each moment), and *stagehands* (deeper passions) in Table 1.2. The "other-suffering" family, such as compassionate care, might be evoked in the visit to a religious building, through its symbols, images, and rites—or even the "other-condemning" family, such as rage. Indeed, moral shame can trigger ostensibly righteous outrage, shifting the blame from oneself or one's group to others as contemptible scapegoats (Scheff 179), through the *melodramatic* "misprojection" of attribution bias, blaming persons rather than situations (Blattman 152-3). This probably involves the left-parietal *costume-body definer* with binary, good versus evil attributions.

Religious buildings may enable such scapegoating with depictions of evil tricksters, as threats to divine goodness. But they can also evoke *tragicomic* compassion with hope for those who suffer, as akin to oneself, through ideals of spiritual kinship, extending primal care bonds. Tragicomic refers to Aristotle's *Poetics*, with complex plot "reversals" in tragedy that shift sympathy and fear through "recognition." But it adds dialectical irony: comic twists in tragedy, or tragic in comedy, as a rebalancing of positive and negative values, through viewer-challenging, immersive yet distancing scenes—unlike the melodramatic temptation of simplistic hero/victim/villain projections, with a linear moral conflict promising ultimate victory.

Churches and temples often inspire Haidt's "other-praising" emotions of elevation and gratitude, with impressive structures, parental figures, and participatory rites. Other-related, moral emotions and religious experiences, along with self-focused ones, involve the visitor's inner *director* (imagining others' views of oneself, including the divine Other's), *stage manager* (monitoring one's behaviors), *light/sound operator* (controlling one's impulses), and *audience* (supporting or contradicting belief ideals through memorable meaning patterns). But these neural networks are also affected by the shifting crosstalk of one's inner *scriptwriter/critic* and *mime-improviser/scene-designer*, including the left parietal *costume-body definer* and right parietal *costume-body designer* of self and Otherness.[25] This left/right

---

[25] Along with Newberg's research on the left superior parietal "orientation area" and left inferior parietal "binary operator," yet right parietal "holistic operator," other scientists' mappings of brains show *left* inferior parietal activity when subjects take a first-person perspective, with the self as an acting agent (Ruby and Decety; Chaminade and Decety). Taking a third-person point of view, or perceiving actions as caused by the other, activates more of the *right* inferior parietal lobe (Farrer and Frith). This may also relate to Persinger's research with temporal-lobe stimulation evoking a God Experience or sensed presence of the Other, and Ramachandran's research on temporal-lobe epileptics, since the inferior (lower) parietal lobe is adjacent to the temporal lobe. Indeed, the temporal parietal junction (TPJ) has been identified as a prime area to activate spirit-like experiences in the lab—the left TPJ for "an illusory shadow person" and the right TPJ for Out of Body Experiences (OBE, also common in Near Death Experiences)—in relation to its normal role of self-motion processing and perspective taking (Nakul and Lopez). See also Blanke and Thut on inducing OBE with TPJ stimulation.

balancing act involves primary and social emotions, including the *rasas* of anger, disgust, awe as respect, and courage, arising from subcortical *stagehands* through left-cortical networks—with grief, fear, lust, and joyful (or rebellious) play surging through right-cortical circuits (Diagram 1.4).

Contradicting the Basic Emotion Theory of Panksepp and Haidt, another theory has emerged in affective science, from James Russell, Lisa Feldman Barrett, and their colleagues. They argue that all emotions are psychological constructions of one's bodily needs, felt in the brain regarding social situations, through "core affects" of pleasure/pain and arousal/calmness, with "scripts" of prototypical feelings (Russell 197–9).[26] In my view, this may relate to Newberg's research on the combined arousal/calmness "spillover effect" in ecstatic spiritual experiences, perhaps involving a paradoxical mix of pleasure/pain as well. And yet, according to Barrett, emotions do not control the mind like a powerful flood or an enclosing trap (as tricksterish forces or maternal womb/tomb). They can be reinterpreted through cultural terms and personal mindfulness, as in centering prayer and meditation—perhaps also through the *rasa*-cathartic effects of art, architecture, and design, in religious spaces and performances.

In this book, I will consider both the "top-down" psychological construction of emotions, regarding core affects, and the "bottom-up" animal-human drives in Basic Emotion Theory (LeDoux 461), with more "output-flexible" activations of mindfulness or more "output-rigid" impulses of our remnant instincts (Scarantino 359), such as survival and reproduction (Kringelbach and Berridge 230–1). My approach does not reduce emotions to "universal" categories. It considers the common human basis for many varieties of spiritual experiences, from animal-human drives to primary and social emotions, through different cultural traditions and religious values, reflected in European churches and Chinese temples.

Family Extensions

Whether we believe in one self, as immortal soul or not, or in multiple souls or no self, our neural networks for staging consciousness are patterned by our animal ancestry and personal experiences. Each of us moves in early life from a primary caregiver, often female, to "transitional objects" in play, school, work, and further social spaces, perhaps of religious buildings, which distance us from her (Watts 18–19; Winnicott). From the *round* worlds of our mother's womb and our early nurturing contact with her body, to the increasingly *rectilinear* and patriarchal environments of home, school, and workplace, we each experience the Other in specific bio-cultural ways that influence

---

[26] For debates about basic emotions, involving Russell, Panksepp, and others, see Zachar and Ellis. For neuroscience research against distinct networks for basic emotions, asking subjects to attend to "body feeling," emotion, and thought, which found "domain-general intrinsic networks" activated, especially the "salience network," coinciding with other tasks, see Oosterwijk et al. 128–30. For a philosopher's proposal of a new Basic Emotion Theory (BET), mediating between traditional BET and psychological constructionism, see Scarantino.

our sense of self, regarding (meta)physical territories, hierarchies, playfulness, belonging, and meaning/purpose. This relates to the softness or strictness of sacred music as a transitional object (M. Clark 35–6). It also relates to curved or angular shapes perceived as matching made-up word sounds in various "bouba-kiki" experiments (Peiffer-Smadja and Cohen; Ramachandran and Blakeslee).[27] Thus, the round or rectilinear aspects of religious buildings, with their music and imagery, may evoke fundamental structures of self vis-à-vis the Other, especially through mother, father, and child/trickster figures, reflecting early life, inner and outer stages.

Particular brain networks develop in each of us during childhood, from proto- to core to autobiographical selves and extended consciousness, through emotional embodied experiences that structure our inner theatre's primal sense of Mother, Father, and social or metaphysical Others. Various people and images might fit these roles during our child to adult development. The Mother or (m)Other, as *primary* caregiver, might not be the birth parent, or female, or the same person throughout childhood. Likewise, the Father, as *secondary* figure who helps us separate from the Mother and gain a distinct ego-identity, with contacts to a bigger social world through rules and symbolic meanings (law and language), might be any gender, a single parent switching roles, or a combination of people. Various tricksters may emerge, too, in our childhood dramas, as siblings, peers, and adults, or within us—through mischievous and rebellious impulses, beyond parental care and limits, especially as hormones, growth spurts, and events change us. Thus, "the non-primal real [may be] functioning to remind the symbolic [patriarchy] of the latter's derivative nature. And yet, ... this is what enables the human being to be free" (Dunlap 108).

Those who grew up in homes with religious imagery, and family trips to a church or temple, may experience the hometown religious building, or a new one elsewhere, through early emotional memory networks of nurturing care, yet sacrificial demands. With each new visit to a sacred building, subconscious *stagehand* and *audience* networks excite conscious neural circuits in the staging of feelings and ideas, positive or negative. Visitors who grew up *without* religious experiences, or those corresponding to the building, might be affected by its architecture and artworks in similar ways, but through "familiar" memories and feelings that are framed by different communal myths, doctrines, and beliefs, secular as well.

Eventually, children make the difficult move, in specific personal ways, beyond nurturing ties with the mother's body (or primary caregiver's), which involve powerful mammalian emotions of care when she is there or panic and grief when she is not. We each find transitional objects, such as a soft blanket or stuffed animal, but also move beyond them (often to digital devices). Fantasies are thus evoked about *lost* objects of oxytocin and opioid pleasures, through dopaminergic desires, seeking further substitutes. This also involves the mother's desires, focused on, but going beyond the child, which *alienate* it, creating specific experiences of existential *lack* (Fink 178–9)—and the

---

[27] Cf. Chen et al. for a cross-cultural experiment, which found that the bouba-kiki effect was similar for US and Taiwanese subjects, but with "partly tuned" cultural differences. See also McCormick et al.

potential spiritual yearning for belonging, purpose, and nurturing ideals in a bigger, religious Other.

Such alienation, with or without religious substitutes, helps the child to *separate* from the imaginary Mother and "grow up," to connect with peers and other adults, especially those in the Father's role as symbolic Other. Thus, patriarchal figures (including women) may offer symbolic meanings and moral limits to erotic pleasure/ pain, demanding certain sacrifices of remembered, ecstatic *jouissance* at the mother's body—and of later substitutes. This involves mimetic admiration yet envy, desire yet rivalry (Girard), with peers and adults, reflected in religious buildings with playful or rebellious tricksters, nurtured or conquered by divine ideals of an imaginary Mother and symbolic Father.

A primal, tragic shift from mimetic desire to vengeful rivalry is depicted in Christian mythology with a trickster, the archangel Lucifer, "a thousandfold / Brighter than the sun,"[28] challenging God, falling from heaven, and becoming Satan. Then, as a subhuman snake or worm-dragon, Satan tempts Eve and Adam to rebel against the divine Father, in a similar mimetic way, through the desire to be godlike (Oughourlian 71–2). Such trickster rebellion also relates to the earlier Hebrew myth, given in Genesis 6.1–4, about angels as "sons of God" who mate with humans, disrupting the natural order and requiring a Great Flood to wash away their offspring, the monstrous Nephilim, whose name means "the Fallen Ones" (De La Torre and Hernández 58–9).

At traditional religious sites, parental figures and offspring may appear, as metaphysical *extensions* of the brain's inherited architecture, reprogramed by familial and cultural experiences. Thus, subcortical animal-human (or childlike) drives, motivating right-cortical maternal ideals and left-cortical patriarchal demands, may be expressed in varying degrees and combinations—at supportive/trickster edges of round or rectilinear, multi- or uni-directional, dispersed or focused, open or enclosed, lifelike or abstract designs. Such family extensions in religious buildings, even as "archetypes," are *not* fixed universal absolutes. They continue to develop in each of our lives and subcultures, reflecting "fictive kinship relationships," shown by symbolic costumes, jewelry, and tattoos in earlier stages of human evolution as well, to cooperate within a group, yet also "compete more effectively with other groups" (Winkelman and Baker 262).

Diagram 1.6 offers a map of inner and outer theatres, with extended family dynamics and neuro-performance elements. These involve feedback loops of each person's neural, social, and spiritual networks, at play in everyday life but also in the heightened experiences of a temple or church. This Family Extensions Model relates to several recent trends in religious studies, which use cognitive, neurological, attachment, and adaptation theories borrowed from science (Tremlin 12–29). It includes the brain's inner theatre or "IT" elements (Table 1.2), partially programed by each person's secure,

---

[28] This is said by Lucifer about himself, after God declares his "Ego" as "alpha et omega," then leaves his throne, and the archangel mounts it, in the first play, *The Creation*, of the mid-fifteenth-century Wakefield or Towneley Cycle, one of many medieval, biblical dramas performed in and around churches (*Wakefield* 59–62). See also Pizzato, *Inner Theatres*, 90.

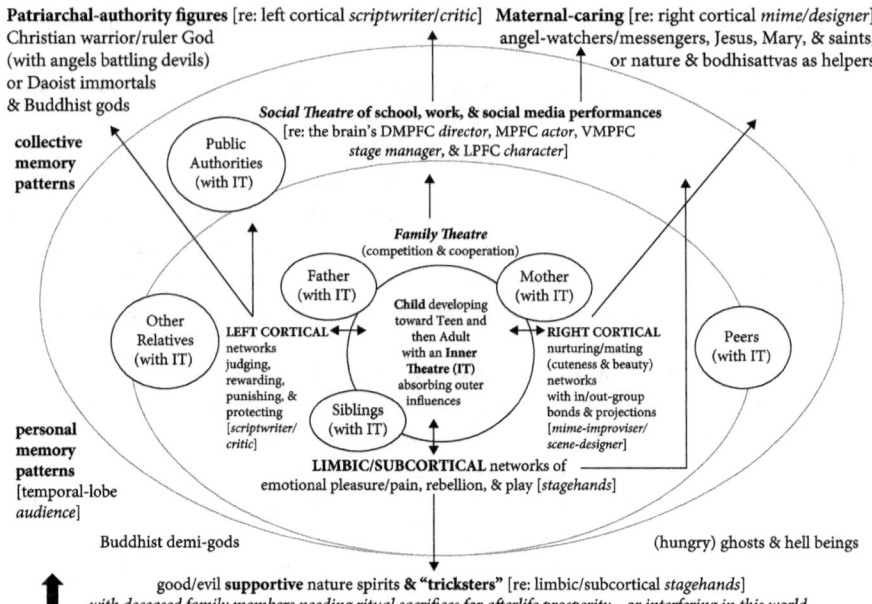

Diagram 1.6 Family Extensions of the Brain's Inner Theatre (IT) toward a Cosmic Theatre.

anxious, or ambiguous attachments to parental figures, as a child and later in life.[29] But it also shows how IT elements extend to the adaptive, group-selective, reprograming environments of social and cosmic theatres, involving religious myth, art, and architecture, with a church or temple as divine "home" and community sanctuary. It draws on neuroscience discoveries about right and left cortical (maternal and patriarchal) functions in relation to subcortical, supportive/trickster drives, inherited from our animal ancestors. Thus, Diagram 1.2 and Tables 1.1, 1.2, and 1.3 are embedded within the embodied, enacted extensions of Diagram 1.6, through this book's dialog between cognitive and affective science, psychology, neuroscience, anthropology, architecture, art history, religious studies, philosophy, and performance theory. Please refer back to the tables and figures in this chapter, adding your interpretations to

---

[29] Cf. Kirkpatrick, especially 34–45, 64–8, on the attachment theory of infant-mother relationships, extending into adulthood, with regard to "God referencing" by believers and God as "a *substitute* or *surrogate* caregiver"—yet also a patriarchal, "just" and "fair" God as "big chief" (42, 80–1, 84, 243–4). I disagree with Kirkpatrick when he "doubt[s] that there is any meaningful relationship between ... attachment processes" and Buddhist "detachment" (99). The Buddhist goal of detachment from egoistic desires reflects a key difference between Western, Christian-influenced ideals of soul-God individualism, shown by a child's "secure" attachment in leaving or returning to the caregiver, and East Asian, dialectical interdependency. For more on Attachment Theory and "internal working models" of parental relationships, see Howe.

Table 1.8 European (and Jerusalem) Sites Selected as Representative

Country	City	Religious Site	Chapter
Denmark	Copenhagen	Lutheran Church of Our Savior	2
England	Canterbury	Church of Saint Martin	2
Finland	Helsinki	Chapel of Silence (Kamppi)	3
		Lutheran Cathedral	3
		Lutheran Rock Church (Temppeliaukion)	3
		Uspenski Orthodox Cathedral	2
France	Fréjus	Cathedral of Saint Leontius	2
	Nimes	Maison Carrée	2
	Strasbourg	Cathedral of Our Lady	2
	Vienne	Temple of Augustus and Livia	2
Germany	Cologne	Cathedral of Saint Peter	2
	Hamburg	Lutheran High Church of Saint Michael	2
	Trier	Constantine Basilica (Lutheran Church of the Redeemer)	2
Greece	Delphi	Temple of Apollo & Tholos	2
Israel	Jerusalem	Cathedral of Saint James	3
		Cenacle	3
		Church of Queen Helen	3
		Church of Saint Alexander Nevsky	3
		Church of Saint Anne	3
		Church of the Flagellation	3
		Church of the Holy Sepulchre	2
		Dome of the Rock (Temple Mount)	2 & 3
		Western Wall (Temple Mount)	2 & 3
Italy	Agrigento	Cathedral of Saint Gerland	2
		Temple of Concord	2
	Brescia	Old Cathedral	2
	Noto	Holy Savior Church	2
	Ravenna	Arian Baptistery	2
		Baptistery of Neon	2
	Ragusa	Cathedral of Saint George	2
	Rome	Basilica of Saint Peter	3
		Basilica of Saint Stephen in the Round	2
		Basilica of Saints Ambrose and Charles	2
		Basilica of Saints John and Paul	2
		Catacomb of Saint Callixtus	2
		Church of Domine Quo Vadis	3
		Church of Saint Agnes in Agone	2
		Church of Saint Agnes Outside the Walls	2
		Church of Saint Andrew of the Thickets	2
		Church of Saint Charles at the Four Fountains	2
		Church of Saint Constantina	2
		Church of Saint Laurence in the Palace	3
		Church of Saints Sylvester and Martin	2
		Holy Stairs	3
		Lateran Baptistery	2
		Pantheon (Church of Saint Mary and the Martyrs)	2

(continued)

Table 1.8 (Continued)

Country	City	Religious Site	Chapter
	Siena	Cathedral of Saint Mary's Assumption	2
	Syracuse	Cathedral of Syracuse	2
Malta		Hagar Qim and Mnajdra temples	2
Spain	Barcelona	Holy Family Basilica	2
	Granada	Basilica of Saint John of God	2
	Toledo	Church of Saint Ildefonsus	2
Turkey	Istanbul	New Mosque	2
N=11	23	53 (out of 532 visited, including other countries)	

Table 1.9 Chinese Sites Selected as Representative

City	Religious Site	Chapter
Beijing	Ditan (Temple of Earth)	3
	Tiantan (Temple of Heaven)	3
Changzhou	Tianning Temple	2
Guangzhou	Chen Clan Ancestral Hall	2
	Hualin Temple	2
	Sanyuan Palace	3
Hangzhou	Lingyin Scenic Area with Feilai Feng (including Longhong, Qinglin, & Yuru Caves)	3
	Lingyin Temple	3
	Lower Tianzhu Temple	3
	Middle Tianzhu Temple	3
	Taoguang Temple	3
	Upper Tianzhu Temple	3
	Yongfu Temple	3
Jinan	Thousand Buddha Mountain (Budai Statue, Guanyin Cave, & Wanfo Dong Cave)	2
Leshan	Giant Maitreya	2
Mt. Putuo	Nanhai Guanyin	4
Shanghai	Baiyun Temple	4
	Baohua Temple	2
	Donglin Temple	2
	Jing'an Temple	2
	Qibao Temple	4
	Yuan Ming Temple	2
	Yufo Temple	2
	Yunxiang Temple	2
Qufu	Confucius (Kong) Family Home	2
	Yan Hui Temple	2
9	28 (out of 138 visited in the research project)	

mine—as we compare various examples of sacred sites, reflecting inner theatre ideals that derive from common animal-human drives with culturally diverse, personal and social effects, historically and today, including monumental conflicts.

Specific Hypotheses

The chapters ahead, selecting eighty-one sites from my visits to 685 across a decade (Tables 1.8 and 1.9), will consider how religious buildings might attract or repel, with pleasure or pain, in arousal or calmness, or both, with melodramatic ideals or tragicomic *rasa*-cathartic effects. An objection may be that I am comparing one East Asian country with ten European (plus Israel). But the Christian tradition spread across Europe through the Roman Empire, then developed various competing identities and styles toward today's European countries. Chinese folk religion, Confucianism, Daoism, and Buddhism (coming from India) developed across several millennia of a mostly united, imperial China, though with shifts between Han, Mongolian, and Manchu rulers, also involving Tibet. Comparing European churches and Chinese temples may provide a visitor or reader with *rasa*-cathartic, immersive yet distancing effects that redesign and rescript one's inner staging of self and Other, rebalancing personal relations to familial, social, and cosmic figures. Of course, this also depends on one's inner and outer performances, including beliefs (or not) about a cosmic theatre of gods and spirits watching and perhaps interacting with humans.

From the theories and research gathered thus far, as a dialog between disciplines, here are five hypotheses for the explorations ahead, related to the ground plans shown in Diagram 1.1 and summaries of cultural psychology research in Tables 1.5 and 1.6.

1. Both European churches and Chinese temples are mostly **rectilinear, upright** monuments, reflecting **left-cortical, patriarchal**, *scriptwriter/critic* cognition and hierarchical, territorial drives, through various cultural extensions. But they also have **curved, inclined** elements and round/polygonal designs, expressing **right-cortical, maternal**, *mime-improviser/scene-designer* circuits and nurturing drives. They have **supportive/trickster** images and edges, too, regarding **limbic** *audience* and **subcortical** *stagehand* networks.
2. European churches are **enclosed, unified** monuments (mostly **stone/brick**-built), reflecting left-cortical, **individualistic** (one-soul/God), patriarchal characteristics. They **dominate nature** and bodily desires, in a **binary polarized** (good versus evil), **objectifying, mechanical** (left hemisphere) way, toward **permanent** melodramatic **victory**, while **focusing** the visitor in a mostly **unilinear direction** toward **HAP** (high-arousal positive) emotions as ideal affects.
3. Chinese temples involve more **holistic, collectivist** right-hemisphere considerations with **multidirectional contexts, open-air** yards, and **dispersed** halls (mostly **wooden** or cave-carved). They emphasize **balanced dialectical** *yin/yang* ideals and feminine/masculine **harmony with nature**, plus **cyclical change**

with a mix of **LAP/LAN and HAP/HAN** (low and high arousal, positive and negative) emotion ideals.
4. European churches, with their land-dominating **vertical** spires and low to high arousal (LA to **HA**) narthex-nave spaces, reflect **more left-cortical,** territorial, hierarchical, **melodramatic, bounded,** individual/group **competition**.
5. Chinese temples, as less vertically monumental and **more horizontally shamanic,** reflect **left and right cortical balance**—with multiple halls embedded in **porous** collective yards, showing more **tragicomic** awareness of **interdependent** relations and **cooperation** between religious traditions.

Religious buildings reflect specific traditions that affect each visitor through personal, yet collective beliefs and rites, involving left-cortical scriptures and rules, combined with right-cortical holistic aspirations, plus limbic/subcortical memory projections, complex feelings, and supportive/trickster motivations. Depending on the visitor's inner theatre, a church or temple offers specific metaphysical meanings and moral emotions to help with the trials of life. Yet it may also evoke ideological conflicts between sacred and secular, or between different religions, perpetuated by rival groups. How much individualism or collectivism, freedom or control, dominance or balance, change or stability do we want—while trying to understand such developments in other cultures?

In sacred sites for the communal gathering of inner and outer theatricality, moral rules and transcendent meanings *frame* each person's identity, beyond human alienation, loss, and mortality. But group identifications and collective emotions may project devilish threats upon others—purifying one's self or group by imagining guilty desires and acts in others. How do churches and temples reflect this danger of cathartic backfire? How do they offer a potential antidote with more *rasa*-cathartic awareness, through immersion, yet distance, with animal-human drives, as emotion flavors, transformed into super-natural ideals? Hopefully, comparing the church and temple examples here with your own experience of such sites will produce a further savoring of emotions. Thus, we may contribute, in the current mutations and selections of cultural evolution, to a better awareness of sacrificial demands, scapegoating temptations, and yet beneficial scripts in sacred places.

2

Monumental Developments in Patriarchal, Maternal, and Trickster Designs

Religious monuments have developed from brain spirits, as animal-human drives and extended consciousness in various cultures, evoked at natural sites and expressed in built environments. A gradual shift emerged from the "horizontal shamanism" of tribal healers, with spirit guides in nature and altered states of consciousness, to "vertical shamanism" with priestly myths, hierarchic rituals, bigger gods, and built temples in Western and Eastern Eurasia (Lewis-Williams and Pearce). This projected strict and nurturing parental figures as various super-natural forms, suppressing trickster rivals or rebalancing their energies. From ancient Egypt and Israel to Greece and Rome (as in China), *patriarchal* gods and rectilinear temples became dominant. Even Athena, patron of Athens as goddess of wisdom, handicraft, and war, was born from Zeus's head in full armor. But there may have been earlier, more *maternal* alternatives.

Maltese Mysteries

On the Mediterranean islands of Malta, female sculptures with plump fecund bodies were carved from 3,600 to 2,500 BCE, ranging in size from 50 centimeters to 2 meters, or 20 inches to six and a half feet (Figure 2.1). Such statues were placed, along with animal bones, near or inside large circular buildings, made of limestone blocks during the same time period, prior to Stonehenge in England and the pyramids of Egypt (Ching et al. 46). Maltese megalithic "temples" had domed roofs, corbeled or timbered and covered with dirt on the outside to form a hill. The remains still have rectangular "trilithon" (three large stone) doorways and round interior chambers (Figure 2.2), some with drum-shaped altars showing evidence of fire sacrifices (Figure 2.3), as at Mnajdra and Hagar Qim, which I visited in June 2012. One of the Mnajdra temples, the central one of three (Trump 148–50), has an etching of its own domed design on a curved inner wall (Figure 2.4). Small, carved models of the temples have also been found, along with the "goddess" sculptures. At Hagar Qim, the rising sun of the summer solstice enters an inner chamber through a precise hole in the temple wall (Skeates 210). At several sites, including Hagar Qim, the temple opening offers a view of the far-southerly moonrise or moonset at key times of year (Cox). In the courtyard of the Tarxien temple, the legs and lower skirt were found of what some theorists today see as "a massive free-standing statue of the Mother Goddess" (P. McNamara, *Spirit* 77). Thus, the Maltese temple builders displayed both vertical, megalithic rectitude (especially with trilithon doorways) and horizontal, domed, maternal inclinations.

Prehistoric Maltese people also carved underground, multilevel hypogea (catacombs) with similar curved walls, domed ceilings, and trilithon doorways, yet with thousands of graves and at least one female figurine, lying on her side as if asleep (Trump 128–35). The temple makers were probably converting the design of their domestic huts into these more permanent, awe-inspiring, womblike domes for the dead and for "Mother Goddess" statues, large and small, with whom they communed below ground and above, perhaps with "ecstatic" rites, like earlier shamans in caves (Gimbutas 151–3; P. McNamara, *Spirit* 78). "Compared to the size of the human body, the monumental facades and colossal sacred statues of the temples remain particularly impressive, and were surely designed to dwarf and overawe.... By contrast, the miniature temple models and engravings and anthropomorphic figurines found within the temples appear to condense the significance and power of the things that they represent..., at the same time as increasing the relative size and potency of the people who experience them" (Skeates 209).

Scholars in the "goddess movement" since the 1970s, inspired by archeologist Marija Gimbutas, view the apparent goddess worship at Malta as being prevalent throughout Neolithic Europe, in mother, maiden, and crone forms—with evidence also at the much earlier Çatalhöyük site in Turkey, nine thousand years ago, and later at Minoan Crete (Goettner-Abendroth, *Matriarchal* 27–32). Such European matriarchies were repressed by patriarchal god cultures in the Bronze Age and subsequent historical periods. (Evidence at Delphi is considered below.) Yet there are remnants in patriarchal religious spaces, such as the maze patterns in the floors of several medieval French cathedrals, reflecting moon goddess dance rituals (Goettner-Abendroth, *Dancing* 38–40).

Regarding prehistoric China, Martin Palmer sees a lack of evidence for matriarchal, earth goddess religions. However, "male and female deities," along with male and female shamans, "worked together ... until the fifth century BC when the firm hand of Confucian patriarchy began to exclude the feminine and the shamanistic" (Palmer et al. 13). In subsequent centuries of inner and outer *scriptwriter/critic* developments, "the whole emotional world was sacrificed to the demands of law, order, filial piety and control."

Some scholars question how current feminist desires might bias interpretations through retrospective awe (Eller; Goodison and Morris 10–21; Malone 156–63). And yet, Gimbutas's work on Old Europe is gaining appreciation among some anthropologists, with *matriarchy* defined as "the role of mothers in the household" becoming a model and economic basis for "female authority in other aspects of life" and women thus having "a preponderance of overall day-to-day power" (Graeber and Wengrow 216–19). Likewise, anthropologists Camilla Power and Chris Knight argue for a reconsideration of seasonal, matri-central elements in many cultures, past and present. These include, in China today, indigenous mountain cultures with a tradition of female shamans, extending back thousands of years with megalithic ancestor temples and dragon cults, as "one of the birthplaces of matriarchies," along with others across Eurasia, Africa, the Americas, and Oceania (Goettner-Abendroth, *Matriarchal* 104–27).

The circular, domed, megalithic temples in Malta, with female sculptures and burial hypogea, suggest shifts from horizontal to vertical shamanism, yet with maternal inclinations as well as patriarchal rectitude. Vast social networks were needed to build (and dig) such extensive worship and funeral sites, converted from domestic hut and womblike designs. These outer performance networks involved inner theatre ones as well. Right-cortical, maternal, nurturing (of the living and dead) circuits connected in new ways with left-cortical, patriarchal, priestly dimensions in figures and temple ruins that survive today, but with myths and rites that are unknown. Subcortical trickster aspects were also involved through inner, cooperative yet competitive *stagehand* and *audience* networks, interacting with prefrontal *director, actor, stage manager, character,* and *operator* circuits (plus parietal *costume-body definer/designer* functions)—inside and between many brains. Together, the perceptions, emotions, and ideas of many people joined in making the Maltese temples. We now reinterpret them through our inner theatres and cultural networks, which include desires for lost mother-goddess myths, rituals, and religions that might evoke supernatural awe and human potency in alternative, matriarchal, perhaps more egalitarian ways, regarding today's bodies and politics.

Chinese Super-Parents and *Yin/Yang*

According to an ancient Chinese (Han) myth, the primordial mother goddess, Nüwa (or Nu Gua), with a human face and snake body, as the waters of creation, made human beings from the yellow clay of earth, with the help of her twin brother and husband, Fuxi (R. Wang 96; Yang and An 172–4). This is one of many creations myths among China's fifty-six ethnic groups (20–1).[1] Yet it also explains the dominant social hierarchy: Nüwa first molded humans from yellow clay, but dragged a knotted cord through the mud to make more, distinguishing the upper and lower classes (Birrell 20).[2] In a silk painting from the seventh century, found in an underground tomb in Xinjiang, Nüwa and Fuxi are depicted vertically, their snake bodies intertwining (Nibley 115). Nüwa holds a pointed compass to measure the heavens; Fuxi holds a carpenter's square (and plumb bob) to measure the earth. The Chinese words for "carpenter's square" and "compass" are *ju* and *gui*, but together they mean "to *establish order*" (Schinz 26). "The carpenter's square also stands for the square that is the symbol

---

[1] In the key Daoist text of Laozi (*Dao De Jing*), all creation emanates from the Dao, rather than a cosmogony by gods (Raman 165).
[2] In other early legends, Green Jade Mother (or Daughter) created all life, including humans, with her brother, Jade Emperor. "*Made* them, not gave birth to them, for there seems to be no tradition in China of an earth mother figure" (Palmer et al. 10). Later, such legends "became overlaid with much more conventionally acceptable patriarchal concepts."

of the earth, while the pair of compasses represent the circle, the symbol of heaven. Fuxi, the male (*yang*), gives order to the earth (*yin*), and Nüwa, the female (*yin*), gives order to the heaven (*yang*)." An interplay of *yin* and *yang* becomes manifest as the primordial mother and her brother give order to the circular, masculine heaven and the square, feminine earth. Such *balanced* geometries also apply to Beijing's round Temple of Heaven and square Temple of Earth, built in the fifteenth to sixteenth centuries for the emperor's sacrifices, as Son of Heaven, in a three-thousand-year-old tradition (next chapter).

Nüwa and Fuxi appeared in the Han period (206 BCE to 220 CE) in tombs and doorways, also linked to the moon and sun (Lewis 578). They were associated with guardian figures (like later temples' lion statues), dividing inner from outer spaces, while establishing the tomb as a distinct realm, protecting it from "the watery forces of pollution and chaos." The combined, male and female images of Fuxi and Nüwa with intertwining (phallic) snake tails "produced a spatial order structured in both the vertical and horizontal dimensions. . . ." In mythic texts, Nüwa restored order by taming a great flood, patching the sky with five-colored stones, and placing the world on four giant tortoise legs—with the earth as the tortoise's body and the sky as its shell (579). She then built mounds of ashes from burning reeds "to dam the surging flood" (Griffith 29) and melted thousands of colored stones to patch the hole in heaven's floor, which then turned into a rainbow (Stevens 31). "Great Mother Nüwa" also saved humans from the God of Plague (sent by the Jade Emperor, Yu Di) and became the "Supreme Matchmaker" fueling their reproductive drive (Yang and An 173–4). But she was demoted "between the classical and medieval eras" at a time when "the position of women was devalued" (Birrell 24). By about "AD 1100, when classical texts were being codified and printed, the history of women was being rewritten by a male academic and literary hierarchy" with an "anti-female bias" regarding "mythical figures" (50). And yet, "a female-friendly counterculture evolved within Daoism, Confucianism, Buddhism, and village folklore," with *yin* versions of such traditions (Griffith 9).

Early Chinese tomb art was produced, unlike texts, "for many people of no literary pretensions" (Lewis 582). It reflects how "female deities played a crucial role throughout the history of Chinese religion," although hidden behind prominent tales of "sage kings." The Queen Mother of the West (Xiwangmu) also appeared in Han tomb art (579–80). Tombs thus reflected, as dwelling places for the deceased, "both the physical and social structure of the household, in which women played a much more important role" than they did in patriarchal lineage and state government (582). This gender tension will be explored in the pages ahead, regarding Chinese temples and European churches as well.

Together, Nüwa and Fuxi suggest *balance*, with the first female measuring the sky as a circle, which has masculine *yang* because of its strength, while the first male measures the earth's square, receptive *yin*. Feminine and masculine, earth and sky, square and circle, receptive and aggressive, darkness and light, horizontal and vertical are not binary opposites, but inter-embedded compliments. This is shown in the Daoist teardrop symbol (*taijitu*) of *yin* and *yang*, forming a whole together, with a drop of each color inside the tear-shape of its partner, in harmonic balance. Thus, Daoism relates to earlier Chinese shamanism, with its many gods, spirits, and magical practices, gaining "control" over natural forces in order "to work *with* nature by assisting the physical and spirit worlds to return to harmony" (Fowler 11). Fundamental to the *I Ching*, or *Book of Changes*, there is "the complementary dynamic relationship" between Heaven as firm, active, creative, energizing, light, incorporeal, macrocosmic *yang*, "determinant of what happens on Earth," and Earth as yielding, receptive, passive, dark, corporeal *yin*, "determined by its upper opposite" (Fowler 47). This may seem averse to modern Western notions of male and female equality, but *yang* and *yin* are not fixed ideals: "change is the nature of reality, nothing is fixed, fate is never decreed."

Pagoda, Eaves, Harmony, and Dragons

Many temples in China have a *ta* or "pagoda" within the walls of the complex or nearby, combining rectilinear and round elements in its polygonal tower (Ching et al. 275)—unlike more rectilinear church steeples. The Chinese pagoda derives from the Indian *stupa* as an upward extension of the Buddhist reliquary, which the pilgrim circumambulates clockwise, offering respect to the right side, "in a haptic reenactment of the fundamental order of space and time," bringing the body into harmony with it (168). The stupa, related to earlier Hindu symbols of female and male generative organs, the *yoni* and *lingam*, also combines a circle inside a square, like the Buddhist mandala (Scranton 89; Snodgrass; Stratton 11–14). In Tibet, the stupa is identified with the Body of the Buddha: its circular base with his crossed legs, dome with his torso, and pointed top with his head (Snodgrass 360–2).

Chinese Buddhist and Daoist temples usually have rectilinear walls—based on the palatial homes of emperors and other wealthy families. The shapes of halls, with columns and peaked roofs, have remained relatively consistent since the Han dynasty, two thousand years ago. Roofs are still connected without nails to the supporting columns by intricate *dougong*, earthquake-survivable brackets. They have wave-like curves and upturned corners on the eaves (*wen*), performing a "meaningful rhythm" of wind-water *feng-shui* (N. Wu 40). So do pagoda roof layers. Such curved corners, with glazed roof tiles, started as early as the fifth century CE, especially in southern China (Lip 19, 27). In my view, *wen* reflect caves inside the earth (sometimes made into temples), as well as the curved sky above, and the roundness of a womb from which each of us emerges to then be rectified, through a specific culture, by patriarchal, linear, more left-cortical *scriptwriter/critic* orders. *Wen* in Chinese temples counterbalance such rectitude with curved, more natural and maternal, right-cortical *mime/designer* inclinations. And yet, male figures are more numerous inside the halls. In Buddhist temples, Guanyin often appears as a nurturing figure, with her vase of elixir inclined toward the viewer, sometimes with boy and girl acolytes, but rarely holding a child and outnumbered by the male bodhisattvas around her.

In traditional Chinese *feng-shui*, the earth has feminine *yin* energy and the sky has masculine *yang* (Lip 23), like ancient Greek mythology with Gaia as earth goddesses and Uranus as sky god. In Chinese mythology, Tiandi, the god of heaven, is male, yet there is also a male earth and wealth god, Tudigong. The three main Daoist deities, as "Pure Ones," are all male with *Tian* (Heaven) in their names, as rulers of separate heavenly realms (Stevens 26–7). Yuanshi Tianzun (God of the Beginning) is the initial creator of the world and rules in Yu-Qing (first realm). Lingbao Tianzun (Heavenly Elder of the Spiritual Treasure) separated *yang* from *yin* and rules in Shang-Qing (second realm). Shenbao Tianzun (Greatest Holy One) gave laws to humans and rules in Tai-Qing (third realm). He also became the human philosopher Laozi, legendary author of the *Dao De Jing* about the Way (*Dao*), which "gives birth to them [the myriad things], … gives them shape, constitutes them, nurtures them, and protects them, … [as] the mother of all under heaven" (Kim 61–3).

Although male figures typically outnumber female images in Chinese temples, a balance between masculine and feminine energies is valued, as between human and natural. Instead of the dominance of male sky gods over female earth gods, or the "dominion" of humans over animals (Gen. 1.28), in the Greco-Roman and Hebrew-Christian traditions, *harmony* is the key in Chinese *feng-shui*.[3] This includes a "balance between the forces of nature and influences of man," or between the eave's *yin* and the roof's *yang* in a temple, whether Daoist or Buddhist (Lip 7, 69). It also involves temple roof ridges with symbolic animals: fish as success, elephant as wisdom, phoenix (*fenghuang*) as beauty and *yin* power, horse as vitality, lion as strength, and fish-dragon (*chiwen*) as *yang* power bringing rain to protect from fire (70). This tradition of roof-ridge animals goes back over fifteen hundred years.

In Roman Catholic and Eastern Orthodox churches, dragons represent Satan and his devils, fought with a sword or lance by St. Michael the Archangel (as in Revelation 12, referring to Genesis 3), or by St. George or Theodore on horseback, or banished by St. Philip the Apostle. This reflects a different religious attitude toward the fish-reptilian otherness of our inner theatres, with the pre-human ancestry and primal emotions of subcortical *stagehand* networks as tricksters, projected onto other people melodramatically or imagined with other spirits as evil threats to holiness. Popular notions today of our "reptilian" brain relate to this Western heritage of understanding our higher-order consciousness as a rational versus instinctual brain—or a "soul" with God-given dominion over the evil Serpent-Dragon in the Garden.

However, subcortical *stagehands* should be considered as our fish-reptilian-mammalian brain, perhaps reflected in various roof-ridge animals of Chinese temples, including the mythical dragon. Even Christ is symbolized as a fish or lamb. But a purely evil version of such subcortical, animal-human legacies appears with Satan having

---

[3] For an exception in the Western tradition, see Raman 165, on the tension of opposites theorized by the Greek philosopher Heraclitus of Ephesus (fifth century BCE), "not unlike the yin-yang duality of Chinese philosophers." See also Bratton 233, on monastic traditions of "care for animals and plants" in both Christianity and Buddhism.

"cloven-feet, horns, and goatee," plus female breasts, drawn from the "pagan" deities Pan and Artemis/Diana (De La Torre and Hernández 138). Inner *stagehands* can help rebalance our self and Other, hyper-reflective, socially vulnerable, monumentally creative, cosmically imaginative consciousness—with supportive and protective as well as trickster forces of nature in us, between us, and in our various environments. So, which aspects of Western churches and Chinese temples, as homes of gods and memorials to ancestors, reflect *dominant control* by left-cortical over right/sub-cortical functions, and by human civilization over the natural world, or *balanced harmony* between them? Which emotions are potentially evoked, in these different traditions, bringing memories and desires into a sacred place?

Domestic to Dominant Sacrifices with Sublime Beauty/Disgust

Christian worship spaces began in private homes and *cubicula*, underground rooms near gravesites, of the Roman Empire (Kilde 18–35). Believers met there for hundreds of years, sometimes under persecution, until Christianity was fully legalized in the fourth century. The New Testament mentions having "church" in someone's house at various points (1 Cor. 16.19; Col. 4.15; and Rom. 16.5). There is archeological evidence, too, for early church gatherings in homes and catacombs, forming the rite of Communion and various cults of heroic martyrdom in Christianity. These gatherings included a nurturing meal, yet also repeated the patriarchal demand for sacrifice. Indeed, the eventual shift from domestic or funeral spaces to "a formal ecclesiastical space ... may mark women's declining power within the Christian community," through a more "hierarchical setting," despite their first-century "public roles" in establishing that religion (Kilde 31).

An early domestic church or small oratory was found in Rome underneath the **Basilica of Saints John and Paul on the Caelian Hill (Basilica dei Santi Giovanni e Paolo al Celio)** when it was excavated in the nineteenth century. The basilica itself was built in 398, remodeling a prior palace, and eventually became known as commemorating two brothers who were former soldiers, retired imperial court members, and illegal Christians. According to a later medieval legend, they were martyred in the basement of their home on that site in 362. Today, the basilica, although destroyed and rebuilt twice, in the ninth and eleventh centuries, "still presents the exterior façade of the third century palace of the Senator Byzantius with its windows filled in" (Dix 27) and the apparent remains of the fourth-century saints under the altar. The interior bears mostly rectilinear elements: a long nave and flat ceiling, with square indentations, yet rounded arches between the square pilasters and roof sections (Figure 2.5). The exterior has a chapel dome to one side, which was added in the nineteenth century, and round columns with its mostly plain façade, with windows and Ionic capitals on the lower level, plus Corinthian on the upper (Figure 2.6). Those capitals, with hair-like scrolls or acanthus leaves, offer the ancient Roman

Figure 2.10 Frescos of people with upraised arms, under Basilica of Saints John and Paul.

symbolism, according to Vitruvius, of mother and maiden, associated by Christians with the Virgin Mary, while Doric columns would be more masculine (D. McNamara, *How* 19–21). Yet the doorway is guarded by male and female Chinese-like lions (Figures 2.7–8).

A nineteenth-century attempt to find the martyrs' bones unearthed a maze of twenty rooms from at least five ancient buildings. One may have been a *vivarium* for exotic animals used in the Colosseum. Another was a small house church, or at least a prayer room (oratory), including third- to fourth-century frescos on the walls, showing Jesus or saints with arms raised in a Christian *orans* gesture (Prandi and Ferrari 128–31), plus mythological and non-religious details, such as sea-goats, birds, winged boys (putti) in boats, naked people, and vegetal vine-branch designs (Figures 2.9–12). There is also "a couple bowing in front of a saint" (Caseau 335). Apparently lacking an altar space, the oratory may have been used for small gatherings, prayers, and "autocommunion with already consecrated Eucharistic bread."

The house is mostly rectilinear. But its arched ceilings and doorways, along with the thirteenth-century arches of an ancient street, the Clivus Scauri, outside the house on a hill running down from the basilica (Figures 2.13–15), may evoke cave-like, maternal, right-cortical associations of wariness, care, and awe in the current visitor, through inner *mime/designer* networks. If the basilica, the house oratory, and the street arches evoke a sense of the *sublime*, this would also involve specific temporal and subcortical areas as inner *audience* and *stagehands*: the inferior temporal cortex, posterior hippocampus, frontal gyrus, fusiform gyrus, basal ganglia, and cerebellum, which are distinct from the brain networks for beauty (Ishizu and Zeki). These three historical sites, visited together and reflected upon afterward, may thus evoke complex emotional flavors, as *rasas* savored at a distance—perhaps also for you, seeing the photos (at the Bloomsbury website).

A sense of *beauty* involves degrees of activation in the orbital frontal cortex (or VMPFC *stage manager*), associated with "rewarding stimuli," and the motor cortex, which signals physical attraction or repulsion (Kawabata and Zeki 1702–03). Also involved with perceptions of beauty are the anterior cingulate (associated with romantic love, musical pleasure, and erotic visual sensations) and the left parietal cortex (*costume-body definer* with a binary operator). However, neural networks for the erotic pleasure of beauty might mix with those for repulsive disgust in the awesome/awful (sublime) experience of desiccated corpses, preserved body parts, and bone relics, or with elaborate images of tortured martyrs and Jesus, found in many European churches. Examples include Agrigento's **Cathedral of Saint Gerland**, Granada's **Basilica of Saint John of God**, Siena's **Cathedral of Saint Mary's Assumption**, Rome's **Basilica of Saints Ambrose and Charles on the Corso**, and Ragusa's **Cathedral of Saint George** (Figures 2.16–22). Such reliquaries and passion images evoke high-arousal negative yet positive (HAN/HAP) affect ideals, with the terror management of mortality and pain sublimated into supernatural exemplars of melodramatic victory over death, nature, and evil.

Roman Catholic art often shows *idealized* beauty, with the sacrificial body bathed in divine light, even while being crucified (Jesus, St. Peter, or St. Andrew), stoned (St. Stephen), shot with arrows (St. Sebastian), or having breasts cut off (St. Agatha of Sicily). Dead body parts, as relics, are often displayed in ornamented cases, evoking a sense of heavenly beauty, "a glimpse of the rewards that will be ours when we go to heaven or reach enlightenment" (Nelson 180), through the inner *stage manager*'s pleasure and reward systems. The disgusting corpse itself, or a grotesque postmortem body-part, or a bloody image of the saint or Jesus, might evoke a repulsive, yet still attractive sense of the sublime, involving the abject, semiotic *chora* (Kristeva).[4] If so, such church objects mix the brain's beauty, ugliness, desire, disgust, fear, surprise, and sublime awe networks,[5] through the left-cortical *scriptwriter/critic*'s meta-narrative judgment, right-cortical *mime/designer*'s holistic appreciation, temporal-lobe *audience*'s intuitive associations, and subcortical *stagehand*'s abject, yet transcendent feelings of mystery.

The aura of the relic or icon, when neared, touched, or kissed by the believer (especially in Eastern Orthodox traditions), like the presence of God in the Communion Host, is intensified through the stories and images of *heroic sacrifice* that it evokes. This may also involve miraculous, nurturing, healing powers of the saint in the physical realm, as well as spiritual, afterlife rewards, with the image, sometimes touchable,

---

[4] Psychoanalytic feminist Julia Kristeva associates the "abject" (and its maternal, semiotic *chora*) with traumatic experiences of death's materiality: "as in true theater, without makeup or masks, refuse and corpses *show me* what I permanently thrust aside in order to live" (3).
[5] According to Charles Darwin, awe is a mixture of surprise and fear (Kandel 327).

representing both. In ancient theatre terms (Indian and Greek), the *bhavas* of disgust, fear, and love, at the sight of a martyr, Mary, or Jesus relic or icon, including the Host, might be refined as tasteful, transcendent *rasas*, through ideals of sacrificial catharsis. With *tragicomic twists* in the artwork's presentation and the viewer's empathetic ethical perspectives (not just melodramatic victim-hero, with righteous courage, versus evil villain), a rebalancing of left and right cortical networks might occur, regarding limbic associations and subcortical emotions, for new ironic insights.

Christianity began with a focus on heroic sacrifice, which also involved nurturing, redemptive powers. This developed through St. Paul's reinterpretation of Jesus's death (influenced by Greco-Roman mystery cults), the persecution of early believers by the Roman Empire, and the subsequent conversion of that empire to Christianity as the state religion (by Theodosius in 380 CE)—with the idealization of Christ and various martyrs for their painful, heroic deaths. Such ideals also derived from the Hebrew version of God demanding a prior sacrifice of the founding father's son, though sending a ram as substitute. This foundational myth of father/son sacrifice was extended into the Roman context through New Testament depictions of Jesus, as God's son, being crucified and his followers embracing such suffering. Christian churches, starting in catacombs with martyrs' tombs and in wealthy believers' homes with a dining room for reenacting the Lord's Last Supper, show ties to patriarchal sacrifices in ancient Rome, as well as earlier kinship cults. Likewise, ancient Chinese tombs involved artworks and rites with a "chief sacrificer" of animals, from the emperor to family heads, yet also "powerful females" of the household, during the Warring States period (475–221 BCE) and early empires, "prior to the rise of institutional Daoism and Buddhism" (Lewis 594).

Buddhists suffered four great persecutions across Chinese history, through Confucian and Daoist rivalries, starting in the fifth century CE, under Emperor Tai Wudi (Cochini 423–52). He ordered the destruction of 30,000 temples, with statues, images, and books also destroyed and monks buried alive. The greatest persecution occurred in the ninth century, under Tang Emperor Wuzong, with Buddhism condemned as a foreign religion that undermined Confucian family loyalty and did not promise immortality like Daoism. More than 4,600 imperial temples and 40,000 smaller temples were demolished, while 260,000 monks and nuns were secularized (Litian 46, 129). Despite such persecutions, however, the focus of sacrificial rituals in China, as in pre-Christian Europe, was toward honoring, communing with, and gaining benefits from multiple gods and family ancestors—not heroic individuals as martyrs. Persecuted victims are usually not depicted in Daoist and Buddhist temples, although quasi-historical figures do appear as deified humans or the Buddha's disciples.

Balanced Ancestor Honoring with Sacrificial Rites and Spirit Tablets

In ancient, pre-Buddhist China, a ritual animal was purified, slaughtered, and burned "to nourish the vital force of the ancestors" (Levi 652). According to one account from the Eastern Zhou period (770–256 BCE), raw meat was meant "for distant and prestigious ancestors," but boiled meat was offered for recent ancestors, considered to be "more 'human.'" This evoked a "communion" between living humans, their dead ancestors, and the gods, through "the smoke of the holocaust," but also "separation" between the living, the dead, and the divine, reaffirming the "different stations" of humans and various gods (653). Although "the living are potential dead persons ... waiting to become gods if only they receive sacrifices," the sacrificial animals prepared for different types of gods "are not interchangeable" (654). The lower level gods, as former ancestors, benefit the living who sacrifice to them, providing protection and "watching over the fecundity" of their descendants. But they also depend on that fecundity and its sacrifices—as spiritual extensions of animal-human drives, especially *survival, reproduction*, and *hierarchy*. "If the patriline disappears, they will disappear with it. ... Moreover, after a certain number of generations, they lose all individuality and are absorbed into the collective and anonymous mass of distant ancestors." Like Catholic saints, Chinese ancestral gods are "never more than intercessors with regard to the great gods of natural forces." Yet the supreme god, Shangdi, Lord of Heaven, exists without any dependence on human kinship lineage.

Located in the home or a special shrine, sacrifices to the ancestors became "the most fundamental and universal form of religious worship," from ancient to medieval China (Knapp 143). During the early medieval period, 100–600 CE, Confucian ritual codes were the norm for rulers and the upper classes, "because the weak monarchs of this period were in dire need of supernatural and classical legitimization" (144). Sacrifices to the ancestors became especially significant for the ruler's prestige, while mourning rites were more important for the literati, though they also "earnestly practiced Confucian ancestral rites" (145). By the Eastern Han dynasty (25–220 CE), the emperor had an "imperial temple" (*Taimiao*) in the capital, dedicated to the founding male ancestor, with separate shrines for six especially meritorious or recent ancestors (146). Each ancestor was represented by a "spirit tablet" (*shenzhu*), a narrow rectangular board with his name on it, inscribed vertically (147). The spirit tablets of other imperial ancestors were put in a "distant kin temple" (*Tiaomiao*). Even today, such spirit tablets are venerated across East Asia, as symbolic effigies of male and female ancestors in many homes and temples, with lit incense sticks and offerings of food and drink placed on a table as the altar (Ching 18; Paper et al. 49). Thus, *interdependent* identities are cultivated in children's inner theatres, at home and when visiting a temple, contrasting with a more individualist emphasis on each person's soul in Western culture, under one God.

Spirit tablets sometimes have an image of the deceased, or a god or buddha, nearby. But they are also venerated without a picture or statue. The latter approach shows a stronger left-cortical, inner *scriptwriter* reverence, with a pure ideogram effigy, while an image evokes more right-cortical, *mime/designer* networks. Yet both approaches involve limbic, memorial *audience* and subcortical, supportive/trickster *stagehand* emotions through spirit-tablet rites. Such emotions include awe and gratitude (with patrilineal prestige), hope (for merit and rewards), fear (with natural disasters attributed to ancestral spirits punishing the living, as restless dishonored ghosts),[6] mournful grief (with personal ties to the deceased), trust (with communal kinship and afterlife beliefs), and loving care (with food, drink, and incense offerings). Ironically, the burning of incense sticks, to honor and nurture ancestral ghosts, especially in temples with collective clouds of smoke, may bring the living closer to them physically. Each "joss stick" produces as much cancer-causing chemicals as a lit cigarette, according to scientific research (MacKinnon).

In early medieval China, "each of the seven emperors' spirit tablets was worshipped individually in his shrine. Each ancestor was given food that he had personally enjoyed in life" (Knapp 147). In special ceremonies every third and fifth year, different spirit tablets, including "retired" ones, were brought together and "worshipped as a group" (148). This expressed the ancestors' collective solidarity with the current ruler, "by sharing a meal together," but with spirit tablets arranged in a certain order to show "status distinctions between them"—and the place of each deceased patriarch "within his lineage." By the Western Han period (206 BCE to 9 CE), royal ancestral shrines were established in various prefectures, demonstrating the ruler's control over such localities (150–1).

Records show multiple daily offerings at imperial graves and shrines with the dead "treated as if they were still alive, to the extent that mausoleums were sometimes called 'eating halls'" (Knapp 151). However, most people did not have an ancestral temple, so they venerated forebears "in their home's main hall" at special festivals (175–7). This involved the head of the household observing a period of purification for three days and then leading his wife and children in offering wine to make the spirits descend (177). In various second-century festivals at different times of the year, rural families also offered wheat, fish, melons, millet, and pigs to ancestral spirits and collective gods. Thus, patriarchal and maternal, hierarchical and nurturing, survival and reproduction balancing acts were performed throughout the centuries, from Chinese homes to temples, rural to imperial, honoring ancestors in order to continue family ties and avoid brain-spirit problems from dishonored ghosts.

Chinese Family Homes as Temple-Museums

Today, in the cities of Guangzhou and Qufu, in southern and northern China, there are examples of large family homes (now open to tourists) with shrines and spirit tablets for venerating ancestors, through food, drink, and incense. The **Chen Clan Ancestral Hall** was built in 1890–94 for ancestor worship and academic study by clan members preparing for imperial exams. It is "classified as a Confucian temple" (Cannon 211), but now houses the Guangzhou Folk Art Museum (Figure 2.23). It includes six courtyards and nine symmetrical buildings, facing south, with a rear hall on the central axis as the main one for spirit tablets and offerings (Figure 2.24). Whether Confucian, Buddhist,

---

[6] See Knapp 189.

or Daoist, Chinese temples face south, the side that gets the most sun, because the majority Han ethnic group "respected the south as the noble seat" (Q. Wang 63).

In Qufu, a much larger complex grew around the **Confucius (Kong) Family Home** and its adjacent temple, plus his gravesite a few kilometers away, honoring the key philosopher of Chinese patriarchal harmony. Just two years after the death of Confucius in 479 BCE, his family home was designated a temple by the king of Lu (Yanxin 66). Grand sacrifices were held there in 195 BCE by the founder of the Han dynasty, Liu Bang, setting an example for many later rulers. But the veneration of Confucius was discontinued in the Communist era with a modern school system replacing temple institutions (Ching 195). This temple was rebuilt and expanded in the seventh, eleventh, fourteenth, fifteenth, and eighteenth centuries (after fires in the thirteenth, fifteenth, and eighteenth), so its buildings date mostly from the Ming and Qing dynasties (Q. Wang 127). They form a model for Confucian temples throughout China (Yanxin 69).

The complex includes several gates, nine courtyards, and a series of halls along a central axis. There is a wall around the entire complex and a performance for tourists each morning at the front gate with costumed soldiers, dancers, and flags (Figures 2.25 and 2.25vid1-9). But a half century ago, during the Cultural Revolution, the Red Guard broke into the temple, damaged the grave tablets of Confucius's parents, burned altars, and dug up the graves of his descendants, dumping their bones on the ground (Griffith 228).

Today, inside the complex, there are various halls with spirit tablets (Figure 2.26). The main building for sacrificial offerings to Confucius, Dacheng Hall ("Hall of Great Achievement"), near the rear of the complex, has a statue of the philosopher (Figures 2.27-28). With its front hall and back bedroom, it combines royal architecture with religious elements (Q. Wang 128). There is also a Resting Hall, dedicated to Confucius's wife. The Kong Family Mansion, adjacent to the temple, dates from the Ming and Qing dynasties (1368-1912). It housed the direct descendants of Confucius, who conducted religious rites honoring him.

Near the Confucius Temple, there is the smaller **Yan Hui Temple**, built in 1290 and then rebuilt on the current site in 1594. It honors the sage's favorite student, Yan Hui, with gates, courtyards, halls, spirit tablets, and statues (Figures 2.29-31). About 500 monuments reside on the Confucius Family Temple grounds, including 21 large tortoise-dragon steles, with many in special pavilions (Figures 2.32-4). There are four similar monuments in the Yan Hui Temple complex (Figure 2.35). Each tortoise-dragon *bixi* (Yang and An 103) has a vertical stele on its back with inscriptions from emperors since the tenth century, praising Confucius and granting him new honorary titles.

In my view, as a tourist to these temples, the buildings, symmetry, and steles show patriarchal, imperial, rectilinear, left-cortical *scriptwriter/critic* order pointed skyward. But the curved roof eaves of various halls and the monumental tortoise-dragons in courtyards suggest maternal, Nüwa, round, right-cortical *mime/designer* nurturing from the earth—in balance with the buildings' containment of veneration spaces and the steles' phallic shape with honorific inscriptions. Perhaps the tortoise-dragon sculptures also recall Nüwa's saving of the earth after a great flood with tortoise leg pillars and shell dome heaven. The bottoms of tortoise shells were used in ancient China for oracle divination—with questions written on them, heat applied, and cracks interpreted by a priestess or diviner who became "possessed by a spirit entity, either the great god Shang Ti or an ancestor spirit" (P. McNamara, *Spirit* 101). Thus, the smiles on the monumental tortoise-dragon sculptures might be seen as a trickster's grin, knowing the twists of fate, including the different eras when Confucius would be valued like a god or despised (Figure 2.36).

From Roman Home Design to Patriarchal Basilica and Baptistery

With parallels to Chinese sacrifices in their location and purpose, early Christian rituals involved homes and tombs (or catacombs), aiming for *extended kinship* between the living, dead, and divine, through hospitality, food, and drink. But Christians also focused on the baptism of new believers and the reenactment of Jesus's Last Supper, with bread and wine as his Body and Blood. This involved a unifying meal of *agape* (love feast) and *eucharist* (thanksgiving), creating a *communion* with one God and his believers, living and dead, especially holy martyrs—instead of animal sacrifices to feed (or incense and other burnt offerings to honor) multiple gods and deceased ancestors.

In first-century Rome, the front half of a typical patrician's house retained yet expanded the floor plan of a peasant's hut from a thousand years earlier (Dix 22). The house had an entrance hall (*vestibulum*), leading to a sky-lit room with pillars (*atrium*), which had a ceiling that was open at the center and a pool of rainwater (*impluvium*) in the floor. This was used as a Christian baptismal pool. Next was an open doorway to the reception room (*tablinum*), usually with a dais and stone table (*cartibulum*), which became the Christian eucharistic altar. Yet, the *tablinum* was originally revered as a "family shrine," with a pagan altar for the "*Lares* and *Penates*, the ancestral spirits and the gods of hearth and home." Other areas of the house, in the garden, kitchen, courtyard, dining room, or atrium, could also serve as a *lararium* with an altar for offerings (Caseau 330–1). On the walls of the *atrium* and the wings (*alae*) of the *tablinum* were portraits and trophies of many generations of noble family members, who "brought honour to the name and house" (Dix 23), like Chinese spirit tablets. Traditionally, for clan meetings, the alpha male *paterfamilias* sat in a special chair on the *tablinum* dais, with patriarchal sub-leaders seated next to him and other family members standing, facing them in the *atrium*.

According to Gregory Dix (an Anglican monk and liturgical scholar), the church's communal performance spaces began in a Roman family setting, with patriarchal figures and ancestral gods, who demanded sacrifices in the past. The household gods, their sacrificial altars, and the sacred hearth with its undying fire were removed. But the chair of the *paterfamilias* stayed in the *tablinum* and became the bishop's throne (23), as the *cathedra* of later cathedrals, symbolizing an extended kinship of Christian believers under one God and priestly patriarch. Virgins and widows were placed safely behind the screens of the *alae*—as with the *matroneum*, a separate upper gallery for women in early churches (Stemp 55). This relates to the screened area for cloistered nuns in later churches, such as the eighteenth-century **Holy Savior Church (San Salvatore)** in Noto, Sicily (Figure 2.37).

The *agape* or "Lord's supper" was performed in a dining room (*triclinium*) near the *atrium*. The symbolic death and rebirth of the Christian initiate, through a sacrificial "immersion of baptism" occurred in the *impluvium*, the rectangular pool within the *atrium*—as with the traditional *mikveh*, a ritual purification bath near the Jewish synagogue. Some scholars today, such as L. Michael White, dispute the details of this "atrium house theory," with church structures and ritual practices "retrojected from third century (or later) sources" (16–17). However, White agrees that the house-church *triclinium*, as dining room for the eucharistic meal, and "perhaps other larger rooms," were prototypes for sanctuaries in later assembly halls and basilicas (19–20).

Eventually, churches were built in "basilica" style, based on the Roman meeting hall, which had judicial and commercial functions, sometimes including a law court at the center. But Christians turned the mall-like breadth of the rectangular basilica space to focus attention toward the east end with its altar, often involving a rounded apse as womblike sanctuary for the tabernacle, bearing consecrated communion hosts as the Body of Christ.

> The democratization of worship required a fundamentally different kind of building from the pagan temple. Thus, what had been a broad, colonnaded interior mall stretching right and left of the entering visitor became a long processional tunnel of space leading the visitor compellingly from the entrance to the holy of holies, the altar space at the opposite end of the nave.
>
> Mathews 94

Unlike Greco-Roman temples, Christian churches allowed not only priests, but also others inside, with a longitudinal, *unidirectional* focus: narthex to nave to elevated altar platform and tabernacle (still an exclusive area for clergy).

The term "nave" came from the Latin *navis*, meaning "ship," which symbolized the community of the faithful traveling toward the rising sun of resurrection in the east. In many churches, a "transept" was added across the nave, giving the entire building a cruciform shape, recalling the Savior's death. The home's *vestibulum* (entryway) became the church's "narthex." The *tablinum* (reception room) became the nave, focused, sometimes with side aisles, toward the main altar (derived from the *cartibulum*), which was set on a raised stage like the theatre's *pulpitum*. The *triclinium* (dining room) thus became the "sanctuary" (or chancel), around and behind the main altar. As the holiest of holy areas, with a decorated tabernacle at the back to hold the consecrated hosts between Masses, it had choir stalls alongside it, a rood screen in front of it (or *templon* iconostasis in Eastern Orthodox churches), and semicircular apse behind it. The *impluvium* (pool) in the open *atrium* of the Roman house became a separate "baptistery" building or a baptismal font in the nave, narthex, or a nearby room.

Unlike the domestic prototype continuing in Chinese temples, with one or more open yards, the open Roman *atrium*, along with other home elements, became fully *enclosed* under the church or baptistery roof. Some early Christian meetings occurred outdoors, but such nature-oriented rites eventually "became associated with heretical groups" (Kilde 18). Thus, Roman Catholicism would "eschew outdoor celebration of the Mass well into the twentieth century, deeming such services too similar to Greco-Roman (i.e. 'pagan') and early Gnostic practices."

The original performance elements in elite Roman homes were based on peasant patterns: the *tablinum* (inner reception room) on the settler's log-cabin, the *cartibulum* (table) on the farmyard chopping block, the *atrium* on the cabin's fore-court, partially roofed over, and the *impluvium* on the "original well or pond beside which the farm had been built" (Dix 22). The latter also showed a shift from a round well or pond to a rectangular pool, with the household *impluvium*. But this design shifted back, with church architecture in subsequent centuries, to a round or polygonal basin as the typical baptismal font, sometimes in its own building or room, especially in Italy and France (Davies, *Architectural*, 13–19). Early examples are the separate **Baptistery of Neon** in Ravenna and baptistery within the **Cathedral of Saint Leontius (Cathédrale Saint-Léonce)** in Fréjus, both from the fifth century (Figures 2.38–42). Thus, the baptistery basin was regarded by early Church Fathers as "the womb of Mother Church," with its roundness signifying "baptismal rebirth" (21–2).

The Baptistery of Neon still has its original mosaic inside the dome, showing Jesus being baptized by John, with God as Holy Spirit descending on him, plus the apostles and St. Paul arrayed in a circular procession around them. The Holy Spirit as dove continued to be a symbol used throughout later centuries. Yet here, unlike in later images of this scene, the genitals of Jesus are shown as he stands in the water, revealing his human materiality. The figure with a white beard next to him, holding a reed and offering a towel, is *not* God the Father, but the River Jordan. He appears like a pre-Christian god personifying nature's power in patriarchal form, along with the Holy Spirit as animal-divine trickster, inside a maternal space of rebirth, built on the site of a prior Roman bath. Thus, at least four inner-theatre networks are reflected around Jesus: the left-cortical, patriarchal *scriptwriter/critic* (River Jordan personified as an old man), subcortical supportive/trickster *stagehand* (Holy Spirit crossing realms), and right-cortical, maternal *mime/designer* (nurturing water from John and the river), in relation to the temporal lobe's memorial *audience* (circular procession and pre-Christian elements).

Catacomb, Mausoleum-Martyrium, and Rectilinear or Round Churches

Even the rectilinear, underground catacombs of Rome, dug outside the city walls, show a mix of patriarchal and maternal spaces, along with trickster powers from beyond the grave. In ancient times, the catacomb was called a *coemetrium* or "dormitory." It had halls, round archways, and collective rooms, where the dead merely slept, awaiting resurrection, in rectangular niches, which are now open but were then covered, as in the **Catacomb of Saint Callixtus** (Figure 2.43). The early Christian saints, as victims of persecution lodged in these underground dormitories, were focal points for later

Figure 2.45 Interior of Saint Constantina.

martyrium-baptistery connections, with round designs of both, for patriarchal sacrifice yet maternal rebirth. Various popes restored the catacombs to honor saints' tombs in the fourth, sixth, and later centuries—with catacombs becoming sites of holy pilgrimage (E. Smith 117). But corpses and relic fragments were also "translated" (transferred) to above ground churches, some of which were circular martyria, patterned after the imperial mausoleum design and often built on the site of a saint's death or grave.

For example, the round church of **Saint Constantina (Santa Costanza)**, along the Via Nomentana in Rome, was built in the fourth century as a mausoleum holding the sarcophagi of Constantina (*d.* 354) and Helena (*d.* 360), the daughters of the first Christian emperor, Constantine the Great.[7] It soon became a baptistery as well (Davies, *Origins* 102). Its rectilinear façade, yet circular walls, with Composite (highest order, doubly feminine, Ionic-Corinthian) columns, round arches, and walkway now revolve around a central altar with relics of Constantina (Figures 2.44–5), thus putting "direct physical emphasis on the person or place to be honored" (Gough 59). It was built adjacent to a much larger basilica honoring St. Agnes (*d.* 304), a twelve- or thirteen-year-old martyr from a half century earlier, whose remains were in the catacombs beneath these churches (Roth 249). According to legend, Agnes refused marriage through her devotion to God and the virgin was then dragged through the streets, raped, sentenced to burning at the stake, and beheaded. Later, Constantina was cured

---

[7] Constantine's daughter Helena was also the wife of a later, neo-pagan emperor, Julian, and the existing mausoleum may have been rebuilt upon Constantina's death, primarily for her. In the seventeenth to eighteenth centuries, the sarcophagi of the two sisters were moved to the Vatican; one is now in Saint Peter's, the other in the Vatican Museum.

of leprosy by praying at St. Agnes's tomb. Only ruined walls of the basilica remain today, but with rounded corners, again suggesting a mix of patriarchal rectangles and maternal circles (Figure 2.46). Thus, the sacredness of the catacomb site, with the underground dorm-room tomb of the holy trickster Agnes, a teen rebel against the pagan empire, was also tied to the round rebirth space of the mausoleum/baptistery, with its elegant, arched-ceiling mosaics (considered further below). Originally, it was made to hold the corpses of the emperor's daughters, one of whom later became canonized (St. Constantina or Constance), like the saint whose postmortem power cured her. Both saints' holy sites, with relics, thus became womblike spaces of heavenly rebirth and Christian initiation.

In the seventh century, another church, **Saint Agnes Outside the Walls (Sant'Agnese fuori le mura)** was built nearby, more directly over Agnes's catacomb tomb. Its rectilinear nave has a second-floor arched *matroneum*, which separated watching women from the men's territorial rite, while a girl's bones sanctified their altar (Figures 2.47–50). Behind the domed altar canopy, an original apse mosaic shows St. Agnes as a Byzantine princess. Yet she is framed by two men, probably popes, including Honorius I, who holds the church they are in, which he commissioned (Figure 2.51). Thus, maternal and trickster, matron and virgin powers, nurturing and fueling sublime brain spirits, are depicted through patriarchal architecture and imagery, reflecting *scriptwriter/critic* networks filtering right-cortical *mime-improviser/designer*, limbic memorial *audience*, and subcortical *stagehand* circuits.

Agnes's skull, which bears miraculous power for devotees, was translated to the seventeenth-century **Saint Agnes in Agone (Sant'Agnese in Agone)** with its mostly rectangular, patriarchal façade, yet circular, maternal interior, in the Piazza Navona of central Rome (Figures 2.52–6). This is the site of the ancient Domitian Stadium, where

Figure 2.50 Interior of Saint Agnes Outside the Walls with *matroneum* and mosaic.

Agnes was martyred in 304, according to tradition, thus giving the church its Italian name, *agone*, as site of the "contest." But it also suggests the *heroic*, competitive, patriarchal aspect of this saint's sacrifice, refusing a Roman husband and dying through loyalty to her divine Father. Yet her church's round nave, with a centralized floor design, Corinthian columns, circular dome, and swirling figures in Baroque paintings and sculptures, creates a womblike *nurturing* space for her skull to be reborn. It is set above a small tabernacle altar (with a lit red candle), to the left of the main one, in a glass case with jewels, as sublime object of trickster power, of paradoxical suffering and triumph, disgust and beauty, grief and joy (Figures 2.57–8). The holy skull of the heroic, martyred girl thus evokes personal interpretations and potential *rasa*-cathartic mindfulness of core body-brain affects: pain/pleasure, avoidance/approach, and arousal/quiescence.

Relics as Postmortem Fuel for Altars, Crypts, Stupas, and the Tallest Pagoda

Medieval European churches often included a saint's relic within the main stone altar (a tradition that continues today) or a tomblike crypt with relics and subterranean archways, built below the rectangular floor plan. This mimicked the early Church's catacomb dormitory, as underground tomb-womb with the bones of a saintly trickster (often a martyred rebel against the pagan empire) whose miraculous powers continued to fuel the patriarchal sacredness and pilgrim attractions above. As early as the fourth century, Gregory of Nazianzus described the "little relics" of saints, whether touched or worshiped, as containing the power of their whole bodies, equal to their holy souls, and thus persisting beyond the grave to cast out devils and heal diseases (qtd. in Dyas 110). Throughout the Middle Ages, "sensory 'stage management'" with beautiful sights, musical sounds, fragrant smells, and touch points at the site of martyrdom or burial, or another place with the transferrable power of relics, created a "spiritual theatre" for belief in the saint's presence, both on earth and in heaven, as a channel of holiness through "closeness to God" (108–10). Thus, the animal-human *salience* of emotional seeking for survival, reproduction, care, alliance-hierarchy, territory, play, and bonding became focused on monumental sites. They were pilgrim attractions and miracle producers, with economic benefits and church structures rising—through competition between cities with sacred crypts, yet also higher and higher (phallic) arches, painted celestial ceilings, and towers with spires.

Like the Basilica of Saint Agnes Outside the Walls, with an altar placed over her catacomb tomb, crypts were built under churches from the mid-eighth century onward "to imitate this circumstance" of a monumental, catacomb-memorial site with holy power (Stemp 54). The body of a revered saint, or an important relic, was "placed in a shrine in the crypt directly underneath the altar, thus making the altar mark a holy site which had not previously existed." Various churches, from Romanesque to later styles, were built with steps going up from the nave to the altar platform (*pulpitum* or "stage") and steps going down to the crypt as oratory chapel. An example in Rome is the **Church** of Saints Sylvester and Martin in the Mountains (San Silvestro e Martino ai Monti) with relics of Ss. Martin, Artemius, Paulinus, and Sisinnius in an oratory crypt from around the year 500 (Figures 2.59–61). Such an architectural combination ties the altar's cooperative, nurturing, right-cortical *mime/designer* dimensions of Last Supper reenactment and Holy Communion sharing to a more left-cortical, patriarchal, *scriptwriter/critic* demand for competitive, heroic sacrifices. Yet this also involves the crypt's limbic/subcortical *audience/stagehand* element, as trickster potential, controlled by biblical readings and sermons from the pulpit.

As Buddhism extended from its origins in India and became more popular across East Asia, round, vertically pointed stupas and pagodas were constructed at thousands of sites for relic veneration, like the crypts and altars of Christian Europe in churches adorned with domes and spires. According to tradition, fragments of the historical Buddha Shakyamuni's bones, the size of rice grains after his cremation, were placed in 84,000 stupas across Asia by the Indian emperor Ashoka in the third century BCE (Hureau 1242). Reliquaries with the Buddha's teeth, hair, nail trimmings, bone fragments, and "contact relics" eventually appeared at numerous sites in China (Robson, "Changing" 91). They even multiplied themselves according to a Tibetan account (Schaeffer 302). But they were typically hidden in a stupa or pagoda, not displayed as with Catholic reliquary *memento mori* artworks.

Postmortem treasures of the Buddha's body and of later holy teachers (sometimes mummified in Tibet) grounded each temple built around the reliquary, along with images of various bodhisattvas. Ordination vows and confession ceremonies "would take place in front of statues," which were seen as embodying a divine spirit, "inhabited by the beings they represented" (Hureau 1241). Furthermore, because "relics (and images) were portable, allowing for the expansion of Buddhist sacred geography," they became "present in the earliest accounts of the beginnings of Buddhism in China" (Robson, "Buddhist" 1359). They were associated with miracle sites (1364), like Catholic relics in catacombs, tombs, crypts, and altars. Stories developed, early in the history of Buddhism, of previous Buddha beings from billions of years ago, whose relics were scattered in this world, plus stupas with relics from Shakyamuni's prior lives (Strong 26–9, 50).

The expansion of sacred geography developed through competition between Buddhism and indigenous religions, as with Christians taking over pagan sites in Europe and their territorial rivalries with Muslims over Spain and Jerusalem, or between Christian sects. However, there was much less religious warfare in East Asia. Sometimes "Buddhism and other religions co-existed (although often with incessant competition) at the same place" (Robson, Introduction xv). Early Buddhists in China generally "settled on mountains with rich pre-Buddhist histories," on or near "sites already deemed sacred by local cults or Daoists" (Robson, "Changing" 94). Related to this, the term for a Chinese temple, *si*, refers also to a government office, which is where Buddhist monks initially resided when moving to China (95). Government officials and elites often donated their mansions, which were then transformed into monasteries, with transported relics sanctifying the site. When Buddhists converted prior Confucian, Daoist, or local cult sites, there was sometimes "resistance to those incursions" (100–04). In some cases, the conversion of sites, along with related myths, went in the other direction, such as a story of the Daoist sage Laozi converting the Buddha, in territorial mimetic rivalry.

A Chinese pagoda (*ta*) elevates the visitor's eyes toward the sky. For those who climb it (when that is permitted), it offers a view over the Buddhist temple and its surroundings, like a territorial watchtower. Yet it bears an earthly fuel of sacred presences with its central relic and many images at various levels. The world's tallest pagoda is part of the **Tianning (Heavenly Peace) Temple** in Changzhou, a city of about four million people, northwest of Shanghai. The wooden pagoda is 154 meters (510 feet) high with thirteen external stories (twenty-six floors) and was built between 2002 and 2007, at a cost of 39 million US dollars ("China"). It represents the miracle of Chinese capitalist growth as much as Buddhist tradition, in a city aspiring for significance in the shadow of its neighbors: Suzhou with its famous gardens and Shanghai with 26 million people as the finance and fashion center of the PRC. The Chan (Zen) temple of Tianning dates back to the seventh century (Tang dynasty), but it has been destroyed and rebuilt five times since then, including full destruction during the Cultural Revolution and rebuilding in the 1980s.

As with most major Chinese temples, the visitor must buy a ticket at the main gate to enter, but with this one, a second ticket is needed for the pagoda (Figure 2.62). The visitor encounters various courtyards and shrines, along a south to north axis, before

Figure 2.67 Incense burner and Mao bust, with other deities, Tianning Temple.

reaching the pagoda at the rear. There is an entryway *Shanmen* (Mountain Gatehouse) with open-mouth Ha and closed-mouth Heng as guardian statues, also representing the Dharma with their names as the first and last letter-sounds in Sanskrit, plus other smaller figures (Figures 2.63–5). Each statue area has an altar for food, candle, and flower offerings, plus a coin box and kneeler. Then, in a courtyard with multiple shrines, statues, and burning areas, a row of figures with altars includes a golden bust of Chairman Mao, with a red scarf tied around his neck, honored like Buddhist saints and Daoist gods (Figures 2.66–8). Banners alongside that display state in Chinese: "Buddha's light illuminates the three-thousand realms," "Law flows to the five continents," and "Beware of thieves." Of all the temples I visited in China, this is the only one where I saw Mao thus honored. Yet it reflects how, in the last several decades, with the resurgence of religion: "Even Mao Zedong himself, an avowed atheist, is mystified into a deity, and worshipped as a secular god" (Yu 95)—as in the Chinese folk tradition of deifying great human patriarchs of the past. And yet, with the many male figures along this yard, there is at least one female, probably Guanyin (Figure 2.69).

Nearby, the Hall of Heavenly Kings, built in the Qing dynasty, displays four large statues of those patriarchs: North and West on one side, South and East on the other, protecting the Dharma, the Buddha's historical teachings (Figures 2.70–4). Their leader, the white-faced King of the North (Duo Wen), associated with winter, is ruler of rain and holds an umbrella as victory banner. He derives from the ancient Indian god of wealth, Kubera. The red-faced King of the West (Guang Mu), associated with autumn, holds a snake or red cord, representing a dragon. He is an eye in the sky, seeing those who do not believe in Buddhism and converting them. The green- or black-faced King of the South (Zeng Zhang) holds a sword. He is associated with summer, rules the wind, and causes roots to grow. The white-faced King of the East (Chi Guo), associated with spring, holds a pipa (stringed instrument). He plays harmonious music, converting people with compassion (Welch 194–5). The images of these kings, as territorial guardians of the four continents in the Indian tradition, developed with Chinese influences in the Tang, Yuan, and Ming dynasties, becoming associated with good weather for crops (Litian 132–4). Thus, animal-human drives of survival and territoriality are reflected in these towering figures with fierce faces, evoking the pain/pleasure of surprise, fear, and sublime awe.

As in most Buddhist temples, at the center of that room, under an elaborate wooden canopy here with dragons, facing north and south, are statues of Wei Tuo (a.k.a. Skanda), a guardian deity as top general for the four kings, and the chubby, laughing Budai, an incarnation of Maitreya, a.k.a. Mile, Buddha of the Future (Figure 2.75). Facing the temple's central hall and guarding the main Buddhas there (Meyer 80), Wei Tuo reflects more left-cortical, patriarchal brain networks, like Heng, Ha, and the Heavenly Kings. But the jolly Budai may evoke more right-cortical, nurturing networks, even as a male figure. Budai might be viewed as a positive trickster, too, "a monk of the Song dynasty who was fat, unkempt, and went about like a simpleton playing games with children" (79). His appearance and behavior were later understood as "disguises to throw off the superficial who could not look beyond a ludicrous exterior. Behind this disgusting, yet playful persona was sagacity and sainthood. People believed that Budai, who promised happiness and wealth, was an incarnation of Maitreya Buddha in his 'body of change.'" Thus, Budai-Maitreya reflects the mammalian play drive in humans, extending toward a cosmic theatre.

Presented together in a glass case, the two figures have their backs to each other, but with offering tables, coin boxes, and kneelers near them, as with the Kings along the sides of the hall, for visitors to interact with them all—exemplifying the multi-directionality of a Chinese temple. An observant Buddhist usually kneels and bows fully, three times, with hands in front of the face, fingertips touching and lifting from the forehead, as if opening the prefrontal cortex spiritually. One might also drop a coin in the box as an offering. Incense is usually burned in the temple courtyard, where the visitor initially enters and bows in the four cardinal directions with several smoking sticks, pointing up from the center of the forehead, held there by both hands, near the inner *director*, *actor*, and *stage manager*.

In comparison, traditional Catholics bow or genuflect to the tabernacle with its communion Hosts, when crossing the church's main aisle, and leave money when lighting a candle by a statue, where there might be a kneeler. But incense is typically used just by the priest or altar boy, swinging a censer. Modern congregants also kneel at various times during the Mass, yet pews with kneelers were not part of ancient churches. Misericords (mercy-heart seats) developed in the Middle Ages, sometimes with trickster figures under the individual pull-down benches, for monks in the choir stalls alongside the altar. Then early modern pews became popular in the nave, through the Protestant Reformation, with kneelers in Catholic churches as well.

Alongside another courtyard at Tianning Temple, glass cases display many statues of arhats, as disciples of the Buddha (Figures 2.76–7). In that yard, there is a stone pillar from 1681 with the names and small images of seven bodhisattvas (Figures 2.78–9). Such images of enlightened beings may evoke awe in the visitor, across the temple complex, and be reminders of each person's many lifetimes, perhaps also as other life forms. Next, there is a Jade Buddha Hall with two, larger than human, seated and reclining sculptures of the Buddha (Figure 2.80). The one lying on his right side (connected with patriarchal, parasympathetic networks of the left hemisphere) shows the Buddha at his death calmly accepting the end of many lifetime cycles (*parinirvana*), thus evoking tragicomic sadness yet joy in the visitor—as historically with his followers, according to early scripture (Parrinder 76–7).

Farther to the north, the Triratna Hall has three floors: Big Meditation Hall, Sutras Depository (closed to visitors), and Nine-Lotus Pavilion with many Buddha statues and the Daoist God of Wealth (twice), plus a view of the big pagoda (Figures 2.81–6). This pavilion, on the third floor, combines religious traditions. It may also evoke nurturing feelings in the visitor, with the cuteness of numerous, identical, tiny Buddha figures (probably from donors)—or a sense of the spirit in each person as interdependent, progressing toward unity. This is suggested, too, by the Triratna or "Three Jewels" of Buddhism: the Buddha, the Dharma (teaching), and the Sangha (community).

At the left side of the last courtyard, in front of the pagoda, are a large digital screen and statue of the bodhisattva Guanyin, with a Guanyin Garden nearby (Figures 2.87–8). In the center of the courtyard is a large, chubby, and laughing Budai-Maitreya statue,

Figure 2.86 Tianning pagoda, Budai shrine, and dragon pillar, viewed from Triratna Hall.

in a glass case and roofed shrine (Figure 2.89). Nearer to the pagoda platform are two tall pillars with writhing dragons (symbols of power, not evil), plus Buddha reliefs and mini-pagoda sculptures along the stairway (Figure 2.90–2). At the highest level of steps, where the pagoda itself begins, eight large elephants and four Heavenly Kings stand guard, with many detailed relief scenes appearing along the white base of the pagoda's multiple sides (Figure 2.93–6). The ear of the metal elephant, nearest the front steps, shows the polish of many visitors' fingers touching it for good luck (Figure 2.97). Thus, fierce protective figures, showing animal-human drives, can still evoke nurturing beliefs through touch, involving both inner *scriptwriter/critic* (left-cortical patriarchal) and *mime/designer* (right-cortical maternal) networks, along with the nearby female Guanyin as merciful bodhisattva and laughing Budai as karmic, fateful, future Buddha.

Most of the temple figures and architectural shapes leading to the world's tallest pagoda are patriarchal. There are some small Guanyin statues near the Mao bust and in the Triratna Hall's top floor, plus the large one at the edge of the pagoda's courtyard. But while current PRC culture has replaced the dominance of Mao's face with older figures, and rebuilt many religious buildings destroyed during the Cultural Revolution, the return of sacred art has not come with gender equality. At Tianning Temple, *rasas* are probably evoked of heroic courage (with Heng, Ha, Four Heavenly Kings, and Wei Tuo), humor (with Budai-Maitreya's big smile), and awe (with imposing statues, including elephants)—more often than feminine nurturing or romantic love (*shringara*). The pagoda itself has patriarchal, "phallic," verticality, especially with its golden spire on top, bearing a 33-ton bronze bell. However, its hexagonal exterior and circular interior, along with specific images inside, involve nurturing, harmonic ideals, evoking left/right cortical balance, rather than dominant control (as in European churches). They suggest cycles of rebirth, gradually progressing toward enlightenment, through non-attachment, equanimity, and yet compassion.

The first floor of the Tianning pagoda is called the Grand Buddha Palace, with a sign over the doorway about "Heavenly Treasure" and four large statues inside of various Buddhas: Vairocana facing south, Samantabhadra (Puxian) west, Guanyin north, and Manjushri (Wenshu) east (Figures 2.98–9). Brass images on the walls include a baby Buddha bathing scene, reflecting the inner theatre's nurturing *mime/designer* networks (Figure 2.100). Steps lead down to an underground level—akin to a medieval crypt—with various wall images and small rooms, including the Tianzi (Son of Heaven) "Silver" Palace, recreated from the Ming period, with 322 small Shakyamuni statues around a large one, all in white marble (Figure 2.101–04). There is also a small, jeweled, stupa-shaped reliquary, offering a window to its treasure (Figure 2.105). Like in a church, this postmortem object of veneration, as supportive/trickster *stagehand* within a womblike *mime/designer* space, increases the *scriptwriter* sanctity of the patriarchal structure above.

Floors 1–5 and 11–13 are also open to the public, displaying Buddhist artworks, some with a kneeler and offering box, indicating sacredness (Figures 2.106–07). There is a quadruple Guanyin statue with numerous arms, spreading like wings, showing the bodhisattva's compassion (Figure 2.108). Another room holds an enormous "Natural Crystal Buddha," as the "treasure of the pagoda," with smaller artworks around it, plus

Figure 2.122 View of temple from Tianning Pagoda.

protective dragons above (Figures Figures 2.109–11). One area has complex wood relief scenes and wood-carved sculptures of Shakyamuni and Guan(shi)yin, the latter with multiple arms to help and eleven heads to "hear the cries of the world," as the meaning of her name (Figure 2.112–15). There are many other artworks, on various levels, mostly of male figures, including wooden sculptures of three arhats, called "Happy," "Smiling Lion," and "Crossing the River" (Figure 2.116). Yet there are also other Guanyin figures (Figure 2.117). A Daoist God of Wealth appears in this Buddhist pagoda: probably Bi Gan, the deified twelfth-century BCE prime minister of the Shang kingdom, or Fan Li, fifth-century BCE political and military advisor to the king of Yue (Figure 2.118). There are *cave-like niches* with Buddhist sculptures, too, replicating ancient grottoes (Figure 2.119). One perhaps shows Yama, Lord of the Underworld, holding the Wheel of Life with his teeth (Figure 2.120). Near the top, there is a balcony with views of the city and the temple complex below (Figures 2.121–2). The "Brahma Voice Pavilion," at the top of the pagoda, contains a huge bell with large paintings on the walls around it, including one of the Buddha preaching with a stupa nearby, reflecting the pagoda's power (Figures 2.123–4).

The picturesque richness of artistic creativity in this recently built pagoda relates to Buddhist myths and figures from millennia ago. The pagoda, as a dramatic climax to the temple courtyards and halls, evokes the visitor's neural networks of awe, joy, playfulness, and courage (climbing high and looking down). Like the temple complex, it reflects the visitor's inner *actor*, *character*, and *stage manager* with exemplary bodhisattva statues and scenes, plus the inner *director* of karmic fate, which can be improved by appealing to more enlightened beings represented there. The temple's multi-directional, dispersed, open to the sky design still has an underground, embedded, material relic beneath its high tower as postmortem fuel—like a church steeple with altar and crypt relics below— perhaps evoking mortal anxieties in the visitor's *audience* and *stagehand* networks, transformed into tragicomic hope and sublime beauty.

From Earth to Heaven: Womblike Caves and Giant Buddhas

The cave-like niches on above-ground floors of the Tianning pagoda reflect the cave temples that were built in mountain grottoes early in the history of Chinese Buddhism, especially from the Northern to Tang dynasties (439–907), while pagoda temples were built on the plains (Litian 129–30). When Buddhism initially developed in China, during the first century CE, wooden monasteries were built with a pagoda at the front or center, which in later designs moved to the back of the complex (Yanxin 76–7; Yuqun 577). However, a doctrine known as "decline of the Dharma" spread through translations of the Mahayana text, *Nirvana Sutra*, predicting the destruction of monasteries and stupas during a dark period 1,500 years after the Buddha's enlightenment (Yuqun 582–3). Cave temples were built as more enduring spaces for meditation and veneration, starting in the fourth to fifth centuries (577). They garnered merit to the builders and cultivated a "field of blessing" for resident monks and visitors, receiving "the protection of the Buddhas" (582). This is akin to Christian churches as sacred spaces, especially with miraculous paintings or a nearby grotto (as at Lourdes) where a vision of the divine occurred. Buddhist cave sites were not revered with the aura of saints' tombs like Christian catacombs. But they drew upon the *qi* of earthly channels in the local lore of prior Daoist beliefs, with mountains as "fecund wombs" (Raz 1404). The cave's *qi* also related to early Chinese views of the Buddha as one of many "transcendents" like Daoist gods and family ancestors (Yuqun 578).

As a transcendent, the Buddha was thought to favor towers (Yuqun 663). Early surface monasteries started with a multilevel pagoda tower, eventually adding a buddha hall with veneration images and a lecture theatre for doctrine teaching along a central axis, plus adjoining buildings such as residence and food halls—at times reaching the scale of an imperial palace (664). This pattern of south to north halls was set in the sixth- to seventh-century Sui and Tang dynasties (Pagani 1340–1). Housing complexes of imperial princes and court ministers were often donated, shaping the courtyard design of Han-style temples for two thousand years (Litian 130). Cave temples included similar elements—stupa/pagoda, image hall, and lecture room—but sometimes added a towering figure of the Buddha carved into the cliff outside the entrance. Some also had a huge Buddha face or reclining body, as an oversize sculpture *within* the womblike cave.

Some caves focused on a central pillar, as "stupa temples," others on "large statues" or multiple images as "buddha hall caves" (Yuqun 579). Meditators used such images to concentrate on some of the thirty-two major and eighty minor "marks of a buddha," which might lead to "visions of the Buddha" and ultimate "union" with him (581). Thus, the towering figure of the Buddha outside the cave, or the many images inside, were not only honoring the transcendent, but producing a *cave theatre* of meditative visions and self-transcendence, like Christian chapels for praying to a statue of a saint or Jesus (though usually not in caves). Today, too, the face and figure of saints, God, or buddhas may *mirror* the visitor, but with an "ideal self" (P. McNamara, *Neuroscience* 53–6) or ideal of non-self as ego dissolution and non-attachment in Buddhism. This mirroring involves various inner-theatre aspects, especially the *character*, *actor*, *director*, and moral *stage manager* of LPFC, MPFC, DMPFC, and VMPFC networks.

At the edge of Jinan, the capital city of Shandong Province in northern China (which includes Qufu), **Thousand Buddha Mountain** offers surface temples, plus cliff carvings created as early as the sixth-century Sui dynasty (Cochini 405). It also includes **Wanfo Dong (Myriad Buddha) Cave**, which is 500 meters long with 28,000 figures, reproduced in the late twentieth century from originals in other caves (Dunhuang and Maiji Shan in Gansu Province, Longmen in Henan Province, and Yungang in Shanxi Province), which were created in the Northern Wei, Tang, and Song dynasties, 386–1279 CE. Outside the cave, there is a huge seated Buddha carving, with gold-painted skin and a yellow-cloth covering, plus veneration areas (Figures 2.125–6 and 2.126vid). There is also a pathway toward the cave entrance (Figure 2.127).

Swirling figures are carved in the rock at the opening to this buddha hall cave, with further figures painted in the initial tunnel (Figures 2.128–32). Two statues, probably

Figure 2.133 Guardian statues near entrance of Wanfo Dong Cave.

of Ha and Heng, guard the entrance farther in, each with a foot holding down a small demon or demigod *asura* (Figures 2.133–4). Nearby, several Buddhas show a peaceful face, some with the right palm raised in the *Abhaya-mudra* gesture of "protection, reassurance, and serenity" (Richie 38). The central one sits with crossed legs on a square pillar with incense offerings on his lap (Figure 2.135). Thus, the visitor is drawn inside the cave, into the mountain's womb, with guards balancing on demons and patriarchal yet nurturing Buddhas transcending such tricksters. Together, they may evoke fear, awe, and trust, through the inner theatre's subcortical *stagehands*, left-cortical *scriptwriter/critic*, and right-cortical *mime/designer*. Ideal affects of high and low arousal, with negative and positive valence (HAN-HAP/LAN-LAP), plus dramatic/contemplative spillover effects, are reflected in harmonious balance.

Further into the cave, there is another Buddha seated on a stool along the wall, guarded by two lions, with his hand held out—and there was money on it when I visited in 2013 (Figures 2.136–7). Other Buddha statues also had money offerings on their laps (Figures 2.138–9). There are many wall paintings, including some with flying *apsaras* as Buddhist celestial nymphs (Figure 2.140). Additional sculptures along the wall show various Buddhas flanked by guards, who are treading on demons, repeating the court contexts and inner-theatre elements of transcendents near the mouth of the cave (Figure 2.141). Shelves in the corridors hold small Buddhist figures—somewhat like the dorm-bed niches for early Christian corpses in catacombs (Figure 2.142). Actual cloaks are worn by some of the statues, with a dual materiality (Figure 2.143).

As the visitor walks deeper into the mountain, hearing the echoes of recorded Buddhist music, a much larger image appears: the head of the Buddha from floor to ceiling (Figures 2.144 and 2.144vid). Like other Buddha heads in the cave, its long earlobes, *bindu* dot in the forehead as "vanishing point," and serene expression signify a prince who gave up his riches to find an answer to his subjects' suffering, which he discovered through a paradoxical mix of detachment and compassion (Richie 34–6). Thus, the huge face may evoke both awe and care networks in the visitor, perhaps with joyful memories of being a child, held close to the face of a much larger human being. Indeed, the Buddha's nose, lips, and earlobes are smooth, possibly through the touch of numerous hands—reflecting various sensory dimensions (Figures 2.145–6).

The passageways between chambers have rounded ceilings, yet also rectilinear frames (Figures 2.147–8). Colorful meditating Buddhas appear along the walls, not tempted by the flying apsaras nearby, even close to the ground (Figures 2.149–51). The visitor also encounters a central stupa-pillar, both rectangular and round, with multiple images of the Buddha and his disciples (Figures 2.152–3). There are animals in some of the wall paintings, including deer, perhaps representing the deer park in Sarnath, India, where the historical Buddha gave his first sermon (Figures 2.154–5). An electric light encircles a Buddha's head, akin to the halos of Christian saints (Figure 2.156). Historically, halos and full-body aureolas were depicted in Buddhist and Greco-Roman art *prior* to Christianity. There is also a reclining (*parinirvana*) Buddha 28 meters long, supported by other heads, perhaps showing prior lifetimes toward a final death and enlightenment—with small pagodas nearby, reflecting the towers and towering figures that honor patriarchal transcendence on the earth's surface (Figures 2.157–9). Thus, a balance between right-cortical, maternal inclination and left-cortical, patriarchal rectitude is shown.

There are veneration rooms, with guards carved into the doorway or banners across it ("Nine Lights of Buddha") and a Buddha in the center of the room, sometimes with small lions, a kneeler, and an offering area (Figures 2.160–3). Deeper into the cave are passages with further Buddha statues, larger than life, like many of the guardian statues (Figures 2.164–7). There are also Buddhas with cloth coverings, standing and reclining, again suggesting upright rectitude and yet relational inclinations (Figures 2.168–70). At the end of the cave is a wide veneration room with a large, well-decorated Buddha statue (Figures 2.171–2 and 2.172vid). Almost all of the statues are male, yet there is at least one of Guanyin (Figure 2.173), perhaps with this imbalance as a counterbalance to the curved, womblike environment.

After returning through the long corridors to the natural light of the entrance and the open sky above, one feels reborn out of the mountain womb, perhaps with a more enlightened life. Ironically, the "ideal self" made present, with each of the many buddha images, some of huge size and solid stone, seems to contradict the idea of "no self" (*anatman*) in Buddhism. But their multiplicity and varying sizes, along with the visitor's passage into and out of the cave, also suggest the "impermanence" (*anitya*) of all physical and mental objects.

Thousand Buddha Mountain has various surface temples, smaller caves, cliff carvings, and huge outdoor statues. A giant Guanyin appears above a cave area, holding her vase of pure water or elixir, symbolizing compassionate wisdom, potentially inclined toward those who venerate her (Figure 2.174). She also gives the *Vitarka-mudra*, symbolizing peace in the teaching of the Dharma (Richie 38). She stands on a lotus flower, or *padma*, akin to the mandala, yet symbolic of "the true essence of all," emerging from the murky depths of the pond where the lotus grows (44–5). Below the huge statue are cliff carvings (Figures 2.175–6) and a tiny cave with many painted statues, plus an offering box that states in Chinese: "Broadly plant happiness in the field" (Figures 2.177–8). There are also multiple buddhas carved around the entrance to a medium-sized cave (Figure 2.179). Inside are many Guanyin images along the tunnel (Figures 2.180–2) and in a larger chamber at its end (Figures 2.183–4), as well as in the return to the surface (Figure 2.185). Compared with Wanfo Dong, the womblike space of this cave involves more right-cortical, maternal, nurturing reflections, above and inside, with its large and small figures, plus potential elixir inclinations. Yet the Guanyin statues also show straight-standing rectitude as transcendent, male-to-female forms.

Not far away is a 20-meter- (66-feet-)high, golden statue, built from 1999 to 2000, of Budai-Maitreya, laughing Buddha of the Future, seated on a lotus flower (Figure 2.186). Relief carvings behind the statue also show the historical Buddha, Shakyamuni, preaching under the Bodhi Tree, and other scenes (Figure 2.187). Although many of the statues on Thousand Buddha Mountain were destroyed during the Cultural Revolution, they have since been rebuilt and new monuments added, such as the huge Budai-Maitreya. A visitor can enter the womblike Guanyin cave, experience compassionate rebirth from darkness into sunlight (like the lotus that grows from the

Monumental Developments in Patriarchal, Maternal, and Trickster Designs 133

Figure 2.186 Laughing Budai-Maitreya at Thousand Buddha Mountain.

lake bottom to the surface), and then walk to the future Buddha, who sits on a lotus flower, sharing humorous joy. Tasting this and other *rasas*, reflected in the cave and outdoor sculptures, might lead to a greater inner-theatre awareness of trickster *stagehands* (or outer-theatre, Trojan Horse tricks), thus refining one's *actor*, *director*, and *stage manager* circuits, perhaps toward the ninth *rasa* of peace.

Near **Leshan** in Sichuan Province, a **giant Maitreya** has been carved into the cliff above the confluence of the Minjian, Dadu, and Qingyi Rivers, facing the holy Mt. Emei (Figures 2.188–9 and 2.189vid). It is not the chubby laughing Budai, but the ruler form of Maitreya, seated on a throne with an *ushnisa* hair style, long earlobes, and the *bindu* dot in his forehead (Richie 34–6). The 1,021 ringlets of coiled hair on his head, plus the ears, collar, and chest, involve a sophisticated drainage system to prevent erosion. This statue was carved out of the cliff in 713 to 803, with ears added as wood forms covered in clay. It was an appeal to the Buddha for economic and religious reasons, with turbulent river waters that hindered shipping and visits by pilgrims to holy sites nearby. The rubble that fell from the cliff during the carving did pacify the water below. At 71 meters (233 feet), it is the tallest, extant, premodern statue in the world, akin to the standing Bamiyan Buddhas in Afghanistan, which were 35 and 53 meters tall, but destroyed by the Taliban in spring 2001.

Visitors streaming down the cliff stairs on the right side of the Leshan statue find small carvings and paintings in niches, where offerings of money and incense have

134 European Churches and Chinese Temples as Neuro-Theatrical Sites

Figure 2.193 Giant Leshan Maitreya cliff carving.

been left (Figures 2.190–2). They also get closer views of the Buddha's fingers on his knees, expressing calmness, along with his meditative face (Figure 2.193). Boats with visitors pass along the river near the bottom of the statue (Figure 2.194). The Buddha's toes are larger than people, but with normal-size offering boxes and an incense burner between his feet (Figures 2.195–6 and 2.195–6vid). During the climb up the many steps to the top of the statue's head—passing the cave where the monk, Hai Tong, resided as initiator of the carving project, thirteen centuries ago—the visitor sees a stream of people going down the other side, like ants (Figure 2.197). Thus, a complex, high/low arousal, negative/positive, fearful/peaceful spillover of awe is evoked around the cliff-carving: at each person's vulnerable insignificance, yet valuable interdependence with others, plus the potential for greater enlightenment in each lifetime.

Rarely are Christian statues so gigantic. (Modern exceptions are the 30-meter concrete and sandstone Christ the Redeemer statue near Rio de Janeiro, Brazil, and the 41-meter aluminum Virgin Mary with wings in Quito, Ecuador). Protestant churches minimize or totally exclude images of God or saints, focusing instead on the Bible and music as ties to the divine, although sometimes showing Jesus, historical founders, and tomb effigies. Catholic churches display many human figures, but most are life-size or smaller, at least in appearance at a distance. Eastern Orthodox churches may have a large image of Christ Pantocrator (All-Ruler) on the inner dome and Mary Theotokos (God-Bearer) in the apse. But they also offer life-size or smaller icons that visitors view on walls, on the iconostasis (altar screen), or in a frame at eye-level and sometimes kiss. Unlike a Catholic "portrait," which may be realistic, the Orthodox icon shows a saint in "the glorious radiance of heaven," stern-faced and gaunt, often with a flat golden background, "freed from the effects of the Fall, radiating the Taboric light of the Transfiguration" (D. McNamara, "Incarnation" 22). The viewer's emotions are not subjectively evoked, but "purified and perfected ... [through] visual asceticism," as in "church buildings" giving a "foretaste" of heaven by "enclosing space into which the Holy Spirit is invited" (23–4) via left-cortical, more abstract, *scriptwriter/critic* networks. This also relates to a biblical metaphor in the First Letter of Peter, circa 60–80 CE, with Christians as "living stones" forming the Church as God's building (24, 29). Thus, in all these Christian traditions, churches do not have gigantic statues like the Leshan Maitreya, which also has temples nearby, or Jinan (Thousand Buddha Mountain) Guanyin and Budai. But the exterior and interior of churches often draw a visitor's eyes upward, with "gigantism in space" (Kilde 111), in awesome left-cortical and awful right-cortical ways, evoking respectful elevation and threatening fear/surprise (Diagram 1.4).

Patriarchal Basilica In-Spirations with Maternal Nurturing and Tricksters

With its expansion across the ancient Roman Empire, Christianity evoked awe across many centuries by shaping vast spaces in cruciform churches, with spires rising skyward. Although also starting with intimate, round, womb-like martyria and baptisteries,

Christians adopted the Roman judicial hall, the "basilica," as their main architectural form. The Aula Palatina or **Constantine Basilica (Konstantinbasilika)** in Trier, Germany, was a palace basilica built by Constantine in 310, with interior elements added in the Middle Ages and later, but then burned with bombing during the Second World War. It was refurbished as the Protestant "Church of the Redeemer," returning to classical simplicity (Figure 2.198). At 67 meters long by 26 meters wide and 33 meters high, it is the largest extant hall from ancient times, similar in length and width to the Leshan Buddha if that cliff carving were laid horizontally (71 by 28 meters).

As an Evangelical Lutheran church, the Constantine Basilica focuses the visitor's attention on an open, rectilinear space with round arches, a simple cross over the altar, and a modern organ in the back—with music rising in the vast space as a way to connect with the divine (Figures 2.199–201 and 2.201vid). Thus, the patriarchal, left-cortical, *scriptwriter/critic* dimension is stressed, from the basilica's original purpose as an ancient legal hall to the modern abstract cross and altar of Christ's dutiful-son sacrifice. Yet the round arches also suggest strong maternal nurturing, along with the organ's music, evoking images and emotions of right-cortical, limbic, and subcortical, *mime/designer*, *audience*, and *stagehand* participation by the inner theatres of persons in the pews.

Early Romanesque churches developed from catacomb and domestic paradigms, including the round mausoleum-martyrium, such as Saint Constantina, with maternal nurturing characteristics, to more patriarchal, rectilinear, basilica and cruciform plans. Medieval Gothic churches added higher and higher towers, as French, German, and Spanish cities with saints' relics competed for fame and pilgrims. Urban cathedrals, especially in France, were usually dedicated to Mary rather than to local saints (Roth 293). They valued maternal archetypes with sculptures and paintings, showing the "Virgin" ideal of "Our Lady," as in courtly romance, yet with patriarchal spires on top and male saints above many altars. Starting in the fifteenth century, with a different patriarchal twist, Renaissance churches returned to classical restraint, geometrical decor, and proportional balance, although with large domes and facades, like ancient Roman architecture, stressing "the earth-bound horizontal" (317). And then, in the seventeenth century, a "superhuman" scale arose again (357), with numerous swirling shapes and angelic figures, adding feminine curves and trickster playfulness (sometimes in ellipsoid naves) during the Counter-Reformation Baroque. The eighteenth- to nineteenth-century Enlightenment and Romantic periods included neo-classical and neo-Gothic styles, which revived earlier horizontal solidity or vertical spires, as a competition between patriarchal orders, fueled by maternal and trickster forces—between "enlightened logic and ennobling probity ... [or] mystery and irregularity of form" (426). Twentieth-century modernist churches stressed abstraction, functionalism, new materials, and pure geometric forms. Subsequent postmodern churches evoked playful mixtures of styles—with or without spires.

The church with the highest twin spires in the world, at 157 meters (515 feet),[8] is **Cologne's Cathedral of Saint Peter (Kölner Dom)**. Initially built from 1248 to 1473,

---

[8] The Lutheran Minster in Ulm, Germany, built from 1377 to 1890, has a single spire fifteen feet higher than the Cologne Cathedral, with its original plan adjusted to be so, showing the rivalry between faiths and cities.

Figure 2.209 Apse view of chancel screen and Three Kings reliquary, Cologne Cathedral.

but left unfinished until the neo-Gothic Romantic period, it was completed in 1880, according to the original medieval plan, with the façade and spires finished in 1911 (Figure 2.202). The cathedral also has the Romano-Germanic Museum near it, built over an ancient Roman villa with a mosaic of the theatre god Dionysus/Bacchus and his followers (Figures 2.203–04). That mosaic was discovered by the Nazis when creating a bomb shelter, so it emerged from the earth like a Nietzschean dream—or nightmare.

Indeed, the cathedral was badly damaged by World War II bombings and then rebuilt. It now has the largest façade of any church, but with human-size figures arranged around the doorways (Figure 2.205), including saints as "pillars of the church" (D. McNamara, *How* 240). Inside, behind a chancel screen, its twelfth-century, basilica-shaped "Shrine of the Three Kings" is thought to hold the bones of the magi who visited the newborn Jesus (Figures 2.206–08 and 2.208vid). After the bones were taken (or stolen) from Milan by Holy Roman Emperor Frederick Barbarossa when he conquered that city in 1164, they inspired the towering heights above with vast interior spaces and pointed Gothic arches evoking awe as well (Figure 2.209 and 2.209vid). A collective belief in the holiness of those early pilgrims as wise magician saints (one depicted as black) fueled the building of a cruciform basilica with twin spires, for further pilgrims to find, across many centuries.

The **Cathedral of Our Lady (Cathédrale Notre-Dame)** in Strasbourg, France, was built from 1015 to 1439, on the site of a former Roman temple and a Romanesque church. It became Protestant for over a century (1521–1681). It has the highest Gothic spire existing from the Middle Ages, at 142 meters (466 feet), although its south tower was never built (Figures 2.210–12 and 2.212vid). Its western façade, added from 1277 to 1399, with patriarchal pointed, Rayonnant Gothic ornaments, has three doorways with tympanums displaying Jesus's infancy, crucifixion, and Last Judgment. The latter, above the southwest door, shows a seated Christ with his hands raised and evil people below him, entering a monstrous hell-mouth with devils to his left (as in the Valenciennes stage design of 1547), while angels with long trumpets raise the dead (Figure 2.213). The Madonna with Child also appears at the peak of a triangle, on the central tympanum, with a bearded male face (God the Father) above her.

Visitors can climb a spiral staircase to an observation deck near the octagonal spire, with many views en route of the medieval church (Figures 2.214–15). The deck offers a closer look at the openwork spire, along with a view of the church square below (Figures 2.216–17). Statues along the roof edges are also visible from the staircase, high above the ground, including one where playful visitors have left coins on its head, probably for the challenge of the toss rather than religious devotion (Figure 2.218). Along with many patriarchal figures, outside and inside this church, a female statue with a scroll (perhaps Mary as queen) can be seen near the roof, plus flying buttresses and gargoyle tricksters extending the structures near her, like subcortical supportive/trickster *stagehands* (Figure 2.219). Here and at other French churches, hundreds of the statues were smashed during the French Revolution as inner-theatre tricksters and group identifications became violent against regal and religious hierarchies. But if damaged, these stone figures, like the tympanums, were later restored.

Figure 2.213 Tympanum with Last Judgment and hell-mouth, Strasbourg Cathedral.

Inside the cathedral, vast vertical spaces and pointed Gothic arches suggest patriarchal authority, like in a Roman basilica, but reaching greater heights (Figure 2.220). There is a cave-like crypt under the main altar, from the prior Romanesque church, suggesting a saintly energy below ground, which serves the ritual space for commemoration of the Son's sacrifice (Figure 2.221). A side chapel contains a complex, nineteenth-century, astronomical clock offering patriarchal measurements of various natural orders (Figure 2.222). Medieval stained-glass windows, most from the twelfth to fourteenth centuries (removed by the Nazis but found by American soldiers after the Second World War), also assert male rule, even with current artworks as authorized tricksters below (Figure 2.223). Yet maternal images appear in the windows with Mary and young Jesus scenes (Figures 2.224–5). The devilish underside to patriarchal authority and maternal nurturing can be seen there, too, with the killing of the Holy Innocents by Herod's soldiers in medieval garb (Figure 2.226). A trickster dimension appears also with animal-human demons, tied up while Jesus revives the dead Lazarus and frees Adam and Eve from hell (Figures 2.227–8).

With such imagery, survival fear yet nurturing hope might be evoked in visitors, past and present, through subcortical *stagehand* networks, along with moral disgust in VMPFC and insula circuits, as *stage manager* and *audience*. Likewise, left-cortical *scriptwriter/critic* seeking, with patriarchal awe, is evoked if the visitor climbs the spiral

140   European Churches and Chinese Temples as Neuro-Theatrical Sites

Figure 2.229 Copenhagen's Church of Our Savior.

stairway toward the spire, or walks the nave toward the altar, or stares upward at the stained-glass scenes. Those images in colored glass, lit by the sun, explained the faith to illiterate medieval believers. So did religious plays performed on set pieces between tree-like columns and in the square outside such churches, involving inner theatres hundreds of years ago. Today's bare stone surfaces of Gothic churches, inside and out, were much more colorful then, with painted figures and scenes to edify their audiences—in a very different, belief and ritual context. Yet the patriarchal hierarchy of Strasbourg's towering spire and high statues, as Jesus sends damned souls into a devilish hell-mouth over the façade doorway, may also affect us today, along with the stained-glass images of Mary's maternal nurturing and animal-human demons' capture.

Surprisingly theatrical as a Protestant (Evangelical Lutheran) building, Copenhagen's **Church of Our Savior (Vor Frelsers Kirke)** was completed in 1695, but got its corkscrew spire in 1752, inspired by the Catholic Baroque tower of Saint Ivo (Sant'Ivo alla Sapienza) in Rome, yet elongating it higher (Figures 2.229–30). Inside, the rectilinear ceiling and walls are plain, stressing their cruciform ground plan (Figure 2.231 and 2.231vid). But the pews have doors with personal titles and floral carvings above them (Figure 2.232). The round baptismal font, to the left of the altar, is even more ornate with cherubic babies (or Cupid-like putti) in its rectilinear railing (Figure 2.233). Angels also stand or sit along the communion rail, with a book, staff, horn, or sword, and hold a chalice behind the altar, challenging Jesus in the Garden of Gethsemane (Figures 2.234–5). Elephants on the back wall appear to support an enormous organ over the entryway, perhaps related to the seventeenth-century Danish-Norwegian East India Company and its colonies (Figure 2.236).

Inside the tower, there are wooden stairs upward to a view of other steeples across the city (Figures 2.237–8). External, ever-narrowing, metal steps can be taken counter-clockwise up the spire, on top of which appears a golden globe and statue of Jesus holding a banner (Figures 2.39–42 and 2.241–2vid). The patriarchal verticality of this spire bears a swirling, feminine elegance, like the angels and cherubs inside the church, suggesting maternal nurturing. Also, the whimsical twist of the spire and the elephants under the organ evoke light-hearted, trickster/supportive *stagehand* elements—akin to yet unlike the animal-human devils in Strasbourg's stained glass.

Multiple spires adorn a more recent, neo-baroque, Catholic church, **Holy Family (Sagrada Família) Basilica** in Barcelona, with eleven of its planned eighteen towers completed as of 2022 (Figure 2.243, from 2011). They will eventually symbolize the twelve apostles, four evangelists, Mary (tower completed in 2021), and Jesus. The central highest tower, representing Christ, will make this the tallest religious building in the world. The basilica was designed by Antoni Gaudí, who started its construction in 1883 and died in 1926, leaving plans and models, most of which were destroyed by anarchists ten years later. But the remnants are now being used to complete his dream. Gaudí combined Gothic and Arte Nouveau styles into his own organic *modernista* forms, both growing and melting, like vegetation and wet sand, as he looked to "'the laws of Nature … [to] collaborate with the creator'" (qtd. in Kilde 176). On the first-built "Nativity Façade," below its four apostle-assigned spires, maternal and trickster energies appear. Mary is crowned by God as Queen of Heaven and the Holy Family escapes to Egypt while Herod's soldiers kill innocent babies instead of Jesus (Figures 2.244–5). Through stories evoked by these Gaudi-designed scenes, along with those in the "Passion Façade" on the west side, completed with sharp angles in a contrasting style, by sculptor Josep Maria Subirachs (Figures 2.246–7), a modern artist's postmortem "genius" fuels patriarchal spires and images, plus maternal and trickster figures—like saints' relics and anonymous designers in prior centuries.

Buddhist images in pagodas, caves, and surface halls (or alternate images in Daoist temples), with statues sometimes rising to great heights, consolidate many prior centuries of Chinese ancestor and nature-spirit worship into *collective* stories and beliefs, evoking various elements of visitors' inner theatres. Likewise, prior "pagan" traditions underlie Christian monuments and rituals in Europe (even the modern festivals of Christmas and Easter), although sublimated with suffering saints and a sacrificed God, rather than Daoist longevity or Buddhist enlightenment. The Western emphasis on redemptive suffering and fighting evil is shown with the *dominance* of patriarchal spires and figures, over the landscape and in art, even with female martyrs as heroic victims following God's will. Buddhist caves and cliff carvings, whether deep in a mountain or monumental in size, retain natural elements through harmonious *balancing* (like wooden temples with yards, trees, and ponds)—as in the confluence of rivers and drainage of rain, redirected by the giant Leshan Buddha.

Spirit Possession or Trickster Rivalry: Columns and Screens

Brain spirits, as animal-human drives and extended consciousness, are reflected at monumental sites, yet cultivated differently. They appear as left-cortical dominance over nature and transcendence beyond the body in European churches or more right-cortical (along with left), holistic, dialectical balancing of *yin* and *yang* in East Asian temples. Both traditions of religious buildings involve the survival drive, especially through desires and fears evoked by sacred spaces, mythic scenes, and ritual actions. Such sites reflect how each ego-soul experiences joy and yet anxiety, regarding hope for an afterlife reward, or fear of eternal punishment, in the Christian framework of conquering evil—and a longer life process or many-lives' progress in the Daoist/Buddhist sense of health and karma (Table 1.1).

Reproduction emotions of love and lust are extended toward cooperative group legacies, involving friendship or greed, with inspiring spires on churches that dominate the landscape and monumental Buddha carvings that reshape a cliff or cave. These collaborative creations attract pilgrims and tourists, also bringing wealth to the area. Territoriality and mammalian care appear in the sanctity of enclosed church spaces, where holy water purifies and Communion nurtures the soul. They also appear in open temple courtyards and curved-roof shrines, with warrior statues, incense, and compassionate figures of safety, respect, and meditation. The alliance-hierarchy drive is evoked in religious monuments toward belonging with the faithful, through moral grooming and holy purity. But how are playful, rebellious "brain spirits," as super-natural extensions of animal-human drives, invoked if good, expelled when evil, or reintegrated if unwise, in European churches and Chinese temples?

Both Greco-Roman-Christian and Chinese traditions involve the veneration of imperial gods and ancestral spirits, plus natural energies in paganism and Daoism. But patriarchal and maternal gods or saints, along with trickster spirits, may have darker aspects, perceived as threatening, cruel, or rebellious. After gaining power through the Roman Empire, the Christian repression of other religions involved a fear of spirit possession in pagans, heretics, witches, and others—sometimes with the exorcism of devilish tricksters or execution of scapegoats for communal purification. This focused general anxieties into specific fears, through the patriarchal metanarrative of supernatural good versus evil, angels against devils, involving the brain's left cortical *scriptwriter/critic* and left parietal *costume-body definer*, especially its binary operator, in melodramatic modes.

And yet, Christian believers valued possession by the "Holy Spirit," regarding the New Testament tale of Pentecost when "a violent wind came from heaven" and visited Jesus's followers, more than a month after his crucifixion, with "tongues of fire that separated and came to rest on each of them," making them "speak in other tongues as the Spirit enabled them" (Acts 2.2–4). St. Paul also preached that Christians must receive the Holy Spirit and become a "son" like Jesus, thus being reborn as Paul was, through his own possession experience (P. McNamara, *Spirit* 143–4). This developed, over many centuries, into a Christian theology of "positive spirit possession," influencing the "exaltation of the individual" in Western culture (144). Even today, Pentecostals and mainline Church charismatics invoke possession by the Holy Spirit, through "speaking in tongues," with such glossolalia considered a divine language. However, there is a crucial distinction between this and demonic possession when self-awareness is lost: "the human self is not canceled out when it comes into union with the deity; instead it is brought to fulfillment when putting on the mind of Christ as Paul advised."

As mentioned in Chapter 1 (and Table 1.4), brain scans of Pentecostals speaking in tongues show increased temporal lobe and midbrain emotions, through the activation of both arousal and quiescent (sympathetic and parasympathetic) nervous systems, with possessed subjects' frenzied outer appearance, yet inner tranquility (Newberg and Waldman 206–08). They also exhibit an increased activation in the left parietal orientation area, indicating that "speakers in tongues do not lose their personal sense of self" (205). In contrast, Catholic nuns praying to Jesus and Tibetan Buddhists meditating without a deity show a deactivation of the left parietal sense of self, as they merge mentally with Jesus or with nothingness (Newberg et al. 117–23).

Daoist *rites* involve the invocation of positive spirits and exorcism of negative ones, as well as helping the dearly departed on their spiritual journeys, especially with divine statues giving authority to temple performances. Likewise, Buddhist *images* may evoke, through the inner theatre's mirror neurons, spiritual mimicry in the viewer of an enlightened being's facial expressions, postures, and gestures—or transcendent meditation with wrathful (Tibetan) deities arousing fear and yet a greater awareness about negative emotions and karma. Christian images also evoke mimetic desires of spiritual union, or transcendent ecstasy, with theatrical scenes of heroic sacrifice, regal judgment, and maternal nurturing. Of course, the particular feelings evoked today, with such images in temples or churches, depend on the visitor's knowledge of and belief in their stories, plus personal memory associations, through the brain's subcortical *stagehands*, right-cortical *mime/designer*, left-cortical *scriptwriter*, and limbic *audience*, staging interactions with the "spirit" of artworks and spaces.

In the Greco-Roman tradition underlying Christianity, most temples were rectilinear, but with round, tree-like columns in an external colonnade (*peristasis*), which may relate to prior rituals involving spirits in a sacred grove (Roth 197). Doric columns were smooth, with height measured at six times the diameter, using male proportions according to the ancient architect Vitruvius. But more slender, Ionic and Corinthian columns, representing mothers and maidens with curled or acanthus-leaf capitals, typically had fluting along the side, like a woman's dress. Many columns had torus shapes at the base, signifying captives' ropes as "slaves of the state" or saintly offerings in the later Christian tradition (D. McNamara, *Catholic* 124–5, 130). Greco-Roman temples presented an external altar for public sacrifices, because the inner room (the *cella* or *naos* with a *pronaos* entryway) was reserved for religious authorities with a private altar, treasury of pilgrims' gifts, and large statue showing the deity's presence.

One of the most sacred sites with such a temple was Delphi, where a young virgin or (later) an elderly priestess sat as an "oracle." She was known as the *Pythia*, a term related to the python believed to be at the center of the earth. Inside the rectilinear **Temple of Apollo**, situated on the mountainside below a circular outdoor theatre (Figure 2.248 and 2.248vid), she inhaled fumes from the earth, becoming possessed in a physically exhausting trance (*enthusiasmos*), and gave cryptic forecasts. There was also a round **Tholos** (domed temple) on another plateau farther below, with a double colonnade of ten columns forming the inner wall, plus twenty freestanding columns around them, and a conical roof (Figures 2.249–51). It may have been associated with a prior cult of Mother Earth (Gaia), the earliest deity worshiped at Delphi, and it was the first area that pilgrims encountered while climbing the mountain toward the oracle. These temples and the theatre above them were built in the fourth century BCE. Such designs influenced the later development of rectilinear/triangular church porticos with Greek columns and yet also round tholos martyria and baptisteries (D. McNamara, *How* 148–9, 164).

It was typical of Greek temples to have masculine and feminine aspects, since their Olympian regime combined patriarchal Dorian sky gods with earth goddesses of the Bronze Age (Roth 188–9). The male Doric columns and inner *cella* were often aligned on an axis pointing to distant twin peaks that were sacred to those earlier goddesses (189). The interior architecture was plain, but the exterior was "lavished with artistic attention" (197). There was also a sacred precinct (*temenos*) around the temple, defined by a low wall, showing the territory of the good spirits worshiped there—reflecting patriarchal and maternal vis-à-vis trickster, inner/outer networks.

Likewise, Daoist and Buddhist temples usually have a walled enclosure around the various halls, aligned on a south to north axis or along a mountain according to its *feng-shui*. Halls have round columns inside and often a short portico in front with an even number of columns, sometimes decorated, as with the writhing dragons at the Buddhist **Hualin (Flowery Forest) Temple** in Guangzhou, which are symbols of imperial power and natural energies, sometimes touched for luck (Figures 2.252–4). The doorway of each hall usually has a high threshold that the visitor should step over, signifying a barrier against evil spirits. Spirit screens (*yingbi*) are sometimes placed parallel to the gate or doorway of a temple, forming a separate, rectilinear, decorated wall to block demons, which can only travel in straight lines according to ancient tradition. The Buddhist **Donglin (East Forest) Temple** in Shanghai (originating in 1308 but redesigned in 2004–07) has such a spirit screen, plus Chinese lions and a canal with bridges protecting the main gate (Figures 2.255–9 and 2.259vid), as considered further below. Chinese lions can also be playful, protective tricksters when animated by puppet-dancers at Lunar New Year, spreading luck and scaring away evil spirits from the previous year.

Unlike Lucifer/Satan (sometimes depicted as a dragon), with his fellow devils, versus God, angels, and saints in Christianity, many gods in the Greek and Roman pantheon were *not* purely evil or good. They had mixed morals in the ancient myths, as superhuman rulers displaying benevolence or cruelty, sometimes through the forces of nature. This depended on political alignments between them, as patriarchal, maternal, and supportive/trickster figures, extending protection/lust, care/vengeance, or play/mischief toward certain humans. Thus, the Greco-Roman temple might be seen as a *spiritual cage* to capture, channel, and restrain the powers of the god it honors—with an inner walled sanctum, private statue, sacrificial altars, and colonnade.

In later centuries, Greek and Roman temples were sometimes converted into Christian churches. The gaps between columns in the external colonnade were filled in to create the walls—and columns were often positioned in the nave—for the spirits of human congregants to commune with divine goodness in a large, public, *interior space*. Thus, the **Temple of Concord** (honoring the goddess Concordia) near Agrigento, Sicily, was preserved from its fifth-century BCE origins on a hilltop near a seaside Greek colony, through its tenure as a Catholic church, to its restoration as an ancient monument (Figures 2.260–4 and 2.264vid). It has a rectilinear design of six by thirteen, Doric, fluted columns, an inner *cella*, and a triangular roof.

In another part of Sicily, the **Cathedral of Syracuse (Duomo di Siracusa)** still shows some of its ancient masculine Doric columns in the side walls and nave, from a fifth-century BCE Temple of Athena, absorbed into a seventh-century CE Byzantine Orthodox basilica (Figures 2.265–7). It was then made into a mosque in the ninth century and converted to a Catholic church in the eleventh, after Arab colonizers were conquered by Norman invaders in 1085. Its front façade was rebuilt with leafy feminine Corinthian columns and further baroque flourishes in the eighteenth century after a major earthquake (Figure 2.268). As with most churches, the entrance is on the west side, so visitors walk toward the main altar (or ancient *cella* area) on the east side, where the sunrise symbolizes resurrection—even with an internal sacred space (Figures 2.269–70). The bishop's throne (*cathedra*) is near the main altar and its dome, with a wooden choir stall and painting between (Figure 2.271). The cathedral also contains the arm-bone of St. Lucy, a local martyr from the fourth century and patron

Figure 2.268 Cathedral of Syracuse.

of the city, with a small painted dome over that relic, its altar, and a painting of the saint (Figures 2.272–4). St. Lucy's bones became so valuable that most were translated to other, competing cities. But relic bones of another saint also appear here in a side chapel (Figure 2.275–6). The baptismal font, near the cathedral entrance, is made from an ancient bowl (Figure 2.277). Thus, saintly spirits and God's Holy Spirit are invoked through relics, artworks, and various rites, especially communion and baptism, inside a multi-style cathedral that repurposes an ancient pagan temple. It adds sky-like domes to the ancient tree-like columns, recalling earlier rites with nature spirits, as well as the arboreal realm of our primate ancestors.

With columns thinning and arches rising pointedly from the Romanesque to Gothic periods, European churches created huge interior spaces with vaulted ceilings. The Gothic "chancel screen," a decorated partition of wood, stone, or iron, sometimes with open tracery, plus a "rood" (cross) or pulpit on top, separated the public from the altar area (Stemp 55)—like the separate *cella* of ancient Greek temples. Churches then became more balanced yet whimsical with such screens reduced to a railing, from Renaissance to Baroque designs. Thicker columns, rounded arches, and domes were added with swirling clouds, flying figures, and edge-arranged cherubs. But the chancel (sanctuary), as the most sacred area around the main altar, was still reserved for clergy. There they performed the role of Jesus at the Last Supper, invoking the Holy Spirit and "transubstantiating" bread and wine into the Body and Blood of Christ. At the back of the chancel, the "tabernacle" held the sacred bread-flesh from previous Masses, inside an ornate reliquary-like box.

Catholic architectural theology points to the ancient Temple of Solomon (*c.* 990–931 BCE), as described in the Hebrew Bible, with its (1) outer porch, (2) inner Holy Place (*hekal*) courtyard, (3) veil, and (4) exclusive Holy of Holies (*debir*) with an altar for animal sacrifices. These areas, symbolizing (1) earth, (2) paradise as Garden of Eden, (3) sublime threshold, and (4) heaven, became paradigms for the church's fully enclosed (1) narthex, (2) nave with vegetal ornaments and treelike columns, (3) chancel screen or communion railing, and (4) sanctuary with altar and tabernacle (D. McNamara, *Catholic* 49–56). Ancient Egyptian temples had a similar plan of walled enclosure, inner yards with columns, and exclusive holiest sanctum, centuries before Solomon's Temple (Wilkinson). But the appropriation of an "Old Testament" design means that each church, in a sense, re-places Solomon's temple. This relates to the long history of Christianity's mimetic-mythic rivalry with its older Abrahamic sibling.

A rood screen, as sublime threshold veil, increased the "drama" and "theatrical" spectacle of the Mass, with the celebrant's back to the medieval audience, who rarely received the communion bread (Kilde 76). Alerted by bells ringing, they watched through the screen's "crosshatches" and "squints" at the elevation of a mystically transubstantiating Host (and wine cup), attracted by such "concealment, exposure, and voyeurism." A chancel fence still exists today in Cologne's Cathedral, considered above. But starting in the sixteenth century, in many Counter-Reformation churches, the screen returned to the lower communion rail of ancient Christianity, based on the Roman judicial basilica design (99). This made the chancel reenactment of the Last Supper more visible to voyeuristic congregants, as divine Body display, like the swirling flesh in Baroque art, "an event similar to theater," although the Mass was still in Latin (99–100). In our post-Vatican II era, with audience participation through vernacular scripts and music, the Mass is often celebrated with more (Protestant-like) communal intimacy. Even in longitudinal cruciform churches, an altar is usually placed at the center of the nave-transept crossing, where the celebrant, in the role of Jesus at the Last Supper, faces the congregants—evoking inner-theatre brain spirits through clerical and divine projections.

In Eastern Orthodox churches, there is a fully opaque screen: a *templon* as iconostasis (icon decorated wall) separating the altar area from the public. This makes the chancel even more like a *cella* as priest-only sanctum. The iconostasis developed "from a low balustrade around the sanctuary in early Byzantine churches," as in the Roman public basilica, "to a high screen by the fifteenth century" (Kilde 60). Typically, Jesus with the Book of Judgment, John the Baptist, and Archangel Gabriel as Messenger (on the deacon door as side entry for clergy) appear to the right of the central doors, known as Royal or Holy Doors, with a Mystical (Last) Supper scene painted above them. To the left of the Royal Doors is Mary holding the Christ Child, the particular patron saint of the church, and Archangel Michael as Defender (on the side-exit deacon door). The Royal Doorway is only used by the bishop (or by other clergy during Bright Week after Easter) and when the priest approaches the people while holding the Gospel book or sacred chalice. Women are never allowed behind the *templon* or on the

Figure 2.282 Iconostasis in Uspenski Orthodox Cathedral, Helsinki.

platform in front of it (except in a nunnery). Yet at times during the service, the central doors open to allow a view inside.

Built in 1862–8, when Finland belonged to Russia (and designed by Russian architect Aleksey Gornostayev), Helsinki's **Uspenski Orthodox Cathedral** has such a *templon*, along with a smaller icon of St. George conquering an evil dragon. Its name refers to the "Dormition" of Mary (her sleep-death with bodily rise to heaven) and the cathedral is dedicated to her. There are no pews because traditionally in Orthodox churches everyone stands, except the elderly, men on the right, women on the left, even if the service is hours long (Papalexandrou 345). Outside, the steeples' golden "onion domes," in the Russian-Scandinavian tradition, add patriarchal points atop their maternal roundness, also with a cross and ball symbolizing Christ's authority over the earth (Figures 2.278–84 and 2.284vid). The central dome represents the Sacred Heart of Jesus and the smaller ones signify the hearts of the twelve apostles ("Helsinki's"). Dominating its hilltop, like the Lutheran Cathedral on another hill at the city center (next chapter), Uspenski is the main site of the Finnish Orthodox Church and the largest church of that style in Western Europe. It thus reflects left-cortical, patriarchal, *scriptwriter/critic* networks of hierarchical, territorial control, with columns and screens, yet also maternal elements such as domes, in relation to supportive/trickster spirits.

The spiritual cages of European churches and Chinese temples screen, control, and yet evoke super-natural tricksters—as monuments of cooperative but competing "memeplexes" (gene-like ideologies using humans as vehicles) with righteous ideals and mimetic rivalries.[9] They reflect and shape our inner theatres, with the ego-self as a memeplex in relation to others: "predicting and outwitting others' behavior," as a "protector" of memes through "beliefs" (Blackmore 229–33). Thus, trajectories of Otherness (with in- and out-groups) frame the staging of self-consciousness from past to future, appearing at sacred monuments. These also relate to *viral* memes as trickster spirits in our current social media—with patriarchal territorial-hierarchic *scriptwriter/ critic* frames and maternal nurturing *mime-improviser/designer* fantasies.

Nurturing yet Dominant Domes and Round Church Images

Shapes and decorations vary greatly, but in Roman Catholic and Eastern Orthodox churches, a half dome often covers the apse area of the main altar and tabernacle, with a larger full dome over the nave-transept crossing, representing the heavens above. Domes and round columns, with the chancel as inner sanctum, evoke spirit possession in a positive maternal sense, as curved breast- and womb-like shapes draw the visitor's eyes upward to the heavens, even with a patriarchal, cruciform floor plan and a cross dominating the top of the church outside. Domes, columns, and chancel screens—like Chinese temple columns, high doorway thresholds, and the spirit screen protecting the main gate—express the *territorial* drive, plus a fear of trickster spirits. This is also depicted with St. George on horseback with a lance (or Archangel Michael with a sword) dominating the devilish dragon or snake, a potential threat to sacred spaces. Such a threat reflects visitors' trickster *stagehands*, filtered by patriarchal *scriptwriter* and maternal *mime-improviser* networks, related also to outer, political and cosmic theatres.

Even prior to Christianity, ancient Roman temples increased their patriarchal domination by altering the Greek prototype, merging walls and columns along the back and parts of the sides, with an open portico only at the front (Roth 217). This can be seen today with the **Temple of Augustus and Livia** in Vienne, France, from the first century BCE, which later became a church (Figure 2.285). The **Maison Carrée** in Nimes, France, shows more merging of columns with the *cella*'s side walls, as a Roman temple from the first century CE, dedicated to Emperor Augustus's two grandsons, who died young (Figures 2.286–7).

The **Pantheon** in Rome, completed in 128 CE under the emperor Hadrian, took the further step of expanding the *cella* as a circular rotunda, with multiple altars for many gods. It added a huge, coffered, concrete dome with an open hole (oculus) for sunlight and rain to come inside—while keeping a rectilinear colonnade at the entrance, under a triangular pediment (Figures 2.288–94 and 2.294vid). The diameter of the dome,

---

[9] See James on various successful memes in the evolving "religion virus" of Christianity: polytheism to monotheism with pragmatic/natural to God-given rules—and a specialist to general-purpose, tolerant to intolerant, local to global, physical to abstract, unlikeable to kind, sexual to asexual divinity, plus guilt, proselytism, heaven/hell, Armageddon, anti-rationalism, ignorance-is-bliss, inerrancy, martyrdom, underdog, and one-nation-under-God memes (42, 75–85, 103–19).

43.3 meters, equals the distance between the oculus and marble floor, forming a perfect spherical space, with the dome symbolizing the sky as it touches the earth (Roth 224). From the seventh century on, this spherical, womblike rotunda-*cum*-dome, with rectilinear, protective entry colonnade, was preserved as the "Church of St. Mary and the Martyrs." Statues of pagan gods, including the deified emperor Augustus, were replaced by figures of the Mother of God and various saints (Figures 2.295–7 and 2.297vid). Later, memorial tombs were added with the remains of Raphael, the Renaissance painter, and of Victor Emmanuel, the nineteenth-century king of Italy, as godlike figures. Holy relics from the catacombs were also set beneath the main altar.

The term "oculus" suggests the Eye of God watching from above, through the lens of the sky (Figure 2.298). Likewise, in northern Italy, the mostly round, eleventh-century **Old Cathedral (Duomo Vecchio)** of Brescia has a chapel dome with the Eye of God (Providence) in a triangle (Holy Trinity) painted at its apex, like the Great Seal of the United States on the one-dollar bill, plus the Holy Spirit as a bird in another dome (Figures 2.299–300). Thus, the circular, womblike spaces of Rome's Church of St. Mary and the Martyrs (Pantheon) and Brescia's Romanesque cathedral bear a patch of divine surveillance, watching from above, as a spirit they possess, reflecting the patriarchal controls of visitors' inner theatres and society outside.

Unlike those round churches, which place the main altar opposite the entrance, Rome's fourth-century tholos-like **Saint Constantina**, already mentioned here as a converted mausoleum, has a *central* altar, with a dome above it showing a host of heavenly Renaissance figures (Figures 2.301–03). Yet there are various altar niches in its circular wall with paintings and sarcophagi (Figures 2.304–07). In the archway above the circular ambulatory, there are fourth-century, palace-style mosaics, showing Dionysian revelers, vegetation, animals, cherubic putti, and geometric designs (Figures 2.308–10). This pagan or secular imagery, according to theological historian Margaret Miles, "may have been deliberately incorporated into christian expressions of creation, the beauty of the natural world, and the promise of eternal life" to show "the christian church as capable of accepting a wide range of meanings" (58). However, such "inclusivity," through the alignment of Christian spirits with the imperial power that had recently persecuted them, produced a "dramatic ... exhilarating tension" with that former hostility—and the lingering "fear ... that Christianity might become a ward of the state."

There are no extant depictions of Christ on the cross from the fourth century, probably because that would have reminded people of the recent, "shameful death of criminals" (Miles 59). There are also no depictions of the Last Judgment from that time, although it became a popular image during the Middle Ages, because the melodramatic division of good and bad souls, going to heaven or hell, went against the initial Christian ideal of universal inclusivity. However, two small apses of Saint Constantina show, in the half-domes above side altars, the earliest extant mosaics of Christ Pantocrator (Ruler of All) made at some point in the fourth century. He is depicted in both apses with imperial robes: as a dark-haired, bearded Jesus giving keys to St. Peter in one mosaic and as a blond, beardless Jesus giving a law scroll to St. Paul in another, where sheep also flock around him—early prototypes of Christ as divine patriarch and yet

Monumental Developments in Patriarchal, Maternal, and Trickster Designs 151

Figure 2.316 Interior of Saint Stephen in the Round.

"Good Shepherd" (Figures 2.311–13). The latter relates to the Greco-Roman god, Hermes/Mercury, as shepherd figure and pagan trickster, demonic but valued by medieval Christian alchemists (De La Torre and Hernández 119, 202). Today, this mausoleum-church evokes nurturing emotions, as a womblike space of death and rebirth, with twelve pairs of columns touched by numerous visiting hands, plus the interplay of light and dark from the central windows into the enclosed arcade. Yet it also shows patriarchal ideals of heroic sacrifice and imperial power, redeeming mortal sorrow with ecstatic joy. Thus, Saint Constantina signifies spirit possession and divine authority, as a martyr's mausoleum, with Christ displayed in mosaic tiles as both patriarchal ruler and caring shepherd, reflecting left-cortical *scriptwriter/critic* and right-cortical *mime/designer* networks.

Rome's fifth-century **Basilica of Saint Stephen in the Round (Santo Stefano Rotondo)**, on the Celian Hill, has a double colonnade of twenty and twenty-eight Ionic and Corinthian columns around its central altar, with two columns closer to it, against the communion rail (Davies, *Origin* 54), unlike the Pantheon's empty spherical space (Figures 2.314–18). Yet its tholos design also has side altars like the Pantheon. Relics of Ss. Primus and Felicianus were translated to this church from catacomb tombs in the seventh century—with mosaics from that time showing them beside a jeweled cross, in a chapel apse along the circular wall (Figure 2.319). Originally, the church may have had a dome, upon the higher circular wall that rises from the inner colonnade, which now has a conical wooden roof (Krautheimer 65). The church had three concentric aisles, with columns between them, bisected by four equal arms, making the floor plan of a Greek cross with several circles, thus combining patriarchal and maternal elements. But its outer ring and three of its arms were torn down in 1450. In the walled areas between the outer columns, thirty-four Mannerist frescos from the 1500s show the martyrdoms of various saints with violent details, plus life scenes at the tops of multiple swords pointing to Mary's holy pain, which stress God's patriarchal demand for heroic sacrifices (Figures 2.320–1).

This church was built on top of ancient Roman soldiers' barracks and a Mithraeum (worship space for the bull-sacrificing Mithras cult), repressing the sacred territory of prior offerings through newly unifying Christian ideals. Today, its ancient, womblike, circular space evokes awe and joy, centered upon the main altar. Yet its Late Renaissance murals with martyrdom scenes evoke fear and disgust, through amygdala and insula networks of the temporal-lobe *audience*, drawing on personal and potential experiences with the visitor's inner staging of self and Other. There are various saints eaten by lions or burned to death, or hanged, or drowned with stones at the neck, or having intestines, teeth, or eyes torn out. St. Margaret is raked and St. Agatha of Sicily has her breasts cut off (Figures 2.322–3).

Such scenes of heroic, redemptive suffering, with serene expressions on martyrs' faces, may elicit various feelings in visitors, through the automatic empathy of mirror neuron signals and mimetic arousal of pain networks (Schott), especially right and subcortical, voyeuristic yet masochistic, holistic prey-wary and trickster circuits. The scenes might create a spillover effect of arousal/quiescence, pain/pleasure, and avoidance/approach in this tomb/womb, as the visitor (or pilgrim) tastes various *rasas*, through left-cortical, meta-narrative recognition of passionate devotion to God and his heavenly reward. Questions may also be evoked, with shifts between the inner *scriptwriter/critic* and *mime/designer*, involving prefrontal *actor*, *character*, and *director* networks, as to why the divine Scriptwriter, Designer, and Director enjoys the martyrs' dramas. Do the paintings show trickster-rebels against the Roman Empire, tied to this church's spirit-possessing relics, as legendary remnants of heroic suffering? Or trickster-torturers, authorized by rulers across human history—and by a divine Father's sacrificial desires as Audience? I leave it to you, looking at the photos, to answer. Yet both aspects relate to the sources of Christianity in the "Holy Land."

Holy Land Sources and Conflicts

The ultimate mausoleum-martyrium in Christianity is the **Church of the Holy Sepulchre** in Jerusalem, with maternal nurturing, patriarchal sacrifice, postmortem fuel, and spirit possession elements in its architecture and art. In the second century, the Roman emperor Hadrian, who also built the Pantheon, filled in the quarry around the tomb where Christians believed their Lord, Jesus Christ, had been buried and rose again. Hadrian constructed a temple to Jupiter or Venus over that site, conquering the sacred territory. However, in the fourth century (325–6), the Christian emperor

Constantine the Great (or his mother Helena) ordered the destruction of that temple and excavation of the dirt and rock around the cave-tomb of Jesus, so that a church could be built over the space (Davies, *Origin* 54). Thus, Constantine's church "proudly announced the triumph of Christianity over the older Roman religion" and created an early "pilgrimage site" in Jerusalem (Kilde 41–2).

The "Anastasis" (Resurrection church) was a "huge rotunda" with a dome, possibly having a central hole, over the "baldacchino" (canopy) that covered Christ's empty tomb (Krautheimer 61). Like Saint Constantina, this "mausoleum-heroon" (hero's tomb and shrine) had a circular ambulatory inside and colonnaded porch outside. Between it and the larger basilica built nearby, there was a courtyard with another sacred site, the rock of Golgotha where Jesus was crucified, according to Catholic and Orthodox traditions. Yet some Protestants today revere a different site, "Skull Hill" with its "Garden Tomb," excavated in 1867.

Constantine's church was burned by Persian invaders in 614 and then rebuilt by Byzantine Christians in 630. From the seventh to tenth centuries, it was protected by the Muslim rulers of Jerusalem, but then destroyed in 1009 by the Fatimid caliph Hakim. In the twelfth century, the church was rebuilt by Crusaders from Europe, who covered the courtyard and Golgotha rock, along with the tomb, under one roof. They continued battling Muslims for possession of the Holy Land across several centuries. In the sixteenth century, Franciscans extended the church and built an "Edicule" over the sacred cave, with marble decorations. They added an antechamber to it, supposedly holding the "Angel Stone," a piece of the rock that had covered Jesus's tomb, which angels rolled away during his resurrection.

After a fire in the nineteenth century, the Edicule was rebuilt with a more rectilinear floor plan. A circular, domed ambulatory now surrounds it, with columns as in Constantine's original rotunda, creating a womb-like space that bears the Edicule as a baby chapel (Figures 2.324 and 2.324vid). The current dome dates from 1870, with restoration work in 1994–7. Restoration work was also performed on the Edicule in 2016–17, fixing cracks in its walls, at the cost of four million dollars. Attached to the larger ambulatory is the Greek Orthodox nave, or "Catholicon," with a smaller dome showing Christ Pantocrator. There are also various chapels along its edges, belonging to Roman Catholics and other Christian denominations, all under a continuous roof and rectangular outer wall with rounded corners, connecting to the Calvary/Golgotha site and its second-floor chapel, near the entrance. (A virtual tour is available at http://www.sepulchre.custodia.org/default.asp?id=4099.)

Today's visitor, as faithful pilgrim or curious tourist, approaches the church through a small archway into a courtyard (parvis) and then through the Crusader façade on its south side (Figures 2.325–6). This is more like Chinese temples than medieval churches, which typically have the main entrance on the west side. Near that door, in the south transept, one encounters the "Stone of Anointing," thought to be a marble slab on which the corpse of Jesus was laid, in preparation for burial, although the stone was put there in the nineteenth century. As part of the story of Jesus being taken down from his cross, it is considered to be the "Thirteenth Station," prior to his burial as the fourteenth. Believers kneel, touch, and kiss (or touch a rosary to) the stone as a relic tied to God's human body, which suffered, died, and rose from the dead (Figure 2.327). A modern mosaic nearby, on the outside wall of the Catholicon, shows the crucifixion of Jesus, his dead body laid on the slab with others mourning, and the corpse being carried toward the cave tomb (Figures 2.328–9). Thus, visitors, especially believing pilgrims, may mimic original followers at the site of their Savior's sacrifice—through inner, artful, social, and cosmic theatres.

Near the Stone of Anointing, stairs rise to the two Calvary (Golgotha) chapels, where Jesus was crucified (Figure 2.330). Mournful awe is evoked, especially in believers' inner theatres, at the Catholic (Franciscan) Chapel of the Nailing to the Cross, with a twelfth-century mosaic of Jesus being nailed to the wooden beams for his crucifixion, at the statue of Mary as "Our Lady of Sorrows," and at the Greek Orthodox chapel with the Calvary rock shown under glass as a relic in situ (Figures 2.331–2). These are the Eleventh and Twelfth Stations of the Cross, where the visitor can sometimes witness Armenian monks chanting (Figure 2.332vid). On the main floor, directly below, is the Chapel of Adam, which also shows the Calvary rock, thought to be where the first human was buried, or at least his skull, under the spot where God offered his Son to redeem all of us from Adam's original sin (Figure 2.333). Survival, reproduction, territoriality, care, alliance-hierarchy, play, belonging-grooming, and seeking emotions are thus evoked, in paradoxical ways.

The maternal mourning and nurturing dimension in these displays of Father-Son sacrifice, with the Calvary site, Our Lady of Sorrows, mosaic of Jesus's nailing to the cross, and Stone of Anointing, also leads the visitor toward the cave tomb, as shown in the wall mosaic. A worker in a black robe (functioning as outer-theatre stage manager) allows tourists into this area when there is room—or stops them when clergy are scheduled for ritual prayers (Figure 2.334). When they are allowed into the space around the Edicule, visitors get in line behind a metal Israeli "police" barricade to enter, near the rear screens of the Greek Orthodox catholicon nave (Figure 2.335). A low doorway makes tall adults stoop when entering the Edicule antechamber with its "Angel Stone" (Figures 2.336–7). There is a marble curtain with an even lower entrance to the inner chamber, where a marble slab covers the supposed tomb of Christ, with a tiny altar and icons almost invisible in the darkness (Figure 2.338). This recreates a womblike cave experience (despite most of the original cave having been cleared away), especially when the visitor leaves again, through the low portals, into the light of the rotunda with its dome above (Figure 2.339). But the tourist/pilgrim can also approach the holy site of Jesus's burial chamber from behind the Edicule, where a tiny Coptic Chapel shows, below its altar, part of the bedrock of that tomb—with its historical emptiness signifying the personal hope for heavenly rebirth of the spirit after death (Figure 2.340). Territorial compromises between Christian denominations are shown here, as with the Greek Orthodox catholicon and Roman Catholic areas, while the black-robed worker regulates access, for clergy and laity, theatrically.

Unlike the peaceful contexts of Saint Constantina and Saint Stephen in the Round, in areas of Rome not frequented by tourists, the Church of the Holy Sepulchre is often packed with people, like the Old City of Jerusalem around it. For many centuries, there has been tension, sometimes erupting into outright conflicts, between the various Christian denominations that claim ownership of certain parts of the Holy Sepulchre Church. This relates to the territorial conflicts between Christian crusaders, Muslim rulers, Jewish leaders, and ancient Roman governors over control of the "Holy Land," with its multiple sacred sites. According to the "Status Quo" agreement, codified by the Ottoman Sultan of Turkey in 1852, Greek Orthodox, Roman Catholic, Armenian Apostolic, and Syrian Orthodox clergy control specific areas of the church. Each group is allowed access to the holiest sites at certain times for its rites. The latter two are part of the Oriental Orthodox communion, along with Coptic (Egyptian) and Ethiopian Orthodox Churches. These two also have specific areas, such as the back of the Edicule and the roof of the church, where there is a small monastery (Deir al-Sultan), but that is an area of conflict, too. In 2002, a fight erupted between Coptic and Ethiopian clergy after a Coptic monk moved his chair out of its assigned spot into the shade. Eleven people were hospitalized. In 2008, a larger fistfight broke out between Armenian and Greek clergy around the Edicule, which was ended by Israeli police. Thus, the "possession" of holy territories reflects divisive spirits of Christianity, throughout its history. And yet, the collective praying, chanting, and singing of groups, at regulated points each day, creates beauty, awe, and hope in the visitor's experience of this church, evoking positive spirits as well.

Cross-cultural influences, yet conflicts, between Abrahamic religions, in circular and rectilinear spaces, involving the right-cortical *mime* and left-cortical *critic*, can also be seen with Jerusalem's **Dome of the Rock (Qubbat as-Sakhra)**. Its design combines round and polygonal shapes with a dome inside an octagon inscribed in a similar octagon (Davies, *Origin* 54). This mosque contains the "Foundation Stone," one of the holiest sites in both Judaism and Islam: thought to be the place where God created Adam, where Abraham was willing to sacrifice his son, and where Mohammed took a "Night Journey" to heaven while still alive. Originally built in 692, with an octagonal wall added in the ninth century, the dome rebuilt in 1023, and its gold plating added in 1961, it was "directly inspired by the work of the Constantinian artists" and made by Byzantine builders (55), with a dome the same size as that on the Anastasis (Holy Sepulchre).

Along with the Al-Aqsa silver (lead) domed mosque, the golden Dome of the Rock sits on the Temple Mount (al-Haram al-Sharif), atop the ruins of the Second Temple, the most sacred Jewish site, with the **Western Wall** and its courtyard below. (These sites are considered again with a photo in the next chapter.) Originally, the Second Temple, following instructions in Ezekiel, was "organized hierarchically" along an axis from the exterior for non-believers to semi-exterior for lay believers, interior for priests, and "holy of holies" for the High Priest (Kilde 7). Currently, even the remaining Wall is restricted to enable believers' proper rites, such as hand-washing before nearing it, putting paper prayers in the cracks, or singing together, with men in one area and women another. Tourists may watch at a distance, but not take photographs near the wall. The Temple Mount with the Dome of the Rock and Western Wall exemplifies, like the Holy Sepulchre, a sacred site of spirit possession, yet spirited *rivalry* between

Abrahamic kin.[10] It involves animal-human drives transformed into religious ideals, staging many positive acts, but also a history of righteous violence. Churches, mosques, and temples reflect the best of brain spirits, with or without angelic figures, through the generous designs and playful creativity of collective energies. Yet they also demonstrate the trickster devils of *natural* ties gone awry, in each of our brain-body theatres, especially when projected onto others as "evil."

Courtyards, Fountains, Fonts, and Fests—Ordered from Above or Balanced Within?

The small courtyard of the Holy Sepulchre church and much larger yards of the Al-Aqsa mosque, Dome of the Rock, and Western Wall are *holding areas of belonging*, with ties to divinity in the sky above. Crowds gather to view the building from the outside and then file through a doorway into it—or dance and pray at the Wall itself, putting prayer notes in its cracks. But mosque courtyards have an area for the ritual washing of the face, hands, and feet. All visitors must leave their shoes before entering the sacred carpeted building and female visitors must cover their heads and bodies with a cloth, sometimes provided by the mosque if needed.

In the Persian-influenced Ottoman style, the washing area may involve a central fountain (*shadirvan*), as well as a porch by the door for leaving shoes. The seventeenth-century **New Mosque (Yeni Cami)** in Istanbul exemplifies this Ottoman design with its courtyard fountain, although water taps along the mosque's south wall are used for ritual ablutions. It also has sixty-six domes and semi-domes, including twenty-four along the yard's columned peristyle, plus two minaret towers, yet an overall rectilinear design (Figures 2.341–2 and 2.342vid). As in most mosques, its interior has a pulpit for preaching and a *mihrab* showing the holy direction (*Qibla*) of Mecca for personal prostrations. Geometric designs and stylized Arabic appear on its domes, walls, and carpet—with human and animal imagery forbidden, especially depictions of Allah, as potential idolatry. There is a separate area in the rear for women, like the *matroneum* in early Christian churches (Figures 2.343–5 and 2.345vid). One might see here, as with churches and temples, but in distinctive ways: feminine, maternal, more right-cortical elements of the courtyard fountain, domes, and women's area serving the dominant, left-cortical structures of Mecca alignment, preacher's pulpit, and pointed minarets—directed toward the ultimate, creative Patriarch. Like church bells, minaret *muezzins* (or recordings on loudspeakers) remind the public of sky-God rules, calling for prayers

---

[10] "Operation Al-Aqsa Flood" was what Hamas militants called their brutal incursion into Israeli territory on October 7, 2023, partly to avenge the storming of the Temple Mount (Al-Aqsa Mosque Compound) by over 800 religious Jews two days before, who claimed the right to worship there, against the Status Quo agreement, and related violence by Israeli police inside the mosque six months earlier. It led to another Gaza war, far worse than others before—with both sides in melodramatic victim-hero vengeance against villain mode, showing collective repetition compulsions of biblical proportions.

five times each day, while their towers point to the divine *scriptwriter/critic* and *director*, ordering submission from above.

Although not enclosed in the same way as a Turkish mosque or Chinese temple courtyard, the squares around European churches served in medieval times for theatrical performances and, as often today, for food and souvenir markets. They sometimes have a domed baptistery with a font inside (somewhat like an Ottoman mosque fountain), separate from the church, for the one-time ritual purification of a baby or convert. Baptisteries are often octagonal, with their near roundness signifying the womb and rebirth, while the eight sides symbolize the seven-day Creation week in Genesis plus "the day of Christ's Resurrection" (Davies, *Architectural* 15–16). They thus offer a maternal, reproductive-nurturing, natural inclination, along with patriarchal, survival-territorial-hierarchic, abstract (more left-cortical) ordering.

Early Byzantine examples of this in Ravenna, Italy, are the fifth-century Orthodox Baptistery of Neon (already mentioned) and the sixth-century **Arian Baptistery** (Figures 2.346–7). Both have a mosaic in the dome with John baptizing a naked Jesus in the River Jordan while the Holy Spirit as a dove descends on him, plus an old man personifying the river, with apostles in a procession around them, each carrying a crown. This scene appears above the font at the center of the baptistery, reflecting the holy water below, where people were ritually possessed by divine goodness. Yet the mosaic also represents the sky as a dome over the church square outside—with the dove arriving from that sky-dome above. Arianism, declared a heresy in 325 under Emperor Constantine, but continuing under later Roman emperors and Italian kings, held that Jesus was semi-divine, begotten in time and not co-eternal with the Father. The Arian Baptistery, constructed by the Ostrogothic king, Theodoric the Great, near his palace, shows a more androgynous Jesus, with wide hips, sloping shoulders, and

Figure 2.347 Interior dome mosaic of Ravenna's Arian Baptistery.

bulging breasts, perhaps akin to the Greco-Roman, wine, fertility, and theatre god Dionysus (Jensen 124–6; Mathews 138). This suggests a transformative balance between left-cortical patriarchal authority and more right-cortical maternal nurturing with emotional sensitivity (in both men and women).

Christian baptisteries reflect an earlier tradition of the Jewish *mikveh*, or ritual bath, near a synagogue (Figure 2.348), although such a sacred pool often involves steps going down, connecting pre-temple purification to nature's tomb/womb. The *mikveh* is so important that it must be built prior to the synagogue. It is traditionally used for full immersion to purify the body before entering the temple, including all of the hair on the head, by women after menstruation or childbirth, by men after ejaculation, and by a new convert to Judaism, or for washing a corpse prior to burial, or for new cooking utensils.

Early in Christian history, adult initiation through the purification rite of baptism involved immersion of the body, at least up to the ankles, with the pouring of water over the head and body (affusion), as in the ancient Roman *frigidarium* of the public baths (Davies, *Origin* 103). The **Lateran Baptistery**, a.k.a. San Giovanni in Fonte, was built in 315 as the first baptistery in Rome and became a model for subsequent ones. Like the Roman home's atrium with *impluvium*, yet octagonal (more like a tholos) with a circular sunken floor as water basin and a central font, it suggests the ritual of "immersion with affusion as the normal practice." Its font originally had water coming from the mouth of a golden lamb on the rim, which represented sacrifice (Jesus as the Lamb of God). It still has octagonal outer walls from Constantine's time. But the interior was remodeled in the fifth, seventh, twelfth, and seventeenth centuries. It eventually gained a double level colonnade, Baroque paintings of Constantine, including his Milvian Bridge battle victory with the Christian Chi-Ro symbol, and the Holy Spirit as bird at the center of the dome (Figures 2.349–52 and 2.352vid).

The Lateran Baptistery also has several rectilinear chapels. One is dedicated to St. Venantius, with translated relics and an apse mosaic showing two saints named John on either side of Jesus, related to the full title of the Lateran Basilica nearby: Archbasilica of the Most Holy Savior and of Saints John the Baptist and John the Evangelist in Lateran (Figures 2.353–4 and 2.354vid). Thus, patriarchal angles and figures grew to dominate the initial womblike rebirth space. The fully enclosed fountain of this baptistery, as the model for many others, evokes visitors' left-cortical *scriptwriter/critic* with ideals of heroic sacrifice, as well as their right-cortical *mime/designer* with nurturing ritual feelings, especially during a central baptism or side chapel communion service. And yet, the supportive/trickster *stagehands* of each person's animal-human drives and the memorial *audience* of early life experiences are reflected (and sublimated) with the Holy Spirit bird above and baptisms performed below.

Unlike Chinese Buddhist temples, many European churches are not monastic. But when they are, they often have an adjacent "cloister" with a walkway, colonnade, and central well or pool, as at the seventeenth-century **Saint Charles at the Four Fountains (San Carlo alle Quattro Fontane)** and **Saint Andrew of the Thickets (Sant'Andrea delle Fratte)** in Rome (Figures 2.355–60 and 2.360vid). The latter's cloister now has fish in its pool and artists in its surrounding rooms. Such a courtyard offers a particular

Monumental Developments in Patriarchal, Maternal, and Trickster Designs 159

Figure 2.350 Lateran Baptistery interior.

balance of rectilinear and round, manmade and natural elements. But traditionally, it was reserved for monks or nuns, as the term "cloistered" suggests, and the fountain was not used for ritual ablutions as in mosques.

Instead, most Catholic churches have "holy water fonts" just inside the doors, sometimes held up by an angel, into which believers can dip their fingers while entering. They then make the "sign of the cross" by touching the wetted fingers to the forehead, chest, and each shoulder (while whispering, "In the Name of the Father, the Son, and the Holy Spirit") as a purification rite recalling their earlier baptism. The baptismal font is usually inside the church, near the entry doors, as a nurturing area for infant baptism (as in the Syracuse Cathedral, mentioned above). But some Protestant denominations have returned to adult baptism with partial or full immersion in a pool of water to purify the body and invoke the Holy Spirit, signifying self-sacrifice with descent into water, and then nurturing rebirth. Thus, American "Baptist" churches position a tub of water as the focal point of worship, above and behind the sanctuary platform and pulpit—reordered through belief in the Divine director.

Like Ottoman mosques, Chinese temples have *imbedded courtyards*, often on a south-to-north axis with pools of water and trees as nurturing elements, inside rectilinear walls, serving various ritual functions under the dome of the sky. These courtyards become packed with crowds on New Year's Eve (in the Chinese lunar calendar). People pay extra for entry, believing they will gain the spirit of good luck if present at the first ringing of the temple bell after midnight. At the **Yuan Ming (Perfect Light) Temple** in Shanghai, visitors pay for a ticket on New Year's Eve, although usually no ticket is needed (Figure 2.361). They pack into the front courtyard, lighting candles and incense, and then join the crowd in the main hall and its yard or in smaller rooms upstairs (Figures 2.362-4, 2.363vid1-3, and 2.364vid1-7). This temple, as Lecture Hall of the Pure Land School, was converted from a wealthy donor's home in 1934 (Cochini 107).

Not far away, at the much larger **Jing'an (Peace) Temple**, people pay more than ten times the normal entrance fee, crowding into the main courtyard, while fireworks explode around the city, lit in the streets by numerous citizens (Figures 2.365-8). In 2014, an estimated five to six thousand people paid 600 RMB (96 US dollars) to enter, but in 2015, entrance was limited to three thousand for safety reasons (Min). This temple, first established in the third century near a river, now has a thirteenth-century Southern Song design, housing monks in the Mi Zong (Tangmi) Esoteric and Pure Land Schools (Cochini 110). It was rebuilt in the 1980s after becoming a warehouse during the Cultural Revolution.

On ordinary days, visitors pay a small fee to enter the Jing'an Temple courtyard, buy incense (joss) sticks, light them over an open flame, bow to the four cardinal directions, and put the smoking sticks in a metal censer, or burn spirit money in it, even with snow falling (Figures 2.369-70 and 2.370vid1-2). They also go to various halls and statues for more bowing. Ritually, visitors kneel in each hall, on the cushion provided there, bow three times to the floor, with open hands near the forehead, and then leave money in the metal collection box. At Jing'an Temple, this happens at the top of a large staircase in the main "Mahavira Hall," which has a silver Shakyamuni, wooden reliefs of his life, and a bell (Figures 2.371-5). It also happens in the Guanyin hall on the east side of the yard, with its camphor-wood statue of the "Goddess of Mercy," who pours healing water or elixir from an inclined vase (Figure 2.376). It happens, too, in the Shakyamuni Hall on the west, with the largest jade sitting-Buddha in China (Gautam 64; Leighton 74), his fingers pointing to the Earth Goddess below, to verify his enlightenment when tempted by the demon, Mara (Figure 2.377). The layout of wooden shrines, arranged around a central courtyard with trees, connects with the five traditional Chinese elements. They are new *yang* wood (trees), full *yang* fire (incense lighting), full *yin* water (Guanyin's vase and the yard's openness to rain or snow), new *yin* metal (burners and collection boxes), and *yang-yin* balanced earth (sand in burners, soil beneath trees, and jade Buddha pointing downward). Thus, ideal affects of high and low arousal are cultivated in this Chinese temple, with a courtyard festival crowd or with its ordinary permeability to nature's balances of sun, rain, and snow.

Spirit Money, Playfulness, and Consumerism

Lay Buddhists sometimes fold special sheets of silver or gold paper into ingot-shaped "spirit money" in the ground-level meeting hall under the main one at Jing'an (Figures 2.378-9 and 2.379vid). I have only seen women do this, here and in various Buddhist

Monumental Developments in Patriarchal, Maternal, and Trickster Designs 161

Figure 2.386 Coin play and incense bow in Jing'an Temple.

and Daoist temples. According to C. Fred Blake, such folding is related to traditional women's roles in making dumplings, birthing children, and binding feet (*Burning* 126). Yet both men and women light the colored paper on fire at the incense burner in the courtyard—nurturing a dead family member who can use the money in the afterlife, or honoring the gods, as the smoke rises. Thus, emotions of social bonding (grooming/gossip purity), grief, fear, hope, care, and honor, are cultivated in a temple hall and courtyard with the folding and then burning of spirit money, plus incense and other offerings.

At Jing'an Temple, there are sometimes large gatherings of laity and clergy in the ground-level meeting hall, which has various Buddha images (Figures 2.380-3 and 2.381vid). There are also private rites in the small halls alongside the courtyard, involving family members and temple monks (Figures 2.384 and 2.384vid). More playfully, visitors may toss coins at the large symbolic brazier in the center of the courtyard, trying to reach the top for luck, even while others bow respectfully nearby and chant in the hall (Figures 2.385-7 and 2.387vid1-2). People also leave coins along the stone relief of dragons in the middle of the stairway to the central Mahavira Hall, even during rain (Figure 2.388-9), and in an empty stone well of an east side hall near the entrance (Figure 2.390). Creative playfulness is in the spirit of Jing'an Temple, transformed as an animal-human drive, along with survival, reproduction, territoriality, care, and alliance-hierarchy, toward personal enlightenment and communal harmony, even with ancestral ghosts. The tragicomic *rasas* of such drives are also reflected, from dramatic compassion to contemplative wisdom, with high and low arousal, negative and positive affects *in balance*, through the serene faces of various bodhisattva statues. This is unlike the low to high arousal, negative to positive (HAP) church images of suffering martyrs and a crucified Christ, as melodramatic heroes of goodness conquering evil.

Typically, a Chinese temple has a large bell or bell tower, as bright sound *yang*, to the right or east of the main entrance and a large drum or drum tower, as dull sound *yin*, to the left (Meyer 78). At Jing'an a visitor can walk along the upper level of the temple's front wall, seeing its bell tower in the southeast corner, which holds a Ming dynasty copper Hongwu bell weighing 3.5 tons (Gautam 64), its drum tower in the southwest, and its Budai-Maitreya hall in between (Figures 2.391–3). From the upper-level walkway, one can also see various temple hall rooftops with fish-dragons (*chiwen*) and other creatures, like church gargoyles but protective, plus the city's nearby commercial areas (Figure 2.394–6). On the ground level, facing the yard, there is a temple shop with religious objects and a votive hall for ancestral tablets and offerings (Figures 2.397–8).

Rites with patriarchal, maternal, and trickster elements extend from the central courtyard and its trees to the rectilinear arrangement of halls, walls, and towers around it, with monks living and eating in upper-level areas on the sides and back of the temple. Mass-marketing ads are visible as well on Shanghai skyscrapers beyond the temple yard and buildings (Figure 2.399 and 2.399vid1–2). China's rapid conversion to global capitalist consumerism, in the last half century, might be seen here as a trickster spirit, in relation to Buddhist ideals of non-attachment, at the edges of the temple's sanctuary. But Jing'an's visitors still offer traditional devotion to ancestors and gods in burning spirit money and incense in the courtyard, as ritual props that can be bought in the temple shop or others nearby, through the interdependent, filial duty economy, with Buddhist equanimity and compassion—while fire consumes and smoke is shared, for better or worse, in spiritual or physical health.

Tricksters and Offerings

Traditional tricksters appear as demigods (*asuras*) under the feet of the Four Heavenly Kings, in the entrance hall near the courtyard of some Buddhist temples, such as the **Baohua (Jade Flower) Temple** in Shanghai. It originated in the thirteenth-century Song dynasty and was rebuilt in 2003. It includes two side halls, perhaps as drum and bell towers, with round roofs symbolizing heaven (Figures 2.400–09 and 2.408–09vid). The entrance hall demigods under each king are akin to the devil and dragon figures dominated by Archangel Michael and St. George in European church imagery—but more as a balancing with than conquering of the trickster rival. When I visited this temple, there also seemed to be a mournful, yet trickster aspect to the procession of monks and laity from the inner courtyard to the larger entry yard, carrying and then burning spirit money, plus a cardboard house, which passed through the flames into the spirit realm (Figures 2.410–11 and 2.410–11vid).

Such offerings are akin to the lighting of candles by Catholics (and Orthodox Christians) near a statue and to the swinging of a censer by clergy or "altar boys" during Mass, except that those rituals are typically performed inside the building—in a *bounded* environment. The rising smoke symbolizes personal or congregational prayers, seeking supportive interventions from above, from saints or angels as divine stagehands in relation to the animal drives in persons and groups. However, in Chinese temples, much

Figure 2.410 Monk and family with offerings for burning, Baohua Temple.

more is burned in an *open* courtyard, not just candles and incense. Special facsimiles of metal ingots (from folded *yuanbao* paper as spirit money), plus miniature paper houses, cars, clothing, servants, fans, phones, or other items (*zhizha*), sold in the temple and "paper shops" nearby, are burned and sent upward in the smoke to honor and help the spirits (Blake, *Burning* 164; Scott 4–5). This theatrical use of props, to give spirits "property" (also as collective family wealth), includes large boxes or "mailing bags" of paper ingots, which are burned after being folded, or purchased as pre-folded, with the name of a designated recipient sometimes written on the bag (133, 228).

Believers hope this gains them blessings from gods or bodhisattvas (especially with gold), or helps their ancestors (with silver), or avoids reprisals from the other dead (with copper or Hell Money cash) as positive supporters or negative tricksters (Blake, *Burning* 104). Gods, as heavenly spirits (*shen*), do not need the money but believers hope they will redistribute it to needy spirits and give similar blessings here in this world, especially with Chinese characters, such as "long life," printed on the cash (Scott 22). Human ghosts (*gui*),[11] especially those who are like "beggars," not supported by living relatives, may cause harm if ignored. Spirit money burned for them, especially at the Hungry Ghost Festival each fall, is "believed to ease the sufferings of the souls of those who died violently or unknown and far from home" (21, 91–6). In temples at other times, food and drink offerings, such as fruits, cakes, packaged items, canned drinks, and bottles of water are also placed near the images of bodhisattvas to honor

---

[11] See Poo 175–83, on the historical development of the characters for *gui* (representing the ancient shaman's death mask) as ghost and *shen* as natural/divine spirit, or *guishen* as more general, yet *rengui* as human ghost and *tianshen* as heavenly spirit or god, plus *ligui* as an evil, haunting, dead human ghost "who did not receive proper burial and sacrifice" (178).

them and gain aid—or left by the name plaque of a deceased loved one as a nurturing gesture. After a short time, the spiritual aspects of such offerings have gone to their destinations. The food may be taken home and consumed by people, thus sharing a meal with the departed or deities (122).

In Catholic and Orthodox faiths, God *orders all* from above and his saints are intercessors for the living, helping individuals with personal problems and protecting them from external evils. In the more collectivist Chinese tradition, from folk religion to Daoism and Buddhism, many gods, enlightened figures, intercessor spirits, good deceased souls, or orphaned ones (not remembered, honored, or given proper burial by family members) might benefit or harm the living. Offerings in smoke, food, and drink seek to *rebalance* such relations and potential threats, through animal-human drives of survival, reproduction, alliance-hierarchy, and nurturing, with various emotions, such as grief, fear, and hope. Like Christian rites of candles and incense, or the more regular offering of bread and wine as God's Body and Blood, shared at Holy Communion, such performances may trigger a spillover effect in the brain's staging of self and Other consciousness. Arousal emotions in the sympathetic nervous system may combine with quiescent feelings in the parasympathetic, evoking inner theatre networks of transcendent peace through the intersubjective pain/pleasure sacrifices of personal tragedies given new meaning, as *rasa*-cathartic flavors mix, regarding supportive/ trickster spirits and orphaned souls.

Coins, Fish, Monstrous Statues, and Memorials

Playfulness appears, as an animal-human-divine drive with paradoxical spillover effects, at the **Donglin Temple** of Shanghai, already mentioned above regarding its spirit screen, as rectilinear protection from straight-line traveling phantoms. Across the open thoroughfare from that screen, visitors choose one of three bridges, crossing a small rectangular pool, to reach the *Shanmen* entry gate (Figures 2.412–14, see also 2.255–9). Above it are five lotus flower ornaments, plus various standing and meditation-seated figures (Figure 2.415). Inside are two guardian statues, Heng and Ha (Figure 2.416). Once in the main courtyard, visitors meet a 5-meter tall, enamel-covered "Child of Wealth" (Shancai Tongzi, attendant to Guanyin), where they can toss coins toward the mouths of eight copper fish, which appear in the pool around him (Figures 2.417–19). Bringing such fish play to life, they can also buy a real carp in the *Shanmen* and release it into the pool (Figure 2.420).[12]

This temple has a central hall for Shakyamuni with a sunken panel dome (caisson) over his head, two attendants with him, and arhats along the sides (Figures 2.421 and 2.421vid). There are smaller halls with various bodhisattvas, including Manjushri (Wenshu) as male "Mother of the Buddhas" riding a lion (Quinter 591), which

---

[12] The Chinese character for *fish* (*yú*) is a homophone for superfluidity and thus abundance (Scott 197).

Monumental Developments in Patriarchal, Maternal, and Trickster Designs 165

Figure 2.415 Donglin Temple entry gate.

symbolizes nobility and courage, and Samantabhadra (Puxian) on an elephant with six tusks, symbolizing purification of the six senses (Figures 2.422–3). Adding to these animal-human figures, nearby halls include Ksitigarbha (Dizang) as "Earth Womb" (Leighton 94, 124, 207), Medicine Buddha, and the Pure Land trinity of Amitabha with two female bodhisattvas (Mahasthamaprapta as Shih Chih and Avalokiteshvara as Guanyin), plus Master Hui Yuan, founder of Pure Land Buddhism (Figures 2.424–7). Donglin Temple also displays a 34-meter-high, gilded, wooden, "thousand-armed, thousand-eyed" Guanyin on a 66-petal lotus flower, the largest indoor statue of its type in the world, with 9,999 mini-statues of her in the walls of the cave-like space, inside a fictive mountain with huge bronze doors, inscribed with 999 buddha images (Figures 2.428–30). Along with these patriarchal and maternal statues, there is a metallic sculpture at the top of the fictive mountain with a trickster mix of various figures in one large head: Guanyin with dragons as nose, Guan Yu (Garan Bodhisattva) as right ear, and Wei Tuo as left. Also, the Tathagata (Dhyani) Buddhas of the five cardinal directions are in the crown: north Amoghasiddhi, west Amitabha, center Vairocana, south Ratnasambhava (Baosheng), and east Akshobhya (Figures 2.431–32).

Various emotions might be felt by visitors in this temple: inner *scriptwriter/critic* awe and courage, especially with the huge statue, or *mime-improviser/designer* care and joy, with a fish release or coin toss at the pool. And yet, the temple also reflects *stagehand/ audience* trickster drives and personal memory associations—mediated by different aspects of self and Other (*actor*, *character*, *director*, and *stage manager*), perhaps toward detachment yet compassion. While the left-cortical, patriarchal ordering of nature is stressed through monumental, animal-human, and monstrous statues, a more right-cortical, maternal nurturing with playful aspects also becomes valued, in the temple's creative flourishes, as a balance of cooperative and competitive, contemplative and dramatic networks.

Like Baohua, **Yunxiang (Flying Cloud) Temple** in Shanghai (Tang dynasty style, rebuilt 2000 to 2004) shows the Four Heavenly Kings balancing on demigod *asuras*, but more colorfully and comically depicted (Figures 2.433–37). There is also a quadruple version of multi-headed, multi-armed Avalokiteshvara on a lotus blossom at the center of that hall, displaying prodigious compassion (Figure 2.438). Further inside, there is a small shelter for a laughing Budai-Maitreya (Figures 2.439–40) and a Mahasthamaprapta Hall with small Daoist statues clothed in robes, probably city or earth gods and goddesses (Figures 2.441–3). There is also a Samantabhadra Hall (Figure 2.444) and Manjushri Hall (Figure 2.445). The larger Mahavira Hall displays three similar Buddhas: Amitabha, Shakyamuni, and the Medicine Buddha (Bhaisajyaguru) from left to right (Figures 2.446–7). Along the sides of this hall are seated arhat statues with reliefs under them of animal and mythic figures, such as fish, deer, lion, dragon, phoenix, and apsaras (Figures 2.448–9). All these halls are arranged in and around a central courtyard with grass, bushes, and trees, open to the sky (Figure 2.450).

Figure 2.438 Multi-headed, multi-armed Avalokiteshvara in Yunxiang Temple.

There was scaffolding on the Mahavira Hall for its external refurbishment when I visited in 2014. Inside, at the back of the central Buddha figures, visitors playfully stuck a coin to a wooden painting, which somehow held it vertically (Figures 2.451–2). Orange-robed monks performed chants in private services in the side halls (reminding me of the Catholic rosary, sometimes prayed collectively in church). They also led the laity to the courtyard to burn paper offerings (Figures 2.453–5).

Under the central courtyard, there is a Buddha Hall with many ancestor tablets and a large statue of Ksitigarbha (Dizang in Chinese), who vowed not to achieve nirvana until all hells are emptied (Figures 2.456–7). Some memorials have photos, small animal figures, lotus candles, plastic ingots, trees, and fruit, or real fruit decaying (Figures 2.458–60). At the surface again, to the east of the central courtyard and bell tower is a "Seven-Treasure Pond" with live turtles and fish (Figure 2.461). On the west side of the temple, at the rectangular "Eight-Merit Water" pond, like at Donglin's Child of Wealth statue, visitors can buy a fish and release it, as a compassion ritual (Figure 2.462), which is typical of many Buddhist temples (Meyer 78). This offers a playful opportunity, too, for those who feed or touch the many fish (Figure 2.463).

At the rear of **Yufo (Jade Buddha) Temple** in Shanghai, there is a similar carp pond, where visitors feed fish—even letting them suck on fingers (Figures 2.464–5 and 2.465vid1). Such playful nurturing of animal life at a pool, like the respectful bowing with incense or burning of ghost money in the courtyard, or pouring oil as an offering, or ringing a bell, or chanting with monks, or singing near the burner, performs an inner/outer balancing act of various emotions (Figures 2.465vid2–7). These performances and observances may lead to a tasteful cathartic awareness of tragicomic *rasas*, including melodramatic temptations, whether or not they are watched by patriarchal orders from above.

Older Christian churches sometimes have a *graveyard* nearby, as communal connection to the life/death cycles of nature, akin to the inner courtyards and memorial rooms of a Chinese Buddhist temple, or the monks' graves, usually outside the north wall (Meyer 78). The oldest church in England, **Saint Martin's** in Canterbury, has a graveyard on several sides of it, which includes tombstones with Celtic-style ringed crosses and interlaced designs (Figure 2.466). Saint Martin's still has ancient thin red bricks and a Roman tomb built into its chancel wall (Figure 2.467). According to St. Bede in 731, it was built and used by Christians while the Romans still occupied Britain, prior to 409. It was renovated in the sixth century as the private chapel of Queen Bertha of Kent, a Frankish princess, and has Saxon walls along the nave from that time, showing the remains of a north-side doorway used until 1840 (Figures 2.468–72). It also became the center of Augustine of Canterbury's missionary work, when he was sent from Rome to England in 597. Its narthex entryway and tower are from the fourteenth-century Norman era. Videos and an inside tour are available at https://www.martinpaul.org/stmartins.htm.

There are memorials inside the church from the sixteenth to eighteenth centuries. The churchyard tombstones are from later centuries, yet they also form a communal connection across time, between the living and the dead, for those entering the building. As visitors approach the altar, with a sacristy and organ to the left, a female statue to the right (Bertha in a Saxon doorway), and stained-glass windows above, they may hope for spiritual rebirth and afterlife survival—like the dead in the yard before they passed away (Figures 2.473–89). Thus, the patriarchal tower and rectilinear entryway have a maternal/trickster aim: from left-cortical, theological order to right-cortical, metaphysical openness and subcortical, *stagehand* malleability, involving others in the earth. Yet church memorials and churchyard graves also reflect the inner *audience* of unique personal memories in each visitor.

The interplay evoked between brain-body theatres of living visitors extends toward dead and divine figures through interior controlled spaces and exterior tombstones. Here it involves, near the entry door, a twelfth-century baptismal font with a covered pool of holy water, plus a current play area with table and toys for the next generation (Figures 2.490–4). Like Yunxiang Temple with its underground room for honoring the dead, and its playful possibilities with a koi pond, Saint Martin's mixes a monumental heritage with various directions for seeking *beneficial* immortality. From its ancient Roman Catholic to Renaissance Anglican traditions, there are balancing acts of natural cycles and regenerative hopes in its chancel, nave, and graveyard elements, especially with the baptismal vessel, children's area, ancient bricks, and memorial stones.

Summa: Monumental Domination and Balancing Acts

A church or temple is an "outer theatre" involving performances (people, imagery, spaces, and designs), audience members (human and possibly divine), and backstage areas. Such elements reflect collective imaginings about a cosmic theatre—with Daoist gods, or Buddhist supernatural beings, or a Jewish, Muslim, or Christian God, plus angels and saints, watching and judging us, performing examples for us, and potentially interacting with our animal-human and natural orders.[13] Yet a religious building also reflects "inner theatre" elements in the staging of self/Other consciousness, within and between brains, *projecting* higher orders of control, nurturing, and support or mischief. In each of us, that inner theatre involves a developing, emotional awareness of mortal losses: personal aging, the death of loved ones, and the separation from natural being through symbolic language, stories, and abstractions.

From prehistory to various historical periods, aging, grieving, and hopeful humans created monumental dwellings for their ancestors and divinities. In Europe and China, they drew on sacred, domestic, judicial, and burial designs: from Greco-Roman *cellae*, homes, law courts, and catacombs—or family altars, imperial palaces, and caves. Believers used religious buildings to define sanctuaries, gather communities, send offerings, seek spiritual help, and dominate or rebalance threatening forces with good ones.

---

[13] Cf. Shults, "Problem" 53, on Pascal Boyer's cognitive theory of religion, summarizing "three different ways in which supernatural agents are connected to morality: the legislator, exemplar, and interested party models."

European churches show more of the *dominance* approach with towering spires above focused enclosures, low to high narthex-nave ceilings, exclusive sanctuaries, burial crypts with holy relics, and water fonts for purification rites in self-blessing or clerical baptism. These aspects of monumental churches reflect a cultural emphasis on patriarchal dimensions, evoking more of the visitor's left-cortical, *scriptwriter/critic* networks. But maternal, right-cortical, *mime-improviser/scene-designer* circuits are also involved, especially with the nurturing spaces of baptismal fonts, children's play areas, and graveyards, plus the central communion altar and tabernacle. Yet the latter are typically marked off as sacred territories of the chancel, where male clergy and their assistants perform on a higher platform, as with the pulpit there or midway along the nave.

In Catholic, Lutheran, and Anglican churches, there may be choir stalls near the high altar, originally for monks or other clergy, and a rood screen or communion railing, which sets off that special stage area. In Eastern Orthodox churches, a *templon* as iconostasis creates a barrier as well, with painted figures blocking a full view of the altar. Yet the central doorway is open during the service, allowing a framed glimpse of the Last Supper reenactment, when the priest stands at the altar with his back to the people. Such theatrical frames evoke inner *actor*, *director*, *stage manager*, *character*, and *operator* networks, with hubs in the prefrontal cortex. Thus, the visitor stages conscious associations of what is experienced in church, alone or with others, while the self performs for a potential divine Other—regarding cosmic conflicts of good and evil.

Many churches, such as the Lutheran **High Church of Saint Michael (Hauptkirche Sankt Michaelis)** in Hamburg (1786) and Catholic **Cathedral of Saint George** in Ragusa, Sicily (1718), display the Archangel Michael with a cross, conquering Satan as a bat-winged humanoid, or St. George on horseback with a lance, attacking that devil as a dragon (Figures 2.495–504). The Jesuit **Church of Saint Ildefonsus (San Ildefonso)** in Toledo (1765) even shows the Virgin Mary with a spear, fighting the serpentine Satan at her feet, while holding the baby Jesus and with baby John the Baptist nearby (Figures 2.505–09). Such scenes demonstrate patriarchal, heroic domination over nature and evil—as do Protestant churches with fewer images and a simple cross rather than a crucifix, stressing the Word of God from the pulpit and voices of a lay choir.

Churches' melodramatic good-versus-evil figures also reflect the God-given "dominion" of Adam over the animals, which he names in Genesis 2.19, using left-cortical verbal networks. However, Eve shows more right-cortical (Devil's Advocate) alternative views, along with the trickster-snake, representing subcortical animal-human mischief, as they tempt Adam into the original sin of disobedience. Yet, in the Catholic interpretation of the New Testament, Mary becomes the heroic "New Eve" getting *melodramatic revenge*. This involves a gender change in the fourth-century Latin Vulgate, with God's prophecy to the snake in Genesis 3.15. "I will put enmity between you and the woman, and between your seed and hers; she [or 'he' if referring to seed, as in the Greek, yet ambiguous in the original Hebrew] will crush your head, and you will lie in wait for her [or his] heel."

The devilish trickster of our animal drives, through subcortical *stagehands* and the temporal-lobe *audience* (as personal ghosts), continues to threaten the Catholic "communion of saints," including the faithful on earth, with mischievous temptations and abject losses. Ecclesiastical tricksters also appear with Gothic gargoyles, Baroque cherubs, and miracle-making reliquaries. The latter, believed to bear the positive trickster power of saints or Christ, relate to memorial tombs inside churches and in graveyards where the faithful may someday resurrect. All such monumental elements, along with spires, columns, domes, raised platforms/pulpits, screens, altars, reliquary crypts, and cruciform layouts, reflect the *conquering* of evil and death (God's punishment for original sin) through Christ's victory over Satan, as the "New Adam." This also involves each believer's moral control over nature's bodily temptations. The emotional drives of survival, reproduction, territoriality, and alliance-hierarchy are thus *sublimated* in European churches, through playful, nurturing, yet purifying (grooming/gossip) scenes and rites, toward spiritual meanings. These drives and meanings, reflected in European churches, are often projected from higher-order inner-theatre networks onto the dominant, mimetic-mythic, melodramatic framework of good triumphing over evil.

On the other side of Eurasia, Chinese temples deal with the fear of death and evil by *rebalancing* natural and supernatural energies. Daoism, building on Chinese folk religions, developed techniques for increasing the body's health, with the aim of immortality, sometimes with sexual rites (Schipper 144–5). Rather than viewing the flesh as tempting the soul toward evil, as in the Christian tradition, Daoist "Inner Alchemy puts sex at the center of its practice, just as it locates sex in the very center of the body" (154). Historically, this involved ascetic rites, with "elixirs," potentially extending one's life toward immortality. The human body was believed to be "a small universe in itself, [and] had its own spirits of the Four Seasons and Five Elements [wood, fire, water, earth, and metal], parallel to those outside the body" (Yun 27). Sometimes elixirs backfired, however, as with the deaths of various emperors from the third century BCE to the eighteenth century CE. Mercury (cinnabar) or arsenic was often used, which killed the emperor but preserved the corpse from decay, encouraging a belief in his immortality.

The Daoist rebalancing of heat and coolness in the body, through diet, medicinal herbs, and the circulation of *qi*, relates to the *feng-shui* ("wind-water" geomancy) of Chinese temples, optimally facing the sun's warmth in the south, with open-air courtyards and multiple shrines dispersed along a central axis. Roofs have curled corners (as if upturned by the wind) and auspicious animals on their ridges, not to show dominance over nature, but to balance with its forces. Mountain temples are arranged along preexisting contours, with shrines at various levels, on a shifting axis, following the Dao (the Way) of nature—as considered in the next chapter with Buddhist and Daoist temples. Inside the main Daoist hall, large regal statues (usually of the founder Laozi, the Three Pure Ones, or the Three Emperor-Officials) exemplify wise leadership, in a tradition of the Emperor as "Son of Heaven," who has a filial duty to make offerings to the gods and ancestors, thus ensuring nature's kindness and generosity toward his people. Other gods are also arrayed in smaller shrines, including birth-year figures, for visitors' offerings, prayers, and fortune-learning. Evil spirits are redirected away from the temple with guardian statues at the entrance (and sometimes a "spirit screen"), plus high thresholds at each hall's doorways, which the human visitor should step over, not on.

Buddhist temples, like Daoist, face south, along a centrally balanced or flowing axis, with "feminine curves on the roof ... [as] the natural line ... among mountains," plus ponds, bushes, and trees arrayed in the paved courtyards (Y. Wang 213). Instead of or along with Daoist gods, various enlightened beings are displayed, sometimes with huge statues. Typically, the laughing Future Buddha (Budai-Maitreya) greets the visitor in the first hall, with the Protector Buddha (Wei Tuo) on the other side of him, facing the center of the temple complex. Often the Four Heavenly Kings or Heng and Ha are nearby as guardians. Next (or in place of Budai) is the compassionate Guanyin, a female nurturing bodhisattva pouring aid from a vase or with multiple arms and heads to help others, across many lifetimes, especially those who bow with incense in the courtyard and leave money near the statue. Guanyin was originally male in India, as Avalokiteshvara, "Observes Without Obstacles" (or "With Compassion"). But he became female in China after the eighth century, as Guan Shih Yin, "The One Who Hears the Cries of the World" (Palmer et al. 5–7).

The main or side halls may have various other figures. Ksitigarbha holds a staff and jewel because he vowed to live in the hell realm, with the staff for opening it, helping others there until all sentient beings evolve beyond it. Samantabhadra rides a six-tusked elephant, showing the meditative practice of purifying the body's six senses. Manjushri exemplifies wisdom while riding a powerful lion. Amitabha, the Buddha of infinite light, promises a Pure Land as "Western Paradise" to those who chant his name and give offerings. The main elevated hall usually has a large statue of Shakyamuni, the historical Buddha, sometimes with two figures, the older Mahakashyapa on the left and young Ananda on the right, identically posed as early disciples and patriarchs. Or Amitabha and Medicine Buddha, or Samantabhadra and Manjushri, may pose on each side of the Buddha Tathagata (or Vairocana) in serene contemplation (de Visser 137–9, 202). Along the sides of the temple complex are lecture, meditation, library, dining, and residence halls for the monks.

As inspiration for religious monuments, the human fear of death and evil is resolved in a Buddhist temple through the natural *balance* of left-cortical detachment and yet right-cortical compassion for all living things. This re-solution involves supernatural progress through multiple lifetimes, beyond the suffering caused by attachments, while developing equanimity about change. Evil beings are viewed compassionately, too, with demons suffering from bad karma, like hungry ghosts, animals, and many humans—but all capable of developing toward higher levels of merit and wisdom. Some temples, such as Baohua and Yunxiang, have large statues of the Four Heavenly Kings in the entry hall, as guardian forces of the four cardinal directions, stepping on demigods (*asuras*) that envy them. But they are not angels or saints conquering devils, as in Christian iconography. They exemplify transcendent rulers in the divine realm, balancing on semi-divine beings below, holding them down to teach them, in realms above the human, as all beings progress, through meditation and merit, toward enlightenment.

There are many patriarchal figures in Daoist and Buddhist temples, along with rectilinear designs, evoking left-cortical, symbolic, *scriptwriter/critic* networks in the visitor. Yet to some degree, they are balanced with natural, nurturing, right-cortical, *mime/designer* elements: curved eaves on dispersed shrines in courtyards open to the sky, with ponds and plants, plus Queen Mother of the West and maternal Mazu/Doumu or compassionate female Guanyin and Shih Chih statues. There are hints, too, of subcortical, animal-human, *stagehand* drives, in supportive/disruptive balances, with dragons and other animal figures on columns and roof ridges, or with Samantabhadra and Manjushri riding trickster beasts. Each figure, as a distinctive character with stories and symbols, displays a balance of left-cortical meditative focus, right-cortical compassionate openness, and limbic/subcortical emotional drives, refined through multiple lifetimes. Of course, such palatial temples also depend on the favor of earthly rulers and wealthy believers to be built, restored, and maintained, as mostly wooden structures (with stone platforms and outer walls) from centuries ago and from recent decades when the Communist Party began valuing these monuments again—after destroying them earlier or turning them into factories—for national pride, moral order, and economic growth.

Westerners typically leave flowers at gravesites, inside and outside churches. Chinese burn lots of incense, spirit money, and other symbolic objects, such as cardboard houses, while also leaving food, candles, and flowers for departed ancestors, gods, and bodhisattvas. Both traditions thus express *abject* loss and yet the hope of positive returns from the Real of the spirit realm (Kristeva).[14] The burning of offerings, with smoke rising, poses real dangers in this one: to the wooden structures, the lungs of participants, and the natural environment. Yet courtyard incense burners manifest a continued connection between the living and the dead, with persistent filial ties and duties. This *collectivist* dimension of East Asian identity involves right-cortical *mime/ designer* reproductive/nurturing emotions and subcortical *stagehand* survival drives, with serious mourning and playful hopes, through maternal and trickster performances, as well as patriarchal demands. When people die in this context, they believe they will be honored in the future—because their spirits may threaten relatives from beyond the grave if they are not.

Collectivist networks of the living, honoring and indebted to the dead, involve Confucian ideals of filial loyalty, along with personal ghosts of the inner theatre's temporal lobe *audience*. But Daoist temple rites help individuals, for a donation fee, to exorcise spirits or aid family members in migrating across afterlife realms. Great men of the past also become *deified* individuals, memorialized in Confucian and Daoist temple statues (Puett). Likewise, Buddhist temples display large images of certain persons as exemplary individuals, paradoxically showing huge faces and bodies

---

[14] Kristeva relates the abject to eruptions of the Lacanian Real, because it "draws me toward the place where meaning collapses" (2). Yet she also finds it at the edges of meaning-making in religion and art: "The various means of *purifying* the abject—the various catharses—make up the history of religions, and end up with that catharsis par excellence called art, both on the far and near side of religion" (17). She associates the abject with rites of defilement, exclusion, and taboo, from "paganism" to monotheistic religions, as well as "*transgression* (of the Law)." Specifically, she defines it as "integrated in the Christian Word [of God] as a threatening otherness—but always nameable, always totalizeable."

(sometimes cut into cliffs or caves) as *egoless* ideals of devoted meditation. In comparison, monumental European churches, built in stone, emphasize vast spaces of divine immortality, with tall towers and vaulted ceilings inspiring ego-soul transcendence. Yet they contain mostly life-size or smaller images of Catholic/Orthodox saints and Christ, or the Protestant purity of humans preaching and singing hymns without such images.

Monuments to God, gods, or bodhisattvas have been created at great cost throughout human history, often reflecting ideologies in conflict with rival groups for holy territories—with more left-cortical, patriarchal dimensions in rectilinear, altar-focused designs and male figures. The vertical shamanism of religious hierarchies, West and East, became expressed in basilicas, cruciform churches, spires, pagodas, palace-like temples, large statues, and cliff carvings. But many churches and temples also have maternal images or curved, natural, contextual designs, especially with martyria, baptisteries, cave spaces, and open courtyards with vegetation, evoking right-cortical, nurturing networks. These images, designs, and networks mediate the otherness of subcortical trickster impulses: mischievous play, personal or group rivalry (especially between Abrahamic siblings as Children of God), and outright rebellion. Such dynamics in religious buildings might evoke a *rasa*-cathartic recognition of the trickster otherness in each of us, in our animal-human drives—not to purify self or group through sacrifice and *scapegoating*, but to become more aware of our inner/outer theatres of cruelty, repression, and projection. Thus, religious monuments may point toward a better evolution of human minds/souls (and their gods) with bio-cultural drives and emotions tasted at a discerning, respectful, yet questioning distance.

In recent centuries, there has been a shift toward left-cortical dominance with European monotheistic churches and Western individualism. This shift appears especially in Protestant churches where a verbal focus on God is stressed through abstract symbols (such as the cross), Bible readings, and preaching—more than in Catholic and Orthodox churches. Those traditional faiths maintained right-cortical evocative, figural images, including Marian tragicomic scenes, plus bread/wine "transubstantiation," Holy Communion, and confession rituals, along with incense, candles, and relics.

As with Augustine traveling from Rome to preach at Canterbury in the sixth century, Western values have spread to new territories, especially in the last half millennium, through European missionaries colonizing Asia, Africa, and the Americas. Such Westernization eventually involved, in the secular realm, objective reason, advanced technologies, and capitalist abstractions (fetishizing money, automation, and consumerism), as competitive extensions of left-cortical functions and animal-human dominance drives of territory and hierarchy. While China and many other nations around the globe have embraced individualist consumerism, that value system is also becoming more collectivist in the West through mass and social media, even as China maintains collective top-down authority through the Communist Party.

Degrees of worship, sacrifice, and playfulness are extending now from churches and temples of the past to new physical and virtual sites, with monumental investments of money, time, and energy. Hopefully, the exploration here of Western and Eastern traditions will help readers to play a better role in shaping the evolution of religious and secular values, on many stages and screens. Melodramatic fear of suffering and death, through abstractions from nature in prior religious contexts, may fuel the left-cortical, *scriptwriter/critic*'s objectifying of certain places, things, and people as supernaturally good or evil. This has led to conflict and bloodshed, from animal sacrifices and personal mortifications to warfare (especially with Abrahamic rivalries) and genocide. Churches and temples are monuments of such ideological competition—and yet also of beneficial cooperation between persons and groups.

We can do better in the future by understanding Western and non-Western expressions of the subcortical, animal-human, sometimes abject, trickster *stagehands* in us, between us, and projected by us onto others—regarding our temporal-lobe *audience* ghosts and right-cortical *mime/designer* (holistic Devil's Advocate) improvisations. Through *rasa*-cathartic awareness, tasting our emotions reflectively, even while immersed in a religious building (or virtual screen space), we can shift our brains between right-cortical, sympathetic openness to complex contexts and left-cortical, parasympathetic abstractions, thus clarifying our personal associations and primal drives. We can choose to *reconfirm* the moral values of inherited traditions—or to *alter* their altars of abject, bloody, heroic sacrifices, especially with monumental conflicts of righteous values. Thus, the next chapter compares sacrificial altars and environments from the past, in Europe and China, as neuro-theatrical spaces of cooperation and competition, of morality and consumption, of tragicomedy and melodrama, with patriarchal, maternal, personal, and supportive/trickster networks, evolving toward the future—through us.

3

Places and Spaces with Super-Natural Translations

The last chapter considered monumental developments in the historical styles of European churches, from homes and catacombs to cruciform or curved designs. Ancient *cellae*, basilicas, and mausoleums were altered with spires, domes, columns, and screens. These elements showed the dominance of patriarchal divinity over trickster natures, through moral ideals and political hierarchies. That chapter made comparisons between such enclosed, altar-focused, mostly rectilinear, often vertically vast interior spaces, in various church designs, and those of Chinese temples, influenced by imperial palaces. They involved multiple open yards and dispersed memorial halls along the earth's surface or carved into caves and cliffs, with pools, plants, trees, pagodas, and huge statues. Such temples expressed a dialectical balance of *yin* and *yang*, natural and supernatural, inclined and upright, tragicomic-contemplative and melo-dramatic, horizontal shamanism and vertical religion.

This chapter will continue to explore design elements in exemplary churches and temples, as holy or contested sites, regarding how space is *shaped* by the architecture and *performs* around the visitor, with specific artworks and rites. Religious buildings shape not only sacred spaces, but also human brains, grooming their purity within the authorized moral group by evoking inner theatre networks. These include the behavior-monitoring *stage manager*, plus the left and right parietal *costume-body definer* and *designer*, which construct a verbal first-person and spatial third-person sense of self and Otherness—sometimes with sacrificial demands and scapegoats, through the animal-human seeking of symbolic meaning and narrative purpose.

Outer Spaces and Inner Networks

The performance of space around the visitor becomes especially meaningful in a sacred building, where it evokes a spiritual resonance of aura and awe, between outer and inner theatricality. Such resonance involves animal-human drives, shared across cultures yet fashioned differently in each brain through familial, social, and religious (or secular) frameworks, with Chinese and European, porous and bounded, group and ego characteristics. Thus, architectural layouts of sacred places reflect natural, cultural, and super-natural dimensions of inner, outer, and cosmic theatres. Gods, ancestors, saints, angels/devils, or Buddhas possibly watch and perform, too, as ideal scriptwriter, director, designer, stage manager, or actor/character. (With Buddhism, there is also "karma" as an automatic, metaphysical, stage manager of multi-life justice.) These dimensions and spirits may attract the visitor with believable meanings in one's life: toward *sacrificial submission*, controlling trickster pleasures and disruptive emotions through moral values, which sometimes conflict between religious groups. Yet sacred spaces may also offer a *rasa*-catharsis (emotion-contagion flavor awareness) of desires and fantasies—especially through cross-cultural interplay, if we compare differences between religious buildings with open minds.

Rectilinear, cruciform shapes became dominant in European church architecture, through narthex-nave-chancel and transept designs, sometimes with pointed arches and towers, expressing left-cortical analytic *scriptwriter/critic* functions with patriarchal authority and sacrificial demands (Table 1.3). Church spaces were thus places to evoke yet tame the trickster *stagehands* of animal-human drives within and between brains. Left-cortical functions are reflected in (and reprogramed by) the channeling of visitors from narthex to nave, along the main or side aisles, focusing them toward the raised altar and high ceilings of sacrificial and vertical awe.

In churches across Europe, round elements in columns, arches, domes, and apses became popular as well, especially in pre- and post-Gothic periods. These added right-cortical holistic *mime-improviser/scene-designer* inclinations with maternal, nurturing aspects. There were also circular, ellipsoid, or polygonal alternatives, in church floorplans or baptistery buildings, akin to the ancient Roman Pantheon and Christian martyr mausoleums. Many churches had fourteen "Stations of the Cross" along the walls, for believers to meditate on the cruel, painful, and sacrificial tricks of fate, apparently desired by God the Father as divine spectator.

Circumambulating these stations, even in a rectilinear space, believers' inner theatres meditate on each scene of Christ's passion, using left-cortical, sequential, mythic *scriptwriter/critic* and right-cortical, empathetic, mimetic *mime/designer* networks. This personal rite developed in the fifteenth century, with stations initially outside churches, reflecting the "Via Dolorosa" sites in Jerusalem. Such re-imagined sites were created after medieval Crusaders conquered the Muslim territory and St. Francis (whose bleeding stigmata imitated the wounds of Christ) founded the Custody of the Holy Land in 1217. Franciscan friars have led pilgrimages there since the fourteenth century. For pilgrims who believe they are walking in the tragicomic footsteps of Christ's passion, the climax is the Church of the Holy Sepulchre, site of his hilltop death, cave burial, and transcendent resurrection—as considered in the last chapter. Other parts of that story will be explored here, through historical sites and biblical territories, involving the Virgin Mother also. Visitors are encouraged to identify with these divine tricksters, Jesus and Mary, plus other saints, who transform physical pain, sexual abstinence, political failure, and existential loss into holiness at mimetic-mythic places, reflected in church spaces.

Chinese temples, across various dynasty styles, developed a consistent use of *yang* roofs, coming down from heaven, with upturned eaves (for over a thousand years), round *yin* columns, rising from earth, and other curvilinear aspects of rectilinear gates, walls, and halls. Temples harmonize the five elements/phases with their colors and directions: blue-green wood east, white metal west, yellow earth center, black water north, and red fire south. They also balance Confucian and Daoist principles from the *Lüshi Chunqiu*, compiled by Lü Buwei (239 BCE): *shi* (well-suitedness) with moderate *yin* space and *yang* height, both inside halls (*yin*) and outside (*yang*)—using symmetry and rhythm, like harmonious music (S. Cook 332, 335). "If the house is large, there is an excess of Yin; if the tower is high, there is an excess of Yang" (Knoblock and Riegel 69).

Each temple complex shapes its spaces through open courtyards, natural contexts, and mostly horizontal planes—yet also with vertical columns and sometimes pagodas, drum/bell towers, and huge statues. Visitors are drawn in various directions by multiple halls, which often have dragons, animals, or other protective tricksters as *wenshou* on roof ridges. Thus, patriarchal *scriptwriter/critic*, maternal *mime-improviser/ designer*, emotional-memorial *audience*, and supportive/trickster *stagehand* aspects are explored in further examples here from China (with Buddhist ties to India) and Europe (with Christian ties to Jerusalem). This chapter reveals how design elements shape the spaces, figures, and scenes performing around the visitor, regarding the historical, mythical, or natural significance of each site—interacting with inner theatre networks.

Church styles changed historically (more than Chinese temples) from ancient to medieval. Romanesque judicial solidity developed toward more vertical Gothic aspirations in thin columns, pointed arches, and colorful stained-glass windows, with external gargoyles, flying buttresses, and high towers. Renaissance churches moved back to classical balance and restrained humanism, yet included *Madonna Lactans* paintings, with Mary's bare breast (sometimes at odd angles) feeding the baby Jesus, especially in the late fourteenth to early sixteenth centuries. With Protestant Reformation threats, Catholic churches developed dramatic, swirling, even fleshier, Baroque designs (e.g. Saint Agnes in *Agone*), countering the splinter Christians' abstract, symbolic, and sometimes iconoclastic purifications with right-cortical, nurturing, angelic fantasies, including chubby cherubs as sanctioned tricksters. (The Catholic Council of Trent, 1545–63, limited nudity in religious art, so as not to excite lust, yet validated holy imagery.) After Neoclassical and Gothic Revival movements in the eighteenth to nineteenth centuries, modernist designs in the twentieth began incorporating Protestant purities toward cleaner *scriptwriter/critic* forms, following "function" with non-ornamented, geometric designs. Yet postmodern styles featured playful, right cortical *mime-improviser* and subcortical trickster-*stagehand* elements—as considered in this chapter.

Wood and Stone, Harmonizing or Controlling Translations

Chinese temples have long expressed a dialectical balance between permanence and change, involving authority, sustenance, and playfulness. Their *wooden* structures were destroyed and rebuilt many times across the centuries, while maintaining similar styles. Traditionally, most European churches were made of *stone*, stressing dominance over the landscape and transcendent vertical rapture, in a shift of ancient traditions from Greek to Roman (Jones 2: 269–70). Church graveyards also use tombstones as durable memorials in a tradition extending back, perhaps, to the monoliths of Stonehenge five thousand years ago (161–2). Instead, Chinese temples have small wooden "spirit tablets" commemorating deceased ancestors, although some sites include stone pagodas, as enduring reliquaries, and stone steles with imperial messages. Even the carved spaces and sculptures of Buddhist cave temples employ *feng-shui* (wind-water) principles to flow in harmony with the local *qi*, rather than dominating nature.

European churches are built around translated relics or upon mythic, yet contested sites, as are Chinese temples. But church spaces often stress the *melodramatic* ideal of heroic sacrifice to redeem suffering and death, as punishments for original sin, while *dominating* nature and *controlling* devilish temptations. These elements contrast with Chinese folk religion's more *tragicomic* sense of sacrifice through *debt* to ancestors and *supplication* to gods, Daoist *balancing* of natural forces, and Buddhist *harmonizing* of karmic desires toward non-attachment and mindful awakening.

Some European churches are built to blend with their natural environments (Geva). Yet Chinese and Tibetan Buddhism, along with Daoism, has a stronger tradition of "sacred landscapes" as expressions of the "natural and potential ... Spark of Awakening" in each person (Winters 152). Such West and East Eurasian differences become reflected in the more focused or dispersed, sequential or contextual, closed or open, mechanically controlling or naturally blended spaces of churches and temples. Thus, sacred sites and materials evoke various participatory emotions—through inner, social, and cosmic theatre resonance. Comparisons also involve competitive and cooperative, progressive or conservative styles, which stress individualist or collectivist meanings with different types of sacrifices, through spatial networks performing around visitors, who are both spectators and actors.

Holy Land to Europe translations of Jesus, Mary, and martyred saints, as ideals of heroic, suffering individuals, are shown at dominant sites with relic attachments. These reflect inner theatre networks differently from Daoist and Buddhist ideals of natural harmony and ego dissolution in Chinese temple spaces. In the Christian case, left-cortical *scriptwriter/critic* demands are stressed, in a fixed filtering of right-cortical *improviser/designer* feelings and subcortical *stagehand* drives. Thus, believers' brain spirits interact with patriarchal, maternal, and trickster reflections in church spaces, especially through ties to holy territories and Stations of the Cross. The participation of an individual mind (or soul) in the "communion of saints" through the imitation of Christ (*imitatio Christi*) hinges upon a transcendent mystery, set theatrically at certain Jerusalem sites. Why did God the Creator-Father desire to watch his Son suffer and die for the sins of humankind, while becoming that victim, too, in loving pain, through a woman's role in the sacrifice, against devilish temptations to forego it? Through God's will, relic translations, and church spaces, how does the suffering ego of each believer mimetically transform from victim to hero, with group identifications as good versus evil projections, controlling natural drives? How has this *melodramatic* mode created historical sacrifices of self and others?

Terra Sancta Territories

A sacred site evokes awe by giving a religious context for fears of death, hopes of healing or immortality, and yet rivalries over territory. Paradoxically, the brain-body systems of pleasure and pain, arousal and quiescence may activate together in ecstatic moments, with believers' inner theatres finding connections to history and myth, through animal-human, competitive and cooperative, territorial and hierarchical drives. "Sacred" spaces, where the divine touches the human, are tied to the costly signaling "sacrifices" demanded of group members and sometimes of rivals. The Latin word *sacer* means something set apart from daily life as holy or accursed. A church as "sanctuary" may be a site of safety or threat, of community or conflict, with evil attracted to its holiness and humans contending for its super-natural resources, especially when "religions" hold related yet rival beliefs (from *religare*, to bind).

Many sites in Jerusalem became sacred spaces through rivalry, such as the territory of the Temple Mount (al-Haram al-Sharif) with its **Dome of the Rock (Qubbat as-Sakhra)** and Al-Aqsa Mosque, holy to Muslims, plus the **Western Wall**, holy to Jews as a remnant of the Second Temple (Figure 3.1). Jesus visited that Herodian Temple, challenging its animal sacrifices and currency exchanges, according to the New Testament. In 1099, medieval Crusaders turned the Dome of the Rock into an Augustinian church and the Templar Knights believed it to be the site of Solomon's original temple, along with the Al-Aqsa mosque, which they expanded and turned into their headquarters, as part of the king's palace (with a stable for horses). The Crusaders made the Dome of the Rock, as *Templum Domini*, a model for their round churches and banking centers across Europe, such as Temple Church in London. But both buildings became mosques again in 1187, when Saladin and the Muslim Ayyubids reconquered Jerusalem.

Likewise, the "Via Dolorosa" became a popular route for medieval European pilgrims in Jerusalem, commemorating various historical-mythical sites, from Jesus's condemnation to crucifixion soon after his temple disruption (in the Synoptic Gospels). Since the eighth century, pilgrim-tourists have walked various versions of the route, stopping in awe at supposed locations for the Passion of Jesus (Figure 3.2). In the Middle Ages, "passion plays" enacted that drama in European towns and a dozen Crusades were launched, across several centuries, to take and retake Holy Land territory from Muslim rivals. Today, inside or near many European churches, "Stations of the Cross" offer Passion images, increasing brain-spirit ties to exotic Jerusalem sites along the Via Dolorosa (Stations 1–9), as well as the yard and interior of the Holy Sepulchre (10–14). Praying at the Stations in other churches, too, or with related Mysteries of the Rosary (using a string of beads as performance prop), believers transform their personal grief, aligned with Mary and Jesus's Passion, into the Creator's sacrificial demands of love, will, and knowledge. Yet they also align their little lives with Europe's colonial expansions, across Mediterranean and global territories, as God's apparent crusading and missionary plan—with wars, conversions, and sacred spaces.

The **Church of the Flagellation** (Figure 3.3), in the Muslim Quarter of Jerusalem's Old City, stands on the site where, according to legend, Jesus was tortured with whips and a crown of thorns. This church is part of a Franciscan monastery, along with the Church of the Condemnation and Imposition of the Cross, as Second Station. They are near the Umariya madrasa as the First, at the site of the ancient Antonia Fortress, where Jesus was supposedly condemned by the Roman governor, Pontius Pilate. Although current scholarship disagrees, Franciscan clergy have led pilgrims from this area to other Stations since the fourteenth century. A similar route was taken hundreds of years earlier.

The Flagellation church was completely rebuilt in 1929, but in a twelfth-century style, with a narrow nave, neo-Romanesque arches, and stained-glass windows showing scenes of Christ's Passion, which ostensibly occurred there. A window above the altar depicts the bound Christ (Figure 3.4). Another shows Pilate washing his hands to absolve himself during his judgment of Jesus (Figure 3.5). The dome over the altar depicts the Crown of Thorns placed on Jesus by Roman soldiers mocking him (Figure 3.6). A tile on the floor claims the site as "Terra Santa" (Italian for Holy Land) in the custody of the Franciscan Order (Figure 3.7). Such details in this symmetrical, rectilinear nave, with its curved columns and arches, demonstrate left-cortical, patriarchal *dominance* over the space, in relation to right-cortical/limbic sympathy for suffering and loss, exemplified by the Son of God. Personal fear of divine judgment, with the patriarchal demand for sacrifice, yet grief at Jesus's suffering for the sins of humankind, plus hope at God's redemptive power, might be evoked in visitors through their own limbic *audience* ghosts and subcortical *stagehands*. Christian pilgrimages to the site, across the centuries, are thus fueled by inner theatre scenes, in each believer's brain, of Jesus as filial heroic trickster, rebelling against the Roman Empire, while submitting to his Father's will. Yet this attractive, melodramatic metanarrative might also be viewed, with tragicomic *rasa*-cathartic aftertastes, as fueling the economics of historical and spiritual tourism—with bloody mimetic-mythic conflicts over Terra Sancta (in Latin).

Not part of the Via Dolorosa, yet near where it begins and also popular with pilgrimage tours, the **Church of Saint Anne** in Jerusalem (Figures 3.8–9) evokes the joyful site of Mary's birth and childhood, in the home of her father Joachim and mother Anne, according to medieval Crusaders. The doctrine of Mary's Immaculate Conception in the womb of Anne involves Roman Catholic efforts, across the centuries, to purify Mary, as later God-bearer, from prior Greco-Roman stories of gods, such as Zeus/Jupiter, impregnating human females. Mary's sinless origin was debated by male theologians in the Middle Ages, such as Bernard of Clairvaux and Thomas Aquinas, in relation to the earlier doctrine of Augustine that all humans are born into "original sin" through the sexual act of conception. While Bernard and Aquinas objected to the popular notion of Mary as free from sin, even in Anne's womb, it continued until Pope Pius IX, on the advice of his bishops, converted the idea to dogma in 1854, based on tradition rather than scripture (Gribble). Bernadette Soubirous's mystical vision of Mary confirmed this, at the cave-grotto of Lourdes in 1858, when the apparition declared: "I am the Immaculate Conception." This defines Mary as a paradoxical ideal for Catholic women, with left-cortical purity, yet right-cortical nurturing as "Virgin Mother." It relates to frequent depictions of her as youthful throughout life, with idealized, light-colored skin, because untouched by original sin and its punishment of aging in Genesis. Yet Black Madonnas also exist, perhaps as earth-mother figures, showing the influence of ancient Egyptian Isis-Horus images (Begg 13–15).

A Byzantine basilica was built in the fifth century near the legendary site of Mary's conception and Anne's home, over the ruins of a Roman temple to Asclepius or Serapis, which included two pools of healing water. They were thought to be the pool of Bethesda, where Jesus healed a paralyzed man, violating Sabbath rules, according to John 5.1–13. The basilica was destroyed by Persian invaders in 614 and after its reconstruction was destroyed again by the Muslim ruler al-Hakim in 1009 (like the Holy Sepulchre). The current, Romanesque Church of Saint Anne was built by Crusaders in 1131–8, and then turned into a madrasa by Muslim rulers. It later became a garbage dump, but the medieval church was restored in 1856 and then administered by French missionaries. The rectangular stone columns, yet round, slightly peaked arches and curved, cross-vaulted ceiling in its three-aisled nave (Figures 3.10–12) express not only left-cortical, patriarchal, *scriptwriter/critic* security in this enclosure of holy spaces, but also right-cortical, nurturing, *mime/designer* networks, over a womblike crypt as home-site of Jesus's mother and grandparents. The ruins of the Byzantine basilica, earlier Roman temple, and healing pools exist nearby (Figures 3.13–17), again evoking historical domains of patriarchal, territorial power and yet maternal healing, tied to miraculous trickster *stagehands*.

Spatial Rivalries

Among many other sacred spaces in Jerusalem involving the life of Jesus is his Last Supper location in the "Upper Room" of the **Cenacle** on Mount Zion. At least since the fourth century, it has also been valued as the site where Christ appeared after his resurrection, confronting the disbelief of Thomas, and where the Holy Spirit descended on the apostles at Pentecost in tongues of fire (Clausen 15). Today, just foundations of the ancient building exist, plus walls that are probably Byzantine and a ceiling with Gothic rib-vaulting. Thus, the Upper Room space shows the remains of a large Crusader basilica, with a *mihrab* from 1524 when Ottoman rulers took it from the Franciscans and turned it into a mosque (Figures 3.18–20). Yet the area has been valued, too, since the sixth century, as Mary's Jerusalem home and death site, commemorated by the nearby Church of the Dormition, which means "falling asleep," because Mary was assumed into heaven (Re'em and Berkovich 60–2). The Cenacle is also located over the legendary "Tomb of David," as a treasured space for brain-spirit projections by many generations of Jews, Christians, and Muslims, sometimes in conflict.

Another memorial space, the Coptic Orthodox **Church of Queen Helen**, adjacent to and below the Holy Sepulchre, now belongs to the Armenian Apostolic Church. It has images of Constantine's mother, St. Helena, plus other figures, and a stairway leading down to a large cistern of water, supposedly used by her forces during their pilgrimage quest (Figures 3.21–7). In 326–8, they translated many relics from Jerusalem to Rome, including the "True Cross" and its nails, ostensibly used in the crucifixion of

Jesus three centuries before. Thus, patriarchal and maternal spaces of awe and care, territoriality and possessiveness, abound in Jerusalem, with modern trickster problems of authenticating its historical treasures—such as splinters from the True Cross venerated in churches across Europe. The vital role of water for survival, especially in a dry climate, is also exemplified by the cistern within this church, as with the Bethesda pool ruins at the Church of Saint Anne. The animal-human need for water is likewise associated with spiritual rebirth and purity, as shown by baptismal spaces and holy water fonts in Catholic churches worldwide.

The nineteenth-century Russian Orthodox **Church of Saint Alexander Nevsky**, masked by an ordinary building façade, contains remnants of Constantine's Holy Sepulchre church. It also houses the ostensible "eye of a needle," as a hole in the ancient stone wall (Figure 3.28), through which it is easier for a camel to pass than a rich man to enter heaven, according to Jesus (Matt. 19.24). The hole was probably used by travelers who arrived at the city wall when the gate was closed. The round archway of a stone gate was discovered (Figure 3.29), along with the wall's hole as needle's eye, when workmen were digging the foundation for a Russian pilgrims' hostel in 1883. Archeologists dated the gate's wall to the second century and column to the eleventh, not to the time of Jesus. Nevertheless, the excavation also found the bottom of a wide stairway (Figure 3.30) going up from the gate toward the lost Constantinian church, which made a fortuitous connection to the Roman emperor who founded the central city of Eastern Orthodoxy, Constantinople (today's Istanbul), and legitimized the Christian Church. A chunk of the rock of Calvary from the Holy Sepulchre was moved here and a wooden crucifix placed in it, to connect these theatrical spaces of sacred, sacrificial history, which involve the current visitor as both spectator and actor (Figures 3.31–2).

The modern Orthodox chapel upstairs, dedicated to a thirteenth-century Russian warrior-saint, has the traditional *templon* wall with icons blocking the holiest area, accessible only to priests, plus a stone altar in front of it and a coffin shaped reliquary with an icon on top (Figures 3.33–4). Patriarchal authority is clear here with rectilinear design elements and *templon* icons. But there are smaller, female icons, horizontally and vertically arrayed on stands and walls, under glass or behind a metal frame for kissing (Figures 3.35–8). There was also a devoted nun chanting from a prayer stand when I visited with my son Luke in 2012, adding to the sense of awe I felt with the medieval and ancient elements, through the modern scaffolding (Figure 3.39).

Not to be confused with the Russian Orthodox or other Eastern (Orthodox Catholic) Rites, the Armenian Apostolic Church, like the Egyptian Coptic, is one of six Oriental Orthodox Rites that have much smaller populations than the Roman Catholic Church worldwide, yet have traditions going back to the start of Christianity. Ancient Armenia included what is now eastern Turkey, where Armenians suffered a genocide under the Islamic Ottoman Turkish Empire in 1915–18, with about a million people killed. The Armenian Apostolic Church, which traces its identity to the missionary work of Jesus's apostles, Bartholomew and Thaddeus, is the oldest state-authorized form of Christianity. It started in the early fourth century, prior to Constantine's conversion as Roman emperor, and it separated from the authority of Rome and

Constantinople in 554. One of its centers or "sees" is the Patriarchate in Jerusalem and it has a strong presence along with other denominations in the Holy Sepulchre, through the "Status Quo" decree issued by the Ottoman Sultan in 1757. In the Armenian Quarter of the Old City, and inside the Armenian Patriarchate compound, the **Cathedral of Saint James** (1142) has a modest façade and entry gate with various external images and two wall altars (Figures 3.40–2). Services were permitted *only* at those outside altars when the church was closed under Islamic Sultan Saladin in the twelfth century. The cathedral is dedicated to both James the Greater (older or taller) and James the Lesser or the Just (also an apostle and possibly the "brother" or cousin of Jesus). It claims to have the skull of the former, at the site of his martyrdom, and the tomb with body of the latter, who was the first bishop of Jerusalem, according to tradition, and also martyred (Pringle 170).

A cloth covers the entryway, under an image of Jesus's face on Veronica's cloth (Figure 3.43). The wide, rectangular chancel has icons, hanging lamps, and a dome overhead with a six-pointed Star of David design. The main altar area includes the tomb of St. James the Lesser under a baldachin (Figure 3.44). On the left side is a door to a chapel with the head of St. James the Greater, at the traditional site of his beheading (Figures 3.45–6), and a balcony with a cantor during the service (Figure 3.47), plus upper level icons extending around the nave (Figures 3.48–9). At the service, clergy in red and white, red and gold, or purple robes, some wearing black hoods, hold candles, chant hymns, and swing metal censers, spreading the scent and smoke at the icons and congregants—in a patriarchal, authoritative, yet maternal, nurturing atmosphere of outer/inner theatricality (Figures 3.50–1 and 3.51vid). There are side chapels with semi-dome images of Mary with the child Jesus holding an open book, the sacrificial Lamb of God in swirling branches tied to patriarchal figures, and Mary with baby Jesus, as male authorities honor them (Figures 3.52–4). There are also zodiac figures in the floor tiles (Figure 3.55). Such spaces evoke awe, grief, and hope against historical, personal, and cyclical tricksters, especially those arising between religious or ethnic groups, as stressed by a poster in English outside the church about the Armenian genocide, which has not been acknowledged by Turkish authorities, over a century later (Figure 3.56).

Domination and Translation, From the Holy Land to Rome

Various Christian faiths, along with Judaism and Islam, vie for sacred sites in the "Holy City" of Jerusalem, showing animal-human territoriality turned into metaphysical ideals of survival and reproduction, through mimetic rivalry among the "Children of God" across two millennia. Sacred relics of super-natural survival have also been translated from Jerusalem to Rome, which is the European center for Catholic Christians, with its Vatican City as an independent country. Its many sacred sites involve martyrdom locations of St. Paul, who spread Christianity across parts of the Roman Empire, and St. Peter, an apostle of Jesus who became the first "Pope," as Bishop of Rome—in rivalry with other Christian leaders and their cities, including Bishop

James in Jerusalem. Peter was also the first Patriarch of Antioch (in Syria), according to the Eastern Orthodox tradition. Thus, evangelical care, sectarian alliance/hierarchy, and patriarchal grooming/purification drives, with related emotions and ideals (Table 1.1), circulate in the monumental church spaces of Rome, with ties to Jerusalem's biblical sites, through the seeking of meaning and purpose beyond mortality in the Roman Catholic tradition.

In Rome, **Saint Peter's Papal Basilica (Basilica Papale di San Pietro**, 1506–1626) dominates its Vatican site with a rectilinear building and spherical yet pointed dome, designed by Michelangelo (Figure 3.57). Built on a westward slope, it faces east, unlike most churches (D. McNamara, *How* 83). Statues of Jesus, St. John the Baptist, St. John the Evangelist, and the apostles adorn the top edge of its picturesque Baroque façade (Figure 3.58), designed by Carlo Maderno. He also extended the nave beyond Michelangelo's balanced Greek-cross floorplan, diminishing the significance of his central dome. There is a huge piazza or "square" projecting outward from the front of the basilica with its wide platform of steps that has statues of Ss. Peter and Paul at its corners (Figure 3.59). Two long narrow buildings extend from wider points at the sides of the basilica, far beyond the steps, creating a trapezoidal courtyard space. These extensions continue as a roofed colonnade, built in 1656–67, four columns wide, climaxing as an oval embrace of the piazza. It is open at the other end, but was designed as a full enclosure by Gian Lorenzo Bernini (Figures 3.60–1). With 140 statues of saints on its roof, the double colonnade encircles the piazza, its obelisk, and two fountains (Figure 3.62), as the "arms of Mother Church" according to Bernini, embracing believers in a mix of patriarchal and maternal, light and shadow ideals (Sparavigna).

At the center of the piazza is an ancient Egyptian obelisk, over four thousand years old. It was brought from Alexandria to a nearby site by Emperor Caligula in 37 CE, for the spine (*spina*) of an oblong "circus" or circular racetrack, where Peter was later martyred. The obelisk was moved to its current location in 1568. A century later, Bernini used it as the center of his piazza, shaped somewhat like the circus racetrack. It has four bronze lions near its base and acts as a sundial, with its noon shadow reaching toward an appropriate zodiac figure in the pavement around it, depending on the time of year. Saint Peter's Square evokes awe in visitors, with ties to nature through history and art, even as they wait in a long line to enter the largest church in the world, which has security fears, yet offers monumental hope, through its beauty.

St. Peter was martyred in *c*. 64–8 CE, along with many other Christians during the reign of Nero, as entertainment for crowds at the ancient Roman circus where the Egyptian obelisk stood. Peter was then buried in a cemetery nearby—a site now under the basilica's main altar (Figure 3.63). However, his skull has been kept since the ninth century, along with the skull of St. Paul and wood from the Last Supper table, in the Papal Archbasilica of Saint John Lateran in Rome. Peter's supposed tomb, under the Vatican basilica, is accessible through the multiple "grottoes" of its crypt, which include columns and memorial slabs from the original church built by Constantine in 360.

The "crossing" of the main floor, where nave meets transept at the central altar over St. Peter's tomb, thus becomes a key site of Roman Catholic lineage and authority, in "the 'topographical transfusion' of Jerusalem to Rome ... as the second Jerusalem"

(Lavin, qtd. in Jones 2: 120). The basilica was initially conceived as a memorial church, connecting the martyrdom of Peter with the divine symmetry of a circular ground plan, by architect Donato Bramante (191). But that design was rejected in favor of a Latin cross with a huge nave for congregations and processions. Thus, the crossing became crucial as the patriarchal heart of the church—a mixture of *scriptwriter/critic* (revised with theatrical authority) and *mime-designer* (nurturing) spaces, plus *audience* (memorial) and trickster *stagehand* (cryptic) sites, interacting with visitors' left, right, limbic, and sub-cortical networks.

Eight spiraling, ancient Greek, "Solomonic" columns from the earlier church were moved to the crossing, with pairs of them placed in four small balconies below the corner pendentives that support the dome and show images of the four gospel writers (Figure 3.64). Beneath the pendentive showing St. John the Evangelist (Figure 3.65) and its pair of ancient pillars, to the right of the main altar, is a statue of Constantine's mother, St. Helena. The sculpture shows her holding the True Cross that she found in Jerusalem when she was about eighty years old, in the 320s (Figure 3.66), perhaps traveling there in grief after Constantine executed her grandson, Crispus. According to a later legend, shown in a fourteenth-century fresco by Piero della Francesca in the Church of San Francesco in Arezzo, Helena discovered the remains of Jesus's cross by torturing a local Jew, who knew where it was buried. But three crosses were found, perhaps including those of the two thieves crucified with Jesus. So, they were tested on a terminally ill person, who was healed by only one of them, and then Helena brought it to Rome.

Other pendentive corners in the transept-nave intersection bear statues of St. Longinus (whose spear pierced Jesus on the cross) and St. Andrew (brother of Peter). The fourth corner, to the left of the main altar, displays a statue of St. Veronica holding the veil with which, according to a medieval legend (and the sixth Station of the Cross), she wiped the face of Jesus as he carried his cross (Figure 3.67). Miraculously, the veil retained an image of Jesus's face—with Veronica's name meaning "true image" in Latin. That veil (or its fabrication), plus fragments of the True Cross and Longinus's spear, are kept in a chapel behind Veronica's statue. They are displayed each year on "Passion Sunday," a week before Easter, from the balcony above the statue, between the Solomonic columns, as theatrical props for a processional rite, with numerous spectators gathered in the nave. Like the statue of Helena with the True Cross, the statue of Veronica with the True Image idealizes patriarchal sacrifice, maternal care yet possessive control, and the "blood relic" as trickster fetish (Morgan 61)—even when it is not displayed.

The spiraling columns from Constantine's basilica inspired the four, hollow bronze, Baroque pillars of Bernini's 1633 baldachin, which stands 29 meters (95 feet) tall, over the main altar (Figure 3.68). In the marble bases of Bernini's columns, shield designs show seven stages of a woman's face during childbirth and then a child's face, acknowledging the pain of mothers at the origins of patriarchal aspirations. Below the baldachin and in front of the altar, there is an opening in the floor to show the site of Peter's tomb, at the other end of a holy lifetime, suggesting his supportive-trickster power as faithful martyr (Figures 3.69–70). Likewise, at the top of the baldachin are angels at the four corners and cherubs between, holding the papal crown and St. Peter's keys to heaven, as promised by Jesus (Figure 3.71). Thus, the rectilinear, cruciform design of the overall basilica focuses its vast indoor spaces on the sacred underground site of Peter's tomb—yet involves curved columns, canopy, angels, crown, and dome above, with feminine, Baroque, hyper-theatrical flourishes (plus Helena and Veronica as prominent figures).

The Holy Spirit as a dove appears in the center of the canopy (Figure 3.72) and in the stained-glass window of the apse behind it, transforming our animal-human trickster drives into the third person of the Trinity, as intermediary between Father, Virgin Mother, and Son (Figures 3.73–4). Another relic also appears in the apse: the chair that St. Peter ostensibly taught from, or pieces of it, or a throne representing it since the Middle Ages ("The Chair"), covered with oak, iron, and bronze, plus ivory plaques showing the labors of Hercules (Figure 3.75). Bronze statues of four Doctors of the Church, two Roman Catholic and two Greek Orthodox, stand beside it, in a continuous tradition of unifying truth, believed to come from Jesus as God, through Peter as "rock" of the Church (Matt. 16.18), to the many subsequent popes, with the dove flying across history.

Below the current floor, tombs of numerous popes and saints were built around Peter's burial site, during the twelve centuries that the original Constantine basilica existed. But many of them, including the tombs of over seventy-five popes, were demolished in the sixteenth century and their relics relocated by Bramante, who became known as "Maestro Ruinante." This destruction and reconstruction of predecessors' tombs was initiated by Pope Julius II in the early 1500s, allegedly for his own tomb, to be designed by Michelangelo, which was never completed (Reardon). Subsequent popes continued the demolition, authorizing the construction of the grandest church in Christendom, with Michelangelo, Maderno, Bernini, and others as architects, over the site of another basilica and the earlier Roman racetrack.

With this and other churches full of Baroque splendor, the Counter-Reformation Church doubled down on the power of figural art to lure people into Catholic sanctuaries, in contrast to Protestant buildings, which focused on preaching and singing, purified from idols (Seasoltz, "Christian" 121–3). At Saint Peter's Basilica, sixteenth- and seventeenth-century popes recolonized a sacred site of ancient gaming and martyrdom, with its twelve centuries of prior architecture and worship as the center of Roman Christianity's imperial expansion. The popes' territorial demolition and rebuilding project, with playfully ornate artwork, was partially funded by the very "indulgences" that disgusted the Protestants: selling believers the clergy's special rites to reduce their afterlife prison time for sins, in the tortures of Purgatory, or that of their departed loved ones. Grief and fear thus became redemptive hope and joy, through the examples of saints and angels in Baroque artwork. Obedience to "Mother Church" and its patriarchate would transform the devilish *stagehands* and ghostly *audience members* of believers' brains into moral *actors* and upright *characters*, with heavenly destinies, inspired by holy relics as historical props: bone, chair, veil, spear, and cross fragments, in various basilica spaces.

Today's visitor, whether pilgrim or tourist, enters the basilica through a columned portico, as the narthex, with an ornate ceiling already hinting at the Baroque theatricality inside (Figures 3.76–7). To the far left is a sculpture by Agostino Cornacchini (1725) of Charlemagne on horseback, as an early medieval champion of the "Holy Roman Empire" and Catholic Church (Figure 3.78). To the far right, visible through glass, is a sculpture by Bernini (1670) of ancient Roman Emperor Constantine on horseback, seeing Christ's cross as a guiding vision while in battle (Figure 3.79). To the right of the normal entry doorway, there is the "Holy Door" or *Porta Sancta* (Figures 3.80–1), which is only opened every twenty-five years, with great fanfare in a Jubilee of the Church, such as 2025. This may also give a reason for tourists to return, benefitting the local economy. The sixteen bronze panels on the door show the banishment of Adam and Eve from Paradise and then various stories from the New Testament, plus the door's opening in the last panel—putting that theatrical entry point in a mythic context, even while preventing it, except in the Jubilee year. Pilgrims also get an indulgence for their confessed sins up to that point, thus reducing Purgatory penalties, by walking through the Holy Doorway in the Jubilee Year.

After visitors enter through the normal doorway (Figure 3.82), the first main attraction, opposite the baptistery chapel on the far left (Figure 3.83), is Michelangelo's Pietà in a chapel to the right (Figure 3.84), with a cupola over that area showing people rising to heaven (Figures 3.85 and 3.85vid). The tragic Pietà, with its title suggesting piety through pity (from the Latin *pietas*, devotion), was carved in 1499 when Michelangelo was just twenty-four. It shows in delicate, seemingly soft, marble details an ever-youthful Mary, with her dead Son draped between her legs, where she had also given birth to him three decades before (Figure 3.86). Currently, the sculpture is protected by a transparent acrylic screen because it was damaged by a hammer-swinging Hungarian-Australian in 1972, who climbed on it and broke off Mary's forearm and parts of her nose and eye, while shouting, "I am Jesus Christ. I have risen from the dead." The statute itself rose again to its idealized, nurturing, life/death form, after the marble was restored. A mosaic of Peter, holding the keys to heaven, appears to the right of the Pietà, closer to the entry doors, and huge cherubs hold a holy water font to the left of it, along the main aisle (Figures 3.87–9). Together, they exemplify the three major brain networks evoked throughout the basilica: left-cortical patriarchal authority, right-cortical maternal care (and grief), and subcortical trickster playfulness as holy ideals. Yet the mentally disturbed visitor with a geologist's hammer also showed the negative tricksters that might be evoked in the inner theatres moving through such spaces.

The north aisle of the basilica stretches from the Pietà toward the transept (Figure 3.90), with elite tombs and saintly chapels (Figure 3.91). The south aisle, to the left of the entrance, extends from the baptistery to the transept (with the basilica facing east, unlike most churches). Walking along the main aisle, with its coffered ceiling and angel reliefs flying off edges, the visitor approaches on the right, near the central altar, a medieval bronze statue of St. Peter, seated in his throne, with a canopy over it, holding the keys to heaven (Figures 3.92–3). Taken from the original Constantine basilica, this statue's feet are worn smooth by numerous visitors touching and kissing them for blessing or good luck (Figures 3.94–5 and 3.95vid). Especially when dressed in a costume, with a ring on its finger, on the saint's feast day (June 29), this statue performs

Figure 3.94 Visitor touches Peter's statue in Saint Peter's Basilica.

an immortal connection between believers of the past and present, across hundreds of years, showing the touch of numerous hands, with hope through art, theatricality, and holy spaces.

Most of the artwork in the basilica shows male figures, including the statues of thirty-nine founders of religious orders, positioned along the main aisle and transept, just nine of whom are female. Yet Mary plays a key role throughout, from the sorrowful Madonna figure in the Pietà of the north aisle to the joyful child being presented to the temple priest in a scene by Romaneli (1642) in a south aisle chapel (Figure 3.96), next to the baptistery. Ss. Helena and Veronica play mythic roles, too, as nurturing ideals and relic creators, near the central altar. Likewise, other feminine figures and curved elements in this Baroque basilica (Figures 3.97–8) evoke visitors' right-cortical, maternal *mime-improviser/designer*. But the left-cortical *scriptwriter/critic* is also reflected by male figures, rectilinear forms, and hierarchical orders of controlled territories in the vast architectural spaces of verticality, challenged by playful twists and cherubic tricksters. The dominant elements assert patriarchal ascendency over maternal care and trickster playfulness, as with the keys Peter holds in his statue and mosaic—or Michelangelo's huge dome (completed by Giacomo della Porta), with an elderly white-bearded man as Almighty God at the center, sometimes directing sunlight on the statue of St. Peter (Figures 3.99–100).[1] Likewise, the scene inside an ellipsoid

---

[1] See also: https://stpetersbasilica.info/Interior/Dome/dome-GodtheFather.jpg.

dome near the baptistery and Presentation of Mary chapels depicts God as an old white man in the sky, gesturing toward Mary, a fair-skinned lady from the Middle East, while his cherubs hold a crown over her head (Figures 3.101–02).

As in many European churches, images of holiness in Saint Peter's Basilica groom visitors' brain spirits. This involves patriarchal ideals of Pietà-like grief, mortal fear (at Peter's martyrdom site), and yet playful joy with the awe inspired by vast enclosed spaces, performing around and dwarfing people who pass through them. Here, Baroque designs reflect many centuries of vertical shamanism, especially the Counter-Reformation ambition to build the biggest church in the world, which continues to attract and groom visitors with visions of white holiness. This theatrical ideal reimagines the divine spectatorship of an ancient, Middle Eastern YHWH, who desired human sacrifices, but then acted as his own heroic, submissive, redemptive, trickster-like victim, who transfigured suffering and death. Unfortunately, some visitors may over-identify with such a sacrificial ideal and perform hyper-theatrically, like the Hungarian-Australian with a hammer. Even worse, though, are melodramatic patriarchal leaders, religious and secular, who project inner tricksters onto others as heretical, demonic, or political scapegoats and territorial threats.

Peter as Trickster with Spatial Returns

A very small church in Rome, outside the city's ancient walls and near a catacomb, commemorates a fearful mistake made by the first patriarch from Palestine, despite his magical trickster powers—like Jesus who was depicted in early Christian art with a wand, before he became the medieval crucified Christ. "Peter's magic was a favorite theme in the early Church," recorded even in the canonical Acts of the Apostles, which tells of Peter healing the sick with his shadow, making the lame leap, slipping out of chains, and bringing death with a curse (Mathews 84). According to the apocryphal *Acts of Peter*, probably written in Asia Minor a century after the events it describes, Simon Peter challenged a gnostic magician, Simon Magus, to a miracle contest in Rome. Simon Magus made a recently dead man raise his head and open his eyes, but then Simon Peter made him sit up, take off his burial clothes, and speak again. Simon Magus flew in the air but Simon Peter prayed to God, making the rival magician fall and break a leg, leading later to his death.

Yet Peter had also angered many Roman men, whose wives and concubines had converted to Christian celibacy through his preaching, and they wanted revenge. On the advice of his followers, Peter dressed in disguise and left Rome secretly, so that he could continue his mission. Along the Appian Way, outside the city wall, Peter had a vision of Jesus and asked him: "Lord, whither goest thou?" (*Acts*, section 35), or in Latin, "*Domine, quo vadis?*" Jesus replied that he was going to Rome to be crucified again, yet he then ascended to heaven. Peter took this to mean that his own mission was to be crucified. So, he returned to Rome and told his followers the story. Later, at the circus site, he asked to be crucified "head downward" (section 37) because he was unworthy of dying in the same way as Jesus. While on his cross, Peter explained to his audience that it symbolized rebirth, since he also came into the world head downward.

The **Church of Domine Quo Vadis** (Santa Maria in Palmis) is located at the site, according to tradition, where Peter conversed with the risen Jesus (Figure 3.103). A Christian church may have existed there since the ninth century, but the current one was built in the seventeenth. It is also the possible location of an ancient shrine with a sacred field, honoring Rediculum, Roman god of "the return," who reassured worried travelers leaving on a long journey. Today's visitor can still walk on the Roman road, the Appian Way, and see the city wall from the church site, like ancient travelers (Figure 3.104).

Just inside the church's threshold is the imprint of two bare feet on the floor, supposedly left by Christ (Figures 3.105–06). The current imprint is a copy of what was probably a devotional offering by an ancient Roman, grateful for his safe return. The original was moved to the Basilica of St. Sebastian Outside the Walls, above a Christian catacomb, commemorating the martyrs originally buried there, whose bones were also translated. Thus, Domine Quo Vadis, even as a small, simple, rectilinear church, conquers an earlier religion's sacred territory, appropriating a remnant votary object. The church's narrative of patriarchal sacrifice and transcendence includes Peter's apocryphal theatrics, dominating a rival magician, in melodramatic competition.

On the left wall near the entry door, a mural shows St. Peter preaching, with a halo around his head, along with several framed pictures as Stations of the Cross (Figure 3.107). The same wall, nearer to the altar, shows Peter being crucified with his head downward, plus a framed picture of Mary beaming light from her heart to devotees, along with more Stations (Figure 3.108). On the right wall, in parallel areas, Jesus is shown preaching and being crucified, head upward (Figures 3.109–10). Above the altar, a smaller image shows Mary with the child Jesus (Figure 3.111), acknowledging maternal love as a foundation for the patriarchal ordering and trickster powers of St. Peter, along with the adult Jesus, submitting to, yet overcoming death. Hence, the spaces and images of this small church perform around the pilgrim, promising returns to home and family, but also transcendent extensions of them—through inner/outer theatre networks and the magical ideal of a competitive, fearful, yet faithful martyr. Visitors who identify with Peter and the Madonna have their brain spirits groomed, to some degree, with potentially disruptive, subcortical, trickster *stagehands* rewired toward the Christian path of returning to God. Such grooming also involves moral *stage manager* and superego *director* circuits, in relation to the individual ego as *actor* and *character*. Purifying identifications include the patriarchal *scriptwriter/critic* and maternal *mime/designer* as well, with translated meanings and feelings.

Holy Stairs and Original Icon

With her cross-historical identifications and super-natural relic translations, St. Helena, mother of the first Christian emperor, Constantine, not only brought the True Cross and its nails to Rome, but also the alleged stairs of Pilate's praetorium palace, where

Jesus was judged and tortured in Jerusalem. The twenty-eight white marble steps of the **Holy Stairs (Scala Sancta)**, encased in wood for protection since 1723, are located in a former papal palace, near the Archbasilica of Saint John Lateran in Rome. The rectilinear stairs have Renaissance murals on the walls beside them and on the curved ceiling, which pilgrims can contemplate while they climb the steps on their knees (Figure 3.112). They thus perform with the space and imagery around them, recreating the aura of Christ's passion, while imagining other places and times, in this sacred theatre of fear, grief, care, and sublime awe. Their ecstasy may approach what Lutheran theologian Rudolf Otto called a century ago the "numinous," involving "a tranquil mood of deepest worship," submerging us in the "*mysterium tremendum*" of Otherness, which becomes "thrillingly vibrant and resonant" (qtd. in Crosbie, "Calling" 226). Perhaps this is related also to the paradoxical, ecstatic, "spillover effect" of parasympathetic calmness and sympathetic arousal, in Newberg's neurotheology research. According to Otto, the numinous can be experienced in sacred spaces through semi-darkness, silence, and emptiness, the last of which he valued in Chinese architecture, with its sublime horizontals, "unfolding courtyards, and vistas—capturing nothingness" (Crosbie, "Calling" 227–8).

In Roman Catholic doctrine, revised over the centuries by various popes, a penitent believer gets a plenary indulgence for oneself or a deceased person—in climbing the Holy Stairs with a mind detached from sin, while praying for the Pope's intentions, after receiving Holy Communion and confession. That person gets a full remission from punishment in Purgatory for sins committed since baptism. (This means the soul would go straight to Heaven if the pilgrim died at that moment.) The Catholic sacrament of confession gives the believer "forgiveness" of sins, but not purification from all punishment. And yet, a plenary indulgence offers this, using the inexhaustible "treasury" of *merit* from the suffering, prayers, and good works of Christ and the saints, through the authority of the Pope, granted by Jesus to Peter in the Bible.[2] Of course, if a believer sins again after receiving the plenary indulgence, punishment in Purgatory might still occur. A pilgrim can only receive the indulgence once per day, but can get multiple ones across several days and send them to various souls already in Purgatory, including departed loved ones—in the spiritual economy of the Catholic cosmic theatre. From the Middle Ages to the Renaissance, the Church's selling of indulgences helped fund the creation of great churches and their artworks, such as Saint Peter's, yet also led to Protestant revolts.

On each side of the Holy Stairs in Rome, two replica staircases were built, with bare marble and similar murals, when it was relocated in 1589 (Figures 3.113–15). There are statues near it, too, that some pilgrims revere (Figures 3.116–17). At the top of the five

---

[2] "And I tell you that you are Peter, and on this rock I will build my church, and the gates of Hades will not overcome it. I will give you the keys of the kingdom of heaven; whatever you bind on earth will be bound in heaven, and whatever you loose on earth will be loosed in heaven" (Matt. 16.18-19). However, Jesus also says the part about binding and loosening again in Matt. 18.18, apparently to all his disciples. On the Catholic "Treasury of Merit," see http://www.calledtocommunion.com/2011/01/indulgences-the-treasury-of-merit-and-the-communion-of-saints/.

staircases, a doorway leads to a rectilinear chapel known as the **Church of Saint Laurence in the Palace at the Holy of Holies (Chiesa di San Lorenzo in Palatio ad Sancta Sanctorum)**, which served as a private oratory for various popes during the Middle Ages (Figures 3.118–20). It is known as the "Holy of Holies" because it contains the relics of many saints, plus a special painting, the *Uronica* (original icon), an image of Christ Pantocrator supposedly started by St. Luke the Evangelist at the request of Mary and finished by angels. The *Uronica* and its altar are now visible to pilgrims through a grilled window near the chapel, with the Latin phrase: "There is no place holier than this" (Figures 3.121–3). It has layers of medieval overpainting and a metal *riza* covering, as in the Eastern Orthodox tradition. The original painted surface is reportedly dangerous, blinding a pope who dared to look at it, according to Gerald of Wales, *c.* 1215 (Belting 542). In the Middle Ages, this icon was carried in elaborate processions, thus performing across the city as a supernatural artwork (Bolton). In this chapel, it creates the aura of a holy space that pilgrims peer into, tasting fear across the centuries, if they know the resonant stories.

Likewise, pilgrims' inner theatre emotions, imaginations, and beliefs have interacted with the Holy Stairs across the centuries. Their intimate contact with this sacred site, transported from Jerusalem to Rome, promises the transport of souls from Purgatory to Heaven. Knees pressed to each step, surrounded by other believers' bodies and elaborate paintings, in a tunnel upward to the Uronica chapel, a pilgrim might feel the sublime awe of a spiritual rebirth canal, while also sending suffering souls in Purgatory to Heaven. Through mortal fears, immortal hopes, and political rivalries, which brought the Holy Stairs to Rome centuries ago, pilgrims share in the beauty, wealth, and power of this site—especially if they believe that Peter's aristocratic successors can free souls from afterlife punishment, with inner theatres *translated* to God.

Divine Desire Watching

God the Father's biblical desire for the sacrifice of sons, from Isaac to Jesus, involves Mount Moriah in the Hebrew Bible, thought by Jews to be the current location of the Temple Mount, and Mount Calvary (Golgotha) in the New Testament, included now in the Church of the Holy Sepulchre. God allowed Abraham to substitute a ram for his son, as sacrificial offering, and then became the offering himself, suffering and dying on the cross as Jesus. But for Job, suffering increased, from his livestock, servants, and family to his own body, because God allowed Satan, as fatal trickster, to torment a good person in a game of superpowers, which demanded further offerings.

Christians visiting biblical sites in Jerusalem (and other locations), walking the Via Dolorosa in imitation of Christ, or acting in rites around translated relics believe they are *performing* in a cosmic theatre for an all-knowing, all-powerful, always present Creator. He watches, allows evil in, and once acted as heroic victim in the drama of human suffering. Believing in such a God as Father, Son, and Spirit, with Mary as divinized Virgin Mother, through image identifications, *grooms* brain networks, inherited animal drives, and various emotions (Table 1.1) toward a meaningful metanarrative of theatrical purpose. This magnifies each person's *individual* experiences of pain and pleasure beyond the flesh, as transcendent joy in God's Love. Mary's submission to the Father, Jesus's divine passion from the Holy Stairs to Golgotha, and Peter's painful martyrdom (along with that of other saints) exemplify this patriarchal logic of heroic victim/trickster sacrifice, in sublime pain, as melodramatic or tragicomic. Thus, the sacred spaces around their images and relics promise miracles of physical healing and spiritual meaning to suffering believers. Yet, in the melodramatic mode of evil projection, even the "stirrings" of inner-theatre desire are sinful, with "flesh as the root of all evil," according to the Catholic tradition, especially since the Counter-Reformation (Foucault 19–20). How does this Christian logic of spatial performances—seeking goodness (against projected evil) in visits to Holy Land sites or with relic translations to European churches—relate to Chinese Buddhist temples?

In Buddhism, there is no Creator God, as individual super-ego ideal, who watches and judges human suffering and sin, as divine spectator of deeds and inner theatres. So, there is a different cosmic-theatre relationship to devotees. More like elder siblings than a divine Father-Judge, bodhisattvas become enlightened, like all sentient beings, through a very long process of many lifetimes, practicing detachment and accepting change, which dissolves ego ideals. And yet, they delay their ultimate nirvana through compassion for others. As gods (which today's humans might eventually become), they watch and potentially help people who suffer from ego attachments and cravings. Visitors at temples honor them with offerings of incense, candles, food, drink, and money, not only to get spiritual aid for departed loved ones, or protection from evil spirits, or miraculous improvements in physical fate, but also for inner-theatre grooming and emotional meaning—as mindful observation. This may involve more of the tragicomic, *rasa*-cathartic mode (awareness over ignorance) than melodramatic, good versus evil. An increasing awareness of porous, *interdependent* selves becomes valued, rather than the independent soul (as child of God) in Western Christianity or as the modern bounded (and postmodern virtual) self in secular media. How do Chinese temple spaces and their mythic translations reflect such alternative, animal-human and super-human, ego and superego performances?

Cyclical, Open, Dispersed, and Natural Spaces

Buddhism's key idea of "karma" involves a treasury of merit similar to Catholic doctrine, but with merit from the good deeds of various bodhisattvas, in their multiple *cycles* of life and death, potentially available to supplicants, especially in the Chinese Mahayana tradition. Lay people bow, kneel, and give offerings to such figures, hoping for gradual progress toward a better next-life realm. Yet this would not be a sudden, complete, melodramatic, plenary indulgence, but an eventual, tragicomic *balance* of detachment and compassion—as shown in the meditative performances of statues, like living monks and nuns. Buddhism started in India with the teachings of Shakyamuni Buddha (Siddhartha Gautama, 563–483 or 480–400 BCE), remembered orally and in later written sutras. Reliquary "stupas" were built across India, especially during the reign of Emperor Ashoka in the third century BCE—with later legends extending such translated holy sites to China and Southeast Asia (Strong 124). Eventually, the mendicant order of wandering monks and nuns, which the Buddha founded as travelers, turned into various branches of monastic communities with temples across Asia. They present images of bodhisattvas, for contemplation and supplication, with relics and supernatural powers believed to help visitors, especially those offering donations.

Buddhism spread along the "Silk Road" to China—but not as suddenly as Christianity spread across Europe when adopted by Roman (then Byzantine) emperors and other rulers after the fall of Rome. Gradually, Buddhism became more popular in East and Southeast Asia than in India, where Hinduism and Islam dominated. Probably the first of many monks who traveled to China, An Shigao, translated and taught sutras there in the second century CE, after settling in Luoyang, capital of the Eastern Han dynasty, where the White Horse Temple was built (Xinjiang). Buddhism eventually blended with indigenous Daoism, sometimes through conflicts, vying for the patronage of various emperors across the dynasties and their territories.

Hangzhou became an early center of Chinese Buddhism, especially with the founding of **Lingyin Si (Temple of the Soul's Retreat or Hidden Spirits)** in 326 CE, by the traveling Indian monk Huili (Cochini 63; Shahar, "Lingyin" 216). It was enlarged in the sixth century, destroyed during a persecution period in the ninth, and then rebuilt in the tenth (Shahar, "Lingyin" 198), with many later renovations, especially during the Qing period (1644–1912). It was mostly saved from destruction during the Cultural Revolution (1966–76), reportedly due to Premiere Zhou Enlai. As a monastery of Chan Buddhism (akin to Japanese Zen), it is now one of the largest and wealthiest temples in China.

Upon entering the **Lingyin Scenic Area**, after paying the entrance fee, a visitor sees a stone reliquary with the ashes of Huili. It was first built in 975 and then rebuilt as a hexagonal, seven-layer, pagoda-shaped sculpture in 1590 with Buddha images from the fourth layer upward (Figure 3.124). Near the entrance, there is also **Feilai Feng (Peak Flown from Afar)**, so named by Huili because it looked to him like a mountain from India, perhaps Vulture Peak, a legendary living place of Shakyamuni, where he taught monks and celestial beings, according to *The Lotus Sutra* (Palmer et al. 4; Shahar, "Lingyin" 205–06). Thus, a sacred connection was made between Chinese and Indian sites—like (yet more natural and holistic than) the objective ties between Rome and Jerusalem through translated relics of the holy stairs, cross, nails, spear, veil (Veronica), and painting (Uronica).

More than 470 Buddhist figures have been carved in high relief from the rock surfaces and small caves of Feilai Feng, with a dozen dating back over a thousand years, but most to the Yuan dynasty (1271–1368). These lead the visitor toward the *natural* elements of rock and water, with a stream nearby, along the Flown Peak, on a *cyclical*, open-air journey with *dispersed* sites, prior to reaching the main temple. The LAP awe evoked in such spaces is unlike that of Saint Peter's *linear*, *mechanical* courtyard with its ancient obelisk, sequential colonnade, and direct *focus* on the church façade. Yet some of the carved rock sculptures have a smooth gloss from the touch of numerous visitors

Figure 3.126 Cliff-carved Buddhas and sutra trip, Felai Feng.

over the centuries (Figure 3.125), like the feet of the bronze statue of St. Peter in his basilica. Some represent historical trips by Buddhist monks bringing sutras from India to China in the first, third, and seventh centuries, including the Tang monk, Xuanzang, heralded in the sixteenth-century novel, *Journey to the West*, where he has animal-human helpers (Figures 3.126–8). Thus, the question asked by St. Peter at the site of the small Quo Vadis church outside the ancient Roman wall (Where are you going?) is answered in a different way with such figures, carved onto the Flown Peak and within it. They are not returning to the capital for a sacrificial heroic fate, but returning multiple times to the Indian sources of knowledge for Chinese progress in morality and freedom—revising our animal-human brain spirits of extended consciousness.

At Feilai Feng, **Longhong Cave**, also known as Leading to the Sky Cave (Tong Tian Dong), has a carving of Guanyin and a "Thread of Heaven" (Yixian Tian) with sunlight coming through an opening above (Figures 3.129–34). **Yuru (Jade Milk) Cave**, with its name referring to limestone drips calcified from the ceiling, is also called Arhat Cave with many such figures in its walls, plus the Six Patriarchs of Chan Buddhism carved in 1026 (Figures 3.135–41). One figure has polished hands due to numerous living hands touching it for luck, although there is now a fence protecting it (Figure 3.142). Thus, visitors today participate in the theatre of Buddhist contact and detachment, though at a visual distance, unlike the visitors touching Peter's toes in his basilica.

Qinglin Cave, also known as Tiger Mouth because of the shape of its opening, has a carving above it created in 1282 of the three saints of the Huayan School, which influenced Chan Buddhism: Manjushri left, Vairocana center, and Samantabhadra right (Figures 3.143–4). To the right of the opening, there is also a relief scene of the Locana Ceremony, with Samantabhadra on the left, riding his six-tusked elephant, Vairocana at the center on a lotus flower, symbolizing purity over the six senses, and Manjushri on the right, riding his lion, representing wisdom as "Mother of the Buddhas," in control of mind (Figures 3.145–8). Inside, there is the oldest carving at Feilai Feng, made in 962, showing the Three Saints of the West: Mahasthamaprapta (Dashizhi) left, Amitabha (Amituofo) center, and Avalokiteshvara right (Figure 3.149). Near the opening there is also a row of eighteen arhats above a natural rock bed known as the "Bed of Daoji" because a famous, rule-breaking, yet kindly monk from the twelfth century (Daoji or Jigong) reportedly slept there (Figure 3.150). Historical, mythic, and sacred auras circulate around the visitor passing through the cave temple spaces, resonating with inner theatre aspects reflected in figures, symbols, and stories—even memorializing a trickster. This may be like Domine Quo Vadis or Saint Peter's Basilica, but here in a natural nurturing, rather than confrontational hierarchic environment.

Along the hillside near these caves, there are various carved figures (Figures 3.151–3), many of which show the influence of Tibetan Buddhism (Zi 87). These include Ushnishavijaya (Victorious One with ushnisha head-bump), as Crested Ultimate Tara, with three faces and eight arms, and Syamatara, as protective, maternal Green Tara, thus reflecting left and right-cortical networks (Figures 3.154–6). Budai-Maitreya also appears as a joyful trickster (Figure 3.157). Another scene of chubby, laughing Budai with his followers (Figure 3.158) is the largest carving at Feilai Feng, exemplifying Song dynasty art of the tenth to thirteenth centuries (Zi 88). It suggests, at least to this visitor: right-cortical, male nurturing ties to subcortical trickster-*stagehand* playfulness.

Samantabhadra appears again on his six-tusked elephant, showing left-cortical purity and control over the senses (Figure 3.159). Likewise, the Heavenly King of the North, ruler of rain, carries his iconic umbrella banner and rides a lion, inside a roofed shrine (Figures 3.160–1). A Yuan carving shows Mahasthamaprapta, symbolizing wisdom as a key buddha of Pure Land, his name meaning "Arrival of the Great Strength," with robes flowing over the edge of the rock frame (Figure 3.162). Amitabha appears again, too, promising a "Western Paradise" to Pure Land devotees (Figure 3.163). Many of the carvings, although cut in a rectilinear frame, blend with the curves of natural rock around them (Figure 3.164). One of these shows Yang Lianzhenjia, a powerful thirteenth-century monk in Hangzhou who destroyed imperial tombs, reconverted temples from Daoist to Buddhist, forced conversions, accumulated wealth, and was implicated in four deaths (Figure 3.165). Today, some people view him as a demon who should not be worshiped, yet his carving is preserved here with others he commissioned.

A few carvings have curved or triangular frames, while including Avalokiteshvara or Shakyamuni giving various hand mudras: fearless, alms giving, meditative, and demon quelling (Figures 3.166–8). Looking up at the various carved reminders of enlightened beings may inspire awe in the visitor, at their commanding yet serene presence. These include a 700-year-old Yuan (Han Buddhist) carving of Shakyamuni with his right hand raised in the Dharma teaching mudra, while his left holds a mendicant begging bowl (Figure 3.169). Another shows him gesturing to the earth as verification of his serenity when tempted toward melodramatic lust or anger by Mara's daughters and warriors (Figure 3.170). Thus, the awe evoked in this natural context, with hillside trees, plants and stream, plus cyclical paths and dispersed images, is very different from the totally man-made, mechanical majesty with linear, focused order of Saint Peter's Square and Basilica.

Halls along a Hillside with Flower, Immolation, and Trickster Ideals

When one reaches the entrance to Lingyin Temple, it seems modest, with a small doorway to one side of the first hall (Figure 3.171). Yet the various stone carvings of Feilai Feng leading to this entrance connect the natural environs to the wooden structures inside, with stone Sutra Pillars near the arched entryway, as historical reliquaries from the tenth century (Figure 3.172). Inside, the visitor sees an open courtyard with many trees and plants, plus a round central burner for incense and other offerings, with people bowing while holding incense to their foreheads (Figures 3.173–7). People gather at incense-lighting stands for their individual yet collective offering rites (Figure 3.178). There are also rectangular burners with lion-dragons (*suan ni*) twisting around their supports (Bates 59–60). They are aligned on the temple's main axis, which flows up the mountain, from the Hall of the Four Heavenly Kings, as a "Mountain Gate" (*Shanmen*), to higher level shrines (Figures 3.179–81). Thus, the multiple spaces of Lingyin Temple, with its rectilinear halls, harmonize with the hillside's natural inclinations.

In Chan Buddhist temples, the initial Mountain Gate, with its three arched doorways, is also known as the Gate of the Three Liberations (emptiness, no-aspects, and desirelessness), often with two guardian statues, Heng and Ha. Here, it displays the Four Heavenly Kings, two on each side, with workers sometimes cleaning around them (Figures 3.182–4). At the center of the hall, the guardian Buddha, Wei Tuo (Skanda), faces toward the courtyard, framed by a mix of round pillars with dragons, hexagonal lantern, rectilinear canopy, and curved eaves (Figures 3.185–6). This camphorwood statue is the oldest in the temple, dating back more than 800 years to the Song dynasty (Malik 119). Behind him, balancing with Wei Tuo's left-cortical, patriarchal, and aggressive protection of the temple, a golden statue of the future Buddha, Maitreya, appears in a more maternal, smiling, well-fed, and nurturing Budai form, though also adorned with dragons as natural forces (Figures 3.187–8 and 3.188vid).

Walking clockwise around the initial, open-air courtyard, one reaches, after a shop with religious objects, the 500 Arhats Hall (Figures 3.189–90). It shows statues of the Buddha's legendary disciples, who attended the early councils of monks and had supernatural skills: knowing the thoughts of others, their own prior lives, and their destiny and death, with abilities to fly, change shapes, and appear or disappear (de

Figure 3.185 800-year-old Wei Tuo statue, Lingyin Temple.

Visser 202). As shown by the wooden "Visit Map" in the courtyard (Figure 3.191), this building has a swastika form, an ancient symbol of eternal cycles and good fortune, used by Hinduism and Buddhism for millennia before its misappropriation by German Nazis. The four bent arms of the building contain hundreds of similar yet distinctive bronze statues of the Buddha's key followers, like Catholic saints in a church, yet all apparently male. Several hold a child, however, or have a nearby animal in a nurturing pose (Figures 3.192–5).

Supernatural and heroic stories are suggested here, through the arhat (luohan) imagery, but not in the martyrdom vein of Christianity. For example, Gobaka (Kaixin) was a prince who revealed the Buddha nature of his heart by actually opening his chest, to convince his brother he did not want to fight him for rule of their kingdom (Figure 3.196). This is akin to the "Sacred Heart of Jesus" shown outside his body in Catholic images since the seventeenth century, offered to the viewer in romantic-erotic relations of divine love and sacrifice, evoking sympathetic arousal, passion, and debt (Morgan 111–36). The "Immaculate Heart of Mary" is also shown outside her body, sometimes pierced by one or seven swords.

In a more peaceful LAP vein, various arhats in this hall have tamed wild creatures. Pindola Bhradvaja (Qilu) rides a deer. Kalika (Qixiang) rides an elephant. Vijraputra (Xiaoshi) plays with a lion cub. Pindola (Fuhu) has a tiger, whom he fed vegetarian food from the temple. Nantimitolo ("Happy Friend," Xianglong) has a dragon, whom

Figure 3.201 Manjushri and arhats, 500 Arhats Hall, Lingyin Temple.

he subdued to save sutras. The latter two show the influence of Daoism, extending the number of key arhats from 16 to 18 in the tenth century (de Visser 201). Another arhat, Maha Panthaka (Pantha the Elder, Tangshou), has a very long, magical arm—which grew that way after he was born beside a road with his twin brother (Figures 3.197). When his widowed mother died, he became a monk as the "Long-Armed Arhat" who helped others, like his brother, Pantha the Younger (Kanmen), the "Gatekeeper Arhat."

Believers circumambulate the hall with hands folded together at the chest (like traditional Catholics), stopping at certain arhats they value and bowing to the statues (Figures 3.198–200). Rounding the corners of the swastika arms, the visitor eventually returns to the center with its four Bodhisattvas, facing outward in the cardinal directions, under a large canopy with dragon pillars, together forming the tallest solid-bronze sculpture in the world at 12.62 meters, with kneelers and coin offering boxes at each of the four sides (Figure 3.201). The figures include Manjushri holding a sword and riding a lion, as wisdom taming mind, and Samantabhadra on his six-tusked elephant, with those tusks representing the six bodily senses and the six *paramitas* or perfections: generosity, morality, patience, diligence, contemplation, and wisdom (Figures 3.202–03). There is also Ksitigarbha with his staff and Guanyin sitting meditatively on a fish-like sea dragon, pouring elixir from her vase, as the sole female figure (Figures 3.204–05). Despite the dominance of males among the hundreds of statues here, as the superior gender for reincarnation, women were the majority of

Figure 3.212 Amitabha flower-burning rite, Lingyin Temple.

worshipers that I saw, as is often the case in temples and churches (Figure 3.206). In the collectivist, patriarchal culture of China, Buddhism offers the hope of personal help for women as well as men, evoked by arhat and bodhisattva figures—in one's inner-theatre progress, across multiple outer-theatre lifetimes, toward nirvana.

Near the 500 Arhats Hall, in the initial courtyard, I saw a group of pilgrims, mostly women, making paper lotus flowers (Figures 3.207–08 and 3.208vid). Then they circled and approached a round burner in a ritual line, two by two, carrying the flowers (Figures 3.209–10 and 3.210vid). Each pair bowed three times and then put the flower offerings into the fire (Figures 3.211–14). The group chanted, "Amituofo," honoring Amitabha, the key figure of Pure Land Buddhism, who promises his followers a Western Paradise en route to nirvana. Some also took photos of others during the ritual, or bathed in the smoke and waved a purse over the burner for further blessings (Figures 3.215–16 and 3.216vid). Thus, the sacred site of this temple gives hope to many visitors, through different types of belief, seeking connection with ideal figures of life/death, nature/culture transcendence, along with good luck in personal possessions. This occurs through ritual spaces and flower-fire-smoke performances, involving social and cosmic as well as inner theatres.

Along the temple's central axis, up the stairs to another open area and burner, one finds the Mahavira Hall, which contains a statue of Shakyamuni, the historical Buddha, carved from camphorwood in 1953 and covered in gold leaf, the largest wooden Shakyamuni statue in China (Figures 3.217–20). There are also multiple kneelers and banners, rectangular and circular, at the front of the hall, near the big Shakyamuni (Figure 3.221). To the left and right of this main statue are the eighteen principle arhats (Figures 3.222–5; Malik 119). Behind it, the female Guanyin stands on a fish-dragon (probably as Mistress of the Southern Sea), pouring out compassion, with divine attendants and 150 smaller figures around her, including arhats and *Journey to the West* characters (Figures 3.226–32 and 3.232vid). Visitors are drawn within this hall in many directions toward various locations with patriarchal and maternal elements—to stare in awe, kneel, bow, and perhaps leave an offering in worship. Some leave money, flowers, or fruit, perhaps seeking to keep what they have in this life, or gain more, while others may want help with the Buddhist goal of detachment, as each lifetime forms an act in the divine tragicomedy.

Behind the Mahavira Hall are more burners and racks for lighting incense sticks and candles, along with a retaining wall and steps up to the next hall (Figures 3.233–4). That one holds a large seated statue of the Medicine Buddha, Bhaisajyaguru, and two standing attendants, Surya-prabha on the left with a sun wheel and Candra-prabha on the right with a moon wheel, symbolizing light and coolness (Zi 43–4). When I visited in July 2013, monks and lay people were seated at tables, perpendicular to those statues and their background panel, chanting with drumbeats and chimes, in a space with fans and ice nearby, due to the summer heat (Figures 3.235–7 and 3.237vid1–2).

In this hall, there are large colorful warrior figures along the walls and an altar with small statues in back (Figures 3.238–40). The ceiling and its lanterns are intricately decorated as well (Figures 3.241–2). Such artistic touches inspire believers to submit physically with bows and offerings to the Medicine Buddha, or with hours of chanting,

Figure 3.236 Lay women and monks near Medicine Buddha.

hoping for divine intervention in their own or loved ones' illnesses—as maternal nurturing from the patriarchal figure towering over them. He is also associated with the legendary Medicine King (Bhaisajyaraja), who immolated his own body in an oil-soaked cloth, as a supreme offering to the Buddha for the sake of others (Ching 148–9). He was then reborn with healing powers and praised by Shakyamuni in the *Lotus Sutra* (Reeves 353–5), which inspired monks and nuns across the centuries to burn their fingers, toes, or entire bodies in this type of self-sacrificing martyrdom and spirit-healing purification (Benn 59–62)—but not with the idealization of suffering in Catholic martyrdom or Christ's crucifixion.

East of the Medicine Buddha Hall is Master Jigong Hall (Figures 3.243–4). It includes a "cultural relic" display for visitors, with sculptures and painted wall-screens, completed in 2011, of the famous monk Jigong (a.k.a. Daoji, 1130–1209), who was kind-hearted yet eccentric (Figures 3.245–52). Trained at, but then expelled from Lingyin Temple for breaking many rules, especially getting drunk and eating meat, he wandered the area in dirty, torn robes and became a folk hero, reportedly with supernatural powers, healing the sick and fighting injustice. He thus exemplifies the positive trickster aspects of bottom–up, mischievous yet supportive (subcortical) *stagehands*, from inner to outer theatres. He rebelled against patriarchal *scriptwriter/ critic* rules, yet with maternal *mime/designer* nurturing and redesigning acts, for an *audience* in his time and apparently across history. Even today, some devotees bring "carved sandalwood effigies of the god," the deified Jigong, to Lingyin Temple to have them blessed (Ni 101).

The fourth hall on the main axis is the Zhizhi (Strait to the Heart) Dharma Hall and Sutra Library, which has a detailed relief, with playful lions, on the retaining wall leading up to it, and then the Chinese characters for "Chan" Buddhism on a courtyard wall (Figures 3.253-6). Inside the hall, on a platform in the middle room, is a "lion seat" for the master monk to give readings and interpretations, with a Dharma Wheel above it (Figures 3.257-9). According to the Lingyin Temple website, the chair's name refers to how the Dharma (Buddhist teaching) can overpower evil spirits like a lion's roar—in a cosmic theatre involving animal, human, and divine levels. Yet playful imagery is balanced with serious teaching, both involving lions, in such sacred spaces.

The last major building up the hillside is Huayan Hall, with a courtyard ringed by bamboo trees and a view of the area around Hangzhou's West Lake (Figures 3.260-3). Inside are large statues of Manjushri and Samantabhadra, representing wisdom and ethical purity as human figures holding flowers, on each side of the central Buddha, Vairocana—all seated in meditation with similar faces (Figures 3.264-70; Welch 190). Their elaborately decorated bases combine curved lotus-blossoming wholeness (and swirling cloud scenes) with rectilinear framed firmness, plus animal-face feet at the corners, reflecting right- and left-cortical, care and control networks, plus subcortical drives (Figures 3.271-2). Outside, with the sky's round openness, the rectilinear walls have circular relief images (over windows) of a mother elephant with babies and the Buddha teaching his followers, again reflecting maternal *mime/designer* and patriarchal *scriptwriter/critic* networks (Figures 3.273-4). The courtyard also has a round fountain, with a sphere in the center and dragons at the edges, plus lion guards standing nearby (Figures 3.275-8). Together, these details suggest a balance of right and left cortical, receptive *yin* and projective *yang* elements with nurturing, teaching, and guarding figures in a natural spatial context (Figure 3.279).

The Zhizhi and Huayan Halls, as the farthest uphill, were constructed from 2000 to 2002, extending the temple along the contours of the natural environment. On the sides of the monastery complex are dining and residential halls (Figures 3.280-1). There is also a Dragon Palace museum with precious objects (Figures 3.282-3), such as a carved piece of pink jade, one of only four in the world that large (Cochini 66). Of special note are two stone pagodas, on either side of the Mahavira Hall, which are octagonal, nine levels, and 12 meters high, carved in 960 (Figures 3.284-5). Thus, the Lingyin temple complex includes structures from a thousand years ago, along with others built more recently. This reflects the drama of Chinese history, shifting from millennia of imperial religious traditions to modern communist atheism, with the destruction or closure of religious buildings during the Cultural Revolution, and then to a resurgence of government-authorized religions, justified by an apparent morality crisis, plus an increasingly capitalist environment for pilgrims and tourists.

The interplay between patriarchal, maternal, and trickster aspects can be seen in each Lingyin building, with its inner images and outer courtyards, along the natural contours of the mountain, evoking visitors' *scriptwriter/critic*, *mime/designer*, and *audience/stagehand* networks. There is a particular connection between this temple and the *Journey to the West* (*Xiyou Ji*) story, novelized in the sixteenth century, about a Tang monk, Xuanzang (Tripitaka), who traveled to India in the seventh century to get holy sutras with the help of a supernatural warrior, Monkey King (Sun Wukong). With his frenetic wariness and fighting of demons, Monkey King represents, in my view, the alternative, holistic, contextual networks of the right cortical *mime-improviser/designer* and the disruptive animal drives of subcortical, trickster *stagehands*. The serene, yet at times overly confident Tang monk represents the left-cortical *scriptwriter/critic*, controlling Sun Wukong's "monkey mind" (a Buddhist phrase for an unsettled mind during meditation) with a special chant that activates a gold band Monkey wears on his head, given to them by the compassionate bodhisattva Guanyin. Lingyin Temple was founded by an earlier monk, Huili, who traveled from afar in the fourth century, bringing the Buddha's teachings like Xuanzang. It became known for its local monkeys (gibbons, which are actually apes), drawn to the courtyard with food, raised by monks, and sometimes given the surname "Sun," prior to the Tang period (Shahar, "Lingyin" 199–203). In the Arhat Hall, I noticed a similar depiction, relating to a sutra about an arhat initiating a monkey into his monastic order (210–11), which suggests the taming of our monkey mind through meditation as well (Figure 3.286).

Further inner-theatre networks are involved in the staging or changing of consciousness at this temple. Lingyin evokes the inner *actor* of one's self-knowledge, the *character* of one's imagined appearance (especially while bowing, lighting incense, or performing other rites), and the *director* imagining others' views (with bodhisattva statues as well as other people). The outer theatricality of this temple also evokes the visitor's inner *stage manager*, monitoring one's behavior, and the *operator* controlling it, plus the *costume-body definer* and *designer* of self (or no-self) and Otherness. Like the authoritative site of Saint Peter's Basilica, built where he was martyred and symbolizing Vatican control, Lingyin is a key temple of Chan Buddhism, built where a founding father experienced transcendence. And yet, on the day I visited, it also evoked performers from a different branch of Buddhism (probably stage-managed by a pilgrimage tour-guide) to create and burn paper flower offerings with the belief that Amitabha was watching their characters, as divine director, and might reward each actor's eternal essence (Buddha nature) with a place in paradise.

Unlike Saint Peter's and other Christian churches, this Buddhist temple does *not* funnel all believers toward one central altar (or its reliquary crypt) in a linear journey of the soul, representing one lifetime ending with eternal reward or punishment. Instead, multiple halls with numerous altars and figures draw the visitor in various directions, much more so than the side chapels in a Catholic church. Here, the visitor chooses to observe and perform in dispersed spaces: lighting incense in open-air yards, perhaps chanting with paper flowers burned in communal order, or kneeling and bowing closer to statues inside halls, while circumambulating the temple complex, or joining in more formal chanting with the monks at one hall.

In the collectivist culture of China, with right- and left-cortical, contextual yet analytical, *yin-yang* dialectical cognition (Li), the dispersion of worship spaces mixed with natural elements still enables an individual focus on specific arhats and bodhisattvas as superhuman exemplars, guides, and helpers. This focus depends on each person's unique inner *audience* of karmic life experiences, in temporal-lobe networks, exciting or inhibiting which percepts, concepts, and outward performances become staged in the brain—possibly toward a more enlightened awareness of the desires and fears that cause suffering. But unlike Catholic ideals of suffering saints, painful sacrifices are not shown as redemptive melodramatic victories over evil. Even the self-immolation story of the Medicine King, like his meditative Buddha image in Lingyin Temple, exemplifies non-attachment, not the value of pain as an offering to God (or tie to Christ). Statues appear with LAP emotions: serene, cheerful, or protective faces and poses, *balancing* a middle way between asceticism and joy, nihilism and survival—not being tortured to death with heroic sacrifices justifying a painful, ecstatic transformation, like Jesus and the martyred saints, pleasing the divine Father-Spectator. Paradoxically, at Lingyin and other Buddhist temples, the large images of enlightened beings, as ideal spectators, do not represent a transcendent ego, but its dissolution. They exemplify multi-life wisdom and compassionate magnanimity, helping visitors who identify with or appeal to such beings, with engaged emotions, yet distanced, interdependent, changing flavors, toward the ninth *rasa* of peace.

Balancing Patriarchal and Maternal, Buddhist and Daoist

Another temple founded by Huili, **Yongfu (Happiness Forever)** is also in the Feilai Feng scenic area, with halls flowing along Shisun Mountain, to the west of Lingyin (Figures 3.287-9).[3] The first hall, with lion guards in front, holds fierce-looking Heng and Ha statues, their feet balanced on demigods (Figures 3.290-4). There is a pool with a small figure nearby and then a green walkway with stairs toward further halls uphill (Figures 3.295-7). First, one finds a laughing, chubby, golden Budai-Maitreya in a glass case and then, on the other side of it, a flat wood engraving of Wei Tuo (Figures 3.298-300). Together, they might be seen as nurturing/playful maternal/trickster and protective patriarchal figures, along with Heng and Ha, encountered earlier in the temple's spaces.

After Puyuan Purity yard with its round burner, a multi-armed Avalokiteshvara appears (Figures 3.301-02). This male form of the bodhisattva shows nine arms on each side, representing a thousand arms, each holding a symbolic object of compassion. According to legend, he vowed to help all sentient beings toward freedom from the cycles of reincarnation (*samsara*). But this vow split his head into eleven pieces, which were then reformed by Amitabha into eleven heads, and his arms into a thousand with helpful hands, sometimes shown also on Guanyin, the female version of Avalokiteshvara. Such an image reflects the numerous networks of the brain's inner theatre, as they interact with mixed gender, maternal, patriarchal, and positive trickster ideals.

---

[3] Cf. Gildow about the schedule of rituals posted on Yongfu signboards.

Another walkway with much greenery leads to the gateway sign, "Divine Melody Overflowing the Cup" (Fan Lai Liu Shang), and then the Kalavinka Preaching Courtyard with its Fan Lai Lecture Hall (Figures 3.303–07). Next are steps further uphill, beside a small stream and waterfall, through a gateway with lion guards, to the Guxiang Meditation Courtyard (Figures 3.308–13). Beyond it, the Hairi Building displays the "Three Saints of the West," with lotus flower kneelers and a side altar (Figures 3.314–18). These bodhisattvas, Amitabha ("Infinite Light"), Mahasthamaprapta ("Arrival of Great Strength"), and Avalokiteshvara ("Lord Who Gazes Down"), promise to meet believers after death, helping them toward a Western Paradise. Most of the designs throughout Yongfu, with walkways, yards, and buildings, are rectilinear, evoking left-cortical rule-based authority. And yet, like the compassion of these male bodhisattvas, the natural surroundings, round burners, and upturned roof corners suggest nurturing, maternal aspects as well, balancing patriarchal rectitude with right-cortical inclinations.

A further walkway curves along the mountain's *feng-shui* (wind and water) contours, as shown by a sign, and then continues along a straight, covered passageway to the Ziyan Wisdom Courtyard with Great Hero and Fuxing Halls (Figures 3.319–22). The yard offers views of the West Lake valley and modern city of Hangzhou (Figures 3.323–6). Inside the Great Hero Hall, central statues depict Shakyamuni and his key disciples, young Ananda and older Mahakashyapa (who became the first patriarch), with circular column-like banners nearby (Figures 3.327–30). To the left of their platform, in the corner, is a statue of Samantabhadra on his elephant (Figures 3.331–2). Behind the central platform of the heroes is a depiction of Guanyin, with many smaller figures around her and attendant children beside her, the girl Longnü (Water Dragon Princess) and boy Shancai (Good Talent or Sudhana), plus a meditation picture of buddhas with an offering table along the back wall of the hall (Figures 3.333–5). In the corner, to the right of the central heroes, or ahead as one circumambulates clockwise around them, is Manjushri on his lion (Figures 3.336–7). These typical figures and placements show a predominance of patriarchs as "Great Heroes." But there is also a key role for the feminine, nurturing Guanyin, facing the opposite way, behind the central altar platform—as if suggesting (along with natural elements outside) alternative viewpoints of the brain's right-cortical, *improviser/designer* networks, regarding left-cortical, *scriptwriter/critic* demands (Figures 3.338–9).

Across the courtyard, Fuxing (Revival) Hall has a roundel on its outer wall, on each side of the doorway (Figure 3.340). One shows a *qilin*, a mythical creature with dragon's head, antlers, and scales on an equine or ox-like body. It is a Daoist symbol of protection, prosperity, and fertility, sometimes shown with flames, yet walking on water or clouds, as here, because the *qilin* does not want to hurt any blades of grass. People have playful placed coins on the relief carving, perhaps for good luck (Figure 3.341). Inside the hall is the Blessing Star Guardian God, a patriarchal Daoist figure, again showing the dialectical mix of religious traditions in this Buddhist temple (Figure 3.342). In the courtyard, a round water container with floating leaf pads also suggests nurturing, nature-aware, right-cortical alternatives (Figure 3.343).

Figure 3.342 Daoist Blessing Star Guardian God in Yongfu Buddhist Temple.

Another Trickster, Natural Fluidity, and Baby Holding

A long stairway up the mountain (Beigao Feng or North Peak, northwest of Lingyin Temple) leads to **Taoguang (Hide Your Light) Temple**, founded by Master Taoguang of the Tang dynasty, on a site where the "immortal Lui Dong-bun practised," according to an initial sign (Figures 3.344–6). Lü Dongbin is one of the Eight Immortals of Daoism, former humans who exemplify wisdom and the cultivation of immortality, becoming divine despite their personal flaws. He flirted with women, got boisterously drunk, and had a bad temper, even while developing supernatural powers. Yet he was an early master in the *neidan* tradition of internal alchemy during the late Tang dynasty (618–907) and a prolific poet. Eventually, he was valued by Buddhists, too, who claimed he was converted to their religion by Chan Master Huanglong, near Hangzhou, despite throwing a sword into his room, thus showing the rivalry between Daoism and Buddhism (G. Wu 583–5). In return, some Daoist schools view Lü Dongbin as an incarnation of Manjushri Buddha (Wong 159). In inner theatre terms, he may represent subcortical *stagehand* trickster drives, with more right-cortical *improviser* awareness, like Jigong and Monkey King, valued even with their disruptive potential—not just repressed as sinful, bestial, or demonic.

En route to the temple and its view of West Lake, there are stone gates and a worship platform without a statue, suggesting reverence for the natural environs and punctuating the many steep steps, arrayed along the mountain's contours (Figures 3.347–52). The first courtyard has a hall, Daxiong Baodian, with Shakyamuni, Samantabhadra, and Manjushri statues (Figures 3.353–61). There is also a protective *qilin* screen in the yard (Figure 3.362). A small hall, to the right of the main one, displays three statues on each side, all versions of Guanyin, including one holding a half-naked baby, as the child-giving bodhisattva, related to a Daoist fertility goddess, Songzi Niangniang (Figures 3.363–9). Another Guanyin, on the opposite side, stands on a dragon, as Mistress of the Southern Sea. These figures evoke right-cortical, nurturing, natural dimensions, balancing with left-cortical, regal aspects of male bodhisattvas in the larger hall. Likewise, the rectangular designs of halls and yard are in dialog with the curved elements of upturned roof eaves, akin to the surrounding trees and leaves, lifted by the wind (Figures 3.370–1).

Going through that small hall, and then across a bridge and pond, the visitor meets a hexagonal building with uplifted eaves. It contains a large Guanyin statue with a halo around her head and a Pearl of Light in her fingers, a gift from the underwater Dragon King (Figures 3.372–3). There is a fountain nearby with mountain spring water coming out of a dragon's head and a long bamboo pole with cup attached, available for thirsty pilgrims (Figures 3.374–5). Unlike in Christian churches, dragon figures in China

Figure 3.365 Three Guanyin figures in Taoguang Buddhist Temple.

represent forces of nature, wisdom, and luck (Meccarelli), related, I would say, to the fish-reptilian drives that humans inherit from animal ancestors. Here, they are allies of Guanyin and other deities (or thirsty pilgrims)—not devils to be conquered, as with images of Mary, St. George, or Archangel Michael violently dominating a serpentine dragon in Europe.

Up more steps on this mountain, there is a gate and another courtyard with a view of the landscape, plus a teaching hall (Figures 3.376–83). Then there are further steps, with a view and sound of the mountain stream's waterfall, up to an open shrine with two female statues wearing fabric cloaks and headdresses (Figures 3.384–6 and 3.386vid). The larger appears to be the virgin, He Xiangu, one of the Daoist Eight Immortals, and the smaller perhaps her mother. More steps lead to the highest yard with forest views and a statue of the Daoist immortal Lü Dongbin (Figures 3.387–92 and 3.392vid). Behind that hall, there is a sacred cave with small statues and an offering area, perhaps an ancient furnace for creating Daoist pills of immortality, in the mythical practice of Lü Dongbin (Figures 3.392–7). In another hall along the same yard, to the left of the cave, the bronze meditating figure of Master Yan Guangtao offers a modern realistic ideal, with a banner stating: "Beautiful light flashes forever" (Figures 3.398–401). The view outside offers a spectacular chance to consider the performance spaces of halls, forest, hills, lake, and distant city, around oneself or non-self, mixing Daoist balances with Buddhist detachments (Figures 3.402–04).

In contrast to Catholic churches as historical holy sites with a linear, enclosed focus on the main altar of Christ's redemptive sacrifice (ritually repeated with bread and wine), Buddhist temples with various halls rising up the hills of Feilai Feng draw the visitor through open, natural environments toward multiple, collective points of personal, meditative reflection. Sacrificial pain is not valued, but detachment from ego desire is, along with personal offerings of incense, candles, money, food, and drink (somewhat like the side altars in Catholic churches, with individuals lighting candles and depositing coins). The Amitabha worshipers that I observed in the first Lingyin courtyard showed divine-aid hopes as alternatives to that temple's Protestant-like, Chan tradition, which focuses on texts and inner development. Likewise, the variety of arhat, bodhisattva, and Daoist images in Lingyin, Yongfu, and Taoguang, even as Buddhist temples, expresses more fluidity between Chinese traditions than do cruciform Christian denominations and their competitive European spaces.

Three More (Including a Nunnery) with Many Animals and a Missing Statue

Near Feilai Feng's caves, cliff carvings, and temples, rising up Tianzhu (Ancient India) Hill, at the foot of Baiyun Mountain, are three more temples, each with a history of over a thousand years. The first, **Lower Tianzhu** or Fajing Temple, is the oldest, at more than 1,700 years ("Three"). Yet it burned to the ground in 1861 and was rebuilt in 1882 ("Buddhist"). It is now the only Buddhist nunnery in Hangzhou, which has over ten million people. As typical of Chinese temple design, the first hall holds the Four Heavenly Kings, two on each side, with Budai-Maitreya and Wei Tuo in the center (Figures 3.405–10 and 3.410vid). They assert patriarchal control, yet several of them show their dominance while smiling and the chubby Maitreya suggests playful, pleasurable emotions as well.

The next yard, with flags overhead, leads to the main hall, where nuns with shaved heads in brown robes chanted and circumambulated, to the beat of a wooden drum, when I visited (Figure 3.411 and 3.411vid). Another hall nearby has a central statue of the Medicine Buddha, with serene and warrior figures below him (Figure 3.412). They are Shakyamuni with the six buddhas who preceded him (Vipashyin, Shikhin or Shiqi, Vishvabhu, Krakucchamda or Detaining Sun, Konagaman or Kanakamuni, and Kashyapa), plus twelve Yaksha Generals—with all of them protected by a glass wall, where people leave cash offerings (Figures 3.413–17). Thus, the historical founder of Buddhism is not the only begotten Son of God, like Jesus, but just one of many enlightened compassionate beings.

The final hall shows the Three Saints of the West (Amitabha, Avalokiteshvara, and Mahasthamaprapta/Dashizhi), plus various arhats in the back corners, including Asita (Changmei in Chinese), a hermit with long eyebrows who predicted Shakyamuni's greatness (Figures 3.418–22 and 3.419vid). On the tall, narrow doors, there are cranes, deer, boar, horses, and dragons (Figures 3.423–7). Around these halls are various plants, trees, small lantern ornaments, round openings, a pond, and *wenshou* figures on the upturned roof eaves (Figures 3.428–35). There is also a memorial hall with name plaques of departed relatives and a large figure holding a staff, riding an animal, and wearing a crown, perhaps Ksitigarbha (Dizang), who promises to help them, or Shakyamuni or Bhaisajyaguru (Medicine Buddha) as the "Lion's Roar" (Figures 3.436–7). There is a yard with living quarters and flags leading to a teaching hall in the back, plus another yard with a teaching hall on the side (Figures 3.438–42). Of course, visitors also light incense or candles in such yards and leave offerings in the halls (Figure 3.443). Despite the mostly rectilinear designs of shrines, with patriarchal warriors and serene male bodhisattvas, this nunnery also has typical elements that might be viewed as feminine: curved roof eaves and gateways, plus round columns, burners, planters, and hanging lanterns. These are consistent with male monasteries, but a bit more prevalent here, shaping spaces around the visitor as natural and nurturing.

The road and walkway uphill between Tianzhu temples, along a stream, passes some of the local tea plantations, for which Hangzhou is famous (Figures 3.444–8). **Middle Tianzhu Temple** (also "Fajing" with the same sound character but different name character in Chinese) was originally built in 597, renovated in 1892, damaged by fire in 1947, and then restored ("Buddhist"). After passing the first gate and posted map, the visitor reaches the "Palace of Heavenly Kings" with Guanyin facing forward in an ornately carved frame with altar, dragon faces, bats (*fú*, homophonic with "blessing" in Chinese), and muscular guardians below (Figures 3.449–58). Behind her is an eight-armed, three-headed figure, with one pig head (the Hindu goddess of light, adopted by Tibetan Buddhism as Vairocana Piluchana, removing obstacles and giving happiness), instead of the usual Budai-Maitreya in front and Wei Tuo behind (Figures 3.459–62).

The sign above the statue states: "Work Hard for Treasure Palace." More typically, but with unusual props, the sides of this hall present the Four Heavenly Kings, each standing on a large *asura*, showing patriarchal dominance over, yet balance with their rivals (Figures 3.463–70). When I visited, there was a human attendant as guard, near the kings, too (Figure 3.471).

The back doorway opens onto a yard with a round burner, which has dragon handles (Figures 3.472–3). Three-story residential buildings line the sides of the yard and its central pool with small fish, turtles symbolizing longevity, and coins left for luck, tossed playfully into underwater bowls, as natural and trickster elements (Figures 3.474–80). On the bridge over the pool, there is a rectangular burner with dragon handles, plus steps to another round burner and the second hall, which states over its doorway "Clean and Solemn" (Figures 3.481–3). The stairway's banister has protective lions, as does the base of the upper burner, where people have also left coins (Figures 3.484–6). The steps beyond the burners lead to a bare landing and the second hall's doorway (Figure 3.487–8). A vent on the outer wall of that hall shows the arhat Pindola (Bintoulu or Fuhu) riding a tiger that he trained to become vegetarian, Subinda (Tuoda) holding a pagoda as the last disciple to see the Buddha alive, who then treasured his bone relics, and Budai with his big belly, along with other arhats (Figure 3.489). Thus, the yard's spaces, animals, and artworks perform around the visitor, with its openness to the natural sky and the pond's fish and turtles, as well as plants at the edges, plus burners with supernatural figures and coin offerings. Even wall vents may evoke further stories.

Inside Yuantong Hall, a tall, "thousand-armed" (with fewer shown), and eleven-headed Avalokiteshvara greets the visitor, with an ornate lantern above and sculpted lotus blossoms on the base, plus small figures on the altar and a round offering burner (Figures 3.490–3 and 3.493vid). There are elaborate paintings on the side walls, which were being refurbished when I visited, showing the seven buddhas of the past, perhaps with apsaras below them, and Manjushri from the *Vimalakirti Sutra* (Figures 3.494–500). A drum and bell were positioned in one corner of the hall, probably moved from the front corners due to the renovation (Figure 3.501). The back of the central statue does not have another statue, but its detailed cloak is visible, with many flower sculptures above (Figures 3.502–03). Even from the back, the Avalokiteshvara figure appears monstrous with its multiple arms, hands, and props, showing the masculine origins of Guanyin's compassion. It evokes awe, through surprise and fear, as well as hope for help from the bodhisattva, while a column speaks of helping all beings toward enlightenment (Figure 3.504). Through these spaces and images, the visitor's inner *mime/designer* and *scriptwriter/critic*, along with *audience* of memory systems and *stagehand* drives, might be evoked in reshaping the self toward a *rasa*-cathartic savoring of various emotions, while reflecting on the self-awareness yet selflessness of transcendent, peaceful beings.

Behind that second hall, an ivy-covered retaining wall with decorated vents mixes the natural and artful, as steps nearby lead up to the next courtyard (Figures 3.505–08). It offers a rectangular burner and further views of green hills, plant life, and yellow temple buildings (Figures 3.509–14). Inside the next hall, Daxiong (Big Bear) Palace, practitioners kneel before three large, almost identical, black metal figures: Amitabha holding a lotus flower, Shakyamuni center, and Medicine Buddha with a bowl and small ball or pill (Figures 3.515–17). Along with a human attendant and desk in the left corner, a statue stands guard (Figures 3.518–19). He is probably Guan Yu (Guandi), a famous general in the early third century, deified later in the Sui dynasty (581–618). He continues to be revered in Chinese folk religion, Daoism, and Buddhism—typically shown, as here, holding his long beard in his left hand and a weapon in his right (Welch 160).

A series of bronze arhats line the sides of the hall (Figures 3.520–1). More colorful statues of Samantabhadra on his six-tusked elephant and Manjushri on his lion appear in the rear corners (Figures 3.522–8). Between them and behind the three Buddhas, there is a picturesque scene with a large Guanyin pouring her compassion from a vase, while standing on a fish-dragon. Around her are her acolytes, Dragon Princess and Shancai (Sudhana), plus many smaller figures: the fifty-three spiritual advisers that Shancai met on his pilgrimage toward enlightenment, including twenty women, such as Shakyamuni's deceased mother, his wife, and a former prostitute, as told in the *Gandavyuha Sutra* (Figures 3.529–35 and 3.535vid). At the back of this hall, near Guanyin, a tall window shows the natural hillside behind it, thus mirroring the bodhisattva's ties to nature and nurturing fluidity (Figure 3.536).

Continuing around to the front, the various arhats along the wall include Asita (Changmei) with his long eyebrows, opposite the double shrine at the center of the hall

Figure 3.529 Guanyin scene and Samantabhadra in corner, Middle Tianzhu Temple.

(Figures 3.537–40). Also, a statue of Wei Tuo stands guard in the front right corner of the hall, with an attendant's desk, near the three Buddhas (Figures 3.541–2). Spaces and figures perform around the visitor: from the offering area in front of the three serene Buddhas to the guardian Guan Yu in the front left corner, to the arhats along the left wall (each suggesting a story), to Samantabhadra and Manjushri in the back corners on their colorful mounts, to the explosion of colors with many picturesque figures around Guanyin, and again to monochrome arhats along the wall with another guard, Wei Tuo, near the three calm Buddhas at the front.

Balance, not dominance, is emphasized through the focal directions, multiple figures, and use of colors in this rectilinear hall—as well as the view of nature behind it. Attractions are mostly horizontal, but the visitor's eyes are drawn upward, too, especially with the Guanyin spectacle at the back of the hall (Figure 3.543). The fish-dragon with horns at her feet might suggest the evolutionary origins of our deepest subcortical networks, along with nurturing limbic networks from mammalian ancestors and higher-order, right and left cortical, compassionate wisdom in this bodhisattva ideal.

Outside, returning along the main axis, the visitor again sees green hills beyond the various monastic buildings with yellow stucco walls and vent scenes (including deer with coins left, angelic *apsaras*, and a human journey), plus wooden roofs and metal burners with upturned corners—in the interplay of natural and cultural, round and rectilinear dimensions (Figures 3.544–8). As the visitor leaves, the curved gateway also frames a carved stone screen outside, blocking evil, unilinear-traveling spirits from entering (Figure 3.549). Summertime cicadas were rattling on the day that I visited, adding a mysterious sound (Figure 3.549vid). Like the brain's (or a group's) inhibitory circuits, blocking yet needing the trickster *stagehands* of subconscious networks with animal drives, the specific spaces of this temple involve repeated themes of architectural, pictorial, and performative control, built upon fish-turtle survival, mammalian reproduction, and human playfulness, extending toward godlike powers and transcendent meanings.

The sacrifices that developed in Europe, through intergroup competition and in-group idolization, with pilgrimage sites and miraculous objects, are reflected, too, in the nearby **Upper Tianzhu (Shangtianzhu or Faxi) Temple**. It was founded in 939 by the monk Daoyi, but destroyed during the Cultural Revolution and then rebuilt in 1985 and 1991 ("Buddhist"). Early on, it became famous for a naturally "self-made," sandalwood carving of "White-Robed Guanyin," found inside a piece of driftwood—as described by the Song dynasty poet Su Shi a thousand years ago (Broeskamp 109–10). The natural statue, now lost, was probably the first, highly venerated, white-robed, female form of the bodhisattva, becoming the origin point for "the most popular cult in China." It made Hangzhou an early center of Guanyin worship (Palmer et al. 28–33), although by the fourteenth century, Mt. Putuo Island became a more prominent pilgrimage site.

According to monastery records, the miraculous Guanyin statue granted rain in many years and saved Hangzhou from floods in 1065, 1580, and 1608 (C.-f. Yü 198). It also provided Upper Tianzhu monastery with an "accumulation of wealth" from pilgrims (Broeskamp 201). Zunshi, the monastery's Tiantai abbot, who was installed in 1015, popularized the inner visualizing of Guanyin by lay performers, while they fasted and offered food to hungry ghosts and departed ancestors—through a manual he wrote on the "Ghost Feeding" ritual (131–3). Akin to the Protestant Reformation in Europe 500 years later, he empowered lay people to realize their "innate Guanyin capacities," without the monk as mediator (132). But that also involved a Catholic-like miraculous icon, for outer/inner-theatre interplay. A pilgrimage to the White-Robed Guanyin statue became especially attractive for women, promising material and spiritual benefits, through invocations and recitations, "not as mere mechanical repetitions but with a sincere and attentive attitude" (134–5).

Today, steps lead up to the temple's initial gate hall, where a round vent displays the arhats Subinda, holding his pagoda, and Nantimitolo, balancing on his dragon (Figures 3.550–2). Beyond that, signs in English point to various halls (Figures 3.553–5). A stone arch bridge crosses a pond with a hexagonal pavilion and many trees nearby (Figures 3.556–7). Then a walkway extends further uphill with lanterns and carved stone pillars, leading to another gate with stone lions guarding it (Figures 3.558–9). Beyond that, a spirit screen appears opposite the Maitreya Hall, protecting it from linear-trickster ghosts with the phrase "Look at the light-hearted Bodhisattva" (Figures 3.560–1). Hall walls have plants outside and round vents with elephant and lion scenes, balancing the natural, manmade, and supernatural dimensions (Figures 3.562–3).

Inside, visitors meet the laughing, chubby Budai-Maitreya, with a decorated ceiling above him and altar scenes below, plus guard dog, cranes, dragons, and angelic, yet nymph-like apsaras around him (Figures 3.564–73). The guardian Wei Tuo stands behind him, also with a guard dog and altar decorations, plus a kneeler for people with incense (Figures 3.574–84). On the sides of the hall, seated on tiger skins, with feet balancing on rival, demigod *asuras*, are the Four Heavenly Kings in the highest reincarnation realm as gods (but its lowest level), according to Indian Buddhism as well. Guang Mu (Virupaksha in Sanskrit), king of the west, who sees all, holds a snake-dragon and pearl (Figures 3.585–7). Duo Wen (Vaisravana), protector of the north and ruler of rain, who hears everything, holds his umbrella-banner and pagoda, with mountains on his knees like the others (Figures 3.588–91). Chi Guo (Dhritarashtra), king of the east and god of music, has his stringed pipa, converting others to Buddhism through compassionate harmonious playing (Figures 3.592–7). Zeng Zhang (Virudhaka), king of the south and wind, who causes the growth of roots, holds his sword to protect the Buddhist Dharma (Figures 3.598–9). People kneel to honor them and make offerings, with the outside elements connected through a decorated vent hole (Figures 3.600–03). Thus, the balancing act of natural and supernatural wind and rain, or harmonious and omniscient rule, appears with the Heavenly Kings, their feet supported by demigod *asuras*—like the higher-order awareness of the human brain with its subcortical networks.

In the courtyard, the visitor can walk on a bridge between long rectangular pools, which have statues of Guanyin's acolytes, Dragon Princess on a dragon and Shancai on lotus blossoms, with coins that others have tossed (but not with "lotus feet"), while trees and lanterns from above are reflected in the water (Figures 3.604–09). Steps lead to the

Figure 3.592 Kings of the East and South, with feet on *asuras*, Upper Tianzhu Temple.

next level of the yard, where there are round and hexagonal burners with dragons, plus another hexagonal structure showing the Great Compassion mantra of Guanyin and more dragons (Figures 3.610–15). The visitor can also look back and see Wei Tuo in the doorway of the previous hall, as persistent guardian bodhisattva (Figure 3.616). Closer to the second hall are oil lamp stands, a wooden kneeler, a long, decorated, offering box, and a table of books (Figures 3.617–19). But this does not prevent worshipers from bowing with incense toward the statues on the other side of the table, inside the hall (Figures 3.620–1). When I visited, a worker was washing the concrete floor of the hall, yet access was still allowed to the statues, in the stage-managing of their theatrical spaces (Figures 3.622–3).

There is a large drum in the front left corner and bell in the front right (Figures 3.624–6), as is typical in temples that do not have them housed in separate towers at the front of the complex. A golden Buddha, in relief, offers an exemplary pose above the small Guanyin statue of the central shrine, perhaps a replica of the original "White-Robed Guanyin," along with pedestal scenes (Figures 3.627–9). In front and above them are a decorated lamp and ceiling (Figure 3.630). There are also side altars with statues and kneelers, plus a shrine with a dragon banner frame and multiple Guanyin images (Figures 3.631–5). The sunlight coming into the hall, reflecting off the wet floor and the columns, adds a distinctive beauty to the performance of inner spaces and to the high threshold at the doorway, meant to keep out bad spirits (Figures 3.636–42). Sunlight also illuminates a decorated vent hole and windows above it, with banners hanging near them, beside the central shrine (Figures 3.643–4). While I was there in summer 2013, watching a worshiper kneel, an attendant added a candle's light to the altar, changing its appearance (Figures 3.645–9). The interplay in this hall between light and darkness, open and enclosed spaces, individual and collective identities (along with the Buddhist doctrine of no-self and the Chinese tradition of seeking help from idealized immortals) reflects the dialectical, contextual, more right-cortical networks of cognition, which are characteristic of East Asian cultures, in comparison with Western (Li).

Outside the hall, there are stairs upward to another level (Figures 3.650–1). Its yard has a large, round, pagoda-like burner, plus a rectangular one, with fanged faces on their legs (Figures 3.652–6). Red lanterns hang from the tree branches above (Figures 3.657–9). On the hall's wall, a round vent hole shows a scene of mountains, clouds, and a curved bridge (Figure 3.660). While in the yard, reverential visitors, mostly women, bow in the four cardinal directions with incense held at their foreheads, then place it in the burner and proceed up the steps to the next hall—a typical, personal rite in all Chinese temples (Figures 3.661–6).

Many potted plants appear along the stairs and beside them (Figure 3.667). Buddha figures inside are visible through the open doorway, which states: "Majestic Hero Palace," a typical name for the main hall (Figure 3.668). Once inside, the visitor finds kneelers, an offering box, candles, and three serene statues: Amitabha, Shakyamuni, and Medicine Buddha, almost identical in their mindfulness, yet disrupting the viewer's attachment to one ideal as ego image (Figures 3.669–71). Framing them are circular banners, ceiling tiles, a hanging lantern, and an ornate dragon banner, with Chinese

Figure 3.674 Visitor bowing below arhat wall, Upper Tianzhu Temple.

characters above it stating: "Buddha's light shines everywhere" (Figure 3.672). Thus, the spaces in the hall, along with its imagery, perform around the visitor, who has an "audience" with transcendent figures as enlightened brain spirits.

After kneeling and donating there, the visitor may also do so along the sides and back of the hall, honoring many, colorfully displayed arhats, such as Maha Panthaka with his very long arm (Figures 3.673–7). They appear at the back of the central shrine, too, leaning out toward the visitor, who may kneel and bow there (Figures 3.678–82). The arhats are placed high above, as if on a mountainous cliff or in a cave, and nearer on waves, including Asita (Changmei) with his long eyebrows (Figures 3.683–6). There is also a small Guanyin statue on the ornately decorated altar, plus a smaller offering table (Figures 3.687–90). The arhats have animal figures around them: birds, a rabbit, an octopus, fish, an ox, a boar, and others (Figures 3.691–7). Vijraputra has a lion cub in his hand (Figures 3.698–9). Gobaka also appears with his heart's Buddha-nature revealed, near another arhat on a crab (Figure 3.700). Apsaras fly along the base of the shrine, beside more natural scenes of bird, trees, and mountains (Figures 3.701–03). Along the back and side walls of the hall, arhats ride a deer (as Pindola Bhradvaja), donkey, giraffe, turtle, fish, elephant (as Kalika), birds, and other animals (Figures 3.704–14). Nantimitolo tames a dragon and Subinda holds his pagoda (Figure 3.715). Pindola rides his tiger, although another arhat (or Pindola again?) has one on a leash (Figures 3.716–17 and 3.717vid). Thus, the animal-human heritage of our body-brain networks are evoked, through their playfulness drive, as in the eighteenth-century Emperor Qianlong's eulogy for Vijraputra (Xiaoshi), as Laughing Lion Luohan: "Playful and free of inhibitions, / The lion cub leaps with joy. / Easily alternating tension with relaxation, rejoicing with all living things" ("Eighteen Arhats").

Behind this hall, there is a decorated retaining wall with further images and stairs to the residential buildings (Figure 3.718). The visitor may then walk back through the shrines with their open doors on each end, into the yards, which have burners for lay people to feed the spirits and a fish drum to call the monks at mealtimes (Figures 3.719–22). One might also meet other visitors, burning their offerings and bowing at statues, in this temple's dispersed staging of various sacred areas (Figure 3.722vid). Its tragicomic participatory spaces may evoke sadness at remembered losses, yet hope for spiritual connections, with mixed arousal and calm, pain and pleasure, rebalancing the brain-body's inner theatre, across right, left, limbic, and subcortical networks, toward a more enlightened awareness and transcendent joy.

Unlike the left-cortical, linear focus of aisles and vertical spaces, with divine and saintly ego models in European parish churches, this Chinese monastery temple emphasizes right-cortical, contextual circumambulation around and within its various halls, through horizontal, dispersed, open, and naturally balanced spaces. There is thus a dialectic of collectivist orders in monastic rites and individual connections to enlightened figures or deceased family members, through ideals of non-attachment and lay rites of material sacrifices (offerings of incense, spirit money, food, and drink). This also involves the dialectic of wisdom and compassion through inner *scriptwriter/critic* and *mime/improviser* networks, interacting with memorial *audience* ghosts and animal-drive supportive/trickster *stagehands*, within and between brains. As typical of

Chinese temples, in contrast to European churches, balance is valued here between good and threatening spirits, *yang* and *yin* elements, high and low arousal, or individual and collective identities—rather than sacrificial domination over evil, sin, and nature. Yet the hierarchical orders of Heng and Ha or Heavenly Kings on demigods, and of Buddhas with princely attributes, reflect levels of being that transcend others. How do Chinese temples, sometimes flowing along hillsides, relate to folk religion's sacrificial sites of dominant imperial rule, between heaven and earth—like and unlike Roman Catholic churches with territorial hierarchies and Holy Land translations?

Shapes of Heaven and Earth with Altar Mounds

The traditional Chinese view of the sky as round and earth as square (Zhongshu) can be seen in Beijing's fifteenth-century **Tiantan (Temple of Heaven)** with its sacrificial altars, expanded in the sixteenth century by the Ming Emperor Jiajing. It includes an open-air stone platform for plant, animal, and human sacrifices. Such altars for imperial offerings have existed in China for about three thousand years, documented since the Western Zhou dynasty (Cannon 203–04). Redeveloped as a cultural attraction and public park, after late nineteenth-century occupations by European armies, the Temple of Heaven complex, to the south of the Forbidden City, also includes two buildings with pointed, circular roofs and walls (Lip 79–83). "In accordance with principles dating back to pre-Confucian times, the buildings in the Temple of Heaven are round, like the sky, while the foundations and axes of the complex are rectilinear, representing the earth. The complex served as the setting in which the emperor, the Son of Heaven, directly beseeched Heaven to provide good harvests throughout the land" (Yanxin 44). Yet "Heaven" (*tian*) did not bear the transcendent, universal Almighty-God ideal of ontological (first-principle) Being in the Western tradition, but rather a zoetological (life-process) sense of Becoming, as collective nature without individual personality (Ames; Ziporyn 285–6).

The sky is masculine (*yang*) and earth feminine (*yin*), yet the sky is round and earth square, with cold *yin* coming from the sky and hot *yang* coming from the earth. "The two intermingle and interpenetrate, and from their union all things are born" (Chuang Tzu, qtd. in Schipper 113). This reflects a dialectical interplay in Chinese culture between the left-cortical, more masculine, patriarchal, rule-based and right-cortical, more feminine, maternal, holistic networks of the human brain, extending to the cosmos. It also relates to the seventh-century Chinese image of a primordial *yang* god and *yin* goddess, Fuxi and Nüwa, as creator-parents of humans, with each measuring the opposite energy of *yin* earth and *yang* sky, using a square and compass, together establishing order (*ju-gui*). Both are reflected in the round Temple of Heaven buildings, with their rectilinear foundations, supporting structures, and connecting axes—or in the numerous round and rectilinear designs of burners and buildings in various other Chinese temples.

Chinese folk religion, according to ancient writings, used a square altar mound of three or nine steps, representing a mountain, with offerings given to various gods seated on the steps (Schipper 92). The enclosure was open air, but with doorways for priests. Likewise, current Daoist temples have a north hall with steps or tables stacked up, leading to one or three key statues, as an inner chamber, yet mountain altar. During rituals, the priest is surrounded by god images in other halls on the west and east, plus patron saints on the south side (front entry), thus placing him inside the sacred mountain of the ancient model, the Space of the Dao (Schipper 93). Related to this, the initial entry hall of both Daoist and Buddhist temples is often called *shan-men* or "gate to the mountain" (Naquin and Yü 11).

Traditionally, the emperor, as Son of Heaven, along with his empress, gave dutiful offerings in a sacred space to bring seasonal benefits of nature to his people, which the Temple of Heaven complex exemplifies (Paper et al. 48–9). Such responsibilities extend back two thousand years in Chinese philosophy, because otherwise "excessive rain results from an emperor's wildness, excessive drought from arrogance, heat from indolence, cold from hasty judgment, and winds from stupidity" (Sharf 88). The ancient emperor's palace had a "Hall of Light," modeling the universe with a round roof and square base. He moved to a special room at each cardinal point for the different seasons, and to the central room, honoring the Earth, in the third month of each season, embodying their cycles and balances. "The colors of his clothing, his food, everything had to be in keeping with the cosmic cycle so as 'not to interfere' and to insure universal harmony" (Schipper 102).

Today, the vast park around the Temple of Heaven, extending 2.73 square kilometers (over a square mile), is both a tourist site and recreational area used by locals with annual passes for entry. At the ticket office of the East Heavenly Gate, a visitor can rent an audio guide that shows a map of the various sites along rectilinear paths (Figure 3.723). A similar signposted map outlines the curved walls at the north side of the park, representing heaven, and the rectangular southern walls, representing earth (Figure 3.724). Nearby, the "Seven-Star" sculptured stones represent the famous peaks of Mount Tai, placed by Ming Emperor Jiajing, with an eighth added by Emperor Qianlong in the 1700s, showing a union of the Chinese and Manchurian people during the later Qing dynasty (Figures 3.725–6). Walking north and west along rectilinear paths, the visitor reaches an intricately decorated corridor, which has animal sacrifice and kitchen buildings alongside it, plus the round Hall of Prayer for Good Harvests (or for a Prosperous Year) visible in the distance (Figures 3.727–9). Locals socialize and play cards at various spots within the corridor (Figures 3.730–3). Security guards in dark uniforms with red armbands also keep order (Figure 3.734). The *yin* and *yang* interplay of these spaces thus involves current games, representative mountains, and Communist authorities, along with mythical, ritual, and historical dimensions.

Further along the corridor, one reaches the North Divine Kitchen, used to prepare animal sacrifices in the past (Figures 3.735–6). It was closed on the Monday when I visited in July 2019, but I still saw its walls and courtyard. Closer to the Hall of Prayer, the walkway rises above a level yard with a side opening to the rectilinear foundation of supportive buildings around the temple (Figures 3.737–42). Once inside the rounded gate, a visitor sees the three-gable, pagoda-like Hall of Prayer with its three-level, circular base and extensive, rectilinear, tiled courtyard (Figures 3.743–4). To the left are two rectangular buildings and a gate forming the southern entrance to the yard along the central axis of the complex (Figures 3.745–6).

The Hall of Prayer for Good Harvests (Qiniandian) was originally built in 1420. It is 38 meters (125 feet) tall and 32 meters (105 feet) in diameter, involving a white marble base, red walls, blue tile roof, and gold top with many intricate, blue, green, and gold design elements (Figures 3.747–8). Composed of wood with no nails, the hall was struck by lightning and burned in 1889, but was rebuilt a few years later. The levels of the marble base have multiple cylinders with worn carvings and drainage spouts stylized as clouds (lowest level), *yin* phoenixes (mid), and *yang* dragons (top), plus round metal burners (Figures 3.749–56). Likewise, rectangular scenes along the stairway show bas-reliefs of mountains with clouds, phoenixes, and dragons (Figures 3.757–8). There is also a direct view of the main entrance gate to the south and corner buildings in the yard (Figures 3.759–61). These views, details, and spaces—despite the many milling and photo-posing tourists (with umbrellas for shade against the sun)—evoke a sense of balanced grandeur, reflecting the sky's vastness above.

Climbing the steps of the white-marble altar mound, the visitor reaches the wooden Hall of Prayer, with a sign above its doorway showing three Chinese characters: to pray, annual, and good harvest/luck (Figures 3.762–3). Multiple *yang* dragons and *yin* phoenixes are painted above the doorways and on the three-tiered roof, often in balanced pairs, near the dougong earthquake-proof brackets (Figures 3.764–70). Visitors are not allowed inside. But peering through an open doorway, they can see twelve outer, twelve middle, and four inner columns, symbolizing twelve daytime hours, twelve months, and the four seasons, around a central altar (Figures 3.771–7).

Just north of this prominent circular hall, on a lower level, is the rectangular Imperial Hall of Heaven, or Hall of Imperial Zenith, with its three-doorway gate (Figures 3.778–84). It was also built in 1420 as the royal warehouse for the Heaven

Figure 3.744 Hall of Prayer for Good Harvests, Temple of Heaven.

God's and imperial ancestors' tablets used for rituals in the Hall of Prayer. A metal sign nearby explains this and states: "The day before the ceremony the emperor came here in person to burn incense sticks and perform the divine greetings for the transference, and then the officials of the Ministry of Rituals transferred the tablets to their appropriate places in the Hall of Prayer for Good Harvests" (Figure 3.785). Today's tourists, mostly Chinese, descend the steps to the Imperial Hall of Heaven and peer inside (Figures 3.786–9). From the doorway, visitors can see several altars on the left and right walls, plus a central one and the decorated ceiling with dragon and phoenix elements (Figures 3.790–4). However, as with the Hall of Prayer, visitors are not allowed inside. This maintains an exclusive sanctuary space in each building, which *performs* for visitors (along with the uniformed attendants) at a certain distance.

These sacrificial halls now function as tourist sites, not active worship places. Yet, they have become cultural relics of an imperial past with a continued *aura*. The lower Imperial Hall warehouse and higher Hall of Prayer, along a north–south axis, reflect the sacrifices still required for interdependent selves to find meaningful orientations of their bio-cultural drives (Table 1.1). The balance between the upper prayer hall's roundness and lower imperial warehouse's rectangularity might suggest the more right-cortical, nurturing powers of the natural sky, in relation to the more left-cortical, symbolic order of earthly rules. Perhaps they also reflect centralized dominance, yet interdependent duties in China's territorial, hierarchical ancestry, continuing in the PRC, as the Communist Party struggles to balance top-down decisions (such as the Zero Covid policy) with popular demands and capitalist rivalries, within the country and along new silk roads.

Leaving the yard of the Imperial Hall of Heaven, the visitor passes again through its rectilinear gate, which frames the round Hall of Prayer for Good Harvests above it (Figures 3.795–6). Walking up the steps toward the three-tiered, round eaves of that hall, one sees scenes of mountains and clouds on the stairway (Figures 3.797–8). At the Hall of Prayer, alternating dragons and phoenixes appear above the visitor, as a repeated, *yang* and *yin* interplay (Figures 3.799–806). The visitor can also look beyond the round courtyard and decorated fence, at the base of the altar mound, toward several rectangular buildings south of it, in the larger, rectangular yard below, with one area cordoned off for repair work when I was there (Figures 3.807–12). Walking down the central steps toward these halls, one can again view a dragon scene between the steps and a phoenix scene below it, plus tourists taking photos, all performing their roles, as does the space around them (Figures 3.813–15).

To the southeast, the rectangular East Annex Hall formerly held tablets honoring "attendant gods," according to the sign near it (Figures 3.816–18). It now offers an exhibit about the central Hall of Prayer, with drawings and models of possible, round and rectilinear designs from earlier periods, including the Western Zhou, Eastern Han, and Tang dynasties, three thousand, two thousand, and fourteen hundred years ago (Figures 3.819–23). On the other side of the forecourt, the West Annex doorway welcomes visitors with decorated lintel and ceiling elements (Figures 3.824–6). Inside, there is another exhibit with images and objects related to the site (Figures 3.827–8). These museum exhibits in the Annex Halls help to shape visitors' inner theatre experiences of the site and its historical spaces, from past events to current imaginings.

Between the two annexes, the visitor reaches a gatehouse (Qinianmen) on the north–south axis, with a blue tile roof, plus dragon and phoenix decorations, mimicking the Imperial Hall of Heaven designs (Figures 3.829–30). It exemplifies "the highest ranking gate system in ancient China," according to a nearby sign (Figure 3.831). There is also a souvenir stand near the gatehouse and one of its dragons (Figures 3.832–3). The central, closed, rectilinear doorway was originally for the imagined God of Heaven's entry, during ritual processions, while the east door was for the emperor and the west for other officials, according to the sign. There is a similar gatehouse beyond it as well, but with rounded openings (Figures 3.834–5). The steps up to the doorway include a balustrade with dragon decorations (Figures 3.836–8). This gatehouse, the second that officials would reach en route to the Hall of Prayer, has side rooms, currently with gift shops, outside and inside the doorway (Figures 3.839–42). Thus, capitalist tourism supersedes ancient tradition at these parts of the formerly sacred site in communist China.

Looking back at the Hall of Prayer, one gets the view of the emperor and imperial officials in their procession toward the sacrificial area (Figures 3.843–4), as "horizontal axis elements" metaphorically rise "in succession one above the other, with the necessary gateways to heaven in between" (N. Wu 44). One can also see a further interplay of gold phoenixes and dragons on the rectilinear frames, with alternating blue and green backgrounds (Figures 3.845–6). The corner roof eaves are curled, almost imperceptibly, with animals along their ridges, including horned *chaofeng* dragons, which "frighten away evil spirits and stave off disaster" (Bates 56), plus the hornless *chiwen* dragon at each apex tip (Figures 3.847–52). Such "ridge-biters" are

Figure 3.848 Gatehouse roof figures, Temple of Heaven.

"fond of swallowing" (Bates 57–8) and "keen on looking long distances," as they protect a building from fire damage (Yang and An 103).

Animals ritually sacrificed in the emperor's prayers for "Good Harvest" at the winter solstice, extending back two thousand years ago to the Han dynasty (Birrell 73), are reflected in such gatehouse rooftops—along with the powers of nature to shelter, nurture, and destroy. Currently, human animals appear to walk freely through the gatehouse in both directions. But their emotions, behaviors, and perceptions are also constructed by the sacrificial demands their bodies and brains have inherited, from natural drives to cultural desires, as communist citizens or capitalist tourists.

Visitors walking in this reconstructed territory of imperial rule are framed by the dragon-phoenix interplay in spaces around them, resonating with the inner theatre *yang-yin* of left and right cortical circuitry. Today's brain networks inherit the need to survive and reproduce, in competition and cooperation with others, through multiple hierarchies from family to government. Leaders must produce benefits from "heaven," while ordering certain degrees of conformity yet change, or be deposed if they fail to bring prosperity. Such inner and outer theatre networks of bio-cultural identity needs, with sacrificial demands, became more apparent in 2020, not long after I visited. Emergency measures were taken by governments to tame the dragon of a novel coronavirus, spreading from China across the globe, while hoping for the phoenix (in the Western sense) of economic recovery, as a return to Good Harvests of the past.

The smaller gatehouse on the south–north axis toward the Hall of Prayer, the first that officials would meet in past processions, does not have side rooms (Figures 3.853–4). Yet its middle doors, designated for the god of Heaven, are still closed today (Figures 3.855–7). Farther along a paved, elevated walkway, the Danbi Bridge, with its view back to the rectangular gatehouse and round temple-hall top, there are side stairs where visitors can leave to find trees and other elements of the surrounding park (Figures 3.858–60). Or visitors can continue along the walkway toward another rectilinear gate near the next hall, the round Imperial Vault of Heaven (Figures 3.861–4).

Taking the departure into the park, one might find local people dancing, performing tai chi, playing, or singing Chinese opera in a group (Figure 3.865 and 3.865vid1–2). One can also walk to the Fasting Palace at the west side of the park, built in 1420 for the emperor to abstain from meat, liquor, music, women, and state affairs for three days prior to the biannual rituals to secure good harvests for the people (Figures 3.866–7). The square Fasting Palace complex has a double wall and moat around it (Figure 3.868–73). A visitor can then walk back to the main, south–north axis with its Achieving Purity Gate (Chengzhenmen), 500-year-old "Nine-Dragon Cypress" (with branches appearing like dragons), Imperial Vault of Heaven surrounded by an Echo Wall, and nearby gift shop (Figures 3.874–9). There, tourists dress as an emperor on a golden throne, finding another way for inner and outer theatres to resonate (Figure 3.880).

Similar to yet smaller than the Hall of Prayer, and with more roundness in its triple-gate Echo Wall, the circular, single-gabled Imperial Vault of Heaven (built in 1530, rebuilt in 1572), has rectangular annexes (Figures 3.881–5). Within its courtyard, the East Annex Hall formerly held tablets honoring the gods of the sun, Mercury, Mars, Venus, Jupiter, polar stars, and other celestial lights. Altars for such tablets were still visible inside, along with dragons in the ceiling, plus weary tourists on the steps outside, when I visited (Figures 3.886–93). The West Annex Hall, formerly held tablets of the moon (Nocturnal Brightness), Clouds, Rain, Wind, and Thunder, with such altars likewise visible now (Figures 3.894–7). An oval "Echo Wall" surrounds these buildings, with special acoustic properties, adding an outer-theatrical dimension that echoes the past (Figure 3.898).

Tourists may face a waiting line to go up the steps and around the balcony at the Imperial Vault of Heaven, with mountains and clouds depicted near the stairs (Figures 3.899–901). But from the top, they can enjoy a view of the yard, gates, burners, lamps, and annex halls, plus dragons protruding from the Imperial Vault's base and decorating its balcony (Figures 3.902–09). Peeking inside, one can see several altars for the imperial ancestors, on each side of the central one for the divine Emperor Above of High Heaven, Haotian Shangdi (Figures 3.910–11). There are also red columns and a golden dragon in the dome above, playing with a "pearl of wisdom," symbolizing its power to ascend to heaven (Bates 96), in the cosmic theatre reflected here (Figures 3.912–13).

The Circular Mound Altar area (built in 1530, enlarged in 1749), with Lingxing Gates, appears at a distance as the visitor walks south of the Imperial Vault of Heaven, through the Echo Wall's triple gate, which like others has its central door closed (Figures 3.914–15). The Circular Mound was built a century after the Hall of Prayer, shifting the center of the "strict symmetrical layout" of cardinal axes in the Temple of Heaven complex "southward to the thoroughfare between the east and west gates. The new position determined the north–south length of the Circular Mound complex, and one-third of that distance became the side length of its square (outer) low wall" (Xinian 346). Thus, right-cortical *mime-improviser/designer* (Devil's Advocate) departures can be seen here, with and against a fully controlled, symmetrical layout, through proportional lengths and strong axes, like and unlike Saint Peter's Square. According to *feng-shui* geomancy, "straight lines of flow" are dangerous and "require that perfect regularity and axiality always be somehow disrupted" (Jones 1: 88).

Approaching the Circular Mound today, one meets the three open frames in two parallel sets of white-marble Lingxing (Star) Gates and their walls, the first rectilinear, the second circular, symbolizing earth and heaven (Figures 3.916–17). The red walls are topped with blue tiles, which include dragons (Figures 3.918–19). Dragon spouts also appear along the three levels of the white mound, below its balustrades (Figures 3.920–3). Climbing the three sets of nine steps to the top platform, which symbolize the nine levels of Heaven, the visitor experiences the "strong *yang*" of nine as the biggest, single-digit, odd number, also associated with dragons (Figures 3.924–5). From the top of this "Heaven Worshipping Terrace," one can look back to the north at the Lingxing Gates and Imperial Vault, or toward the corners and roundness of the earth and heaven walls, with Beijing skyscrapers beyond (Figures 3.926–8). One can also look south at another two sets of Lingxing Gates, plus the red entry (Zhaoheng) gate at the edge of the entire temple complex (Figures 3.929–30), framing the performance of various vast spaces—and evoking right-cortical, contextual networks.

There are also double Lingxing Gates to the west and east of the Mound, making eight in total, each with three frames, or twenty-four frames in all. According to a

Figure 3.926 Circular Mound to Lingxing Gates and Imperial Vault, Temple of Heaven.

nearby sign, these gates are "the Cloud Gates Forming a Jade Forest," regarding the blue-green floor of the Circular Mound, as bluestone tiles extend from its central "Heaven Heart Stone" in multiples of nine, with the materials and design amplifying the emperor's voice (Figure 3.931). Firewood ovens (one with green glazed tiles) are visible, too, along the outer, rectilinear wall—at sites where pine/cypress branches, animals, and humans were burned as offerings.[4] Thus, emperors at the center of the Circular Mound conducted the winter solstice rites, for hundreds of years (Figures 3.932–4). A Kitchen for Sacrifice and Pavilion of Immolation are also positioned east of the Circular Mound's walls, like those east of the Hall of Prayer.

With such reconstructions and signs, material and symbolic *translations* are made from China's past, like Catholic Christian relics *reframed* in church sanctuaries as holy, miracle-giving bones or other saintly items (though without miraculous beliefs). Ritual spaces for emperors in prior generations, as Sons of Heaven, involved animal-human sacrifices, which they led from the Heaven Heart Stone. Sacrifices were sent upward in smoke to bring rain and agricultural prosperity, yet also outward, beyond the Cloud Gates and Jade Forest, to the empire's people. Today, however, such spaces and their framing elements perform as heritage sites in a modern, autocratic, communist-capitalist context, interacting with the animal-human, inner theatres of tourists, perhaps also reflecting the sacrifices of religious groups who are not harmonious with the dominant order.

---

[4] According to a Chinese travel website: "To bid farewell to the gods, human sacrifices were burned in the oven. Next to the oven is a special pit called the Pit of Hair and Blood because the hair and blood of the sacrificial victims were buried here" ("Circular"). The *Ming Shilu* possibly records this during the early Ming dynasty (late fourteenth century), perhaps corroborated by Korean records in the *Dongguk Yeoji Seungnam*.

The consistency of designs across many buildings in the Temple of Heaven complex, such as gates, concentric platforms, and dragon/phoenix figures, reflects the dominance of imperial rule for thousands of years in China, with Beijing as its capital during various northern dynasties, especially the Ming (1403–1644) and Qing (1644–1912). This is shown, too, with **Ditan (Temple of Earth)**, built in 1530 under the Emperor Jiajing, north of his power base in the Forbidden City palace, while he expanded the Temple of Heaven south of it. He also built the Temple of the Moon to the west and Sun to the east, for seasonal rites involving officials but not the common people. Remnants of those two temples survive today just as gates and parks. Damaged during the Cultural Revolution, but partially restored after, the Temple of Earth is also a park for the people (Ditan Park), located near the Second Ring Road (Figures 3.935-7 and 3.937vid).

Inside the red wall, near its south entrance gate, the Earth God Worship House now functions as a one-room museum, the "Cultural and Historical Relic Exhibition Room," although the sign over the doorway says, "Imperial Family Room" (Figures 3.938-45). It has a central altar with representations of sacrificial animals (Figures 3.946-9). It also displays a decorated chair and carrying chair (Figures 3.950-4). The museum shows a model of the temple complex with the summer solstice rite, plus ceramic ritual objects and a terrain model of the open-air altars (Figures 3.955-60). A sign explains that ten days before the rite, sacrificial animals were picked. Three days prior, the emperor, his family, generals, and ministers abstained from meat, alcohol, banquets, and criminal cases to purify themselves. On the morning of the summer solstice, the gods were invited through memorial tables and then sacrifices were conducted by the emperor. The museum also displays spirit tablets, some on stylized mountains like those on the Temple of Heaven's Hall of Prayer stairs (Figures 3.961-4). It shows a drum stand with lions and bell racks with dogs and dragons (including the roaring *pulao* dragon atop the bells), suggesting to me the animal heritage of our inner theatre and cultural ideals, which sometimes demand sacrifices, especially in melodramatic modes (Figures 3.965-74).

Just north of the Earth God Worship House with its "relic" exhibition, a series of Lingxing (Star) Gates appear, like at the Circular Mound Altar of the Temple of Heaven, as entryways to the Square Water Altar, although these gates have doors (Figure 3.975). Inside the outer gate and wall, one finds a grey floor, which replaced the original yellow bricks when rebuilt in 1750 (Figure 3.976). Yellow tiles with *chiwen* dragons appear atop the red walls (Figure 3.977-80). The next gate has lower walls, but also dragons near it (Figures 3.981-2). Further inside, the grey floor continues with three white lanes marking the south–north axis (Figures 3.983-6). The "square water" moat has a grate over it (Figure 3.987). Steps rise to higher levels of two square platforms, with distant Star Gates also visible along the west–east axis, as well as south–north (Figures 3.988-95). A small metal altar with stylized animals (phoenixes?) is positioned at the center, on a square stone slab, with rectangular and round burners along the platform (Figures 3.996-1002). Thus, patriarchal territoriality and maternal (earth) nurturing are reflected in these spaces, balanced with supportive/trickster energies.

Squares within squares became stages for the emperor's summer solstice rite, honoring the Earth God, Houtu, depicted sometimes as female and sometimes as male

(Yang and An 135–6). The emperor expressed humility before the powers of nature, which the Son of Heaven needed to assure prosperity for the people. A key Daoist text, *Laozi* (or *Dao De Jing*), advises: "if you wish to be noble for sure, take humility as the root; / If you wish to be high for sure, take lowliness as the foundation" (Kim 27). Yet this site also shows the emperor's control over his people, at the heart of the magic squares of earthly survival, with bio-cultural drives of reproduction, care, territoriality, and alliance-hierarchy, through *designer* and *scriptwriter*, right and left cortical networks (Figures 3.1003–04).

The south–north axis line continues into the surrounding Ditan Park (Figures 3.1005–06). There is also a west–east axis, leading to other gates and buildings of this former temple complex (Figures 3.1007–08). Tree-lined walkways with side gardens, shelters, and other areas provide natural spaces where locals recreate (Figures 3.1009–13). An outer gate has several *chiwen* and *chaofeng* dragons on its green tile roof (Figures 3.1014–16). Walls within the park contain historical buildings that served the main altar area and some walls have dragons imprinted on their roof tiles (Figures 3.1017–19). The buildings include a Fasting Hall, Bell Tower, and "Holy Horse Cote" (Figures 3.1020–1). One can also find lotus flowers, which are symbols of enlightenment in Buddhism, with beauty blooming above the pond while tied to the muddy earth below (Figures 3.1022–4). The Temple of Earth park is much less touristy than the Temple of Heaven, with simpler translations of the imperial past into cultural "relics," natural environs, and popular recreational spaces—in the capital of the People's Republic.

While Ming emperors were sacrificing animals in elaborate rituals at the Temples of Heaven and Earth, to bring prosperity from the gods to their people, European patriarchs were using new scientific discoveries and military technologies, including Chinese gunpowder, to conquer much of the globe. Fueled by the belief in one Almighty God, as his "Chosen People," although with sibling rivalries between Catholics and Protestants, Europeans crossed oceans with soldiers, guns, and missionaries, plus germs to which they were better immune than the people they conquered. Western cultures eventually developed independent egos and states, with individual rights, yet much inequality across races, genders, and classes. The left-cortical, predatory *scriptwriter/critic* confidence of God-justified colonizers objectified people of other cultures as subhuman and their land as open for the taking, through a "Manifest Destiny." Thus, the sublimation of human sacrifice, from Isaac to a ram and from Jesus to bread and wine, in the biblical tradition, led to the building of churches for communal rites and preaching throughout Europe, the Americas, Africa, and Asia—yet also the real sacrifice of many people.

Likewise, the sacrificing of animals (or humans) by Chinese emperors, to please traditional gods, did not prevent the suffering of many subjects through natural calamities, wars, and revolutions. But compared with European churches, a more right-cortical, *mime/designer* interdependency becomes apparent in the openness to nature of temples along hillsides with their holistic spaces of gates and shrines, as symbolic mountains across vast axes, mimicking earth and heaven while honoring them. Sacred sites in the ancestor, nature, and enlightenment traditions of China, even with its current communist-capitalist trajectory, reflect more bilateral inner-theatre networks, in contrast with enclosed, land-dominating, human-sacrifice-commemorating, main-altar-focused, monotheistic churches of Europe. And yet, the grand horizontal scale of the Temples of Heaven and Earth might also be seen as reflecting modern autocratic collectivist demands for human sacrifices: in the recent Zero Covid policy or the earlier (anti-religious) Cultural Revolution, Great Leap Forward, and Hundred Flowers to Anti-Rightist Campaigns, with hundreds of thousands to tens of millions of deaths, through top-down, left-cortical, melodramatic controls.

Daoist Nature

Akin to Beijing's imperial temples, a Daoist sanctuary in the megacity of Guangzhou shows the grand goal of divine communication, with offerings and benefits, but on a small, ancient, hillside site with terraced yards, tall trees, and many statues. **Sanyuan Palace (Temple of the Three Primes)** was established as Bei Miao over 2,000 years ago, during the Nanyue Kingdom, according to Wikipedia ("Sanyuan"). More sources place its origin 1,700 years ago as Yuegang Yuan during the Jin dynasty (Ichiko 191). It was converted to a Buddhist site and renamed Wuxing Temple in the Tang period over 1,000 years ago. However, it was then reconverted as Daoist with its current name during the reign of Ming Emperor Wanli over 400 years ago. It was occupied, with statues destroyed, by the Red Guard during the Cultural Revolution but reopened in 1982 and was fully restored by 1990. Its name refers to the Three Great Emperor-Officials: Heaven, Earth, and Water, also known as the Great Emperors of Middle Heaven North Star, Pristine Emptiness, and Pervasive Yin.

Entering the temple's walled enclosure creates a contrast with the busy city outside, in the political and cultural center of Guangzhou with over 15 million people (Figures 3.1025–6). A banyan tree in the small initial yard and a steep stairway are early indications of the temple's openness to nature and harmonizing with Yuexiu Hill on its southern side, as a shiny sign in Chinese and English mentions, also offering a map of the various halls (Figures 3.1027–9). A spirit screen as "filial piety stone carving" protects the yard, across from the stairs, with space for cars to park, as well as bike deliveries (Figures 3.1030–40). The stone-carved screen shows episodes from the fourteenth-century Confucian classic, *The Twenty-Four Paragons of Filial Piety*. As the visitor climbs the temple's steep steps, more trees rise from the earth below the temple floor, with multi-columned trunks and arched branches (Figures 3.1041–6). Chinese characters appear around the gatehouse opening, which name the temple and its "Knowledgeable Famous Mountain." With the landing, midway up the stairs, there are offering boxes and guard lions, which local visitors touch for luck, in the temple's initial performance spaces (Figure 3.1047 and 3.1047vid).

A shrine area also appears to the right of the landing, Hall of the Local God of the Land, with several phrases around its arched doorway: "Three beautiful scenes to leave a fairy shadow" on the right, "Secluded forest and beautiful land" at the top, and "Looking for cranes in the ancient forest" on the left (Figures 3.1048–9). Through that

Figure 3.1045 Initial stairway, trees, and guard lions, Sanyuan Palace.

doorway, with another large tree framing the hall's open area, people bow with incense toward the Daoist shrine of local, husband and wife gods (Figures 3.1050–3 and 3.1053vid). They also give such offerings to a small statue of the Buddhist deity Guanyin, holding her elixir of compassion (Figures 3.1054–8). Nearby is a meeting and dining room for the Guangzhou Taoist Association with small statues of the Three Pure Ones, including Laozi (Figures 3.1059–61). In this temple, with its history of conversions, Daoist, Buddhist, and Confucian spaces coexist harmoniously, unlike the whitewashing of walls and iconoclastic removal of statues in the Protestant conversion or destruction of Catholic churches and monasteries in Northern Renaissance Europe—although the Communist Red Guard also performed that here more recently.

Returning to the stairway and guard lions, the visitor may look up in awe at the complex patterns of overarching tree branches, with further stairs up to the Mountain Gate (Figures 3.1062–3 and 3.1063vid). But such high arousal, especially in new visitors, would likely be counterbalanced by the calmness of various statues in regal, meditative, and compassionate poses, such as the Guanyin figure in the local gods' hall and in other areas uphill. Even the dragons carved along the stairway banisters are in balanced, albeit confrontational, pairs (Figures 3.1064–7). The central rectilinear yard at the top of the stairs, with the grey brick walls of various halls arrayed around it, again emphasizes balance, yet also openness to the round sky (Figures 3.1068–72 and

3.1072vid). Thus, over the main hall's opening, Chinese characters state: "the Dao follows nature," "Dao *qi* persists," and "the Dao opens the universe."

The initial Mountain Gate shrine, Wang Lingguan Hall, has a sign explaining that its deity is a "protector of the Taoist dharma," again showing a cooperative mix with this Buddhist term (Figures 3.1073–4). Wang Lingguan is also described as "knowing every little thing that is happening in the world through his three eyes" and alerting people to injustice with the whip in his hand. (But the image was not visible when I visited.) The moral authority and behavioral controls of inner *scriptwriter/critic* and *stage manager* networks are thus reflected with this Daoist deity, as with Christian depictions of God the Father and Christ Pantocrator, especially in the latter's Last Judgment scenes. And yet, Wang Lingguan is a guardian god, not the divine creator of the world as ultimate melodramatic victor over sin and death. Instead, he is a "demonic savior," a divine official who was invoked during exorcisms to express the supernatural powers of the Ming emperor (Naparstek). He was also invoked by Beijing theatre actors in the Qing period, while wearing his mask and using whips to exorcise the stage (Goossaert, "Ritual").

A series of small hall enclaves line the left side of the courtyard, with kitchen areas on the right. First is the Hall of the Wealth God, where visitors kneel with incense to ask help in financial matters (Figures 3.1075–8). Next is Bo Hall with stairs up to a room with small statues of the Three Pure Ones (Figures 3.1079–80). Next to that is a hall for Guanyin offerings with a Tang period statue of the Buddhist goddess, over a thousand years old, plus a smaller version (Figures 3.1081–6). Such interreligious, interdependent balancing, with low arousal figures, contrasts with Christian, competitive, territorial denominations stressing high arousal, negative to positive (HAN to HAP) ideals. Those involve mortal fear, righteous rage, heroic courage, and sublime awe, in enclosed main-aisle-focused church spaces with crucifixion/martyrdom imagery evoking melodramatic, good versus evil emotions. Here, the small, brick and tile halls, around an open courtyard with trees on a hillside, reflect the stone recesses of cave temples and harmony with the *yin-yang* of nature's Way.

There are two, round, multilevel burners in the yard's corners and a long rectangular burner in the center, with space for holding many visitors' incense sticks. Banners near the entryway state: "Legal Dragon," "Blessed be the Fortune God," and "Money and treasures will be plentiful" (Figures 3.1087–93). Both types of burners are decorated with dragons, as super-natural powers between earth and heaven, like the rising incense smoke. Up the stairway to the main hall's portico, miniature bonsai trees line the railing near small guard lions (sometimes with a cash donation), above the large burners and rectangular yard with its trees (Figures 3.1094–7). Dragons appear on roof and burner edges (Figures 3.1098–1101). A table in the main hall portico makes religious props, such as incense sticks and lamp oil, available for visitor and worker performances (Figures 3.1102–03 and 3.1103vid). The main hall displays the "Sanyuan" of Three Great Emperor-Officials with a fenced area and multiple tables bearing images for special rites (Figures 3.1104–10). A view from the portico landing back toward the yard shows big city apartment buildings beyond the temple (Figures 3.1111–14). A wall near the landing also offers a table with religious props and a sign explaining the hall's deities as "the sky god that gives blessings (Emperor Yao), the earth god that grants absolution (Emperor Shun), and the water god that fixes bad luck (Emperor Yu)" (Figures 3.1115–16). Thus, patriarchal figures are displayed but in a nurturing theatrical space, which recognizes yet "fixes" the trickster twists of "bad luck," reflecting left-cortical *scriptwriter/critic*, right-cortical *mime-improviser/designer*, and subcortical *stagehand* networks.

An archway to the left of the main hall leads to Bao Gu Hall with a sign explaining how it honors "Ms. Bao," a Daoist nun who picked a reddish "Artemisia" plant on the same Yuexiu hillside "to cure diseases" and also healed "tumors by acupuncture and moxibution" (Figures 3.1117–18). The central statue in the hall shows a flat-chested Ms. Bao with a stiff high collar, seated in a cross-legged lotus pose, with human and bird attendants on each side, a canopy over her, and altar area in front (Figures 3.1119–20). Also to the left, yet behind the main hall, the visitor finds a shrine honoring Tin Hau (Queen of Heaven), with a sign explaining that she is known as Tianfei (Princess of Heaven) or Mazu (Maternal Ancestor), Goddess of the Sea, who protects fishermen and sailors (Figures 3.1121–4). She was also the historical woman, Lin Moniang, who lived in the tenth century (Bosco and Ho). Ironically, as Maternal Ancestor, she never married nor had children. But this parallels the Catholic view of Mary as the historical mother of Jesus yet a lifelong virgin (although married to St. Joseph). With Jesus as the New Adam and Mary as the New Eve, she became the maternal ancestor of all believers and was often depicted holding a baby, unlike Chinese mother goddesses. Here, Tin Hau is shown as a regal figure, not a Madonna, in an inner area behind a metal fence, containing the statue, its canopy, and an altar. Yet there is also a table and kneeler for visitors to worship at the fence. Together, these female figures, Bao Gu and Tin Hau, along with Guanyin, offer a nurturing maternal counterbalance to patriarchal figures elsewhere in the temple, through their devotional performance spaces.

A male god appears in the next hall, Lord Guan Yu, both a famous historical general and divine "protector of the Taoist dharma," as the sign states (Figures 3.1125–9). Another small hall, behind the main one, displays Laozi, a deity and key historical figure of Daoism (Figures 3.1130–5). Yet a more comical figure appears in a corner area with a shiny metal fence: True Man Sun, the Rain Immortal, Great Sage of wind and rain, in a meditative cross-legged pose on a water buffalo, which also has its legs folded (Figures 3.1136–40). As the sign explains, he ended a drought by bringing rain during the reign of Emperor Qianlong (1711–99). Since then, people have "offered sacrifices to this god" to avoid the wrath of the Year God, Tai Sui, and "there is an endless stream of pilgrims." Thus, at least to this visitor, the "True Man" with a hat hanging on his back becomes a tragicomic figure as rain god alleviating people's suffering during drought, but in a humble form on a "water" buffalo, expecting an "endless" pilgrim "stream," which I did not see. Yet money offerings were left on the statue and its nearby plastic plate as "sacrifices."

In a nearby space along the back of Sanyuan Palace, the visitor finds a small stone bridge over an empty pool, needing or representing water, with turtle and rock sculptures (Figures 3.1141–3). There is also a shrine honoring the immortal trickster Lü Dongbin, known for his drunkenness, yet alchemical skill (Figures 3.1144–9). Along

Figure 3.1140 True Man Sun on a water buffalo, Sanyuan Palace.

the side walkway are tables with religious props for purchase, for temple or home performances, as the visitor returns to the stairs, main yard, and entry spaces with their openness to nature, plus complex banyan trunks and branches rising from earth to sky, but arching also back toward earth (Figures 3.1150–3 and 3.1153vid).

Openness to nature through trees and sky, with the potential for rain or snow in yards, while valuing female and trickster alternatives to patriarchal figures, reflects the Chinese dialectical ideal of tragicomic (HAN/HAP and LAN/LAP), interdependent harmony. This may help to rebalance visitors' inner theatre networks, making filters between right and left hemispheres more flexible, regarding limbic and subcortical circuits, through the temple's outer theatricality. Such emotion-clarifying, *rasa*-cathartic, contemplative "attunement" might be evoked in churches, too, especially with Stations of the Cross along the walls and Nativity, Madonna, or Pietà images in side altar chapels. But the enclosed focus of churches on the raised sacrificial altar-tabernacle, as ultimate sanctuary space, typically involves martyrdom and crucifixion scenes, or at least an abstract cross, signifying victory over sin, death, and evil. This prioritizes melodramatic victim-hero suffering as redemptive spiritual revenge against bodily temptations. Thus, the sacrificial bread and wine, becoming divine Body and Blood, shared in the communion rite, may also reflect a bloody history of Abrahamic rivalries. And yet, recent developments in the built environments of church spaces indicate an evolving awareness, too, of mimetic rivalry and melodramatic conquest as bearing tragic animal-human flaws and temptations.

Neoclassical to Modernist and Postmodern in Helsinki

Like the Orthodox Uspenski Cathedral on a nearby hill (Chapter 2), the **Finnish Lutheran Cathedral (Tuomiokirkko)** dominates its hilltop site in Helsinki, as a key focus for national and religious identity (Figures 3.1154–61 and 3.1161vid). Rising above the political center of the country, Senate Square, which also includes the main building of the city's university, the Lutheran Cathedral was built in 1830–52 as a tribute to the Russian tsar, Nicholas I, who was also Grand Duke of Finland. It was initially named "Nicholas Church." Senate Square includes a statue of the subsequent tsar, Alexander II, who increased Finland's autonomy in 1863 and promoted the Finnish language, against Swedish from the former half-millennium ruler. The cathedral was designed (with Senate Square) by Carl Ludvig Engel, displaying strong classical shapes: round and rectangular Corinthian columns on porticos with triangular pediments on each of four sides in its symmetrical Greek-cross plan, all in gleaming white, plus a central teal dome with a golden ball-and-cross on top (Figures 3.1162–8). There are also small scenes of Christ's passion and resurrection between the engaged pilasters (Figures 3.1169–72). Four towers with smaller domes and twelve pediment-edge apostle statues were added to Engel's exterior, after his death in 1840, by Ernst Lohrmann (Figures 3.1173–9). He put two small white buildings, as a bell house and chapel, at the western and eastern corners of the church square as well (Figures 3.1180–3 and 3.1183vid). Thus, monumental dominance of the hill and its capital city

Figure 3.1162 Finnish Lutheran Cathedral.

is shown with ancient temple shapes, awe-inspiring levels, sky-like domes (the small ones with golden stars), abstract crosses, and human figures in rectangular scenes and pediment edges.

Inside, the cathedral displays Protestant purity with mostly white, classical and abstract shapes: Ionic colonnades under the round balconies of narthex/apse and transept ends, Corinthian pilasters along the walls, and bare domes with a few skylights and chandeliers, plus light brown pews with door-gates (Figures 3.1184–97). The sole colorful painting in the church, a gift from Tsar Nicholas, attracts the visitor's eyes to the altar area (Figures 3.1198–9). It shows "The Deposition," with friends of Jesus holding his gray corpse after the crucifixion. Golden angel sculptures are perched above the painting on its frame and kneel at each side, while a red upholstered communion rail encircles it and the altar (Figures 3.1200–04). The tragic scene, along with a small baptismal font in front of the altar (Figure 3.1205), reflects and evokes compassionate, nurturing, right-cortical *mime/designer* circuits in visitors, counterbalancing the otherwise left-cortical *scriptwriter/critic* emphasis on classical purity throughout the church. This includes an elevated marble pulpit with golden canopy, to the left of the chancel space, for biblical readings and preaching (Figures 3.1206–10).

Another element in the church's architectural grandness gestures again to the right-cortical, contextual, musical aspect of ritual performances, with ties to participants' subcortical *stagehand* emotions: a silver and gold organ pipe display (Figures 3.1211–14).

Yet the only human sculptures in the church are three historical males at the corners of the crossing, like the pulpit at the fourth: Martin Luther, founder of Lutheranism, Philipp Melanchthon, his intellectual companion, and Mikael Agricola, who first translated the Bible into Finnish (Figures 3.1215–23). These figures assert patriarchal rectitude, reflecting left-cortical *scriptwriter/critic* dominance over other neural network and social performance inclinations.

Near the church's entrance there are offering candles that can be lit and placed on a spherical rack, in exchange for a donation, with a sign strictly stating in English: only one candle per holder and per person (Figure 3.1224). But when I visited in June 2016, local Finns had created another sacred area on the steps below the cathedral, with multiple lit candles, responding to recent news from the US with a sign in English: "To the victims of the Orlando shooting, Our thoughts are with you" (Figures 3.1225–6). Thus, right-cortical nurturing *improviser/designer* care extended, with tragic *rasa* compassion, from Old to New Worlds, beyond the church's left-cortical dominance of religious rites and spaces, with supportive/trickster *stagehand* playfulness, through personal memorial *audience* belonging and meaning-seeking. As I write this in 2023, however, the vulnerability of Finns may be greater than Americans in Orlando—living on the edge of a neo-imperialist Russia with a linked history in Helsinki, shown by its two cathedrals and its Senate Square statue of a tsar.

Twentieth-century modernist architects rejected traditional forms and ornamentations, valuing *functionalism*, with new materials and pure geometry. Yet some, such as Frank Lloyd Wright and Le Corbusier, valued architecture itself as sacred, with new and natural shapes forming the awe of "ineffable space" through maximum *intensity* (Crosbie, "Hermeneutics" 45–6). These twin ideals continued to develop as functional constructivist forms for sacred buildings (often in spare concrete) or "intensified, focused natural" forms with a "religion of art," especially through Corbusier's view of the "demiurge artist working in a secular era" (Kilde 185; Fernández-Cobián 379).

Showing both ideals, the **Rock Church (Temppeliaukion Kirkko)** of Helsinki, near the city center, was planned in the 1930s, but delayed by the Second World War, then redesigned and completed in 1969, scaled down to a quarter of its initial intended size. Even in the later design, it was not initially planned with bare rock walls, but with concrete covering them. And yet, that aspect of modernist "form ever follows function" (as Louis Sullivan put it) was reconsidered with acoustics in mind, by the brothers Timo and Tuomo Suomalainen. They developed the hilltop site as a sunken chamber, with rain or melting snow trickling along the natural cliff walls inside, reminiscent of the refugee architects' home island, Suursaari (Gogland), taken by Russia in the 1940s ("Temppeliaukio"). From outside, the church appears with minimally decorated, geometric shapes: a rock circle like a large well and a low copper dome added to the granite hillock (Figure 3.1227). At the street-level entrance, there is a flat concrete wall with an engraved cross and another outlined in red metal. Several noticeboards are also placed there, along with signs for the church café (Figures 3.1228–35).

After paying a small fee to enter and going through a short tunnel, the visitor finds a reception area with religious objects and souvenirs for sale, and then a votive area to the right with an offering box and candles, along the bare granite cliff (Figures 3.1236–49). In the main chamber, awe is evoked by the round ceiling, which has a solid copper-coil center with radiating concrete beams and 180 skylight windows, opening the rock-walled space to outside brightness while also suggesting a womblike cave (Figures 3.1250–64 and 3.1264vid). The concrete floor is almost level, with a slightly raised altar (just three steps), organ pipes and choir space to the left, small baptismal font made of rocks to the right, black and purple pews, and polygonal balcony in the back (Figures 3.1265–80). Rough stones are piled upon the cliff toward the ceiling, with a bit of greenery on each side of the altar (Figures 3.1281–3). Take-away greeting cards are offered in various languages at the back, while the balcony gives various awe-inspiring views (Figures 3.1284–1304 and 3.1304vid1–2). The overall design, with no human figures and no prominent pulpit, suggests horizontal, nurturing, shamanistic awe (rather than vertical, hierarchical, ecclesiastical), balancing HAP with LAP, arousing and peaceful *rasas*, which the visitor may taste through ritual beliefs, communal music, or silent introspection.

Temppeliaukion is a Lutheran church, like the cathedral, and often used for concerts. Yet its ritual and civic performance space of bare rock-wall acoustics involves visual harmony with the earthen hill site, instead of dominance over it. The Rock Church reflects a left and right cortical, patriarchal and maternal, *scriptwriter* and *mime-improviser*, tragicomic response to the melodramatic World War's destructive delay (and

Figure 3.1288 Lutheran Rock Church interior.

Europe's prior imperial rivalries) like a bombed hole or bomb shelter reborn. It also reflects more of an inclination toward, rather than rectitude filtering of personal memorial *audience* and supportive/trickster *stagehand* networks, as individualist and collectivist, inner and outer connections—with round, polygonal, and natural shapes, instead of transcendent cruciform designs or crucifixion imagery. Such limbic and subcortical, interdependent networks are suggested, too, by the church's exterior: a low dome and well-like rock circle, extending to the natural granite and plant environment, with a small playground nearby, while apartment buildings rise above it (Figures 3.1305–12).

Postmodern playfulness appears even more with the 2012 **Kamppi Chapel of Silence** near Helsinki's commercial center. Designed by Kimmo Lintula, Niko Sirola, and Mikko Summanen of K2S Architects, the small, ecumenical, windowless chapel, shaped like the bow of a ship, in light-brown wood treated with nanotech wax, seems to float on the open public concrete square toward the rising tide of the Kamppi shopping mall on the other side (Figures 3.1313–26). The space-ship bow also has a black trim at its top edge, suggesting a deck as roof, though it bears a hidden skylight. The bow points toward the shopping center and its bus terminal, plus an egg-shaped, hexagonal and box grid sculpture in the square (Figures 3.1327–33). It is if the chapel were arriving overland from Helsinki's harbor, on the other side of cathedral hill— from a fluid natural realm beyond the city's stable anthropo-scene. A few trees in

Figure 3.1340 Ground plan and reflection of Kamppi Chapel of Silence in its window.

concrete planters around the chapel also relate to its curved timber planks, which shine in various nanotech ways with the shifting Scandinavian sunlight and shadows (Figures 3.1334–7). These aspects reflect the coordination, too, of creators' and visitors' inner theatres in such religious yet commercial spaces: mythic *scriptwriter/critic* heritages, mimetic *improviser/designer* growth, personal/collective *audience* associations, and trickster/supportive *stagehand* play-work.

A rectangular entry-hall narthex is joined at an angle to the bow-shaped chapel, emphasizing its visual pun as nave (Latin *navis* for "ship") with a ground plan outlined on the glass wall and an equilateral cross on the exterior brick (Figures 3.1338–42). The narthex interior offers a basic corporate space (like many Protestant churches in the US) with a table, chairs, door to offices, and view of the commercial square (Figures 3.1343–4). Yet there are also religious books and information along the wall, near a second entry door, with more diagrams of the chapel's rectangle plus ship-shape design (Figures 3.1345–9). Near the entry door to the nave are offering candles, a signature book, and brochures in various languages (Figures 3.1350–3).

Inside, an oval skylight offers a halo around the ceiling's solid center, like the window rays in the Rock Church, but in a much smaller, womblike nave with curved wooden walls, yet rectilinear pews (Figures 3.1354–64). The small altar-podium, with open Bible and simple cross, plus candle and flower stands beside it, creates a chancel space at the front of the chapel's bow, aligned with the aisles and pews (Figures 3.1365–70). And yet, more playful-looking cushions are piled against the side wall, like large pebbles on a beach (Figures 3.1371–6). The round pillows and curved walls, with natural *inclined* metonyms of pebbles, beach, and ship's hull, contrast with the *rectilinear* pews, though they also reflect the wooden theme, thus balancing maternal, patriarchal, and trickster/supportive aspects. In the back, there is a candle stand, with curved lines drawn in the sand, like a gravel garden in a Japanese Zen temple (Figures 3.1377–82).

Instead of a more left-cortical inspired church with monumental façade and rising towers, dominating its hilltop site, plus a focused interior of low to high ceiling arousal and main aisle to sacrificial altar hierarchy, *awe* and *peace* are evoked in this small chapel, as a curved common nurturing area and playful space of interdependent *rasas*, harmonizing with natural associations. This is akin to Chinese temples, even as an enclosed skylight sanctuary. Thus, from its Eastern Orthodox and neoclassical Western cathedrals to modernist Rock Church chamber and postmodern Chapel of Silence space-ship, Helsinki shows a rebalancing of regal, natural, and playful directions in animal-human-divine motivations, while at the edge of Russia's recurring imperialistic terr(it)or(ial)ism.

Bio-Religious Drives, East and West

The open, mostly horizontal spaces with formerly sacred grandeur at the Temples of Heaven and Earth are very different from the religiously active Lingyin Scenic Area caves and nearby temples, rising up hillsides, like Sanyuan Palace. The Temple of Heaven complex involves a very long, south-to-north, processional avenue: from initial gates to the open-air Circular Mound Altar, to more gates, to the round Echo Wall and Imperial Vault, to further gates on the Imperial Walkway Bridge, and then to the round Hall of Prayer for Good Harvests and rectangular Imperial Hall of Heaven warehouse. But there are dispersed areas of interest, too, drawing the visitor along other axes, walkways, and corridors to further buildings, gardens, and recreational areas—as in the Temple of Earth park, beyond its open-air altar within a series of squares.

The Lingyin Scenic Area attracts the visitor toward various sites, along the Peak Flown from Afar, with its caves and carved sculptures, to the main Buddhist temple, with its open courtyard, axes, and multiple buildings. Nearby, there are five smaller temples along the hillsides, with open areas and dispersed, one- or two-story halls. Likewise, the Daoist Sanyuan Palace emphasizes contextual, natural, and collectivist aspects of religious space. Such temples reflect the visitor's right-cortical, *mime-improviser/scene-designer*, dialectical balancing, holistic harmonizing circuits, along with some degree of left-cortical, *scriptwriter/critic*, sequentially focused, site-dominating desires (more prevalent at the Temples of Heaven and Earth). Also reflected and evoked are limbic personal-memory *audience* and subcortical supportive/trickster *stagehand* networks, especially through offerings given to deities and family spirits.

Historic churches in Jerusalem and Rome evoke both left and right hemispheres, too, as they shape the spaces that perform around the visitor. They may elicit awe at sacred sites tied to holy deaths, plus other emotions, depending on the inner *audience* and *stagehands*, which present memories and drives, regarding ideas and beliefs, in the conscious re-staging of self and Other. But compared with Chinese temples, European churches focus more on enclosed spaces, sequentially experienced along the main aisle or through side chapels and Stations of the Cross, tied to Jerusalem sites. Each church *dominates* the natural environment with stone solidity and transcendent myths about its site, even if it has an open courtyard or a long-armed piazza as at Saint Peter's Basilica. Such churches reflect the divine demand for individual sacrifices, sublimating bio-cultural drives through *painful pleasures*, exemplified by a martyr's crucifixion in Rome, or other sufferings elsewhere, like Christ's in Jerusalem—with sacred relics translated between holy sites.

Likewise, *scriptwriter/critic* networks are reflected and evoked by the neoclassical purity of Helsinki's Lutheran Cathedral. And yet, the city's Lutheran Rock Church and non-denominational Kamppi Chapel display modernist and postmodern designs with circular rock or oval wooden shapes, creating spaces that reflect (and perhaps elicit) more right-cortical *mime-improviser/designer* circuits in balance with left-cortical *scriptwriter/critic* networks. Even more, the traditional Temples of Heaven and Earth in Beijing, Daoist Sanyuan Palace in Guangzhou, and Lingyin area caves and temples in Hangzhou reflect: the emperor's reciprocal duties to the gods and his people as a supernatural *balancing act*, the people's duty to ancestral spirits through nature's Way, and yet transcendent models of *release from suffering* through greater awareness of tragicomic contexts. These ideals might also be seen in China's recent cultural translations from imperial to communist and capitalist frameworks, with improved living standards and consumer opportunities, yet limited rights and autocratic mechanisms, through religious traditions and technological media.

The churches considered in this chapter involve places and spaces tied to historical, yet mythically transcendent and mimetically competitive stories. Such churches exemplify the culturally transformed drives of spiritual reproduction beyond physical survival in the Western tradition: sacred territoriality, ecclesiastical hierarchy, sacrificial care, hagiographic grooming, and divine purpose. Parallels can be found in the Chinese temples explored above, which likewise frame their sacred sites with walls, cardinal axes, and mostly symmetrical, rectilinear designs. But they reflect alliance-hierarchy modes of imperial/Daoist collective offerings and Buddhist monastic self-negation through horizontal levels of gateways, steps, and modest-sized buildings (though also large statues). There are dragon-phoenix, *yang-yin, feng-shui* balancing acts on the flat earth or hillsides—unlike the vertical spires, huge domes, high ceilings, and vast naves of Saint Peter's and many other churches, dominating their sites, with imagery of melodramatic victim-heroes.

There are different implications for sacrificial care in these spaces, West and East Eurasian. Care may extend from playful mammalian parent-child relations to holistic (more right cortical) gods-emperor-subjects and Buddhas-monks-devotees *or* to supra-natural, nurturing yet demanding (more left cortical) God-ministers-believers. Animal-human grooming is also reflected in the spaces around Buddhist statues, sublimating dramatic gossip through saintly ideals and myths, as in Catholic and Orthodox churches. Yet such figures point *upward* in the Christian prayer and spirit-possession traditions, toward God the Father as cosmic spectator, with his Son and Holy Spirit as actors on the human stage, giving divine purpose to all performances of bounded, one-lifetime, good versus evil souls. This contrasts with a more porous, interdependent, yet *inward* sense of meditation, often through collective chanting, on the "Buddha nature" in each person's karmic journey through many lifetimes—and the *outward* view toward nature's Way in Daoist or imperial temples as inner/outer theatres.

And yet, Helsinki's neoclassical, modernist, and postmodern sites show sacred spaces moving in a more inclusive, tolerant, in(ter)dependent, meditative, cathartic direction of tastefully questioning the melodramatic *rasas* of awe, fear, rage and courage. They appear with tragicomic playfulness and environmental awareness of potential peace, against the Western tradition of imperial dominance, Abrahamic rivalry, and sacrificial demands (at the edge of Russia's bellicose returns). Chinese temples have restored their balanced, detached, more tragicomic tradition of sacred spaces, disrupted by twentieth-century iconoclastic Communism. However, they also reveal the persistent dangers of obsessive ancestral duties, with burnt offerings (polluting nature) and collectivist submission to autocratic rulers (not always wise) as Sons of Heaven or Communist Party Leaders. Western religious spaces, despite their focus on soul-self, God-ego power as independent (yet evangelizing and colonizing), show group-grooming identifications and sacrificial scapegoating dangers. These appear, as in current secular media, through mimetic ethno-nationalistic rivalries of good-versus-evil (im)mortal meaning and meta-narrative purpose. So, where are "we" headed with such inner theatre extensions, in the performance traces of this book?

4

Conclusions

This book explores reflections of and *potential* effects on inner theatre networks, through the outer theatrical aspects of sacred sites. The same religious building might evoke various feelings in different visitors, as first-time tourists, believing pilgrims, or community members. Each human brain is unique, with about eighty billion neurons and a hundred trillion connections. Yet viewers of the same video have "inter-subject correlations" in synchronized brain activity, more so with clips of a fictional TV show or movie, but also of an outdoor concert as a less structured real-life event (Hasson et al.; Pizzato, *Inner* 284–5). Likewise, in moving through monumental religious spaces, seeing artworks, sensing in other ways, and participating ritually, *automatic* physical, emotional, and cognitive "contagion" occurs, through motor (facial expression, gesture, action) and autonomic (arousal/calmness) mimicry (Bastiaansen et al.; Prochazkova and Kret). We feel the space as "motor potentials of our body" through "canonical neurons," while subconsciously mimicking other people or images of them through "mirror neurons," as our inner theatre simulates object use and people's actions with a "projective quality" to *under-stand* them (Gallese and Gattara 164–5, 174). Thus, there may be collective inter-subject correlations in church/temple feelings, imaginings, and ideas, from past to present and future, with common brain structures groomed toward meaning and purpose—through melodramatic, good versus evil projections or tragicomic, *rasa*-cathartic awareness of them.

At age twelve, two years after my mother died, I visited the Cathedral of Notre Dame in Paris with my father, on a Catholic pilgrimage tour of Europe. I remember the solemn awe and playful joy that I experienced in the vast nave, suddenly turning into fear when I no longer saw my father or others in our group among the many visitors standing nearby. The panic I felt, alienated by strangers around me, plus towering columns and pointed arches, as I searched in the church for a familiar face, led to joy again when I saw the tour group and found my father. I felt "saved" by good spirits from potential evil. In April 2019, I recalled that experience when I watched the roof of the same cathedral burning on television. The fire consumed its oak roof beams and their lead cover, bringing down the nineteenth-century spire and making large holes in the medieval stone vaulting. Firefighters saved the rest of the building and the holy relics inside, including Christ's crown of thorns. Yet the event revealed how a stone edifice, enduring across seven centuries, might suddenly become vulnerable—like a relic or visitor in it.

Many people feel awe at such a church with its monumental grandeur, hope in its comforting spaces, gratitude in its evocation of divine love, or fear in its reflection of obligations and judgments. Yet for some, a religious building may evoke painful memories, especially regarding foundational social "grooming." This is shown in the American documentary film, *Procession* (2021), with adult survivors of childhood sexual abuse by Catholic clergy meeting several decades later to reenact traumatic events that haunt them. Apparently, they exorcise their inner theatres with outer theatricality: memory sharing, site-specific reenactments, and thus emotion reappraisal and memory reconsolidation. Another documentary, *Deliver Us From Evil* (2014), offers interviews with a pedophilic priest, his victims, their families, and religious authorities who perpetuated the problem. It considers the Catholic tradition of idealizing celibate males in the theatre of church and Church politics, as they alone "incarnate" the body and blood of God, with bread and wine, on the altar of "sacrifice." Tragically, the survival, reproduction, territoriality, nurturing, play, and alliance-hierarchy drives, sublimated toward belonging and immortal meaning-purpose through church spaces, became twisted into the sacrificial grooming of children at the hands of some anointed males (who also held the Body of Christ)—with the misplaced trust of parents and the willful ignorance of Church authorities.

How do European churches and Chinese temples show different cultural extensions of animal-human drives in each of us, reflecting powerful family figures, social authorities, and peer groups that shape our inner theatre of brain spirits from childhood onward, in pleasurable and painful, arousing and calming ways? How might a comparison of such religious buildings, with various cultural dimensions, evoke a *rasa*-catharsis? Hopefully, this book's examples offer the reader a tasteful cleansing of melodramatic feelings through tragicomic perspective changes, shifting between right and left cortical perspectives, especially regarding mimetic ego rivalries and ideological group projections of good versus evil spirits.

Interdisciplinary Research and Theories

Chapter 1 developed the hypothesis that discoveries in cultural psychology and neuroscience about different tendencies in perception, cognition, and feeling—with more left cortical characteristics shown by Westerners, on average, than East Asians—would be *reflected* in European churches when compared with Chinese temples. Theatrical terms were developed in the chapter as metaphors for brain networks found by cognitive, social, and affective neuroscience, in the "staging" of self and Other awareness. These terms were applied to religious ideals through the anthropology of animal-human drives: with primary and social emotions, via arousal/calmness and pleasure/pain, reflected and potentially *evoked* in visitors, through the different cultural traditions of churches and temples.

The initial hypothesis theorized that European churches would reflect more left-cortical *scriptwriter/critic* networks through dominating, conquest-oriented monuments; rectilinear, focused, enclosed designs; and melodramatic, competitive (good versus evil, sacrificial) figures, related to "bounded" identities. In comparison, Chinese temples would reflect more balance between those brain networks and right-cortical *mime-improviser/scene-designer* circuits with natural-harmony-oriented monuments; curved, dispersed, open designs; and tragicomic, cooperative (compassionate) figures, related to "porous" identities. Along with neuroscience correlations, this hypothesis drew on cultural psychology experiments that showed Westerners as more object-focused, analytical, linear-consistent, individualist thinking/feeling, with high-arousal positive ideals. East Asians were more contextual, dialectical, cyclical, interdependent, and high/low-arousal, pleasure/pain balanced. The former developed through predominant Greco-Roman, Christian, and humanist values. The latter emerged through Confucian social/filial duty, Daoist mental/ritual flow, and Buddhist dependent origination, "middle way," non-attachment. Thus, European churches and Chinese temples also reflect limbic memorial *audience* and subcortical supportive/trickster *stagehand* circuits, but in distinctive ways, regarding how left and right hemispheres interact.

In both building traditions, patriarchal aspects relate to the "dominant" left hemisphere's analytical, focused "interpreter" (as neuroscientists say), with *scriptwriter/critic* networks, which evolved from competitive, predatory territory-hierarchy drives. Such networks filter the right's dialectical, holistic *mime-improviser/designer*, evolved from cooperative, prey/mating care-reproduction drives, with stronger ties to subcortical, homeostatic or trickster *stagehands*. Yet European churches and Chinese temples may reflect different dominating or balancing interactions between these neural networks, with patriarchal upright rectitude, maternal relational inclination, and supportive/trickster values. These also involve the limbic intuitive-memorial *audience*, through fixed or flexible filtering between hemispheres, in melodramatic or tragicomic (perspective changing) modes. Differences may include right-hemisphere arousal networks evoked in European churches, yet filtered through the left's *scriptwriter/critic* with linear, main-altar-focused enclosures, competitive monuments, and passionate, objectifying, melodramatic motifs of good triumphing over evil. By comparison, Chinese temples with multiple, curved-roof shrines and dispersed yards may groom more flexible bi-hemispheric ideals/emotions of dialectical holistic fluidity, in cyclical balancing acts between high and low arousal, pain and pleasure, through openness to nature, interdependent rites, and tragicomic warrior-meditator figures.

Animal-human drives of territoriality and alliance-hierarchy appear more in *patriarchal* religious modes. Reproduction and nurturing emerge in traditional *maternal* modes, related to survival as a fundamental supportive drive. Playfulness as a *trickster* tie between these drives (especially in altered states of consciousness and behavior) manifests with mischievous or rebellious brain spirits, designs, and figures—at the edges of church and temple spaces. Grooming/gossip and seeking immortal meaning/purpose, which build on the other drives, are reflected in religious buildings, with characteristic (melodramatic or tragicomic) developments in Europe and China, as beneficial group bonds and transcendent spiritual experiences, yet with dangers in their histories. Such dangers periodically reappear, especially in the shared but contentious spaces of mixed religious traditions, in Jerusalem and elsewhere, with "heritage groups" involving "self- and other-distinguishing communities," which need to maintain boundaries (Hayden 74). The middle chapters of this book explored how specific religious buildings, formed by many generations of interacting brain spirits, reflect and potentially evoke animal-human drives and family paradigms, in positive or negative ways. These drives and paradigms extend from primary emotions, through various cultural expressions, to social emotions and religious values—in distinctive Western and Chinese trajectories of theatrical cooperation, yet also competition.

Monuments as Maternal and Patriarchal, Domestic or Dominant

Chapter 2 considered *monumental* sites as reflections of brains spirits, extending animal-human drives through the self and Other staging of ego and group identities, from prehistoric Maltese megaliths to ancient Greco-Roman paradigms and Christian churches, compared with Chinese sanctuaries. Maternal dimensions seem to be expressed in Maltese "temples" and "goddess" sculptures from five thousand years ago, offering alternatives to later patriarchal dominance in European religious buildings. Likewise, an imperial Chinese tomb image of the primordial parent-twins, Nüwa and Fuxi, shows them with a compass and carpenter's square, ordering heaven and earth, in a *yin-yang* balance of feminine and masculine energies. Nüwa's significance was demoted in medieval texts, along with other goddesses. But they continued to play strong roles in tales of sage kings, related to the *domestic* heritage of ancestor worship in Chinese tombs, reflected also in temples and their designs.

Typically, Chinese Buddhist, Daoist, and Confucian temples, using the pattern of (or converted from) wealthy homes, have an outer wall around open-air courtyards with a series of shrines, dispersed along a central axis and side areas. They often include plants, trees, pools, and (with Buddhist temples) a vertical yet polygonal-rounded *ta* (pagoda) as stupa reliquary. This monumental temple pattern, reproduced consistently for about two thousand years, reflects porous-self, interdependent ideals, in harmonious balance with nature, through dialectical low/high arousal. It also expresses a balance between right-cortical maternal *mime/designer*, left-cortical patriarchal *scriptwriter/critic*, and subcortical supportive/trickster *stagehand* networks, from inner to outer (and outer to inner) theatres, including limbic memorial *audience* and prefrontal-cortex self-Other circuits.

Ancient Christian meetings began with communal rites in catacomb tombs and wealthy Roman homes—through mournful/heroic ideals and patriarchal sacrifice demands, yet also maternal meal-sharing and trickster aspects. After periods of persecution, creating many martyrs, Christianity became the dominant religion of the Roman Empire, starting in the fourth century, consolidating creeds, suppressing heretics, and building monumental meeting sites. These involved the *round* womblike martyrium (or baptistery) and the *rectangular* basilica (Roman market and judicial hall). The latter was turned lengthwise to focus processional and worshipful attention on the sacrificial altar at one end. Maternal, nurturing spaces of the Roman home, especially the atrium (with *impluvium* pool), *tablinum* (reception room with family altar), and *triclinium* (with dining table), were transformed into more patriarchal domains. These included catacomb-crypt, mausoleum-baptistery, and basilica-cruciform designs, with ancestor memorials, convert baptisms, and communion meals.

Church spaces were thus decorated with martyred saints and Christ as heroic figures of goodness and life, triumphing over evil and death, sometimes with devilish tricksters at the edges.

Both the dominant basilica and early domestic paradigms are shown with the Basilica of Saints John and Paul on the Caelian Hill in Rome, including the house church (or private home chapel) excavated below it. Today's visitor, as tourist or pilgrim, might experience sublime awe, especially through *audience* and *stagehand* circuits, at the monumental site with its third-century façade and later rebuilt basilica. They commemorate a home where two upper-class brothers, members of the imperial court, were martyred in the fourth century, with their holy bones still under the altar, according to a later legend. But the visitor might also feel a sense of beauty through VMPFC *stage manager* and left-parietal *costume definer* networks, especially with various Roman frescos on domestic walls under the basilica, of vine branches, birds, sea-goats, putti in boats, naked adults, and clothed people with open arms in a hug-like *orans* gesture of prayer. Such an early mix of patriarchal and maternal reflections already suggests the developing focus on a bounded, individual soul, valued by the Almighty Creator, who demands the redemptive sacrifice of his Son and appreciates further heroic sacrifices by many martyrs, as the divine Spectator.

Bounded and Bonded or Porous and Interdependent

The sacrificial demand for *bounded* souls is also displayed with bejeweled bones as fetishes, justifying the Christian dominance over nature (and prior pagan sanctuaries) with monumental churches, at martyrdom or translated relic sites, focused on soul power as independent from human mortality. In comparison, Chinese spirit tablets emphasize the *interdependency* of mortal and deceased family members, through home and temple offerings—with low arousal names on wood, rather than high arousal crucifixion and martyrdom scenes, with actual bones as sacred Christian devices. And yet, as a memorial mini-monument, the spirit tablet's written nature reflects left-cortical *scriptwriter/critic* networks. Catholic passion, crucifixion, resurrection, martyrdom, and nativity-Pietà-ascension imagery, especially with tragicomic twists of complex characters and holistic relationships, relates to right-cortical *mime/designer* circuits as well. The evidence does not simply line up as Western left cortical and Chinese right.

Involving culturally pruned connections between left and right, Chinese folk beliefs have long maintained that dead brain spirits are *dependent* on their living descendants and vice versa. Such beliefs persist today through patriarchal survival-territoriality-hierarchy and maternal reproduction-care drives, despite Buddhist teachings of non-attachment and non-self, Daoist of non-action (*wu wei*), and Communist atheism. Chinese ancestral spirits are also intercessors, like Catholic saints, to greater gods and natural forces. Ancestors and gods are aided and honored with incense, "spirit money," and other goods such as cardboard houses, sent upward in smoke—beyond health and environmental concerns with such burning. Food and drink are also left for a time as offerings in homes and temples. Special money is burnt for "hungry ghosts," too, through compassion for beggar spirits who lack family care, yet also the fear that otherwise they may plague the living. The Chen Clan Ancestral Hall (Guangzhou), Confucius Family Home, and Yan Hui Temple (Qufu), with spirit tablets and larger monuments, exemplify memorial, interdependent, living-dead, brain spirit sites, along with the deification of great historical men—though now as cultural museums, mainly for tourists.

Christian martyrs and other saints, as transcendent individual souls, do not need help from the living. Yet inside churches, they are offered lit candles, flowers, and prayers for help, plus monetary donations at their statues, icons, and reliquaries, through fears, desires, and hopes for spiritual aid in living brain-bodies. Christ, as teacher, ruler, and heroic victim on the cross, does not demand material offerings like Chinese spirits. But in extending the Father's love, Jesus shows a passionate desire for each human to love him freely in return (or risk eternal damnation for evil). His mother, Mary, as Madonna, Pietà, and Queen of Heaven figure, shows both the costs and benefits of such individual soul passions. She thus represents idealized nurturing care, without requiring anything from us. She demonstrates how our earthly concerns should be focused, beyond immediate relatives, through left-cortical analytical *scriptwriter/critic*, right-cortical holistic *mime/designer*, and limbic memorial *audience* circuits, toward a unifying heavenly family. However, such ego-soul-God bonding, even of *bounded* individuals (with Mary representing Virgin exceptionalism, permeable only to God), has encouraged imperial, nationalistic, and colonizing passions across European and "New World" territories. With expansionist, evangelical ideals in Catholic, Orthodox, and Protestant traditions, monumental churches were built as theatrical brain-spirit sites, creating intercultural conflicts, sacrificial demands, and yet communal growth in sanctuary territories.

Such missionary conversion passions, with left-cortical, patriarchal, hierarchic-territorial sacrifices, but also right-cortical, maternal, reproductive-nurturing transformations, are reflected in linear, narthex to nave, altar focused churches and their round baptistery fonts, with supportive yet trickster edges. Baptisteries are sometimes built as separate monuments from the main church, displaying their own awe-inspiring artworks. The Orthodox Baptistery of Neon in Ravenna, has an early fifth-century mosaic on its inner dome, above its marble font. The circular mosaic shows the baptism of Jesus by John, plus two supportive/trickster *stagehands*: the River Jordan, personified as a pagan-like gray-bearded deity, representing natural forces yet holding a towel, and the Holy Spirit, as a dove descending from heaven. Such a monument exemplifies the *porous*, interdependent aspects of Early Christianity, involving right-cortical, nurturing *mime/designer*, subcortical *stagehand*, and limbic *audience* (with St. Paul and various apostles around the mosaic's rim), as well as left-cortical, more *bounded*, individualist, patriarchal *scriptwriter/critic* networks, with John recognizing the Messiah, whose genitals are visible in the water.

The Arian Baptistery from the same century, built by the Ostrogoth king Theodoric who conquered Ravenna, has a similar mosaic scene. But the River Jordan as old man, on the opposite side of a more androgynous, wide-hipped (Dionysus-like) Jesus, holds a branch with no towel to offer, perhaps reflecting the Arian doctrine that the Son was not co-eternal with the Father. The two Ravenna baptisteries, despite their porous, round, nurturing, maternal elements, relate to a persistent patriarchal rivalry between Early Christian sects. Theodoric allowed them both to exist, but in separate parts of Ravenna. Emperors in Constantinople, starting with Constantine the Great, sided with Orthodox (Nicene) leaders against the Arians, suppressing their "heresy" for hundreds of years, yet two Roman emperors and various local rulers sided the other way, with Arians against the Orthodox. Likewise, in the long history of imperial China, there were several persecutions of Buddhists when emperors favored Daoism and vice versa. Yet there was not the enormous bloodshed of multiple Crusades with Christians against Muslims (and against fellow Christians in Byzantium), the *Reconquista* (with Santiago Matamoros, St. James the Moor-Slayer, as patron of Spain), and the Thirty Years' War between Catholics and Protestants, plus numerous inquisitions, witch trials, and pogroms.

Another example of a round monument, as martyrium-baptistery, is the Church of Saint Constantina (or Constance) in Rome, dating to a crucial transition time, from persecution to power. It was built to honor the daughters of Constantine the Great, in the fourth century, and now bears the titular one's relics in its altar. Likewise, the Church of Saint Agnes in *Agone*, in Rome's Piazza Navona, has a round interior, but with a rectilinear façade and two towers. It was built in the seventeenth century, at the site of the saint's early fourth-century martyrdom in the Stadium of Domitian, which was a warning to the audience when worship of the emperor and Roman gods was required. Even today, the church displays her skull to the left of the main altar, as a holy relic and trickster edge of the womblike, circular, domed nave, behind the patriarchal Baroque façade. Agnes's independence as a teen rebel against the ancient imperial patriarchy also involves, according to legend, her rejection of high-ranking suitors, through devotion to God, as a bounded self with a divine bond, porous only to Him, while dragged naked through the streets and beheaded. Later, Constantine's daughter, Constantina, prayed to St. Agnes and was cured of leprosy, on her way to becoming a saint as well, porous to God, but bounded against this world, with a haloed head, as holy soul, in the medieval legend. According to an ancient historian, however, she was a bloodthirsty ruler, as wife of the Eastern caesar Gallus: "her pride was swollen beyond measure; she was a Fury in mortal form" (Marcellinus 41).

Higher towers, domes, and various other monumental aspects grew above the typical tomb/womb crypt and patriarchal altar, from Romanesque to Gothic to Baroque styles, in churches across Europe, for hundreds of years. Such competitive styles reflect the "schismogenesis" of group identities, territorial boundaries, and creative aspirations (Graeber and Wengrow). Churches competed against one another, with relics of saints' bodies and Christ's passion attracting fame and pilgrims' money, as porous channels to heavenly joy and earthly miracles. Likewise, Buddhist stupas and pagodas were built as reliquary monuments across Asia, with statues and miracle sites also making divinity present. But that involved beliefs in many gods and multiple lifetimes, with the dependent causation of karma—not a bounded ego-soul identified with one alpha-male Creator God, which does not exist in Buddhism.

Patriarchal, Maternal, and Trickster, with Multi- or Unidirectional Dimensions

A more cooperative than competitive, *interdependent* identity, as porous between lifetimes, yet with the transcendent potential to become a god or to attain further enlightenment, is reflected in the Tianning Temple of Changzhou, with its 26-story pagoda, the tallest in the world. The many statues of arhats and deities in this temple, including the reclining historical Buddha calmly accepting non-existence (*parinirvana*), suggest multiple lifetimes and non-attachment to self in the Buddhist tradition. These ideals also relate to multiple souls and non-action (to harmonize with nature's Way) in Chinese folk religion and Daoist tradition, although extending one's life is a prime goal in Daoism. The large Budai-Maitreya and Guanyin statues at the rear of Tianning, plus its tall pagoda, may seem to represent big egos, like huge statues at other monumental sites, such as Leshan's cliff-carved Maitreya, in his ruler form. But it is paradoxically the opposite: they show transcendent non-self.

The *Tathagata-garbha Sutra* (200–50 CE) uses the image of a rag covering a Buddha statue as a metaphor for "defilements like ignorance, hatred, greed, and delusion," which mask the "embryo" of Buddhahood in each of us as "womb," with our potential for "pure and luminous consciousness shining brightly like a jewel" (Mitchell 139). The large shining statues in many temples reflect that enlightened potential in us, behind the rag of ego. Thus, the predominance of male, meditative, sometimes androgynous figures points to the ultimate goal of transcending bodily ego attachments—even if the visitor gives them incense and other things as offerings, hoping for nurturing help in this world. This paradox reflects a Buddhist balancing act of patriarchal *scriptwriter/critic*, maternal *mime-improviser/designer*, memorial *audience*, and supportive/trickster *stagehand* networks, plus *actor, character, editor, stage manager, operator, costume-body definer/designer*, and *director* circuits, interacting with other brain-bodies and the temple artistry, while deities potentially watch.

Tianning Buddhist Temple, as typical of many in China, has large statues of the entryway guardians Heng and Ha—and then of the Four Heavenly Kings, representing the natural forces of each cardinal direction, holding a lute (pipa), umbrella banner, snake-dragon, and sword. These patriarchal figures, as shifting ideals from India to China, reflect the animal-human drives of territoriality and survival (with good weather for crops), as well as hierarchy, like the temple's pagoda. The Heavenly Kings hall usually has a central Wei Tuo, as protector of the Dharma, yet also Maitreya, in his chubby, laughing Budai form. The latter shows a more right-cortical, maternal, compassionate, holistic ideal and playful trickster (with subcortical ties) as Future Buddha, who appeared in disguise historically, as a jolly medieval monk.

At Shanghai's **Qibao Jiao Temple**, a Budai-Maitreya statue includes children climbing on the cheerful monk. He appears that way and in a smaller version without children, but with yellow cloth honoring him, near the pagoda of this temple, to one side of its main hall area, which has an initial gate and yard with burners as well (Figures 4.1–7). A large Guanyin statue also appears in another side area, which was being renovated when I visited in 2013 (Figures 4.8–12). More typically, the initial hall on the main axis shows the Four Heavenly Kings, facing inward, two on each side, and the protector buddha Wei Tuo, at the center, who faces the rest of the temple, back to back with Guanyin who faces the entrance, as an alternative to Budai (Figures 4.13–29). Contrary to my initial hypothesis about left and right cortical balance reflected in Chinese temples, this one, like all my examples, shows a prevalence of male patriarchal figures with left cortical, territorial-hierarchic ideals. And yet, right cortical, maternal, compassionate, reproductive-care functions, with ties to playful, subcortical, supportive/trickster circuits, are also reflected at Tianning, Qibao Jiao, and other examples, with statues of Budai-Maitreya and Guanyin. These reflections are tainted, however, by the patriarchal history of "golden lotus" foot-binding as collectivist, maternal, *sacrificial* care, painfully altering girls' natural growth (with hoof-feet as in the Buddhist myth of a deer-girl)—unlike statues' bare feet, often appearing on lotus blossoms.

The *multidirectional* array of statues and spaces in the Qibao temple, as with various Buddhist and Daoist sites presented here, confirms that part of our initial hypothesis, contrasting with the *unidirectional* focus of the main aisle, from narthex to nave to altar-art, in European churches. Although some churches have a transept and side aisles with additional chapels, and Stations of the Cross along the walls, all of these elements point toward or circulate around the main altar at the top of the cruciform design. Round churches, such as those considered in Rome, may be exceptions that show more of a holistic orientation, like Chinese temples, but they still focus on the main altar. This difference between multi- and unidirectionality correlates with cultural psychologists' findings that East Asians attend more to background, context, situation, changing fortunes, or surroundings—while Westerners focus on foreground objects, internal causes, fixed personality types, consistent trends, or a rod in a box. According to neuroscience findings, the former relates to right cortical characteristics and the latter to left (Tables 1.3 and 1.5).

More focused basilica, cruciform, and round church or baptistery monuments reflect a bounded self/soul ideal: internally caused with a fixed consistent personality. This ideal developed through ancient, medieval, Renaissance, Baroque, and modern religious or secular re-presentations, with increasingly "individualist" societies. It contrasts with porous self, multiple soul/lifetime, cyclic change, and Confucian collectivist or Daoist/Buddhist holistic interdependent ideals in China. Yet current Western and East Asian cultures may be moving toward one another in such ways. Westerners are becoming more collectivist through cooperative social media, although that shift seems to increase melodramatic, victim-vengeful, group bonds with metanarrative conspiracies and stereotypes. East Asians are becoming more individualist through competitive commerce, which can also increase alienation pressures.

Transcendent Giants in Nature or Dominant Structures and Spires on Colonized Sites

Jinan's monumental Thousand Buddha Mountain displays multi-directional, interdependent, porous self (or non-self) ideals in its wooden shrines, medieval cliff carvings, huge statues, and cave temples with thousands of sculptures recreating historical ones across China. Yet these sites also perform ties to their own natural context. Inside one extensive cave (Wanfo Dong), a reclining Buddha, 28 meters long, rests on other heads. There are many bodhisattvas, arhats, guardians, animals, and *apsaras* (angelic nymphs), some with cloth wrappings or electric halos. Together, they reflect permeable possibilities, although mostly carved in stone. Above a smaller cave on Thousand Buddha Mountain, a huge Guanyin statue pours compassionate wisdom on the visitor. In another area of this complex, an even larger statue of Budai-Maitreya, sitting on a lotus blossom, shares joy with visitors whose inner theatres mirror his expression of laughter, perhaps in a dialectical recipe of that arousal *rasa*, along with other quiescent ones, toward a complex sense of peace.

The 71-meter-tall eighth-century Maitreya (in a more patriarchal form than Budai), carved into a cliff near Leshan, to tame the confluence of rivers for ship traffic, shows a *dialectical mix* of natural concerns, human transformations, and divine ideals, involving worldly and transcendent orders. An interdependent view is possible, too, when the visitor goes down the cliff steps, with other people, to the statue's massive feet, and then climbs back up the other side, seeing many people along the opposite edge, looking like ants against the Future Buddha. Ironically, human figures in European churches are typically life-size or smaller, or appear that way, while reflecting a stronger sense of ego-soul identification with Almighty God. However, monumental domination and replacement of the natural environment are often emphasized, even at prior religions' holy sites, with leaf-shaped stone ornaments, tree-like columns, and high spires. Church images show Mary with Jesus, Christ on the cross, and martyrdom scenes, as human-divine transformations, framed by cosmic battles and the Last Judgment of good over evil, sin, and nature (as in the Strasbourg Cathedral tympanum).

Although it is a Lutheran church without such human imagery, the Constantine Basilica in Trier, derived from an imperial palace, expresses ancient Roman and modern Christian *dominance* with its vast interior space and large hanging cross—while also bearing a history of Second World War damage, like many churches in Germany. At the Cologne Cathedral, the highest twin spires of any church in the world were restored, along with the rest of the building, after that war's severe bombing. It continues today to bear the Shrine of the Three Kings near its altar, justifying the huge monument, built from the thirteenth to nineteenth centuries, which dominates the site of an ancient Roman colonial villa. Indeed, a mosaic depicting the theatre god Dionysus was unearthed nearby, by the Nazi government in 1941, and is now covered by a museum building on the church square.

The highest church spire extant today that was completed during the Middle Ages, on the Strasbourg Cathedral, likewise expresses dominance over an ancient Roman temple site, at the city center, but reaches with just one arm toward God, because a second tower was never built. Climbing a spiral staircase in the Gothic façade, opposite the spire, a visitor can see a mix of patriarchal statues on the outside of the cathedral, along with female, plus gargoyle tricksters. Devils also appear inside, in the medieval stained-glass windows, reflecting the bottom-up rebellion of inner theatres over the centuries. Such trickster brains interacted during the French Revolution, destroying many of the cathedral's statues, which have since been restored.

Playful or Evil, Supportive/Trickster Stagehands with Sacred Cages and Screens

Expressing Baroque whimsy, even as a Lutheran building, Copenhagen's Church of Our Savior displays chubby babies (perhaps as cherubs) around its baptismal font, with large angels near the altar, while elephants hold up the organ over the entry doors. It also has a corkscrew spire with Christ Triumphant holding a banner at the top. Such elements reflect playful, supportive/trickster *stagehand* aspects in relation to maternal nurturing *mime/designer* and patriarchal hierarchic *scriptwriter/critic* networks. Even more playfully, the neo-baroque Holy Family Cathedral in Barcelona, designed a century ago by Antoni Gaudi, is still being built with its eighteen towers and many external sculptures in parabolic, vegetative, sandcastle shapes. Such playfulness appears, however, from the beginning of Greco-Roman and Christian monuments, with *trickster brain spirits* as super-natural extensions of animal-human drives, invoked if good, expelled when evil. They also appear, but with different *rasa* tastes, in the Daoist and Buddhist temples of China, rebalanced with more compassion, because they are unwise, not purely evil.

As a collective brain-spirit of animal-human drives, shaped in particular cultural ways, the trickster plays a role in the dominance or balance paradigm of European and Chinese religious monuments. A fear of spirit "possession" developed in Christianity, from New Testament sources about demons to Catholic inquisitions, Protestant witch trials, and (ancient to) modern exorcisms. But joyful, ecstatic experiences of the Holy Spirit also developed across the centuries, as encouraged by St. Paul in the Bible. Yet he taught his followers "how to control these experiences ... rather than [being] controlled by them" (P. McNamara, *Spirit* 144). Such experiences include "speaking in tongues," which continues today among Pentecostals and other charismatics, exalting the individual through communal rites. The Christianizing of the Roman Empire and beyond, through European churches and later colonial ones, involved collective fears of evil spirits, yet valuing Holy Spirit contacts and (for Catholics) saintly miracle-producing relics. This meant repressing pagan sites and rituals, which bore persistent, underground, subversive forces, reflecting subcortical trickster *stagehands*. But it also involved sublimating their supportive, emotional, motivational (Praise Singing) power, identified with one God and group, to dominate evil temptations in our sinful "fallen" nature—while controlling enemy groups or villains in the melodrama of salvation. Thus, the Christian ideal of fighting the flesh became stronger in the neo-Platonic, Augustinian tradition of the soul as "prisoner of the body," from Catholic to Protestant theology, while Aristotelian, Aquinian Scholasticism offered more appreciation of "sense knowledge," with soul as the body's form (O'Malley 40–2).

Greco-Roman rectilinear stone temples, with an external colonnade of round, tree-like columns and inner *cella* containing the god's statue, like the Hebrew temple's Holy of Holies with the Ark of the Covenant, influenced Christian churches as spiritual cages, drawing on good forces within the sanctuary and excluding evil. The more womblike circular *cella* of the Pantheon in Rome, preserved as the Church of Saint Mary and the Martyrs, with its huge dome yet open oculus, also has a rectilinear portico with cylindrical stone columns and triangular pediment as its protective patriarchal entrance. Within Chinese temples, there are many columns, but made of wood, even more like trees—plus spirit screen walls, usually of stone, parallel to the entrance, and a high threshold at the doorway of each hall, to keep evil spirits out, because it was believed they only travel in straight lines near the ground. Thus, the enclosed, unidirectional, more left-cortical (*scriptwriter/critic*) focus of European churches was partly developed from Greco-Roman temples, as spiritual cages and defensive sanctuaries, exemplified by Sicily's Temple of Concord and Cathedral of Syracuse—through rectilinear, domestic/catacomb, basilica, and cruciform plans. These contrast with the open yard, multi-directional, more balanced left and right cortical (*mime-improviser/designer*) orientation of Chinese temples.

The *templon* (iconostasis) screen of Eastern Orthodox churches, such as the Uspenski Cathedral in Helsinki and Russian Church of Saint Alexander Nevsky in Jerusalem, makes the altar area more *cella*-like, even today, defining the holiest territory as off-limits to non-clergy. It also blocks the congregation's view of the mysterious, bread and wine transubstantiation into Christ's body and blood at the climax of the Mass. This is akin to the barred, though transparent tracery of a chancel screen, with a Great Rood crucifix above it, as spiritual cage around the high altar and choir of medieval churches in Western Europe. That screen was typically removed in Catholic countries during the Counter-Reformation. However, some remain in Anglican and Lutheran lands as a rectilinear, patriarchal barrier, reflecting left cortical *scriptwriter/critic* networks (regarding positive and negative tricksters)—like the Protestant stress on Bible reading, preaching, and exorcisms.

High/Low Arousal with Melodramatic and Tragicomic Territories

Circular exceptions to Europe's dominant basilica and cruciform monuments, reflecting more maternal, nurturing, right cortical, *mime/designer* networks, include Rome's Saint Constantina and Brescia's Old Cathedral. But the former has the early patriarchal figure of Jesus as Lawgiver, along with Good Shepherd associations that include the Greco-Roman trickster god Hermes/Mercury, plus Dionysian imagery. The latter church bears the patriarchal Eye of God at the center of a chapel dome, like the Pantheon's oculus as surveillance from above. Rome's Saint Stephen in the Round likewise offers a circular space, built atop an ancient Mithraeum and soldiers' barracks, with two rings of columns around the main altar as nurturing table. It displays gruesome torture and death scenes along its walls, in Late Renaissance frescos memorializing various martyrs, who emulated Christ's heroic suffering, as the divine Father's will.

Such high-arousal negative (HAN) scenes evoke tragic sympathy, resonating with personal and group traumas. But in visitors', especially believers' inner theatres, there may be a shift to high-arousal positive (HAP) melodramatic emotions, with martyrs' victories over evil torturers. Or there might be a shift to low-arousal positive (LAP) emotions,[1] with a divine plan as complex metaphysical script, demanding sacrificial suffering, yet offering heavenly rewards as tragicomic ending, while evil souls are punished melodramatically. If the latter, a "spillover effect" may occur between right cortical, sympathetic nervous system, arousal networks, in the prey-wary heritage of *mime/designer* circuits, and left cortical, parasympathetic, quiescent networks as predatory, competitive *scriptwriter/critic*. This would also involve subcortical, brain-body, supportive/trickster *stagehands*, regarding God as Director and ancestors/saints as Audience. Such an ecstatic spillover of brain spirits, with neural activity in otherwise opposite systems, reflects the religious mysteries of patriarchal sacrifice, maternal care, and trickster rebirth. Thus, Saint Stephen in the Round shows Mary on a cloud, with seven swords at her heart, tied to tragic scenes of suffering in her life, and yet her transcendent, haloed joy.

European churches exhibit animal-human, patriarchal territoriality, in melodramatic (good versus evil) competition with "pagan" traditions—dominating their sites through stone monuments and sometimes converting their prior columns. Churches rise vertically with brick and stone facades, towers, spires, arches, vaulted ceilings, and domes, expressing the hierarchical drive toward one Almighty (alpha male) God. Chinese temples, in contrast, display more cooperative, horizontal, natural aspects with wooden monuments and caves, including Daoist statues at Buddhist sites, or vice-versa, typically with one or two-story halls.[2] They sometimes have huge figures or a vertical pagoda as reliquary. But the key attitude they reflect is tragicomic (*rasa*-cathartic) balance between high and low, negative and positive emotions—as the *yin* and *yang* of nature's Way or as compassionate yet wise equanimity about interdependent karmic change.

Territorial competition between Christian groups extended across medieval Europe, with spiritual attachment to relic sites and inherited nostalgia for the foreign "Holy Land." This involved historical to local fetishes: from Christ's or the saints' miraculous remains in pilgrimage churches, with ornate reliquaries, to credible points of divine contact in the local priest's hands with transubstantiated bread and wine as God's body and blood. Bethlehem and Jerusalem sites were shown through stories in stained glass, or performed in and around churches, prior to the Bible's translation and accessibility for lay readers. Crusading armies killed and plundered in the Name of God (absolved

---

[1] The theatrical mix of positive and negative emotions, along with high and low arousal, may relate to recent research in organizational management studies, finding a value in "ambivalence" as developing flexibility and engagement, with a "paradox mindset" against premature certainty (Rothman et al.; Y. Liu et al.).

[2] Cf. Peng and He on ancient Roman stone arches and domes contributing to vertical architecture, as a "dialogue with the gods," and Chinese wooden dougong brackets to horizontal, with "restrictions on the height, color and style of the roof" in the Tang and Song periods (4).

by the pope from divine punishment) across Orthodox Christian lands in Eastern Europe, en route to conquering Muslim territories in the Middle East. Franciscans and others set up "Stations of the Cross," from local church images to Terra Sancta sites in Jerusalem, for believing pilgrims to travel there. They viewed and touched places where Christ walked and suffered, bringing back bits of holy earth and other souvenirs (via Knights Templar round-church banking). Such pilgrimages continue today, with easier travel, to various European sites and the Holy Land. Likewise, Chinese Buddhism has four holy mountains (or five others with Chan) and Daoism four more, plus numerous pilgrimage sites. But they are within China and without such bloody rivalries over sacred sacrificial territories.

During the Middle Ages, over hundreds of years, Portuguese and Spanish Catholics reconquered the Iberian Peninsula, forcing out the Moors and Jews. Then they extended a God-given manifest destiny to the "New World," returning with gold for Europe's Renaissance. Competing with them, French Catholics, plus English, Dutch, and Danish Protestants, extended the missionary and economic colonizing, through church building and slave trading, also involving Africa and Asia in the "Enlightenment" and later periods. Europeans thus offered predatory *scriptwriter/critic* rationalizations of melodramatic good versus evil conflicts, of "civilized" over "savage" people: heroically saving souls by conquering them and altering their rites, as reflected in dominant church buildings and tragic (or tragicomic) histories.[3]

Holy Rivalries, yet Common Structures

Today, Christians from all over the world visit Jerusalem's holy sites, some of which were treasured already in the fourth century by the Roman emperor Constantine and his saintly mother Helena. Constantine ordered the destruction of a Roman temple, which a previous emperor had constructed on the quarry where Jesus was apparently buried and rose from death, plus excavation of that cave and the building of a round, domed church over it, as hero-tomb-shrine. Although that church was burned by Persian invaders, then rebuilt, and destroyed again by a Muslim ruler, the current stone church was built by twelfth-century Crusaders, who continued to battle for control of the holy territory across many centuries. It was also renovated by sixteenth-century Franciscans. Instead of being in the original courtyard (more like a Chinese temple with a yard and multiple shrines), the Golgotha crucifixion site, as an upstairs chapel, was included with the empty tomb under one rectilinear roof. Yet the burial site became a sculpted Edicule, rather than full cliff-cave like temples in China.

Visitors enter at the side of the Church of the Holy Sepulchre, between the Golgotha chapel and tomb Edicule, instead of along a central narthex–nave axis toward the altar.

---

[3] Both melodramatic and tragicomic dimensions of the Spanish conquest of the Aztecs are shown in the allegorical *Loa* (introduction) to Sor Juana's 1689 play, *The Divine Narcissus*.

This reflects the monument's political tensions, with occasional fights between Christian denominations, which have different territories inside and on the roof. Such conflicts have arisen, too, between Abrahamic faiths in the Al-Aqsa Mosque Compound (Temple Mount), which includes the Dome of the Rock mosque, with its "Foundation Stone" where Abraham was willing to sacrifice his son and where the prophet Mohammed experienced positive trickster ecstasy in a night journey to heaven, above the ruins of the Second Temple with its Western Wall, sacred to Jews.

Patriarchal, territorial, hierarchic competition, and yet cooperation, is apparent, with the overall rectilinear design, plus courtyard and central fountain of the seventeenth-century New Mosque in Istanbul, enabling visitors to enjoy an open-air embracing space, before submitting to the inner domed worship area, with a separate section for women. Likewise, the Archbasilica of Saint John Lateran, originally built by Emperor Constantine as "the center of Christianity in Rome" (Kilde 40–1), now bears a rectilinear neoclassical façade, Baroque interior, two large piazzas with an ancient Egyptian obelisk, and separate baptistery on the side, combining patriarchal authority and maternal nurturing. Its Lateran Baptistery, the first in Rome, displays such nurturing aspects with an ancient design of octagonal roundness and a large central basin for immersion, though it also has an affusion font. There are Baroque decorations, including Constantine's battle victory using a Christian symbol, above and around it. Rectilinear side chapels offer patriarchal *scriptwriter/critic* preaching, as well as Holy Communion *mime/designer* care. These spaces redefine the sublimation of supportive/trickster *stagehand* drives, as groomed brain spirits, through the central baptismal font and Holy Spirit dome. Such a *rasa* mix of competitive and cooperative performance stages, with patriarchal and maternal dimensions, involving hierarchical, territorial, yet nurturing emotions, complicates the brain-spirit picture here and at many sites explored in this book.

Despite territorial rivalries with negative trickster conflicts, across many centuries, among Christian sects and with Muslims, their sacrificial, ecstatic, memeplex monuments share similar elements, such as ritual purification with a baptistery, outside or in a church, or a prescribed hand-, feet-, and face-washing area in the courtyard of a mosque. Churches and mosques also share a unidirectional focus on the main altar (toward the rising sun in the east) or *mihrab* (toward the Kaaba in Mecca). They have a pulpit or *minbar* for preaching and bell towers or *muezzin* minarets for calls to prayer. Churches sometimes have a square in front or a cloister to the side with plants. Mosques may have plants and fountains in their courtyard, connected with a central enclosed space. Some churches have adjacent graveyards, connecting mourners with nature and earth, like the oldest church in England, Saint Martin's of Canterbury. Yet Chinese temples connect more to nature, through multiple dispersed halls with open-air yards between them, involving trees, bushes, and wind-water (*feng-shui*) considerations, such as curved roof eaves. Territorial sanctuary and nurturing soul-care are balanced through cyclic *yang/yin* harmonies, with temples made mostly of wood or carved as caves—rather than skewed toward left cortical, patriarchal, good over evil (melodramatic) characteristics, as with Europe's stone churches and bejeweled reliquaries, dominating nature, sin, and death.

Interdependent, Ritual, and Playful Dialectics

Chinese temple courtyards are open air, but they can be packed with visitors on Lunar New Year's Eve, paying a much higher fee to be there for good luck, during the first bell ring of the year. I witnessed some of this at the Yuan Ming and Jing'an Buddhist temples in Shanghai. Such collective, cyclical, interdependent aspects are complimented by ordinary, more individual practices. For example, visitors buy and light incense sticks, and offer candles or food at statues, in both Buddhist and Daoist temples. Women fold gold or silver paper as "spirit money" to be burned as an offering to gods or ancestors. At some temples, visitors playfully toss a coin into a well or a central brazier (Jing'an), or in a fish and turtle pool (Middle Tianzhu), or leave it on a *qilin* relief carving (Yongfu) and other places, or stick it magically on a painted wall (Yunxiang). More ritually, incense sticks are lit in a collective burner, often with other visitors, and held to the head while bowing in the four cardinal directions, showing interdependent, holistic concerns.

Folding and burning spirit money (which can also be purchased in bags pre-folded) is often a communal or family rite, honoring gods and ancestors, in both Buddhist and Daoist temples. Tossing or leaving coins is more individual and not in every temple, but still a contagious, mimetic activity. In some temples, such playful mimesis also involves a nurturing animal-human connection, for personal karmic merit, with the possible purchase and release of fish in a collective pool, or feeding the fish there, which I saw at Donglin, Yunxiang, and Yufo Buddhist temples in Shanghai. Patriarchal honoring, maternal nurturing, and trickster play are intermixed dimensions of visitors' performances. Monks' and nuns' collective rites, burning offerings with families (as I saw at Baohua and Yunxiang temples) or chanting at tables with layfolk, or chanting while processing around statues, also reflect inner theatre networks and animal-human drives/emotions.

The dialectic of ritual and playful acts in many temples relates to the Four Heavenly Kings in the Baohua and Yunxiang entrance halls, standing on demigod rivals (*asuras*), as patriarchal protectors controlling disruptive tricksters in cosmic, social, and brain-body theatres. These patriarchal warrior and trickster pairs form a balancing act—unlike melodramatic holy figures conquering evil ones in Catholic and Orthodox churches. In statues and paintings, Mary, saints, and angels heroically trample or stab devilish snakes, dragons, and bat-winged humanoids. But Buddhist temples stage mostly serene, meditative figures, along with protective warriors, dragons, and lions. Visitors' rites are also more tragicomic, with the fearful/hopeful nurturing of spirits, plus playful interdependent gestures.

Tossing a coin at open-mouthed copper fish near a boy attendant of Guanyin at Donglin Temple shows mischievous yet permissible play. This reflects subcortical trickster as well as supportive drives, balanced by left and right cortical networks. Such balancing acts are also displayed with statuary at Donglin: patriarchal ideals, such as Shakyamuni, Samantabhadra, Ksitigarbha, and Amitabha, yet also the huge maternal figure of compassionate Guanyin with 9,999 mini-statues (a strong *yang* number). There is also a big Guanyin head on an artificial mountain, with many figures embedded in it, showing interdependence.

As theatrical monuments, European churches and Chinese temples reveal historical, yet current developments in brain-spirit connections between animal-human drives, personal emotions, and divine ideals. European churches display more patriarchal, left cortical, rectilinear, focused aspects and competitive histories with bounded ego/group, good versus evil, *melodramatic*, hero-victim-vengeful, high-arousal, *nature-dominating* characteristics than Chinese temples. Yet churches also show, especially with round martyria and baptisteries (or Madonna figures), maternal, right cortical, cooperative, low-arousal, *tragicomic* nurturing, in mournful meaning and joyful purpose. However, such monuments and artworks still involve territorial, hierarchic, grooming/purifying, and thus scapegoating aspects. Chinese temples display more of a *dialectical*, high and low arousal, interdependent, porous ego and group *balance* between left and right cortical dimensions, plus natural harmony ideals and playful trickster twists (with arhats also). European churches show God the Father and the Virgin Mother as super-parents, with Jesus as super-baby, eventual victim-hero of divine Passion and ruler-teacher-judge, stressing individualist, competitive ideals. Chinese temples depict deities and bodhisattvas as warriors, rulers, and sages—thus as older, wiser, and compassionately helpful siblings (with Guanyin pouring elixir from a vase, not breastfeeding a baby)—unlike the sibling rivalry of Abrahamic religions, with their bloody history as "Children of God."

Chapter 2 considered churches as stone monuments, mostly rectilinear but with curved elements, dominating their environments, often built over and using columns from prior pagan sites, inspired by Greek myths and the Hebrew Bible, with "dominion" over earth given by the Christian Creator to humans. "In their mastery of nature, the creative God and ordering mind are alike. Man's likeness to God consists in the sovereignty over existence, in the lordly gaze, in the command," extending from Europe's ancient to medieval, Renaissance, and Enlightenment periods (Horkheimer and Adorno 5–6). In China, for many centuries, the emperor was considered the Son of Heaven. Yet folk-religious, Daoist, and Buddhist traditions emphasized harmony with ancestral spirits and nature's Way, plus karmic interdependence. This involved balancing the five elements as cyclic phases of change: the *wuxing* of Earth, Wood, Fire, Metal, and Water. Thus, temples are mostly rectilinear like earth, yet open to the sky's roundness with curved roofs on wooden halls, dispersed across a walled yard. It includes bushes and trees planted in earth, plus fire offerings, metal burners, and pools for turtles and fish. But how do such church and temple spaces perform around the visitor, reshaping inner theatre networks through outer theatricality?

Sacred Spaces and Inner Networks

Chapter 3 explored spatial dimensions in religious buildings, characterized by melodramatic domination or tragicomic balance. Such spaces evoked the visitor's animal-human drives, as primary and social emotions, shaped in different cultural ways—with a potential for *rasa*-cathartic (savoring/clarifying) awareness through cross-cultural comparisons. The hypothesis from Chapter 1 was that European churches would reflect inner theatres in more left cortical, patriarchal, *scriptwriter/ critic* ways, through bounded self-Other ideals. Chinese temples would show more of a balance between those and right cortical, maternal, *mime/designer* networks—also expressing subcortical, supportive/trickster *stagehand* and limbic, memorial *audience* circuits—with porous, interdependent selves-others.

Despite significant round theatre exceptions, most European churches channel the visitor longitudinally, from the entrance area into the nave, along the main aisle toward the chancel's highly decorated altar, evoking awe with the aura of a vast, vertical, enclosed space. Initially, the visitor may experience such high-arousal awe outside the church, gazing up at its façade and towers, but lower arousal in the low-ceiling narthex, and then high arousal again in the nave with its high ceiling—like a theatregoer moving from outside through the lobby to a calm, comfortable seat, and then seeing a spectacle revealed. Some churches also have side aisle and transept chapels, facing in perpendicular directions. There might be fourteen Stations of the Cross on the side walls (as in the Quo Vadis Church) or outside, tied to Jerusalem sites of Christ's Passion, which some visitors circumambulate in prayer. But the central focus is still on the main altar's raised stage and transcendent imagery, sometimes seen through rising columns and ceiling vaults, climaxing in a great dome. Outside, the central dome often has a cross and ball on top, signifying patriarchal authority: "Christ's merciful dominion over Earth" (D. McNamara, *How* 209). Even with a Gothic rose window at the back of the church, the sacrificial altar is the spatial focus, reflected in the stained glass as "a picture of the properly centered soul" (Barron 35). Thus, in many European churches, rectilinear and curved structures groom the visitor's animal-human drives, personal feelings, and inner theatre networks with a focused, unidirectional, left-cortical *scriptwriter/critic* bias, especially when compared with Chinese temples.

Buddhist temples often show two warriors, Heng and Ha, in the entrance hall, or four large Heavenly Kings, evoking initial arousal, plus sculptures and banners with lions, dragons, and other animals as protectors, especially along stairs and roof edges. But even with giant statues and a vertical pagoda, at the entryway or deeper into the complex, its open spaces, plants, and dispersed halls, extending horizontally with multiple columns and curved roofs, offer balanced rhythms of high and low arousal, with various worship areas. Typically, they stage serene Buddhas, standing calmly, reclining at death, or seated in meditative lotus positions (although some ride an elephant, lion, or fish-dragon), including the maternal Guanyin pouring graceful help or with multiple arms and heads in compassionate wisdom. The Way of nature performs in Daoist and Buddhist temples, especially those sited along hillsides or on sacred mountains with trees and flowing streams, or inside caves and with cliff carvings, but also in cities with yards open to the sky and weather. This reflects a left-cortical *scriptwriter/critic* and right-cortical *mime/designer* balancing act of porous, interdependent selves, in the low-arousal, non-action (*wu wei*) of equanimity, with cyclic change, non-attachment, and compassion. As Avalokiteshvara/Guanyin explains on Vulture Peak, in the Buddhist *Heart Sutra*, "Form is emptiness; emptiness is form" (Lopez 6–7, 36, 57). Such formal emptiness may involve LAP affect through parietal *costume-body definer/designer* deactivation, as Newberg found with Tibetan Buddhist meditators and Catholic nuns in prayer, perhaps toward a cyclic, LAP/HAP, spillover effect, akin to shamanic trance. In contrast, the Christian tradition often stresses HAP, right-hemispheric *mime/designer* activation through the left parietal *costume-body definer*, toward God-soul identification, as with Pentecostal "speaking in tongues."

With East Asians, experiments find greater activity in the inner *director* with "perception and inference of others' minds in the dMPFC and TPJ," plus the lateral PFC *character*, for social cognition, and the right DLPFC stage/film *editor*, for social affects, helping to "maintain the low-arousal positive emotional states" (Han 69–70). This may also relate to the emphasis on modesty, communication constraints, social harmony, holistic thinking, and saving "face" in Chinese culture (P. Smith). By comparison, more activity in the MPFC *actor* and VMPFC *stage manager* networks of Westerners, specializing in self-knowledge and the self-monitoring of behavior, supports an "enhanced self-focus that makes people behave independently" (Han 70). This also involves the dorsal ACC (anterior cingulate cortex) *stage manager* and insula (part of the temporal-lobe *audience*) for "high-arousal positive emotional states in Westerners." A specific study on Chinese Buddhists "monitoring the conflict between the doctrine of No-self and self-focus thinking" resulted in less activity of "self-relatedness [circuits] in the VMPFC," but greater processing of Theory of Mind, "self-referential stimuli in the DMPFC" (Han et al.), the inner *director* circuit that imagines the Other's view. Anthropologists have also explored how "local theory of mind" differs across various cultures (Luhrmann, "Mind" 15).

European churches reflect *stage manager* (superego control) networks of bounded, individual *actor* egos, collected by an enclosed space and focused on the high-arousal, alpha patriarchal altar, with bread and wine as the Body and Blood sacrifice of a divine victim, the Lamb of God, handled by the role-playing priest. Christ's passionate victory over sin and death on the cross, extending a single life-death journey toward eternity, with Final Judgment, stresses a melodramatic, good versus evil, HAN to HAP, enhanced self-focus framing of animal-human drives (survival, territoriality, and hierarchy). This is shown in European churches, especially when compared with Chinese temples' tragicomic balance. And yet nurturing, joyous, but also mournful scenes, such as nativity/crucifixion, Pietà/resurrection, and dormition/ascension, found in Catholic churches' Marian and other spaces, may offer tragicomic, cyclic alternatives.

Passionate Spaces of Competitive Actor and Stage Manager Circuits

Chapter 3 considered Passion sites in Jerusalem as pilgrimage spaces of the divine melodrama (or tragicomedy), climaxing at the Calvary hill and Resurrection cave, transformed by the Holy Sepulchre Church, with ties to the fourteen Stations of the Cross in or near other churches. Churches of the Flagellation and Condemnation/Cross-Imposition are part of a Franciscan monastery, as Second Station near the supposed site of the First. Its clerical order, as territorial authority, has administered visiting pilgrims for many centuries, after Crusader conquests over Muslim rulers. The twentieth-century, neo-Romanesque Flagellation church collects daily visitors under stone arches, a vaulted ceiling, and thick walls with stained glass windows, showing Passion scenes. There is also a floor tile marking "Terra Santa." Such spaces emphasize each believer's inner *actor*, through superego *stage manager* networks, identifying with Christ's transcendent suffering. Yet various inner-theatre elements and animal-human drives (with *rasas* as emotion-motivation flavors) may be evoked in pilgrims and tourists, including personal memory *audience* and supportive/trickster *stagehand* circuits.

Not part of the Via Dolorosa, but also popular with pilgrims, the Church of Saint Anne offers a sacred enclosed space to commemorate the backstory of Mary, as the Immaculate Conception of a sinless body, inside her mother, St. Anne, at the legendary site of their family home, near ancient healing pools. Outdoor spaces are thus involved at this site, with the ruins of the pools and Byzantine church, built over a Roman temple, prior to the current Crusader church, which became a Muslim madrasa and then a garbage dump, before being restored in the nineteenth century. Its rectilinear, three-aisled nave, rounded (yet slightly peaked) Romanesque arches, and vaulted ceiling, along with the outdoor sites, express patriarchal *scriptwriter/critic*, maternal *mime/designer*, and supportive/trickster *stagehand* dimensions in the memorial melodrama of Father-Mary-Jesus and Christian soul identifications—through historical competition for holy territories.

Competitive spaces are apparent, too, in the Cenacle on Mount Zion, as the legendary site of (1) Jesus's Last Supper, (2) his post-resurrection appearance showing the doubting Thomas his wound, and (3) the Holy Spirit's visit in Pentecostal tongues of fire. It is also believed to be Mary's final homesite, built above the Tomb of David (a key Jewish king), with the promised Messiah in his lineage, possibly via Mary. Today, its rectilinear, probably Byzantine walls and round, Crusader columns bear a Muslim *mihrab* from the sixteenth century when it was an Ottoman mosque.

Such competitiveness between religions is reflected, too, in the Coptic Church of Queen Helen (now belonging to the Armenian Apostolic Church), adjacent to the Holy Sepulchre, with a cistern below it as a cave space that visitors can enter. There, the expeditionary forces of Constantine's mother reportedly found water, in their quest to capture Holy Land relics for transport to Rome and eventually across Europe. Not to be left out, with Greek Orthodox, Roman Catholic, and Armenian Apostolic clergy dominating certain areas of the Holy Sepulchre, the nearby Russian Orthodox Church of Saint Alexander Nevsky houses a chunk of the Calvary rock. It also bears an ancient stairway leading to the lost Constantinian basilica and a biblical "eye of a needle" passageway in its reliquary spaces. Likewise, the Cathedral of Saint James, as center of the Armenian Patriarchate in Jerusalem, claims to include in its rectilinear, iconic, ritual spaces: the head of St. James the Greater, apostle of Jesus, and the tomb of St. James the Lesser, brother or cousin of Christ (and original Patriarch of Jerusalem). But it also shares with visitors outside the church: a poster in English reminding them about the genocide of a million Armenians in Turkey, in the early twentieth century, not acknowledged as such by that government today.

Complex social emotions are reflected by the "square" in front of some churches, extending dominant territoriality, as exemplified by Saint Peter's Basilica in the Vatican (an independent city-state within Rome). Unlike Chinese courtyards, in a walled complex that typically includes multiple halls and natural elements, such as trees, bushes, and ponds, Saint Peter's Square extends from the monumental basilica with a colonnade at each side, as the "arms of Mother Church," according to its seventeenth-century designer, Gian Lorenzo Bernini. This patriarchal abstraction of maternal nurturing includes two fountains and a tall obelisk, brought to Rome from Egypt by the emperor Caligula for the center of a racetrack nearby, where Peter was reportedly martyred. The vast spaces of the "square," façade steps, and portico draw visitors into the largest church in the world, with a gigantic enclosed space. It includes Michelangelo's Pietà near the entryway and then a medieval bronze statue of Peter with feet rubbed smooth by numerous touches for luck, across hundreds of years. There is also a ten-story twisted-column canopy at the crossing, over the main altar and Peter's tomb. All these aspects and more reflect a predominance of patriarchal dimensions, yet mixed with maternal and trickster.

Through many elements, detailed in Chapter 3, the enclosures of the world's largest church evoke key emotions, extending animal-human drives toward religious ideals (Table 1.1). The survival drive might be felt as desire/fear through ego and group pride, yet potential conflicts with others, through courage/anxiety, especially with the martyrdom site and crucifixion relics (shown from a high balcony on Passion Sunday). These reflect human mortality, but also divine melodramatic rewards, as conquering death, sin, and nature. Reproduction and care may be sensed via love/lust and sympathy/panic in the cooperative legacies and self-sacrifices of intense friendship, or of kin and reciprocal altruism, within a faith community. Such animal-human drives, as emotions in social relations, are also reflected by female saint statues and angelic dome images, some with Baroque fleshiness, directed toward beliefs and rites of charity and compassion. Territoriality and alliance-hierarchy might be felt through security and fairness, plus nostalgia and honor with awe (or rage-vengeance and rivalry-envy), at the monument's vertical heights and creative splendor. Thus, Saint Peter's Basilica is at the center of global Roman Catholicism, with the sacredness of this site and numerous related sanctuaries inspiring moral devotion.

Building on those drives, playful joy, surprise, and freedom might be felt (or mischief and rebellion) with giant cherubs holding a holy water font and with other spiritual powers on the walls and domes, plus the Holy Spirit dove in the stained-glass window of the apse. Yet the grooming of brain spirits can also be sensed, with trust (or disgust) in belonging to the Church (or not), while in this huge, fantastically decorated church. It may involve liking as attraction to, being pleasurably like, and feeling a bond with the fleshy Baroque figures (with or without shame/guilt) in surrounding aisles, chapels, and altar areas, through cruciform spaces defining good against evil. Ultimately, the drive of seeking meaning, beyond mortal losses, might be felt as hope, through grief and mourning, toward transcendent gratitude and purpose in the cosmic theatre of God watching and acting through the church (or Church) and its spaces. Of course, any such feelings depend on the visitor's unique inner theatre, especially with Western-emphasized *actor* and *stage manager* circuits of ego enhancement and superego control.

Bounded Patriarchal Grooming (with Complications)

Legends about Peter's trickster and heroic performances relate to a small church at the edge of ancient Rome, Domine Quo Vadis. After defeating a rival miracle-worker, Simon Magus, Peter tried to escape the wrath of others in Rome. But he had a vision of Jesus, inspiring him to return to the city, re-bound for martyrdom. He was crucified like his Lord, yet upside-down so as not to rival him. The church marks the site where Peter asked the risen Jesus, "Lord, where are you going?" and he replied, "To Rome, to be crucified again," mirroring the saint's mimetic-mythic self. It provides a small space with murals of Peter and Christ, preaching and being crucified, plus images of Mary and the typical Stations of the Cross. Yet it also shows, near the entryway, a replica of ancient footprints in stone, perhaps as a pagan offering, transformed into a Christian sign, for today's visitor to ponder, regarding the meaning and purpose of life, death, and potential returns—in mimetic attachment or mythic release.

The holy stairway of the Scala Sancta, in a former papal palace near Saint John Lateran in Rome, provides another space for visitors to feel various animal-human drives, being groomed toward divine ideals. Believers, ascending the stairs on their knees, gain a plenary indulgence, purifying each soul from afterlife punishment for any sins up to that point. At the top of the stairs, they reach the "Holy of Holies" chapel with the *Uronica* icon of Christ Almighty, reportedly painted by St. Luke the Evangelist, with the power to blind a medieval pope. The rectilinear spaces of the purifying stairway and dangerous icon, with a mix of curved ceiling and arches, plus square and round columns, bear maternal, reproductive, nurturing aspects for believing souls—evoking such brain spirits through right cortical circuits. Yet these spaces express mostly patriarchal ideals, also summoning territorial nostalgia and hierarchical awe in believers who climb on their knees the steps of Jesus in his Jerusalem Passion. Through the pope's authority, in this Renaissance palace, pilgrims gain a playful sanctified freedom from Purgatorial pain for their individual souls (or someone they pray for)—through left cortical networks and inner theatre imaginings about the historical past and postmortem future. This involves seeking meaning beyond loss, through subcortical networks of survival fear, yet transcendent hope for a groomed rebirth, in the Holy of Holies' *Uronica* space at the top of the stairs.

Territorial ties to Jerusalem, not only with sites in the Holy Land that pilgrims have visited for centuries, but also sacred spaces around relics in Rome and in numerous, vertically vast, rectilinear churches across Europe, show the patriarchal power of Christianity, reflecting people's inner theatres of the past and shaping believers' brain spirits today. The hypothesis from Chapter 1 that churches reflect the left cortical bias of Western, ancient to modern, religious to secular, *bounded* selves—with porous spiritual possibilities, yet competitive, nature-dominating, patriarchal group bonds—is mostly confirmed with such enclosed spaces and their relics. But there are complications with right and sub-cortical, maternal and trickster aspects, in particular examples. As McGilchrist points out, there are shifting styles of European art and philosophy, showing more right cortical characteristics in ancient Greece, but then a leftward shift with Rome, rightward with the Renaissance, leftward with the Reformation and Enlightenment, rightward again with Romanticism, and leftward with modernism (*Master*). One might add: rightward again with postmodernism. How does the other side of the hypothesis in Chapter 1, using McGilchrist's neuroscience, plus experiments by cultural psychologists, pan out with examples in Chapter 3? Do Chinese temples show more left and right cortical, balanced characteristics, reflecting *porous*, interdependent, low arousal ideals, through open spaces and dispersed halls in contextual harmony with nature? Do they reflect/evoke more *character*, *editor*, and *director* circuits of the inner theatre, contrasting with *actor* and *stage manager* in churches?

Caves, Carvings, and Temples with Low Arousal, Porous Interdependence

Chinese Buddhism is not as hierarchically organized as the Roman Catholic Church or various Orthodox patriarchates. But a key monastery of Chan Buddhism, Lingyin Temple, one of China's largest and wealthiest, near the "Peak Flown from Afar" cave temples and cliff carvings in Hangzhou, offers a possible comparison with Rome's monumental basilicas and Europe's many relic ties to the Holy Land. The peak's title refers to the fourth-century Huili, Lingyin's founding monk, seeing a resemblance to Vulture Peak in India, where Shakyamuni and Avalokiteshvara speak in the Lotus and Heart sutras. This is somewhat like the fourth-century St. Helena taking the Holy Stairs and other Passion relics from Jerusalem to Rome—but with a mythical trick of nature and naming, rather than historical, territory-dominating claims.

Unlike the more left-cortical, patriarchal, focused, mechanical awe inspired by Saint Peter's prodigious basilica (or maternal embrace of its square), Flown Peak's hundreds of cliff-carved reliefs, around small cave temples, draw the visitor in dispersed, cyclical directions through a natural environment with trees, streams, and live animals, toward Lingyin Temple, as a potential soul's retreat with hidden spirits. This difference is reflected in carvings of various bodhisattvas, emerging from, yet still connected with natural cave walls, and of monks traveling to India, many times across the centuries, to get sutras for the cyclical spread of Buddhism in China. There is also a "Thread of Heaven" in one cave, with sunlight coming through an opening in the ceiling—akin to but more natural than the sun shafts in the vast spaces of Saint Peter's Basilica. Some of the caves' carved bodhisattva statues have polished areas, touched by generations of visitors for good luck, like the medieval bronze feet of Peter's statue in his central Vatican basilica, yet with nurturing ties to the natural context as well. The natural, dispersed, and cyclical aspects of caves and cliff-carvings reflect/evoke visitors' inner *character*, *editor*, and *director* networks with carved reliefs, hundreds of years old, of enlightened beings who exemplify the Buddha nature in each sentient creature, while also watching and helping them.

Various patriarchal elements may seem to dominate the spaces of Flown Peak and Lingyin Temple, from the stone pagoda reliquary with Huili's ashes near the park's entrance to the male Buddha carvings, outside and inside caves, to the Four Heavenly Kings in the first hall and many other statues. The walled temple complex and its halls also have rectilinear shapes, correlating with left-cortical networks of focal filtering functions. However, in comparison with Saint Peter's and other European churches, Lingyin Temple offers openness to the sky and weather with its large yards and dispersed halls, rather than an enclosed, main-altar-focused space. Although this temple has a central axis for some of its halls, it flows along the hillside, including many trees and plants inside the complex, instead of dominating the natural site. It also has a swastika-shaped 500 Arhats Hall to one side, where the visitor walks past many bronze statues of the Buddha's disciples, some with animals, toward four large bodhisattvas at the center, and back outward along the four arms, centripetally and centrifugally circumambulating this complex, rectilinear, yet curvilinear space.

When I visited Lingyin Temple, I happened to see a group of pilgrims in the initial courtyard, making large paper flowers and then walking in a circular line, two by two, holding them and chanting praise to Amitabha Buddha, before dropping the offerings in a round metal burner's fire. Some of them also bathed their shoulders or a purse with the holy smoke afterward. Not only did this demonstrate a left and right cortical, low and high arousal, patriarchal and maternal balance around the burner in the open-air courtyard (without a sacrificial altar or heroic statue). It also showed a porous mix of two major schools, with a Pure Land rite in a Chan Buddhist temple, unlike Orthodox, Catholic, and Protestant territorial conflicts across Europe's history.

With an 800-year old Wei Tuo statue (in the Heavenly Kings Hall), the tallest solid-bronze sculpture in the world (at the center of the Arhats Hall), and the largest wooden Shakyamuni statue in China (in the Mahavira Hall on the main axis), Lingyin Temple has several patriarchal monuments. Yet the tall bronze sculpture includes a seated, meditative, female Guanyin along with male bodhisattvas. Behind the giant Shakyamuni, although with less space for worshipers, Guanyin stands on a fish-dragon, with her girl and boy acolytes, plus many smaller figures, as a tall nurturing form, pouring elixir from a vase. Low-arousal, maternal ideals are prevalent in these and other Chinese temple spaces, both Buddhist and Daoist. Guanyin figures often appear in a regal form, more like Mary as Queen of Heaven than Madonna Lactans, actively nursing the baby Jesus, or as Pietà, holding her Son's crucified body. Yet visitors honor Guanyin and Mary in similar ways, seeking compassionate help from her, while offering lit incense or candles, and putting coins in a box by the statue.

Lingyin's Hall of the Medicine Buddha (behind and above Mahavira) shows a meditating statue of that king, who immolated himself in honor of the Buddha and was praised by Shakyamuni for such non-self-attachment, becoming a specialist in healing others. The Medicine King/Buddha is not shown in a high-arousal scene of sacrificial fire, as melodramatic hero, like Christ on the cross, suffering for others' sins and conquering death. Instead, like most Lingyin statues, Medicine Buddha is in a *low-*

arousal meditative form, seated on a lotus flower, with one hand raised, fingers holding a pill to help others. When I visited this hall, there were also yellow-robed monks and lay people seated at tables by this statue, chanting *interdependently*. Yet the hall's doors were open to other visitors, as pilgrims or tourists, and movement around it was allowed, with many other statues along the walls, in this *porous* identity space.

Another hall at Lingyin creates a space to honor a trickster figure, the eccentric monk, Jigong. Although he was expelled from this temple in the twelfth century for rule-breaking, drunkenness, and eating meat, he also became known for healing the sick and fighting for justice in the outer community. This hall, along with various others, creates a balance of trickster play, maternal nurturing, and patriarchal authority elements. Thus, the temple complex reflects sub-, right-, and left cortical brain-spirits, harmonizing with the natural environment and sky above, whatever the weather might be. Such an open, porous orientation contrasts with the more patriarchal, left-cortical, bounded-self, monotheistic focus of many European churches, with enclosed, rectilinear, competitive sites, dominating natural and political threats, although also creating spaces for a nurturing Mary and trickster Holy Spirit to be honored.

More Hillside Temples with Cooperative Natural Spaces

Uphill from Lingyin, Yongfu Temple (also founded by Huili) contains verdant yards and multiple halls with various bodhisattvas, patriarchal and maternal, plus walkways curving along natural mountain contours. Upper halls and yards offer views of Hangzhou and nearby West Lake, which is famous for inspiring poets, painters, and Chinese gardens. One of those upper buildings, Great Hero Hall, shows statues of Shakyamuni and his two key followers, with Guanyin at the back of them, along with her young attendants, Dragon Princess and Shancai. The bodhisattvas Samantabhadra and Manjushri also appear in the back corners, as in the main hall of many Chinese Buddhist temples, with worship spaces in multiple areas. The wall of another upper building, Fuxing Hall, displays the chimeric *qilin*, a sign of good luck, with coins added by visitors, showing a double trickster dimension, positive and playful. A patriarchal figure inside, the Daoist Blessing Star god, honored in a Buddhist temple, thus creates a shared cooperative space between these religions, unlike historical conflicts in Europe.

Another positive trickster, Lü Dongbin, one of the Eight Immortals, is remembered at Taoguang Temple, uphill from Lingyin and Yongfu, at a site where this sage practiced alchemy, cultivated immortality, and developed supernatural powers—despite flirting with women, getting wildly drunk, and showing a bad temper at times. A later story claimed that this serious but playful Daoist sage was converted to Buddhism by Chan Master Huanglong, after throwing a sword into his room. Such stories reflect dialectical, holistic, cooperative, right-cortical *mime/designer* views, yet also analytical, competitive, left-cortical *scriptwriter/critic* ideas, regarding subcortical, supportive/trickster *stagehand* networks. Indeed, Daoists claimed in return that the trickster Lü Dongbin was an incarnation of the Buddhist deity of wisdom, Manjushri, the male "Mother of the Buddhas." Eventually, he was accepted by both Chinese religions, as shown in the natural balances of this mountainside temple, with a statue of him—unlike Europe's territorial conflicts at Christian, pagan, Jewish, and Muslim sites, including the "Holy Land."

Climbing steep steps toward and between Taoguang's halls, which face different directions along the mountain's contours, a visitor finds the major bodhisattvas, Shakyamuni, Samantabhadra, and Manjushri, a *qilin* on a protective courtyard screen, and Guanyin statues. In a small hall, opposite Guanyin on a dragon, something rare appears: a female holding a baby, as one of several forms of Guanyin (as childless yet child-granting), on each side of the hall, evoking the maternal Way, along with compassionate wisdom, in such natural spaces. Outside, a dragon head sculpture offers visitors flowing water from its mouth. Farther uphill, there is a waterfall, and then a view of the city, lake, and trees, plus Daoist statues and a sacred alchemy cave. This again shows a cooperative mix of mountainside spaces and religions. There are dialectical, human and natural, *yang* and *yin* balances, with low-arousal positive (LAP) figures, including Guanyin with a baby—unlike melodramatic crucifixion, martyrdom, and dragon-devil conquering scenes, yet more like Madonna images, in churches.

Three more temples, near Lingyin, Yongfu, and Taoguang, dotted along the hillside with tea farms, further confirm this book's hypothesis, with new variations. They show left and right cortical balances of dialectical *yang/yin* thinking, porous interdependent identities, and natural harmony aims for animal-human drives, with primary and social feelings groomed by religious values—differently from European churches. Lower Tianzhu Temple houses brown-robed nuns with shaved heads. They sometimes chant collectively while circumambulating male and female bodhisattva statues, with a wooden drum beating, as I observed. Various animal figures (cranes, deer, boar, horses, and dragons) are carved on hall doors, showing ties to nature and animal-human brain spirits. In Middle Tianzhu Temple, a male monastery, Guanyin appears in the initial hall, along with a triple-headed figure, Vairocana Piluchana, adapted from a Hindu goddess. There is a central courtyard pool with fish suggesting superfluidity (*yú*), turtles symbolizing longevity, and coins left in underwater bowls by visitors wishing for luck. The second hall holds a huge Avalokiteshvara statue (the male form of Guanyin) with many arms and heads. The third hall shows a female Guanyin, standing on a fish-dragon and pouring compassion, along with her girl and boy acolytes (plus fifty-three spiritual advisers to the latter, including twenty women)—behind the central statues of the male bodhisattvas, Amitabha, Shakyamuni, and Medicine King. There are others at the edges: Samantabhadra, Manjushri, multiple arhats, and Guan Yu. He was a third-century military leader, deified and revered by Daoists as well, again showing interreligious cooperation at this site.

However, Upper Tianzhu Temple bears a history that reflects other aspects of animal-human drive/emotion grooming: intergroup competition and in-group idolization, through trust-sympathy-love-desire and liking-awe-nostalgia (Table 1.1). For centuries, it was a pilgrimage site with a miraculous object, like European churches with relics and Jerusalem as Holy Land. Founded over a thousand years ago, destroyed during the Cultural Revolution, and then rebuilt, it is famous for a naturally made (that is, uncarved) driftwood figure of "White-Robed Guanyin," which used to be housed there. (It is now lost, but became the prototype for numerous other statues.) The temple became wealthy as a medieval pilgrimage site, with its famous statue believed to bring Hangzhou much needed rain and save it from floods in various years. The medieval Tiantai abbot, Zunshi, popularized inner theatre visualizations of this Guanyin figure and outer theatre "Ghost Feeding" rites at Upper Tianzhu. But it eventually became less popular with Guanyin devotees than Mt. Putuo island, which now has more than thirty major temples and a 20-meter-tall **Nanhai Guanyin** statue, built in 1997 (Figure 4.30).

Within Upper Tianzhu's walls, there are dialectical *yang/yin*, porous interdependent, and natural harmony spaces, which reflect the grooming of drives in the past and currently. For example, territorial security is defended with a spirit screen in front of its Maitreya Hall. Yet that hall has external wall vents with lions and elephants, suggesting playfulness with animal-human, primary and social emotions. Inside, there is a chubby, laughing Future Buddha with a guard dog, cranes, dragons, and nymph-like *apsaras* around him, plus the Four Heavenly Kings, seated yet with feet balancing on *asuras* (like the standing Kings at Middle Tianzhu), along with Wei Tuo as the guardian bodhisattva, mixing maternal, animal-human trickster, and patriarchal forms. Before and after this hall, there are several large pools with bridges and statues, plus bushes and trees, adding interdependent natural aspects. Inside the next hall, a large drum and bell, in the corners near the entry door, offer a *yin-yang* balance (like the drum and bell towers in some temples), along with a possible replica of White-Robed Guanyin. Another hall, higher uphill, shows many small arhat figures on waves, on cliffs, and in caves, with fish, tigers, and many other animals, along the walls around the lotus-seated, almost identical Amitabha, Shakyamuni, and Medicine Buddha. This again involves animal-human and divine balancing acts, in images and spaces, with a competition at this temple for pilgrims and tourists against other Guanyin holy sites, across many centuries—but not a long history of bloodshed between religions as in Europe and Jerusalem.

Heaven and Earth in Sacrificial Balance or Neoclassical, Modern, and Postmodern

Beijing's Temple of Heaven complex, south of the Forbidden City, shows imperial competition for divine favor and popular approval extending across vast horizontal spaces, regarding vertical supplications. It reflects survival, reproduction, territoriality, care, and hierarchy emotions, during the Ming and Qing dynasties, when the emperor conducted biannual animal sacrifices, as Son of Heaven, for society's welfare regarding nature, weather, and farming, although only the elite could watch. (It may also commemorate human sacrifices during the early Ming period.) Its round, three-gabled Hall of Prayer for Good Harvests, on a circular platform in a square yard, balancing *yang* dragon and *yin* phoenix decorations, on rainspouts, stairways, and walls, reflects the *yang* power of heaven and *yin* of earth. To the north of that building and below, there is a rectangular storage room, Imperial Hall of Heaven, for the Heaven God's and imperial ancestors' tablets, which were moved to the higher-level Hall of Prayer to be honored during sacrificial rites. There are also East and West Annex Halls in the yard, originally for attendant gods' tablets, now holding exhibits about the main hall. At the edge of the yard, the central doorway of the gatehouse, for the imagined Heaven God's passage, is now closed. But the side doorways, for the emperor and officials, are used by tourists. This gatehouse and another, parallel to it along the procession road, have animals on their curved roof eaves, including horned dragons to frighten away evil spirits and hornless dragons to protect such wooden buildings from fire. This again reflects animal-human emotions of survival desire/fear and territorial security, extending toward supernatural values.

At the Fasting Palace, on the west side of the current Temple of Heaven park, the emperor would fast for three days prior to the animal sacrifice ritual, in order to purify his body by abstaining from women, meat, liquor, music, and state affairs. Back on the main processional axis, the round, single-gabled Imperial Vault of Heaven and its rectangular annexes held spirit tablets for honoring various celestial lights and natural forces, plus the emperor's ancestors. A dragon still appears today inside the dome of the Imperial Vault, playing with a "pearl of wisdom," as ascendant power regarding celestial deities, natural forces, and imperial kin. In my view, it also reflects the animal-human drives of everyone's brain spirits, sublimated through playful feelings into grooming-gossip-purification and transcendent meaning. This involves inner *stagehand*, *audience*, *mime/designer*, and *scriptwriter/critic* circuits, with outer religious and secular networks, in the staging of self and Other as more porous or bounded, interdependent or individualist, in Eastern and Western traditions—but bound to make sacrifices either way.

The type of sacrifice is a key question, whether animal or human, of self or others, physically or psychologically, by the leader or followers, autocratic or democratic, in bounded (and binding) or porous *groups*, with melodramatic good-versus-evil competition or tragicomic compassionate cooperation. South of the Imperial Vault of Heaven, with another triple gate along the processional route, plus two sets of Star Gates on the four sides around it, the Circular Mound Altar shows the site for animal and human sacrifices hundreds of years ago, with three levels of nine steps each, as the strongest *yang* number. Typically, a bull was burned in offering at the Winter Solstice by the emperor and his assistants, to provide a good harvest for the people in the coming year, but with only special officials and the gods as spectators. Now, ordinary visitors can climb onto this stage, with its central Heaven Heart Stone, blue-green floor, white marble balustrade, and view of distant city skyscrapers. It might be seen as the heart of past sacrifices in the People's Republic of China, reflecting current orders, too. The vast Temple of Heaven complex is a restored cultural attraction, with its park used by locals for games, exercises, and communal gatherings, while the government enforces harmony, with "social credit" scores and certain groups scapegoated. Firewood ovens are set along the Circular Mound's outer rectangular wall, where pine, cypress, and human sacrifices were offered to gods in the past, near the Pit of Hair and Blood for their remains, according to a tourist website ("Circular" at www.mybeijingchina.com).

North of the Forbidden City, the modest remains of the Temple of Earth likewise represent past and current sacrifices, especially with its "Relic Exhibition Room," offering objects and information about the summer solstice rites. Visitors can see its altar mound of squares within squares, plus Star Gates, red (fire color) walls, and yellow (imperial, earth color) tiles with fire-protective dragon heads. This former temple is inside a larger recreational park, like the Temple of Heaven and the fragmentary ruins of the Temple of the Moon to the west and Sun to the east.

Together, these four Ming-Qing temples in Beijing, like the Sanyuan Palace on Guangzhou's ancient hillside site, exemplify ancestor and nature honoring, plus multiple deity venerating, through folk religion and Daoist traditions in China, akin to enlightenment seeking, Buddhist temples. They reflect bilateral (and supportive/ trickster) brain spirits, with animal-human drives groomed by open, *yang/yin* balancing, dispersed, five-element and *feng-shui* harmonizing, porous identity, polytheistic spaces. This contrasts with the enclosed, land-dominating, main-altar-focused, monotheistic, nativity-crucifixion-martyrdom commemorating, bounded-identity, good versus evil, and thus more left-cortex-evoking church spaces of Europe. And yet, the Eastern Orthodox and Lutheran neoclassical versus modernist and (ecumenical) postmodern churches of Helsinki show potential shifts of the Western tradition. They might be viewed as moving historically from *melodramatic*, hilltop-dominating, pointed-dome/tower, rectilinear, more left-cortical, hierarchic Cathedrals toward *tragicomic*, postwar, nature-embedded functionalism (Rock Church) and commerce-countering playfulness (Chapel of Silence), with more inclined, curved, right-cortical nurturing and subcortical supportive/trickster dimensions.

Key Takeaways

Comparing how Chinese temples and European churches reflect inner-theatre networks, while evoking animal-human drives, offers contextual *and* focused views, as stereoscopic, not merely stereotypical. Indeed, such comparisons elucidate the dangers of binary, good against evil identifications and projections in the melodramatic victim-vengeance mode of mimetic desire, rivalry, and scapegoating. Visitors to religious buildings or readers of this book (with its images and videos) might taste such emotional evocations, participating as performers, yet also observing the dangers and benefits, with *rasa*-cathartic awareness.

This theatrical approach in church/temple comparisons is akin to "mindfulness training" (MT) in Western psychotherapy, developed from ancient Buddhist techniques and studied by scientists in recent decades. Various forms of MT involve: (1) recognition of the components of experience, including emotional "conflicts" embedded in cognitive narratives; (2) attentional redirection in aroused or depressive states; and (3) development of a decentered, metacognitive, "observing" self, rather than being "captivated by the internal narrative" of self-rumination (Carmody 68–71; Irving et al. 352–3). Even "robot-guided," brain-computer-interface meditation shifts activity toward the right hemisphere, as a study showed, with "increased sensory awareness and open monitoring" (Alimardani et al. 683). Human-guided MT shows right lateralization, too, even with "evoked sadness," decreasing depression by rebalancing "affective and sensory neural networks" (Farb et al. 25). More mindful, right hemisphere (*mime-improviser/scene-designer*) activity may thus involve "'maximizing complexity'... to alter our relationship with the self" (Siegel, "Mindfulness" 262), toward a self-transcendent "spiritual" openness (Miller). Such metacognitive MT performance-cum-spectatorship, as a refined tasting of emotional animal-human drives, cleansing ego and group narratives in *rasa*-cathartic awareness, might decenter ruminative, midline PFC networks (Bowen et al. 399), within and between brains, especially VMPFC *stage manager* and related insula (temporal lobe) *audience* circuits. Rather than "fighting" or "fixing" personal addictions and collective scapegoats, this can bring "an accepting, curious, and compassionate attitude" (400) through the neuro-social networks that religious buildings continue to evoke.

European churches reflect the repeated tendencies of Christian authorities and empires to demand sacrifices of believers and outsiders, as martyrs or scapegoats, in sectarian rivalries. However, Buddhist temples often display Daoist figures and Daoist show Buddhist for a peaceful mix of worship spaces. Cooperative interdependent permeability becomes apparent with balanced *yin-yang*, nature oriented, non-self-attached, harmonious ideals in temple yards, open to changing weather. I observed such openness with several visits to Jing'an Buddhist Temple, sometimes with rain or snow, and at **Baiyun (White Cloud) Daoist Temple** in Shanghai, with snow in the yard, yet offerings performed for Lunar New Year (Figures 4.31–7).

Despite their apparent openness, however, Chinese temples might be viewed as reflecting past imperial and current communist control of collectivist conformers (or of others viewed as independent threats). They also show capitalist fetishes and pilgrim-tourist profit wheels, with spirit money burning, replica statues for sale, entrance fees, and expected donations, enabling more artistic attractions that may again bring more income. There is a long history to this interdependence of sacred and material economies in Chinese Buddhism (Borup), as in the Roman Catholic and Eastern Orthodox traditions of holy reliquaries, ritual offerings, and pilgrimage sites, including the competitive territory of Jerusalem.

Below is a list of findings in this book, confirming yet complicating its initial hypotheses. Admittedly, historical developments are explored more with Europe's and Jerusalem's churches, due to their competitive variations and conflicts. Chinese temples are considered more collectively, because of their cooperative consistency and less conflict between Confucian, Daoist, and Buddhist traditions than Catholic, Orthodox, and Protestant. While I was completing this book, Russia intensified its invasion of Ukraine, which started in 2014, with the Russian Orthodox Church in support, against the Orthodox Church of Ukraine, after they split in 2019.[4] Tragically, this offered yet

---

[4] In March 2022, Russian Orthodox Patriarch Kirill, mimicking Kremlin propaganda, claimed that the Russian invasion of Ukraine was justified as saving Russian speakers in the Donbas region from genocide ("Russia's").

another example in Europe's long history of religious, nationalistic conflicts, through melodramatic heroes ostensibly saving or avenging victims against evil villains—with scapegoat prejudices, projections of evil onto others, and the competitive bonding of insecure groups and their leaders.

1. Confirmed yet complicated: both European churches and Chinese temples are mostly **rectilinear, upright** monuments, deriving from ancient, upper-class, domestic models, thus reflecting **left-cortical, patriarchal** *scriptwriter/critic* networks and survival-territorial-hierarchic drives. Yet they also show **curved, inclined** elements, reflecting **right-cortical, maternal** *mime-improviser/ scene-designer* circuits and reproduction-nurturing drives. They have **supportive/trickster** images and edges, too, regarding **limbic** *audience* and **subcortical** *stagehand* networks. Both types of religious buildings display patriarchal rulers/teachers as deities, stressing imperial, hierarchical territories. But they reflect and potentially evoke porous spiritual experiences, depending on each visitor's inner theatre, while nurturing communal connections, in the group spaces of a religious sanctuary. In Europe, there are various non-rectilinear ground plans, as exceptions to the basilica and cruciform paradigms, especially with round martyria and polygonal or round baptisteries. In China, there are cave temples with naturally curved inner spaces, yet most temple complexes maintain the traditional palace design of rectilinear walls, courtyards, and halls, often rebuilt over time.
2. Confirmed yet complicated: European churches are **enclosed, unified** monuments (though sometimes with an open "square" in front or "cloister" to the side or nearby "graveyard"), reflecting left-hemispheric, patriarchal, **individualistic** aspects—often with the church name idealizing a saint. Major structures are mostly made of **stone or brick** to endure across the centuries (except with stave churches). Their spaces and images typically **dominate nature** and bodily desires, considered as potentially evil in a **binary polarized, objectifying, mechanical** (left hemispheric) way—with materials and artistic scenes showing a **permanent** melodramatic **victory** over time, mortality, and sin. Churches **focus** the visitor from exterior to interior spaces, in a mostly **unilinear direction**, west to east, usually with a lower ceiling portico and/or narthex, and then a higher ceiling nave. The visitor is directed along the central aisle (even without pews) toward the main altar, perhaps with a relic-bearing crypt below it. Male clergy perform on the higher altar platform (and pulpit), in the holier sanctuary area, like the ancient Greco-Roman *cella* and Hebrew Holy of Holies, as exclusive chancel, sometimes with a screen or iconostasis *templon*. Thus, the focus is on low to high arousal, negative to positive (LAN, LAP, HAN to **HAP**)— with Marian, martyrdom, "Passion," and Ruler-Judgment imagery—evoking left to right cortical, respectful but elevating, threatening yet sublime awe. Cruciform churches include a transept, often with side chapels, where the visitor might light a candle and kneel, while giving a coin donation. There may be an apse with small altars behind the main one and Stations of the Cross along the nave walls for

further prayers. Such variations extend the focus in perpendicular *and cyclical* directions, with related baptismal and memorial areas, including graveyards outside. And yet, collective services, sometimes with incense smoke created by a priest or altar boy, focus congregants toward the pulpit and main altar, as well as upward toward the ceiling and window light, with readings, prayers, and Last Supper reenactments of bread-wine becoming the body-blood of Christ (**HAP**).

3. Confirmed: Chinese temples involve more **holistic, collectivist** right-hemispheric considerations with **multidirectional contexts**, from the exterior wall (sometimes with a spirit screen or bridge over a pool) to the entry gate, then to **open-air** yards and **dispersed wooden** halls with many statues. Halls are mostly on the main axis, south to north (for over a thousand years), yet also placed around the complex in many directions, sometimes flowing up a hillside. They emphasize **balanced dialectical** (LAN/LAP/HAN/HAP) *yin/yang* ideals and feminine/masculine, maternal/patriarchal **harmony with nature** (the Dao as nature's Way, involving earth and heaven), akin to cave temples and cliff carvings with earth-channel *qi*. The built hall-and-yard environments include the five elemental forces (Wood, Water, Metal, Earth, and Fire) in **cyclical change**, with plants, trees, open sky (sometimes with rain or snow), and pools, plus burners with sand or fire for visitors' incense, candles, and spirit money, producing smoke clouds and fragrant smells. Visitors bow to the ground near statues and leave coin donations (**LAP**). They *playfully* toss coins toward holes in large braziers or leave coins on animal sculptures, as a trickster dimension (**HAP/LAP**). Monks chant with lay people (**LAP**) or help them with rituals for deities and the deceased (**LAN**), burning offerings that send money or paper objects through the smoke, hoping for aid and less disturbances in return. At some temples, there are fish and turtle pools, where visitors release or feed the animals for karmic merit (**LAP**).

4. Confirmed yet complicated: European churches, with their land-dominating, low to high arousal (LA to **HA**), narthex-nave enclosures and **vertical** spires or pointed domes, reflect territorial, hierarchical, and **more left-cortical, melodramatic** (**HAP** good over HAN evil), **bounded**, individual/group **competition**. This is seen with Romanesque transformations of pagan sites, extending to Gothic peaked arches and rising towers, with flying buttresses and gargoyle trickster edges. Yet styles developed into new left/right-cortical balances with Renaissance symmetry and then Baroque fluidity, involving perspectival dome interiors, heavenly families, and chubby cherubs (as right-cortical maternal and subcortical supportive/trickster aspects). Eventually, there were competitive "neo" movements, plus modernist (more left-cortical) geometric abstractions, and yet postmodern playful mixtures in church designs. Such historical developments involved medieval to modern, pilgrimage, military, and political ties to the "Holy Land" (with its birth/rebirth sites) through bloody Abrahamic conflicts of "good versus evil" rivals, as competitive "Children of God." (Sadly, this has continued with Jewish-Muslim, Israeli-Palestinian, religious and military conflicts, sometimes with Christian supporters.) Also involved were relic veneration, translation, and artistic attachment, or theft and transformation, with belief in

miraculous powers, turning economic as well as spiritual profit wheels. Thus, European churches reflect and evoke more competitive *actor* and *stage manager* networks, with ego, soul-to-God, melodramatic (good versus evil) grooming of animal-human drives, for immortal meaning and purpose.

5. Confirmed yet complicated: Chinese temples are less vertically monumental and **more horizontally shamanic**, reflecting **left and right cortical balance**, in relation to limbic memorial *audience* and subcortical supportive/trickster *stagehand* networks, perhaps represented by fierce yet protective lions, elephants as meditative mounts, and various dragons, plus warrior deities as peaceful guardians (sometimes dancing on demigods). There may be huge human statues and tall reliquary pagodas or drum and bell towers. Yet most of the halls are of modest size, with just one or two levels, even in a large temple complex. This follows ancient Confucian-Daoist principles of moderation and balance: appropriate size of *yin* inner space and *yang* outer height, with symmetry and rhythm, akin to musical harmony. Their design has been mostly *consistent* for over a thousand years: wooden walls and columns connected by dougong brackets to glazed-tile peaked roofs, with overhanging eaves and upturned corners, sometimes with ridge animals, including fish-dragons. Halls are embedded in **porous** collective yards, showing **tragicomic (LAN/LAP and HAN/HAP)** values of **interdependent cooperation**, sometimes mixing Buddhist and Daoist figures, despite past imperial conflicts, while also reflecting Confucian and folk religious, familial ideals. Chinese pilgrimage sites continue from past to present (after Communist and Cultural Revolution interruptions), competing for tourist wealth, yet without the bloody history of religious-nationalistic conflicts in Europe's holy lands. Thus, Chinese temples reflect/evoke more cooperative *character*, *editor*, and *director* networks, with tragicomic grooming of animal-human drives, for immortal meaning and purpose—or contextual awareness of the suffering caused by purposeful attachments.

The key difference between European churches and Chinese temples is the reflection of *more* melodramatic (good versus evil scapegoating), low to high arousal, survival-territorial-hierarchical emotions in churches. This apparently involves left-cortical, individualistic or group competitive, predatory, objectifying networks, as the inner *scriptwriter/critic*, dominating nature, sin, and death—with a fixed filtering of right-cortical holistic awareness. According to findings in cultural neuroscience, it may also mean more activity in MPFC *actor* and VMPFC/dACC *stage manager* circuits. Temples reflect more of a dialectical, low and high arousal balance between left-cortical optimistic (yet confabulating and projecting) networks and tragicomic, reproductive-nurturing-playful emotions. This balancing act would correlate with more interdependent, cooperative, right-cortical circuits as *mime-improviser/scene-designer*, with stronger ties to subcortical supportive/trickster *stagehands*, regarding the limbic intuitive-memory *audience*—in the staging of self and Other, both internally and externally. It may also involve more active LPFC *character*, (right) DLPFC *stage/film editor*, and DMPFC *director* circuits (Han 69–70).

Yet patriarchal (more left cortical) and maternal (right cortical) characteristics, relating to supportive/trickster (subcortical) aspects, are complex in church and temple comparisons. There is also the possibility of tragicomic *rasa*-cathartic awareness in European churches, especially with awe, fear, anger, and courage, through crucifixion/resurrection, martyrdom, judgment, and Madonna scenes, tasted with compassion, disgust, humor, love, and peace—or of melodramatic, good versus evil identifications in Chinese temples. These theatrical mindsets are crucial differences *within* Western and Chinese, religious and secular, out-group/in-group sacrifices, which continue to evolve today, through individualist and collectivist demands.

Our "brain spirits" are interactive, as the rewiring energies of core affects, evolved drives, and family paradigms. We choose how to perform in porous tolerant groups, respecting individual rights, or in bounded competitive ideologies, promoting conspiracies and projecting scapegoats. As conduits from our ancestors to our descendants, we seek (immortal) meaning and purpose beyond loss, with self/other sacrifices of group bonding and mimetic rivalry—or compassion and acceptance. This occurs through the grooming of our inner theatres, in religious buildings and other psycho-social, meta-physical arenas, as embodied subjects in person or as virtual souls online. Yet each of us, drawing on Western and Eastern traditions, can play an active (self-observant) role in the global development of bounded independent and porous interdependent identities, in tight and loose groups: through melodramatic righteous conflict or tragicomic *rasa*-cathartic awareness. How will our animal-human brain spirits, from churches and temples to other theatrical sites, continue to evolve, in more ego/group competitive or non-selfish cooperative ways? You decide.

Works Cited

The Acts of Peter. The Apocryphal New Testament. Translated by M.R. James, Clarendon Press, 1924, www.earlychristianwritings.com/text/actspeter.html.
Adolphs, Ralph. "Emotions are Functional States That Cause Feelings and Behavior." *The Nature of Emotion*, edited by Andrew S. Fox et al., Oxford University Press, 2018, pp. 6–11.
Agnati, Luigi F., et al. "Art as a Human 'Instinct-Like' Behavior Emerging from the Exaptation of the Communication Process." *Art, Aesthetics, and the Brain*, edited by Joseph P. Huston et al., Oxford University Press, pp. 426–50.
Alcorta, Candace S. "Adolescence and Religion." *Science and the World's Religions*, vol. 2, edited by Patrick McNamara and Wesley J. Wildman, Praeger, 2012, pp. 239–66.
Alexander, Jeffrey C. *Performance and Power.* Polity, 2001.
Alimardani, Maryam, et al. "Robot-Assisted Mindfulness Practice." *2020 29th IEEE International Conference on Robot and Human Interactive Communication (RO-MAN)*, 2020, pp. 683–9, doi: 10.1109/RO-MAN47096.2020.9223428.
Ames, Roger T. "'A Leg is not the Same as Walking.'" *Philosophy East and West*, vol. 72, no. 2, Apr. 2022, pp. 517–27.
Ammaniti, Massimo, and Vittorio Gallese. *The Birth of Intersubjectivity.* Norton, 2014.
Anderson, Miranda, et al. "Distributed Cognition and the Humanities." *Distributed Cognition in Medieval and Renaissance Culture*, edited by Miranda Anderson and Michael Wheeler, Edinburgh University Press, 2019, pp. 1–17.
Arbib, Michael. "Toward a Neuroscience of the Design Process." *Mind in Architecture*, edited by Sarah Robinson and Juhania Pallasmaa, MIT Press, 2015, pp. 75–98.
Aristotle. *Politics,* in *Aristotle in 23 Volumes*, vol. 21, translated by H. Rackham, Harvard University Press, 1944, www.perseus.tufts.edu/hopper/text?doc=urn:cts:greekLit:t lg0086.tlg035.perseus-eng1:8.1342a.
Atran, Scott. *Talking to the Enemy.* HarperCollins, 2010.
Baars, Bernard J. *In the Theater of Consciousness.* Oxford University Press, 1997.
Baars, Bernard J. *On Consciousness.* Nautilus, 2019.
Badgaiyan, Rajendra D. *Neuroscience of the Nonconscious Mind.* Elsevier, 2019.
Baldrian-Hussein, Farzeen. "*Hun* and *Po* 魂•魄 Yang Soul(s) and Yin Soul(s)." *The Encyclopedia of Taoism*, edited by Fabrizio Pregadio, Routledge, 2008, pp. 521–3.
Barrett, Justin. "Cognitive Science of Religion: What Is It and Why Is It?" *Religion Compass*, vol. 1, 2007, pp. 768–86.
Barrett, Lisa Feldman. *How Emotions Are Made.* Houghton Mifflin, 2017.
Barrie, Thomas. *The Sacred In-Between.* Routledge, 2010.
Barron, Robert. *Heaven in Glass and Stone.* Crossroad Publishing, 2000.
Bassil-Morozow, Helena. *The Trickster in Contemporary Film.* Routledge, 2012.
Bastiaansen, J. A. C. J., et al. "Evidence for Mirror Systems in Emotions." *Philosophical Transactions of the Royal Society B*, vol. 364, 2009, pp. 2391–404.
Bauer, Wolfgang. "The Hidden Hero." *Individualism and Holism: Studies in Confucian and Taoist Values*, edited by Donald Munro, University of Michigan Press, 1985, pp. 157–98.

Beauregard, Mario, Johanne Lévesque, and Vincent Paquette. "Neural Basis of Conscious and Voluntary Self-Regulation of Emotion." *Consciousness, Emotional Self-Regulation, and the Brain*, edited by Mario Beauregard, John Benjamins, 2004, pp. 163–94.
Begg, Ean. *The Cult of the Black Virgin*. Routledge, 1986.
Bell, Alexander Peter. *Didactic Tales*. LIT Verlag, 2000.
Bellah, Robert N. *Religion in Human Evolution*. Harvard University Press, 2011.
Belting, Hans. *Likeness and Presence*. Translated by Edmund Jephcott, University of Chicago Press, 1994.
Bendor, Daniel, and Matthew A. Wilson. "Biasing the Content of Hippocampal Replay During Sleep." *Nature Neuroscience*, vol. 15, 2012, pp. 1439–44.
Benn, James A. *Burning for the Buddha*. University of Hawaii Press, 2007.
Bering, Jesse. *The Belief Instinct*. Norton, 2011.
Bermudez, Julio. "Amazing Grace." *Faith and Forum*, vol. 4, no. 2, 2009, pp. 8–13, faithandform.com/feature/amazing-grace/.
Bermudez, Julio. "Empirical Aesthetics." *Considering Research*, edited by Philip Plowright and Bryce Gamper, Lawrence Tech University, 2011, pp. 369–80.
Bermudez, Julio. Introduction. *Transcending Architecture*, edited by Julio Bermudez, Catholic University of America Press, 2015.
Bermudez, Julio. "Profound Experiences of Architecture." *2A Architecture and Art*, vol. 17, 2011, pp. 20–5.
Bermudez, Julio, et al. "Externally-Induced Meditative States." *Frontiers of Architectural Research*, vol. 6, 2017, pp. 123–36.
Berridge, Kent C. "Motivation Concepts in Behavioral Neuroscience." *Physiology & Behavior*, vol. 81, 2004, pp. 179–209.
The Bible, New International Version, Biblica, 2011, www.biblestudytools.com/niv/.
Birch, Robert, and Brian R. Sinclair. "Spirituality in Place." *ARCC Conference Repository*, 2013, pp. 80–7.
Birrell, Anne. *Chinese Myths*. British Museum Press, 2000.
Blackmore, Susan. *The Meme Machine*. Oxford University Press, 2000.
Blake, C. Fred. *Burning Money*. University of Hawai'i Press, 2011.
Blake, C. Fred. "Foot-Binding in Neo-Confucian China and the Appropriation of Female Labor." *Signs*, vol. 19, no. 3, Spring 1994, pp. 676–712.
Blanke, Olaf, and Gregor Thut. "Inducing Out-of-Body Experiences." *Tall Tales about the Mind and Brain*, edited by Sergio Della Sala, Oxford, 2007, DOI:10.1093/acprof:oso/9780198568773.003.0027.
Blattman, Christopher. *Why We Fight*. Viking, 2022.
Bloom, Irene. "On the Matter of the Mind." *Individualism and Holism: Studies in Confucian and Taoist Values*, edited by Donald Munro, University of Michigan Press, 1985, pp. 293–330.
Blowers, Geoffrey H. "The Continuing Prospects for a Chinese Psychology." *The Oxford Handbook of Chinese Psychology*, edited by Michael Harris Bond, Oxford University Press, 2010, pp. 5–18.
Bolton, Brenda M. "Advertise the Message: Images in Rome at the Turn of the Twelfth Century." *Studies in Church History*, vol. 28, 1992, pp. 117–30.
Bonnie, Kristin E., and Frans de Waal. "Primate Social Reciprocity and the Origin of Gratitude." *The Psychology of Gratitude*, edited by Robert A. Emmons and Michael E. McCullough, Oxford, 2004, pp. 213–29.

Borup, Jørn. "Spiritual Capital and Religious Evolution." *Journal of Global Buddhism*, vol. 20, 2019, pp. 49–68.
Bosco, Joseph, and Puay-peng Ho. *Temples of the Empress of Heaven*. Oxford University Press, 1999.
Bowen, Sarah, et al. "A Mindfulness-Based Approach to Addiction." *Handbook of Mindfulness*, edited by Kirk Warren Brown et al., Guilford, 2015, pp. 387–404.
Brattico, Elvira. "From Pleasure to Liking and Back." *Art, Aesthetics, and the Brain*, edited by Joseph P. Huston et al., Oxford University Press, pp. 302–18.
Bratton, Susan. "Religion and the Ecosphere." *Science and the World's Religions*, vol. 3, edited by Patrick McNamara and Wesley J. Wildman, Praeger, 2012, pp. 221–51.
Brennan, Teresa. *The Transmission of Affect*. Cornell University Press, 2004.
Brin, David. "Neoteny and Two-Way Sexual Selection in Human Evolution." *Journal of Social and Evolutionary Systems*, vol. 18, no. 3, 1996, pp. 257–76.
Broesch, Tanya, et al. "Opportunities for Interaction." *Human Nature*, vol. 32, no. 1, Mar. 2021, pp. 208–38.
Broeskamp, Bernadette. "The Construction and Dissemination of a New Visual Idiom." *Searching for the Dharma, Finding Salvation*, edited by Christoph Cueppers and Max Deeg, Lumbini International Research Institute, 2014, pp. 109–40.
Brook, Timothy. *Praying for Power*. Harvard University Press, 1994.
Brookshire, Geoffrey, and Daniel Casasanto. "Motivation and Control." *PLoS ONE*, vol. 7, no. 4, 2012, online, doi:10.1371/journal.pone.0036036.
Bruntz, Courtney. "Religion as Financial Asset." *Journal of Human Values*, vol. 21, no. 1, 2021, pp. 72–83.
"The Buddhist Center in Southeast Asia." Zhejiang Provincial Department of Culture and Tourism, 2016–19, https://ct.zj.gov.cn/art/2019/7/27/art_1663781_36144614.html.
Bulbulia, Joseph, and Richard Sosis. "Signalling Theory and the Evolution of Religious Cooperation." *Religion*, vol. 41, no. 3, 2011, pp. 363–88.
Buswell, Robert E., Jr., and Donald S. Lopez, Jr. *The Princeton Dictionary of Buddhism*. Princeton University Press, 2013.
Calvo-Merino, Beatriz, et al. "Action Observation and Acquired Motor Skills." *Cerebral Cortex*, vol. 15, no. 8, 2005, pp. 1243–9.
Calvo-Merino, Beatriz, et al. "Seeing or Doing?" *Current Biology*, vol. 16, no. 19, 2006, pp. 1905–10.
Candea, Matei. *Comparison in Anthropology*. Cambridge University Press, 2019.
Cannon, Jon. *The Secret Language of Sacred Spaces*. Duncan Baird, 2013.
Carmody, James. "Reconceptualizing Mindfulness." *Handbook of Mindfulness*, edited by Kirk Warren Brown et al., Guilford, 2015, pp. 62–78.
Caseau, Béatrice Chevallier. "Spaces of Roman Religion and Christianity in Late Antiquity." *The Oxford Handbook of Religious Space*, edited by Jeanne Halgren Kilde, Oxford University Press, 2022, pp. 327–43.
Cassaniti, Julia L., and Tanya Marie Luhrmann. "The Cultural Kindling of Spiritual Experiences." *Current Anthropology*, vol. 55, supplement 10, Dec. 2014, pp. S333–43.
Cavarero, Adriana. *Inclinations: A Critique of Rectitude*. Stanford University Press, 2016.
"The Chair of Peter." *Catholic Exchange*, 22 Feb. 2018, Sophia Institute Press, catholicexchange.com/the-chair-of-peter.
Chaminade, Thierry, and Jean Decety. "Leader or Follower? Involvement of the Inferior Parietal Lobule in Agency." *Neuroreport*, vol. 13, no. 15, 2002, pp. 1975–8.

Chandra, Vikram. *Geek Sublime*. Graywolf, 2014.
Chau, Adam Yuet. "Efficacy, Not Confessionality." *Sharing the Sacra*, edited by Glenn Bowman, Berghahn, 2012, pp. 79–96.
Chau, Adam Yuet. Introduction. *Religion in Contemporary China*, edited by Chau, Routledge Press, 2011, pp. 1–31.
Chen, Yi-Chuan, et al. "When 'Bouba' Equals 'Kiki.'" *Scientific Reports*, vol. 6, 2016, online.
Chiao, Joan Y. "Cultural Neuroscience of Emotion." *The Nature of Emotion*, edited by Andrew S. Fox et al., Oxford University Press, 2018, pp. 136–40.
"China Temple Opens Tallest Pagoda." *BBC News*, 1 May 2007, news.bbc.co.uk/2/hi/asia-pacific/6610999.stm
Ching, Francis D. K., Mark M. Jarzombek, and Vikramaditya Prakash. *A Global History of Architecture*. Wiley, 2007.
Ching, Julia. *Chinese Religions*. Macmillan, 1993.
Chirico, Alice, and David B. Yaden. "Awe: A Self-Transcendent and Sometimes Transformative Emotion." *The Function of Emotions*, edited by Heather C. Lench, Springer, 2018, 221–34.
Chouchou, Florian, et al. "How the Insula Speaks to the Heart." *Human Brain Mapping*, vol. 40, 2019, pp. 2611–22.
"The Circular Mound Altar." *My Beijing China*. www.mybeijingchina.com/beijing-attractions/the-temple-of-heaven/the-circular-mound-altar.htm.
Clark, Andy. *Surfing Uncertainty*. University of Oxford Press, 2016.
Clark, Margaret. *Understanding Religion and Spirituality in Clinical Practice*. Karnac Books, 2012.
Clausen, David Christian. *The Upper Room and Tomb of David*. McFarland, 2016.
Coburn, Alex, et al. "Buildings, Beauty, and the Brain." *Journal of Cognitive Neuroscience*, vol. 29, no. 9, 2017, pp. 1521–31.
Cochini, Christian. *Guide to Buddhist Temples of China*. Macau Ricci Institute, 2009.
Cohen, Adam B., and Steven L. Neuberg. "Religious Cultures and Religious Conflict." *Handbook of Cultural Psychology*, edited by Dov Cohen and Shinobu Kitayama, 2nd edition, Oxford University Press, 2019, pp. 857–75.
Cole, Alan. *Mothers and Sons in Chinese Buddhism*. Stanford University Press, 1998.
"Communion Shared-Spoon Ritual Unchanged in Orthodox Church Despite Virus." *Los Angeles Times*, 29 May 2020, www.latimes.com/world-nation/story/2020-05-29/communion-ritual-unchanged-in-orthodox-church-despite-virus.
Cook, Amy. "Emergence, Meaning and Presence." *The Routledge Companion to Theatre, Performance and Cognitive Science*, edited by Rick Kemp and Bruce McConachie, Routledge, 2019, pp. 225–34.
Cook, Scott. "The 'Lüshi Chinqiu' and the Resolution of Philosophical Dissonance." *Harvard Journal of Asiatic Studies*, vol. 62, no. 2, Dec. 2002, pp. 307–45.
Corballis, Michael C. *The Recursive Mind*. Princeton University Press, 2014.
Cox, John. "Moonrise over Malta." *Astronomy and Geophysics*, vol. 49, no. 1, Feb. 2008, pp. 7–8.
Cozolino, Louis J. *The Neuroscience of Psychotherapy*. Norton, 2002.
Crosbie, Michael J. "Calling Forth the Numinous in Architecture." *Transcending Architecture*, edited by Julio Bermudez, Catholic University of America Press, 2015, pp. 225–30.

Crosbie, Michael J. "The Hermeneutics of 21st-Century Sacred Space." *The Oxford Handbook of Religious Space*, edited by Jeanne Halgren Kilde, Oxford University Press, 2022, pp. 44–57.
Damasio, Antonio. *The Feeling of What Happens*. Harcourt, 1999.
Damasio, Antonio. *Looking for Spinoza*. Harcourt, 2003.
Damasio, Antonio. *Self Comes to Mind*. Pantheon, 2010.
d'Aquili, Eugene G., and Andrew B. Newberg. *The Mystical Mind*. Fortress Press, 1999.
Davies, J. G. *The Architectural Setting of Baptism*. Barrie and Rockliff, 1962.
Davies, J. G. *The Origin and Development of Early Christian Architecture*. Philosophical Library, 1953.
de Bary, William Theodore. "Neo-Confucian Individualism and Holism." *Individualism and Holism*, edited by Donald Munro, University of Michigan Press, 1985, pp. 331–58.
Dehaene, Stanislas. *Consciousness and the Brain*. Penguin, 2014.
De La Torre, Miguel A., and Albert Hernández. *The Quest for the Historical Satan*. Nashville: SuperStock, 2011.
De Leersnyder, Jozefien, et al. "Feeling Right is Feeling Good." *Frontiers in Psychology*, vol. 6, article 630, May 2015, pp. 1–12.
Demaree, Heath A., et al. "Brain Lateralization of Emotional Processing." *Behavioral and Cognitive Neuroscience Reviews*, vol. 4, no. 1, Mar. 2005, pp. 3–20, https://pubmed.ncbi.nlm.nih.gov/15886400/.
Dennett, Daniel. *Consciousness Explained*. Little, 1991.
Dennett, Daniel. *Darwin's Dangerous Idea*. Simon, 1995.
de Visser, M. W. *The Arhats of China and Japan*. Oesterheld, 1923.
de Vries, Hent. "Phenomenal Violence and the Philosophy of Religion." *The Oxford Handbook of Religion and Violence*, edited by Mark Juergensmeyer et al., Oxford University Press, 2013, pp. 496–520.
de Waal, Frans. *The Bonobo and the Atheist*. Norton, 2013.
de Waal, Frans. *Our Inner Ape*. Penguin, 2005.
de Waal, Frans. *Primates and Philosophers: How Morality Evolved*. Princeton University Press, 2006.
de Waal, Frans. "Putting the Altruism Back into Altruism." *Annual Review of Psychology*, vol. 59, 2008, pp. 279–99.
de Waal, Frans. "The 'Russian Doll' Model of Empathy and Imitation." *On Being Moved: From Mirror Neurons to Empathy*, edited by Stein Braten, John Benjamins Publishing, 2007, pp. 49–72.
Dix, Dom Gregory. *The Shape of the Liturgy*. Dacre Press, 1945.
Domínguez, Juan F., et al. "The Brain in Culture and Culture in the Brain." *Progress in Brain Research*, vol. 178, 2009, pp. 43–64.
Donald, Merlin. *A Mind So Rare*. Norton, 2001.
Douglas-Klotz, Neil. *Revelations of the Aramaic Jesus*. Hampton Roads, 2022.
Downey, Daniel H., and Greg Lende. "Neuroanthropology and the Encultured Brain." *The Encultured Brain*, edited by Lende and Downey, MIT Press, 2012, pp. 23–65.
Dox, Donnalee. *Reckoning with Spirit in the Paradigm of Performance*. University of Michigan Press, 2016.
Dunbar, Robin. "Gossip in Evolutionary Perspective." *Review of General Psychology*, vol. 8, no. 2, 2004, pp. 100–110.

Dunbar, Robin. *Grooming, Gossip, and the Evolution of Language*. Harvard University Press, 1996.
Dunbar, Robin. *How Religion Evolved*. Oxford University Press, 2022.
Dunlap, Aron. *Lacan and Religion*. Routledge, 2014.
Eagleman, David. *Livewired*. Pantheon, 2020.
Eberhard, John P. *Architecture and the Brain*. Greenway Press, 2007.
Eberhard, John P. *Brain Landscape*. Oxford, 2009.
Ebisch, Sjoerd J. H., and Vittorio Gallese. "A Neuroscientific Perspective on the Nature of Altered Self-Other Relationships in Schizophrenia." *Journal of Consciousness Studies*, vol. 22, no. 1–2, 2015, pp. 220–40.
Edelman, Gerald M. "Naturalizing Consciousness: A Theoretical Framework." *PNAS*, vol. 100, no. 9, 2003, pp. 5520–4, doi.org/10.1073/pnas.0931349100.
Edelman, Gerald M., and Giulio Tononi. *A Universe of Consciousness: How Matter Becomes Mind*. Basic Books, 2000.
"Eighteen Arhats." *Wikipedia*, Wikimedia Foundation, en.wikipedia.org/wiki/Eighteen_Arhats.
Ejova, Anastasia. "Awe as a Social Emotion." *e-Rhizome*, vol. 1, no. 2, 2019, pp. 160–6.
Eller, Cynthia. *The Myth of Matriarchal Prehistory*. Beacon, 2000.
Farb, Norman A. S., et al. "Minding One's Emotions." *Emotion*, vol. 10, no. 1, Feb. 2010, pp. 25–33.
Farrer, C., and C. D. Frith. "Experiencing Oneself vs. Another Person as Being the Cause of an Action," *NeuroImage*, vol. 15, 2002, pp. 596–603.
Faure, Bernard. *Visions of Power*. Princeton University Press, 1996.
Fernández-Cobián, Esteban. "The Religious Landscape and its Architecture in Contemporary Europe." *The Oxford Handbook of Religious Space*, edited by Jeanne Halgren Kilde, Oxford University Press, 2022, pp. 376–90.
Fernyhough, Charles. *Pieces of Light*. HarperCollins, 2012.
Fields, R. Douglas. *The Electric Brain*. BenBella Books, 2020.
Fine, Cordelia. *Testosterone Rex*. Norton, 2014.
Fink, Bruce. *A Clinical Introduction to Lacanian Psychoanalysis*. Harvard University Press, 1997.
Fisher, Gareth. "In the Footsteps of the Tourists." *Social Compass*, vol. 58, no. 4, 2011, pp. 511–24.
Fiske, Allan Page. "Using Individualism and Collectivism to Compare Cultures—A Critique of the Validity and Measurement of the Constructs." *Psychological Bulletin*, vol. 128, no. 1, 2002, pp. 78–88.
Foucault, Michel. *The History of Sexuality, Volume One: An Introduction*. Vintage, 1990, 1976.
Fowler, Jeaneane. *An Introduction to the Philosophy and Religion of Taoism*. Sussex Academic Press, 2005.
Frankfurter, David. "The Construction of Evil and the Violence of Purification." *The Oxford Handbook of Religion and Violence*, edited by Mark Juergensmeyer et al., Oxford University Press, 2013, pp. 520–32.
Freedberg, David. "From Absorption to Judgment." *Empathy*, edited by Vanessa Lux and Sigrid Weigel, Palgrave Macmillan, 2017, pp. 139–80.
Freedberg, David, and Vittorio Gallese. "Motion, Emotion and Empathy in Esthetic Experience." *Trends in Cognitive Sciences*, vol. 11, no. 5, 2007, pp. 197–203.
Fuentes, Augustín. *Why We Believe*. New Haven: Yale University Press, 2019.

Fung, Helene H., and Sheung-Tak Cheng. "Psychology and Aging in the Land of the Panda." *The Oxford Handbook of Chinese Psychology*, edited by Michael Harris Bond, Oxford University Press, 2010, pp. 309–26.
Gallese, Vittorio. "The Empathetic Body in Experimental Aesthetics—Embodied Simulation and Art." *Empathy*, edited by Vanessa Lux and Sigrid Weigel, Palgrave Macmillan, 2017, pp. 181–99.
Gallese, Vittorio, and Alessandro Gattara. "Embodied Simulation, Aesthetics, and Architecture." *Mind in Architecture*, edited by Sarah Robinson and Juhani Pallasmaa, MIT Press, 2015, pp. 161–79.
Gan et al. "Common and Distinct Neurofunctional Representations of Core and Social Disgust in the Brain." *Neuroscience and Biobehavioral Reviews*, vol. 135, Apr. 2022, https://doi.org/10.1016/j.neubiorev.2022.104553.
Gautam, Neeraj. *Buddha: His Life and Teaching*. Mahaveer and Sons, 2009.
Gazzaniga, Michael S. "On Determinism and Human Responsibility." *Neuroexistentialism*, edited by Gregg D. Caruso and Owen Flanagan, Oxford University Press, 2018, pp. 223–34.
George, David E. R. *Buddhism as/in Performance*. D. K. Printworld, 1999.
Geva, Anat. "Symbolism and Myth of Mountains, Stone, and Light as Expressed in Sacred Architecture." *Architecture, Culture, and Spirituality*, edited by Thomas Barrie and Julio Bermudez, Routledge, 2015, pp. 109–21.
Gibson, James J. *The Ecological Approach to Visual Perception*. Houghton Mifflin, 1979.
Gildow, Douglas M. "The Chinese Buddhist Ritual Field." *Journal of Chinese Buddhist Studies*, vol. 27, 2014, pp. 59–127.
Giljov, Andrey, et al. "Facing Each Other." *Biology Letters*, vol. 14, no. 1, Jan. 2018, pp. 1–5, https://royalsocietypublishing.org/doi/epdf/10.1098/rsbl.2017.0707.
Gilligan, Carol. *In a Different Voice*. Harvard University Press, 1982.
Gimbutas, Marija. *The Language of the Goddess*. Harper, 1989.
Gintis, Herbert. *Individuality and Entanglement*. Princeton University Press, 2017.
Girard, René. *Violence and the Sacred*. Translated by Patrick Gregory, Johns Hopkins University Press, 1977.
Goettner-Abendroth, Heide. *The Dancing Goddess*. Boston: Beacon Press, 1991.
Goettner-Abendroth, Heide. *Matriarchal Societies*. Peter Yang, 2012.
Goffman, Erving. *The Presentation of Self in Everyday Life*. Doubleday, 1959.
Goh, J.O., and D.C. Park. "Culture Sculpts the Perceptual Brain." *Cultural Neuroscience*, edited by Joan Chiao, Elsevier, 2009, pp. 95–112.
Goodison, Lucy, and Christine Morris. Introduction. *Ancient Goddesses: The Myths and the Evidence*, edited by Goodison and Morris, University of Wisconsin Press, 1998, pp. 6–21.
Goossaert, Vincent. "Ritual Techniques for Creating a Divine Persona in Late Imperial China." *Journal of Chinese Religions*, vol. 50, no. 1, May 2022, pp. 45–76.
Goossaert, Vincent. "Territorial Cults and the Urbanization of the Chinese World." *Handbook of Religion and the Asian City*, edited by Peter van der Veer, University of California Press, 2015, pp. 52–68.
Gordon, Amie M., et al. "The Dark Side of the Sublime." *Journal of Personality and Social Psychology*, vol. 113, no. 2, 2017, pp. 310–28.
Gottschall, Jonathan. *The Storytelling Animal*. Houghton Mifflin, 2012.
Gough, Michael. *The Origins of Christian Art*. Praeger, 1973.

Graeber, David, and Marshall Sahlins. *On Kings*. Hau Books, 2017.
Graeber, David, and David Wengrow. *The Dawn of Everything*. Farrar, 2021.
Graham, Jesse, et al. "Liberals and Conservatives Rely on Different Sets of Moral Foundations." *Journal of Personality and Social Psychology*, vol. 96, no. 5, 2009, pp. 1029–46.
Graziano, Michael S. A., and Sabine Kastner. "Human Consciousness and its Relation to Social Neuroscience." *Cognitive Neuroscience*, vol. 2, no. 2, 2011, pp. 98–133.
Graziano, Michael S. A., et al. "Toward a Standard Model of Consciousness." *Cognitive Neuropsychology*, vol. 37, nos. 3–4, 2020, pp. 155–72.
Gribble, Father Richard. "Understanding the Immaculate Conception." *Simply Catholic*, https://www.simplycatholic.com/immaculate-conception/.
Griffith, Brian. *A Galaxy of Immortal Women: The Yin Side of Chinese Civilization*. Exterminating Angel Press, 2012.
Grigg, Richard. "Religion and Magical Thinking." *Science and the World's Religions*, vol. 3, edited by Patrick McNamara and Wesley J. Wildman, Praeger, 2012, pp. 195–219.
Guan, Fang, et al. "The Neural Correlate Difference Between Positive and Negative Awe." *Frontiers in Human Neuroscience*, vol. 13, no. 206, June 2019, pp. 1–13.
Guthrie, Stewart. *Faces in the Clouds*. Oxford University Press, 1993.
Haidt, Jonathan. "The Moral Emotions." *Handbook of Affective Sciences*, edited by Richard J. Davidson, Klaus R. Scherer, and H. Hill Goldsmith. Oxford University Press, 2003, pp. 852–70.
Haidt, Jonathan. *The Righteous Mind*. Pantheon Books, 2012.
Haidt, Jonathan, and Craig Joseph. "Intuitive Ethics: How Innately Prepared Intuitions Generate Culturally Variable Virtues." *Daedalus*, vol. 133, no. 4, 2004, pp. 55–66.
Hamilton, J. Paul, et al. "Depressive Rumination, the Default-Mode Network, and the Dark Matter of Clinical Neuroscience." *Biological Psychiatry*, vol. 78, no. 4, 2015, pp. 224–30.
Han, Shihui. "Understanding Cultural Differences in Human Behavior: A Cultural Neuroscience Approach." *Current Opinion in Behavioral Sciences*, vol. 3, 2015, pp. 68–72.
Han, Shihui, et al. "Neural Substrates of Self-Referential Processing in Chinese Buddhists." *SCAN*, vol. 5, 2010, pp. 332–9.
Hansen, Chad. "Individualism in Chinese Thought." *Individualism and Holism: Studies in Confucian and Taoist Values*, edited by Donald Munro, University of Michigan Press, 1985, pp. 35–56.
Harrell, Stevan. "The Concept of Soul in Chinese Folk Religion." *The Journal of Asian Studies*, vol. 38, no. 3, 1979, pp. 519–28.
Harries, Karsten. "Transcending Aesthetics." *Transcending Architecture*, edited by Julio Bermudez. Catholic University of America Press, 2015, pp. 208–22.
Harvey, Peter. *An Introduction to Buddhism*. Cambridge University Press, 1990.
Hasson, Uri, et al. "Intersubject Synchronization of Cortical Activity During Natural Vision." *Science*, vol. 303, 2004, pp. 1634–40.
Hatfield, Elaine, et al. *Emotional Contagion*. Cambridge University Press, 1994.
Hayden, Robert M. "Shared Space, or Mixed?" *The Oxford Handbook of Religious Space*, edited by Jeanne Halgren Kilde, Oxford University Press, 2022, pp. 71–84.
Hecht, David. "Cerebral Lateralization of Pro- and Anti-Social Tendencies." *Experimental Neurobiology*, vol. 23, no. 1, Mar. 2014, pp. 1–27, http://dx.doi.org/10.5607/en.2014.23.1.1.

"Helsinki's Lutheran Cathedral Facing Its Russian Orthodox Cathedral." *Rick Steves Classroom Europe*, https://classroom.ricksteves.com/videos/helsinki-s-lutheran-cathedral-facing-its-russian-orthodox-cathedral.

Hoffman, Donald. *The Case Against Reality*. Norton, 2019.

Holtmann, Olga, et al. "Lateralized Deficits of Disgust Processing After Insula-Basal Ganglia Damage." *Frontiers in Psychology*, vol. 11, no. 1429, 30 June 2020.

The Holy Bible, King James Version. Cambridge Edition: 1769; *King James Bible Online*, 2016, www.kingjamesbibleonline.org.

Horkheimer, Max, and Theodor W. Adorno. *Dialectic of Enlightenment*. Stanford University Press, 1987, 2002.

Howe, David. *Attachment Across the Lifecourse*. Palgrave, 2011.

Hrdy, Sarah Blaffer. *Mother Nature*. Ballantine, 1999.

Hureau, Sylvie. "Buddhist Rituals." *Early Chinese Religion, Part Two*, vol. 2, edited by John Lagerwey and Lü Pengzhi, Brill, 2010, pp. 1207–44.

Hurlbut, William B. "Desire, Mimesis, and the Phylogeny of Freedom." *Mimesis and Science*, edited by Scott R. Garrels, Michigan State University Press, 2011, pp. 175–92.

Iacoboni, Marco. *Mirroring People*. Farrar, 2008.

Iannaccone, Laurence R. "Sacrifice and Stigma." *Journal of Political Economy*, vol. 100, no. 2, 1992, pp. 271–91.

Ichiko, Shiga. "Manifestations of Lüzu in Modern Guandong and Hong Kong." *Daoist Identity*, edited by Livia Kohn and Harold D. Roth, University of Hawai'i Press, 2002, pp. 185–212.

"In Greece, a Clergyman's Death Reignites Communion Spoon Debate." *The World*, 30 Nov. 2020, www.pri.org/stories/2020-11-30/greece-clergyman-s-death-reignites-communion-spoon-debate.

Irving, Julie Anne, et al. "Mindfulness-Based Cognitive Therapy for Chronic Depression." *Handbook of Mindfulness*, edited by Kirk Warren Brown et al., Guilford, 2015, pp. 348–66.

Ishizu, Tomohiro, and Semir Zeki. "A Neurobiological Inquiry into the Origins of Our Experience of the Sublime and Beautiful." *Frontiers in Human Neuroscience*, vol. 8, 2014, pp. 1–10.

Jablonka, Eva, and Marion J. Lamb. *Evolution in Four Dimensions*. MIT Press, 2014.

James, Craig A. *The Religion Virus*. CreateSpace, 2013.

Jensen, Robin Margaret. *Understanding Early Christian Art*. Routledge, 2000.

Johnston, Adrian, and Catherine Malabou. *Self and Emotional Life*. Columbia University Press, 2013.

Johnstone, Brick, and Daniel Cohen. *Neuroscience, Selflessness, and Spiritual Experience*. Elsevier, 2019.

Jones, Lindsay. *The Hermeneutics of Sacred Architecture*, Harvard University Press, 2000, 2 vols.

Joseph, Rhawn. *The Transmitter to God*. University Press, 2001.

Juergensmeyer, Mark. "Religious Terrorism as Performance Violence." *The Oxford Handbook of Religion and Violence*, edited by Mark Juergensmeyer et al., Oxford University Press, 2013, pp. 280–92.

Kandel, Eric. *The Age of Insight*. Random House, 2012.

Kawabata, Hideaki, and Semir Zeki. "Neural Correlates of Beauty." *Journal of Neurophysiology*, vol. 91, 2004, pp. 1699–1705.

Keltner, Dacher, and Jonathan Haidt. "Approaching Awe, a Moral, Spiritual, and Aesthetic Emotion." *Cognition and Emotion*, vol. 17, no. 2, 2003, pp. 297–314.

Kilde, Jeanne Halgren. *Sacred Power, Sacred Space*. Oxford University Press, 2008.
Kim, Hongkyung, translator. *The Old Master*. State University of New York Press, 2012.
Kimball, Charles. "Religion and Violence from Christian Theological Perspectives." *The Oxford Handbook of Religion and Violence*, edited by Mark Juergensmeyer et al., Oxford University Press, 2013, pp. 424–34.
King James Bible Online, www.kingjamesbibleonline.org/.
King, Karen L. "Christianity and Torture." *The Oxford Handbook of Religion and Violence*, edited by Mark Juergensmeyer et al., Oxford University Press, 2013, pp. 293–305.
Kirkpatrick, Lee A. *Attachment, Evolution, and the Psychology of Religion*. Guilford Press, 2005.
Kitts, Margo. "Violent Death in Religious Imagination." *The Oxford Handbook of Religion and Violence*, edited by Mark Juergensmeyer et al., Oxford University Press, 2013, pp. 351–60.
Knapp, Keith N. "Borrowing Legitimacy from the Dead." *Early Chinese Religion*, part two, vol. 1, edited by John Lagerwey and Mark Kalinowski, Brill, 2009, pp. 143–92.
Knight, Chris. *Blood Relations*. Yale University Press, 1991.
Knoblock, John, and Jeffrey Riegel, translators. *The Annals of Lü Buwei*. Stanford University Press, 2000.
Knott, Kim. *The Location of Religion*. Routledge, 2005.
Ko, Dorothy. *Cinderella's Sisters*. University of California Press, 2005.
Ko, Dorothy. *Every Step a Lotus*. University of California Press, 2001.
Konior, Jan. "Confession Rituals and the Philosophy of Forgiveness in Asian Religions and Christianity." *Forum Philosophicum*, vol. 15, 2010, pp. 91–102.
Krautheimer, Richard. *Early Christian and Byzantine Architecture*. Penguin, 1967.
Kringelbach, Morten L., and Kent C. Berridge. "Brain Mechanisms of Pleasure." *The Psychological Construction of Emotion*, edited by James A. Russell and Lisa Feldman Barrett, Guilford Press, 2015, pp. 229–48.
Kristeva, Julia. *Powers of Horror*. Columbia, 1982.
Lacan, Jacques. *Écrits*. Translated by Bruce Fink, Norton, 2006.
Lakoff, George. *Moral Politics*. University of Chicago Press, 1996.
Laland, Kevin N. *Darwin's Unfinished Symphony*. Princeton University Press, 2017.
Lanteaume, Laura, et al. "Emotional Induction after Direct Intracerebral Stimulations of the Human Amygdalae." *Cerebral Cortex*, vol. 17, no. 6, 2007, pp. 1307–13.
Larsson, Marcus, et al. "Reply to M.A. Persinger and S. A. Koren's response to Granqvist et al." *Neuroscience Letters*, vol. 380, no. 3, June 3, 2005, pp. 348–50, doi.org/10.1016/j.neulet.2005.03.059.
Lau, Hi-Po Bobo, and Cecilia Cheng. "The Yin-Yang of Stress." *The Psychological and Cultural Foundations of East Asian Cognition*, edited by Julie Spencer-Rodgers and Kaiping Peng, Oxford University Press, 2018, pp. 573–94.
Lavin, Irving. *Bernini and the Crossing of St. Peter's*. New York University Press, 1968.
Lawtoo, Nidesh. *The Phantom of the Ego*. Michigan State University Press, 2015.
Lawtoo, Nidesh. *Violence and the Oedipal Unconscious*. Vol. 1, Michigan State University Press, 2023.
LeDoux, Joseph. "Afterword." *The Psychological Construction of Emotion*, edited by James A. Russell and Lisa Feldman Barrett, Guilford Press, 2015, pp. 459–63.
Lehrner, Amy, and Rachel Yehuda. "The Social Nature of Emotions." *The Nature of Emotion*, edited by Andrew S. Fox et al., Oxford University Press, 2018, pp. 143–7.
Leighton, Taigen Daniel. *Bodhisattva Archetypes*. Penguin, 1998.

Lembke, Anna. *Dopamine Nation*. Dutton, 2021.
Leuzinger-Bohleber, Marianne. "Embodied Empathy—Clinical and Developmental Perspectives in Psychoanalysis." *Empathy*, edited by Vanessa Lux and Sigrid Weigel, Palgrave Macmillan, 2017, pp. 49–91.
Levi, Jean. "The Rite, the Norm and the Dao." *Early Chinese Religion*, part one, vol. 1, edited by John Lagerwey and Mark Kalinowski, Brill, 2009, pp. 645–92.
Lewis, Mark Edward. "The Mythology of Early China." *Early Chinese Religion*, part one, vol. 1, edited by John Lagerwey and Mark Kalinowski, Brill, 2009, pp. 543–94.
Lewis-Williams, David, and David Pearce. *Inside the Neolithic Mind*. Thames and Hudson, 2005.
Li, Peter Ping. "The Epistemology of Yin-Yang Balancing as the Root of Chinese Cultural Traditions." *The Psychological and Cultural Foundations of East Asian Cognition*, edited by Julie Spencer-Rodgers and Kaiping Peng, Oxford University Press, 2018, pp. 35–80.
Li, Wanqing, et al. "The Default Mode Network and Social Understanding of Others." *Frontiers in Human Neuroscience*, vol. 8, 2014, pp. 1–15.
Lieberman, Matthew D. *Social*. Crown, 2013.
Lip, Evelyn. *Feng Shui Environments of Power*. Academy, 1995.
Litian, Fang. *Chinese Buddhism and Traditional Culture*. Routledge, 2019.
Liu, Shi S., et al. "Ingroup Vigilance in Collectivistic Cultures." *PNAS*, vol. 116, no. 29, July 16, 2019, pp. 14538–46.
Liu, Yanjun, et al. "Thriving at Work." *The Journal of Applied Behavioral Science*, vol. 56, no. 3, 2020, pp. 347–66.
Lloyd, Michael. "The Fallenness of Nature." *Finding Ourselves After Darwin*, edited by Stanley P. Rosenberg. Baker Academic, 2018, pp. 262–79.
Londero, Alain, et al. "The Vestibular System and Artistic Painting." *Aesthetics and Neuroscience*, edited by Zoi Kapula and Marine Vernet, Springer, 2016, pp. 3–18.
Lopez, Jr., Donald S. *The Heart Sutra Explained*. State University of New York Press, 1988.
Luhrmann, T. M. *How God Becomes Real*. Princeton University Press, 2020.
Luhrmann, T. M. "A Hyperreal God and Modern Belief." *Current Anthropology*, vol. 53, no. 4, Aug. 2012, pp. 371–95.
Luhrmann, T. M. "Mind and Spirit." *Journal of the Royal Anthropological Institute*, vol. 26, no. S1, Apr. 2020, pp. 9–27.
Luhrmann, T. M. *When God Talks Back*. Knopf, 2012.
Luhrmann, Tanya Marie, et al. "Sensing the Presence of Gods and Spirits across Cultures and Faiths." *PNAS*, vol. 118, no. 5, Feb. 2, 2021, pp. 1–8, doi.org/10.1073/pnas.2016649118.
MacKinnon, Ian. "Burning Joss Stick 'As Deadly as Traffic Fumes or Cigarette Smoke.'" *The Guardian*, 30 July 2008, www.theguardian.com/world/2008/jul/30/health.
Mai, Cuong T. "The Guanyin Fertility Cult and Family Religion in Late Imperial China." *Journal of the American Academy of Religion*, vol. 87, no. 1, 2019, pp. 156–90.
Malik, Akhtar. *A Survey of Buddhist Temples and Monasteries*. Anmol, 2007.
Mallgrave, Harry Francis. *The Architect's Brain*. Wiley-Blackwell, 2011.
Mallgrave, Harry Francis. "What Designers Can Learn from the Contemporary Biological Sciences." *Mind in Architecture*, edited by Sarah Robinson and Juhania Pallasmaa, MIT Press, 2015, pp. 9–31.

Malone, Caroline. "God or Goddess." *Ancient Goddesses*, edited by Lucy Goodison and Christine Morris, University of Wisconsin Press, 1998, pp. 148–63.
Marcellinus, Ammanius. *The Later Roman Empire (AD 354–378)*. Trans. Walter Hamilton. Penguin, 1986.
Marinkovic, Ksenija, et al. "Right hemisphere has the Last Laugh." *Cognitive, Affective & Behavioral Neuroscience*, vol. 11, no. 1, Mar. 2011, pp. 113–30, www.ncbi.nlm.nih.gov/pmc/articles/PMC3047694/.
Mason, David V. *The Performative Ground of Religion and Theatre*. Routledge, 2019.
Masuda, Takahiko, and Richard E. Nisbett. "Attending Holistically Versus Analytically." *Journal of Personality and Social Psychology*, vol. 81, no. 5, 2001, pp. 922–34.
Mateo, M. Martínez, et al. "Essentializing the Binary Self." *Frontiers in Human Neuroscience*, vol. 7, no. 289, June 2013, pp. 1–4.
Mathews, Thomas F. *The Clash of Gods*. Princeton University Press, 1993.
Mavelli, Luca. *Neoliberal Citizenship*. Oxford University Press, 2022.
McAvan, Emily. *The Postmodern Sacred*, McFarland, 2012.
McCormick, Kelly, et al. "Sound to Meaning Mappings in the Bouba-Kiki Effect." *CogSci*, vol. 2015, 2015, pp. 1565–70.
McDaniel, June. "Hinduism." *The Oxford Handbook of Religion and Emotion*, edited by John Corrigan, Oxford University Press, 2008, pp. 51–72.
McGilchrist, Iain. *The Master and his Emissary*. Yale University Press, 2009.
McGilchrist, Iain. *The Matter With Things*. Vol. 2, Perspectiva, 2021.
McNamara, Denis R. *Catholic Church Architecture and the Spirit of the Liturgy*. Hillenbrand, 2009.
McNamara, Denis R. *How to Read Churches*. Rizzoli International Publications, 2011.
McNamara, Denis R. "Incarnation and Transfiguration." *Sacred Architecture in East and West*, edited by Cyril Hovorun, Marymount Institute Press, 2019, pp. 19–34.
McNamara, Patrick. *The Neuroscience of Religious Experience*. Cambridge University Press, 2009.
McNamara, Patrick. *Religion, Neuroscience, and the Self*. Routledge, 2020.
McNamara, Patrick. *Spirit Possession and Exorcism*. Vol. 1, Praeger, 2011.
Meccarelli, Marco. "Discovering the *Long*: Current Theories and Trends in Research on the Chinese Dragon." *Frontiers of History in China*, vol. 16, no. 1, pp. 123–42.
Mee, Erin B. "Dancing on the Tongue." *Performance Research*, vol. 22, no. 7, 2017, pp. 29–34.
Mee, Erin B. "Rasa on Screen." *Mantichora*, vol. 6, 2016, n.p.
Melley, Timothy. "The Melodramatic Mode in American Politics, and Other Varieties of Narrative Suspicion." *symploke*, vol. 29, no. 1–2, 2021, pp. 57–74.
Mesquita, Batja, et al. "The Cultural Psychology of Emotions." *Handbook of Emotions*, edited by Lisa Feldman Barrett et al., Guilford, 2016, pp. 393–411.
Meyer, Jeffrey F. "Chinese Buddhist Monastic Temples as Cosmograms." *Sacred Architecture*, edited by Emily Lyle, Edinburgh University Press, 1992, pp. 71–92.
Michl, Petra, et al. "Neurobiological Underpinnings of Shame and Guilt." *Social Cognitive and Affective Neuroscience*, vol. 9, 2014, pp. 150–7.
Mignerot, Vincent. "Heuraesthesia." *Aesthetics and Neuroscience*, edited by Zoi Kapula and Marine Vernet, Springer, 2016, pp. 19–30.
Miles, Margaret R. *Image as Insight*. Wipf and Stock, 1985.
Miller, Lisa. *The Awakened Brain*. Random, 2021.

Min, Hu. "Temples to Limit Visitor Numbers at Lunar New Year in Name of Safety." *China Daily*, 28 Jan. 2015, p. A3, archive.shine.cn/metro/society/Temples-to-limit-visitor-numbers-at-Lunar-New-Year-in-name-of-safety/shdaily.shtml.
Mitchell, Donald W. *Buddhism*. Oxford University Press, 2002.
Mollier, Christine. *Buddhism and Taoism Face to Face*. University of Hawai'i Press, 2008.
Morgan, David. *The Embodied Eye*. University of California Press, 2012.
Mozina, David J. *Knotting the Banner*. University of Hawai'i Press, 2021.
Munro, Donald. Introduction. *Individualism and Holism: Studies in Confucian and Taoist Values*, edited by Munro, University of Michigan Press, 1985, pp. 1–32.
Nakatani, Hironori, et al. "Respect and Admiration Differentially Activate the Anterior Temporal Lobe." *Neuroscience Research*, vol. 144, July 2019, pp. 40–7, https://doi.org/10.1016/j.neures.2018.09.003.
Nakul, Estelle, and Christophe Lopez. "Commentary: Out-of-Body Experience during Awake Craniotomy." *Frontiers in Human Neuroscience*, 21 Aug. 2017, doi.org/10.3389/fnhum.2017.00417.
Naparstek, Michael E. *Figuring on Salvation*. Dissertation, ProQuest, 2018.
Naquin, Susan, and Chün-fang Yü, editors. Introduction. *Pilgrims and Sacred Sites in China*, University of California Press, 1992, pp. 1–38.
Narvaez, Darcia. *Neurobiology and the Development of Human Morality*. Norton, 2014.
Nedostup, Rebecca. *Superstitious Regimes*. Harvard University Press, 2009.
Nelson, Kevin. *The Spiritual Doorway in the Brain*. Dutton, 2011.
Newberg, Andrew, and Mark Robert Waldman. *Why We Believe What We Believe*. Free Press, 2006.
Newberg, Andrew, et al. *Why God Won't Go Away: Brain Science and the Biology of Belief*. Ballantine, 2002.
Ng, Emily. "The Mind and the Devil." *Journal of the Royal Anthropological Institute*, vol. 26, no. S1, Apr. 2020, pp. 95–113.
Ni, Xueting Christine. *From Kuan Yin to Chairman Mao*. Weiser, 2018.
Nibley, Hugh. *Temple and Cosmos*. Deseret, 1992.
Nietzsche, Friedrich. *The Birth of Tragedy and The Case Against Wagner*. Trans. Walter Kaufmann, Random, 1967.
Nisbett, Richard E. *The Geography of Thought*. Free Press, 2003.
Norenzayan, Ara. *Big Gods*. Princeton University Press, 2013.
O'Malley, John W. "Trent, Sacred Images, and Catholics' Senses of the Sensuous." *The Sensuous in the Counter-Reformation Church*, edited by Marcia B. Hall and Tracy E. Cooper, Cambridge University Press, 2013, pp. 28–48.
Oosterwijk, Suzanne, et al. "The Neuroscience of Construction." *The Psychological Construction of Emotion*, edited by James A. Russell and Lisa Feldman Barrett, Guilford Press, 2015, pp. 111–43.
Oughourlian, Jean-Michel. *The Puppet of Desire*. Stanford University Press, 1991.
Pagani, Catherine. "Visual Arts, Buddhist: China." *Encyclopedia of Monasticism*, edited by William M. Johnston and Christopher Kleinhenz, Routledge, 2000, pp. 1337–41.
Pagels, Elaine. *The Origin of Satan*. Vintage, 1996.
Pallasmaa, Juhani. "An Architecture of the Seven Senses." *Questions of Perception*, edited by Steven Holl et al., a+u, 1994, pp. 29–37.
Pallasmaa, Juhani. *The Eyes of the Skin: Architecture and the Senses*. John Wiley, 2012.
Palmer, Martin, et al. *Guan Yin*. Thorsons, 1985.

Panksepp, Jaak. *Affective Neuroscience: The Foundations of Human and Animal Emotions.* Oxford University Press, 1998.
Panksepp, Jaak, and Lucy Biven. *The Archaeology of Mind.* Norton, 2012.
Papalexandrou, Amy. "Presence and Performance." *The Oxford Handbook of Religious Space,* edited by Jeanne Halgren Kilde, Oxford University Press, 2022, pp. 344–58.
Paper, Jordan. *The Spirits are Drunk.* State University of New York Press, 1995.
Paper, Jordan, et al. *Through the Earth Darkly.* Bloomsbury, 2016.
Park, BoKyung, et al. "Neural Evidence for Cultural Differences in the Valuation of Positive Facial Expressions." *Social Cognitive and Affective Neuroscience,* vol. 11, no. 2, 2016, pp. 243–52.
Parker, Suzanne C., et al. "The Science of Presence." *Handbook of Mindfulness,* edited by Kirk Warren Brown et al., Guilford, 2015, pp. 225–44.
Parrinder, Gary. *The Wisdom of the Early Buddhists.* New Directions, 1977.
Peiffer-Smadja, Nathan, and Laurent Cohen. "The Cerebral Bases of the Bouba-Kiki Effect." *NeuroImage,* vol. 186, Feb. 2019, pp. 679–89.
Pellis, Sergio, and Vivien Pellis. *The Playful Brain.* London: Oneworld, 2009.
Peng, Shengjie, and Ming He. "The Comparative Study of Classical Architecture in Tang and Song Dynasties and in Ancient Rome." *IOP Conference Series: Materials Science and Engineering,* vol. 592, 2019, doi:10.1088/1757-899X/592/1/01210.
Pérez-Gómez, Albert. "Mood and Meaning in Architecture." *Mind in Architecture,* edited by Sarah Robinson and Juhania Pallasmaa, MIT Press, 2015, pp. 219–35.
Persinger, Michael A. *Neuropsychological Bases of God Beliefs.* Praeger, 1987.
Persinger, Michael A. "The Neuropsychiatry of Paranormal Experiences." *Journal of Neuropsychiatry and Clinical Neurosciences,* vol. 13, no. 4, 2001, pp. 515–23.
Philipchalk, Ron, and Dieter Mueller. "Glossolalia and Temperature Changes in the –Right and Left Cerebral Hemispheres." *The International Journal for the Psychology of Religion,* vol. 10, no. 3, 2000, pp. 181–5.
Piff, Paul K., et al. "Awe, the Small Self, and Prosocial Behavior." *Journal of Personality and Social Psychology,* vol. 108, no. 6, 2015, pp. 883–99.
Pizzato, Mark. *Beast-People Onscreen and in Your Brain.* Praeger, 2016.
Pizzato, Mark. *Ghosts of Theatre and Cinema in the Brain.* Palgrave, 2006.
Pizzato, Mark. *Inner Theatres of Good and Evil: The Mind's Staging of Gods, Angels and Devils.* McFarland, 2011.
Pizzato, Mark. *Mapping Global Theatre Histories.* Palgrave, 2019.
Poceski, Mario. "Buddhism in Chinese History." Edited by Mario Poceski, *The Wiley Blackwell Companion to East and Inner Asian Buddhism,* Wiley-Blackwell, 2014, pp. 40–62.
Pollock, Sheldon. "From Rasa Seen to Rasa Heard." *Aux abords de la clairière,* edited by Caterina Guenzi and Sylvia d'Intino, Brepols, 2012, pp. 189–207.
Poo, Mu-chou. "The Concept of Ghost in Ancient Chinese Religion." *Religion and Chinese Society,* edited by John Lagerway, vol. 1, Chinese University Press, 2004, pp. 173–91.
Power, Camilla. "Sexual Selection Models for the Evolution of Language." *The Cradle of Language,* edited by Rudolf Botha and Chris Knight, Oxford University Press, pp. 257–80.
Prandi, Adriano, and Guy Ferrari. *The Basilica of Saints John and Paul on the Caelian Hill.* Quintily, 1958.
Preston, Stephanie D., and Frans B. M. de Waal. "Empathy." *Behavioral and Brain Sciences,* vol. 25, 2002, pp. 1–20.

Pringle, Denys. *The Churches of the Crusader Kingdom of Jerusalem: Volume III, The City of Jerusalem*. Cambridge University Press, 2007.
Prinz, Jesse. *Beyond Human Nature*. Norton, 2012.
Prinz, Jesse. *The Emotional Construction of Morals*. Oxford University Press, 2007.
Prochazkova, Eliska, and Mariska E. Kret. "Connecting Minds and Sharing Emotion through Mimicry." *Neuroscience and Biobehavioral Reviews*, vol. 80, 2017, pp. 99–114.
Prothero, Stephen. *God Is Not One*. HarperCollins, 2010.
Puett, Michael J. *To Become a God*. Harvard University Press, 2004.
Quinter, David. "Manjusri in East Asia." *Brill's Encyclopedia of Buddhism*, vol. 2, edited by Jonathan A. Silk, Brill, 2019, pp. 591–9.
Ramachandran, V. S. *The Tell-Tale Brain*. Norton, 2011.
Ramachandran, V. S., and Sandra Blakeslee. *Phantoms in the Brain: Probing the Mysteries of the Human Mind*. William Morrow, 1998.
Ramachandran, V. S., and William Hirstein. "The Science of Art: A Neurological Theory of Aesthetic Experience." *Journal of Consciousness Studies*, vol. 6, no. 6-7, 1999, pp. 15–51.
Ramachandran, V S., and E. M. Hubbard. "The Phenomenology of Synaesthesia." *Journal of Consciousness Studies*, vol. 10, no. 8, 2003, pp. 49–57.
Raman, Varadaraja V. "Perspectives on Cosmogony." *Science and the World's Religions*, vol. 1, edited by Patrick McNamara and Wesley J. Wildman, Praeger, 2012, pp. 151–82.
Raz, Gil. "Daoist Sacred Geography." *Early Chinese Religion*, part two, vol. 2, edited by John Lagerwey and Mark Kalinowski, Brill, 2009, pp. 1399–1442.
Reardon, Wendy J. *The Deaths of the Popes*. McFarland, 2004.
Re'em, Amit, and Ilya Berkovich. "New Discoveries in the Cenacle." *New Discoveries in the Archaeology of Jerusalem and its Region*, vol. 10, 2016, pp. 56–92.
Reeves, Gene, translator. *The Lotus Sutra*. Wisdom Publications, 2008.
Reis-Habito, Maria. "The Bodhisattva Guanyin and the Virgin Mary." *Buddhist-Christian Studies*, vol. 13, 1993, pp. 61–9.
Renoult, Julien P. "The Evolution of Aesthetics." *Aesthetics and Neuroscience*, edited by Zoi Kapula and Marine Vernet, Springer, 2016, pp. 271–99.
Ricard, Matthieu, and Trinh Xuan Thuan. *The Quantum and the Lotus*. Three Rivers Press, 2001.
Richie, Cristina. "Symbolism in Asian Statues of the Buddha." *Intermountain West Journal of Religious Studies*, vol. 5, no. 1, 2014, pp. 32–51.
Ritzinger, Justin, and Marcus Bingenheimer. "Whole-Body Relics in Chinese Buddhism." *The Indian International Journal of Buddhist Studies*, vol. 7, 2006, pp. 37–94.
Roberts, Robert C. "The Blessings of Gratitude." *The Psychology of Gratitude*, edited by Robert A. Emmons and Michael E. McCullough, Oxford, 2004, pp. 58–80.
Robson, James. "Buddhist Sacred Geography." *Early Chinese Religion*, part two, vol. 1, edited by John Lagerwey and Mark Kalinowski, Brill, 2009, pp. 1353–98.
Robson, James. "Changing Places." *Images, Relics, and Legends*, edited by James Benn et al., Mosaic, 2012, pp. 90–105.
Robson, James. "Faith in Museums." *PMLA*, vol. 125, no. 1, Jan. 2010, pp. 121–8.
Robson, James. Introduction. *Images, Relics, and Legends*, edited by James Benn et al., Mosaic, 2012, pp. vii–xxv.
Rodríguez, Guillermo. "The Taste of Art and Transcendence." *Transformative Aesthetics*, edited by Erika Fischer-Lichte and Benjamin Wihstutz, Routledge, 2018, pp. 48–67.
Roepstorff, Andreas, and Chris Frith. "What's at the Top in the Top-Down Control of Actions?" *Psychological Research*, vol. 68, 2004, pp. 189–98.

Roepstorff, Andreas, et al. "Enculturing Brains through Patterned Practices." *Neural Networks*, vol. 23, no. 8-9, Oct.-Nov. 2010, pp. 1051-9.
Rolls, Edmund T. "Neurobiological Foundations of Art and Aesthetics." *Art, Aesthetics, and the Brain*, edited by Joseph P. Huston et al., Oxford University Press, pp. 453-78.
Rossano, Matt J. *Supernatural Selection*. Oxford University Press, 2010.
Roth, Leland M. *Understanding Architecture: Its Elements, History and Meaning*. Westview, 1993.
Rothman, Naomi, et al. "Understanding the Dual Nature of Ambivalence." *Academy of Management Annals*, 2017, vol. 11, no. 1, pp. 33-72.
Roughgarden, Joan. *Evolution's Rainbow*. University of California Press, 2004.
Ruby, Perrine, and Jean Decety. "How Would You Feel versus How Do You Think She Would Feel?" *Journal of Cognitive Neuroscience*, vol. 16, no. 6, 2004, pp. 988-99.
Rudd, Melanie, et al. "Awe Expands People's Perception of Time, Alters Decision Making, and Enhances Well-Being." *Psychological Science*, vol. 23, no. 10, 2012, pp. 1130-6.
Rufford, Juliet. *Theatre and Architecture*. Palgrave, 2015.
Russell, James A. "My Psychological Constructionist Perspective, with a Focus on Conscious Affective Experience." *The Psychological Construction of Emotion*, edited by James A. Russell and Lisa Feldman Barrett, Guilford Press, 2015, pp. 183-208.
"Russia's Orthodox Church Paints the Conflict in Ukraine as a Holy War." *The Economist*, 21 Mar. 2022, online.
Ryff, Carol D. "Ideal Ends in Emotional Development." *The Nature of Emotion*, edited by Andrew S. Fox et al., Oxford University Press, 2018, pp. 396-9.
Sagan, Carl. *The Dragons of Eden*. Random, 1977.
"Sanyuan Palace." *Wikipedia*, https://en.wikipedia.org/wiki/Sanyuan_Palace.
Scarantino, Andrea. "Basic Emotion, Psychological Construction, and the Problem of Variability." *The Psychological Construction of Emotion*, edited by James A. Russell and Lisa Feldman Barrett, Guilford Press, 2015, pp. 334-76.
Schaeffer, Kurtis R. "Salt and the Sovereignty of the Dalai Lama." *Images, Relics, and Legends*, edited by James Benn et al., Mosaic, 2012, pp. 288-322.
Schechner, Richard. *Performance Studies: An Introduction*. Routledge, 2002, 2013.
Schechner, Richard. "Rasaesthetics." *TDR*, vol. 45, no. 3, 2001, pp. 27-50.
Scheff, Thomas J. *Goffman Unbound*. Paradigm, 2006.
Schimel, Jeff, et al. "A Consideration of Three Critical Hypotheses." *Handbook of Terror Management Theory*, ed. Clay Routledge and Matthew Vess, Academic Press, 2019, pp. 1-30.
Schinz, Alfred. *The Magic Square*. Axel Menges, 1996.
Schipper, Kristofer. *The Taoist Body*. University of California Press, 1982, 1993.
Schott, G. D. "Pictures of Pain." *Brain*, vol. 138, no. 3, 2015, pp. 812-20.
Schroeder, Timothy, and Carl Matheson. "Imagination and Emotion." *The Architecture of Imagination*, ed. Shaun Nichols, Clarendon Press, 2006, pp. 19-39.
Scott, Janet Lee. *For Gods, Ghosts and Ancestors*. University of Washington Press, 2007.
Scranton, Laird. *China's Cosmological Prehistory*. Inner Traditions, 2014.
Seasoltz, Keven. "The Christian Church Building." *Transcending Architecture*, edited by Julio Bermudez, Catholic University of America Press, 2015, pp. 113-29.
Seghier, Mohamed L. "The Angular Gyrus." *The Neuroscientist*, vol. 19, no. 1, 2013, pp. 43-61.
Seigworth, Gregory J., and Melissa Gregg. "An Inventory of Shimmers." *The Affect Theory Reader*, edited by Gregg and Seigworth, Duke University Press, 2010, pp. 1-25.

Senft, Nicole, et al. "Within- and Between-Group Heterogeneity in Cultural Models of Emotion Among People of European, Asian, and Latino Heritage in the United States." *Emotion*, Feb. 2022, advance online publication, http://dx.doi.org/10.1037/emo0001052.
Shahar, Meir. "The Lingyin Si Monkey Disciples and the Origins of Sun Wukong." *Harvard Journal of Asiatic Studies*, vol. 52, no. 1, 1992, pp. 193–224.
Shahar, Meir. "Violence in Chinese Religions." *The Oxford Handbook of Religion and Violence*, edited by Mark Juergensmeyer et al., Oxford University Press, pp. 183–96.
Shapiro, Yakov, and J. Rowan Scott. "Extraordinary Knowing Within the Framework of Natural Science." *The Supernatural After the Neuro-turn*, edited by Pieter F. Craffert et al. Routledge, 2019, pp. 148–71.
Sharf, Robert H. *Coming to Terms with Chinese Buddhism*. University of Hawai'i Press, 2002.
Sheldrake, Philip. *Spaces for the Sacred*. Johns Hopkins University Press, 2001.
Shiota, Michelle N., et al. "Transcending the Self." *Handbook of Positive Emotions*, edited by Michele M. Tugade et al., Guilford Press, 2014, pp. 362–77.
Shive, Glenn. "Conclusion." *Chinese Religious Life*, edited by David A. Palmer, et al., Oxford University Press, 2011, pp. 245–54.
Shubin, Neil. *Your Inner Fish*. Random, 2008.
Shults, F. LeRon. "The Problem of Good (and Evil)." *Science and the World's Religions*, vol. 1, edited by Patrick McNamara and Wesley J. Wildman, Praeger, 2012, pp. 39–68.
Shults, F. LeRon. "Science and Religious Supremacy." *Science and the World's Religions*, vol. 3, edited by Patrick McNamara and Wesley J. Wildman, Praeger, 2012, pp. 73–100.
Siegel, Daniel J. *The Developing Mind*. Guilford Press, 1999.
Siegel, Daniel J. "Mindfulness Training and Neural Integration." *SCAN*, vol. 2, 2007, pp. 259–63.
Siep, Nicolette, et al. "Anger Provocation Increases Limbic and Decreases Medial Prefrontal Cortex Connectivity with the Left Amygdala in Reactive Aggressive Violent Offenders." *Brain Imaging and Behavior*, vol. 13, 2019, pp. 1311–23.
Simmonds-Moore, Christine, et al. "Exceptional Experiences Following Exposure to a Sham 'God Helmet': Evidence for Placebo, Individual Difference, and Time of Day Influences." *Imagination, Cognition, and Personality*, vol. 39, no. 1, 2019, pp. 44–87, doi.org/10.1177/0276236617749185.
Siviy, Stephen M. "Play and Adversity." *American Journal of Play*, vol. 2, no. 3, 2010, pp. 297–314.
Skeates, Robin. "Making Sense of the Maltese Temple Period." *Time and Mind*, vol. 1, no. 2, 2008, pp. 207–38.
Smith, Eric C. *Foucault's Heterotopia in Christian Catacombs*. Palgrave, 2014.
Smith, Peter B. "On the Distinctiveness of Chinese Psychology." *The Oxford Handbook of Chinese Psychology*, edited by Michael Harris Bond, Oxford University Press, 2010, pp. 699–710.
Snodgrass, Adrian. *The Symbolism of the Stupa*. Motilal Banarsidass, 1992.
Solms, Mark. *The Hidden Spring*. Norton, 2021.
Solms, Mark, and Oliver Turnbull. *The Brain and the Inner World*. Other Press, 2002.
Solomon, Sheldon, et al. *The Worm at the Core*. Random, 2015.
Sparavigna, Amelia Carolina. "Light and Shadows in Bernini's Oval of St. Peter's Square." *Philica*, no. 540, 2015, n.p.

Spencer-Rodgers, Julie, et al. "What is Dialectical Thinking?" *The Psychological and Cultural Foundations of East Asian Cognition*, edited by Julie Spencer-Rodgers and Kaiping Peng, Oxford University Press, 2018, pp. 1–34.

Stellar, Jennifer E. "Self-Transcendent Emotions and Their Social Functions." *Emotion Review*, vol. 9, no. 3, 2017, pp. 200–7.

Stemp, Richard. *The Secret Language of Churches & Cathedrals*. Duncan Baird, 2010.

Stevens, Keith G. *Chinese Mythological Gods*. Oxford University Press, 2001.

Stratton, Eric. *The Evolution of Indian Stupa Architecture in East Asia*. Vedams, 2000.

Strong, John S. *Relics of the Buddha*. Princeton University Press, 2004.

Stump, Eleonore. "The True Self and Life After Death in Heaven." *Death, Immortality and Eternal Life*, edited by T. Ryan Byerly, Routledge, 2021, pp. 65–81.

Sundararajan, Louise. "Religious Awe." *Journal of Theoretical and Philosophical Psychology*, vol. 22, no. 2, 2002, pp. 174–97.

Sussman, Ann, and Justin B. Hollander. *Cognitive Architecture*. Routledge, 2015.

Tardif, Twila, et al. "Putting the 'Noun Bias' in Context." *Child Development*, vol. 70, no. 3, May/June 1999, pp. 620–35.

Tarocco, Francesca. "On the Market." *Religion*, vol. 41, no. 4, Dec. 2011, pp. 627–44.

Taves, Ann. *Religious Experience Reconsidered*. Princeton University Press, 2009.

Taylor, Charles. *A Secular Age*. Harvard University Press, 2007.

Taylor, Jill Bolte. *Whole Brain Living*. Hay House, 2021.

Teasdale, John. *What Happens in Mindfulness*. Guilford, 2022.

"Temppeliaukio Church." *Zest & Curiosity*, www.zestandcuriosity.com/2021/03/25/temppeliaukio-church-the-rock-church-helsinki/.

"Three Temples at Tianzhu." wgly.hangzhou.gov.cn/art/2013/7/7/art_1229495371_58931665.html.

Thurman, Robert A. F., translator. *The Holy Teaching of Vimalakirti*. Pennsylvania State University, 1976.

Tinoca, Carlos A., and João Ortiz. "Magnetic Stimulation of the Temporal Cortex: A Partial "God Helmet" Replication Study." *Journal of Consciousness Exploration & Research*, vol. 5, no. 3, 2014, pp. 234–57.

Tomkins, Silvan S. *Affect Imagery Consciousness*. 2 volumes, Springer, 2008.

Topa, Wahinkpe (Four Arrows), and Darcia Narvaez. *Restoring* the *Kinship Worldview*. North Atlantic Books, 2022.

Tremlin, Todd. "The Origins of Religion." *Science and the World's Religions*, vol. 1, edited by Patrick McNamara and Wesley J. Wildman, Praeger, 2012, pp. 3–38.

Trimble, Michael R. *The Soul in the Brain*. Johns Hopkins University Press, 2007.

Trump, David. *Malta: Prehistory and Temples*. Sta Venera, 2002.

Tsai, Jeanne L. "Ideal Affect." *Perspectives on Psychological Science*, vol. 2, no. 3, 2007, pp. 242–59.

Tsai, Jeanne L., and Magali Clobert. "Cultural Influences on Emotions." *Handbook of Cultural Psychology*, edited by Dov Cohen and Shinobu Kitayama, 2nd edition, Oxford University Press, 2019, pp. 292–318.

Tsai, Jeanne L., et al. "Good Feelings in Christianity and Buddhism." *Personality and Social Psychology Bulletin*, vol. 33, no. 3, March 2007, pp. 409–21.

Turner, Jonathan H. *The Problem of Emotions in Societies*. Routledge, 2011.

Turner, Victor. *From Ritual to Theatre*. PAJ Publications, 2001.

Vail, Kenneth E. III, et al. "Terror Management Theory and Religion." *Handbook of Terror Management Theory*, edited by Clay Routledge and Matthew Vess, Elsevier, 2019, pp. 259–85.

Vanderschuren, Louk J. M. J., et al. "The Neurobiology of Social Play and Its Rewarding Value in Rats." *Neuroscience & Biobehavioral Reviews*, vol. 70, Nov. 2016, pp. 86–105. https://www.ncbi.nlm.nih.gov/pmc/articles/PMC5074863/.

Varela, Francisco J., et al. *The Embodied Mind*. MIT Press, 1991, 2016.

Vartanian, Oshin, et al. "Impact of Contour on Aesthetic Judgments and Approach-Avoidance Decisions in Architecture." *PNAS*, vol. 110, suppl. 2, 2013, pp. 10446–53.

Virtanen, Keijo. "The Concept of Purification in the Greek and Indian Theories of Drama." *The Pursuit of Comparative Aesthetics: An Interface Between East and West*, edited by Mazhar Hussain and Robert Wilkinson, Ashgate, 2006, pp. 55–84.

Vosko, Richard S. "Trends in Christian Places of Worship." *Sacred Architecture in East and West*, edited by Cyril Hovorun, Marymount Institute Press, 2019, pp. 131–58.

The Wakefield Mystery Plays. Edited by Martial Rose, Doubleday, 1962.

Walter, Yoshija. "Neural Structural Changes Associated with Ritual Glossolalia." *Social Science Research Network SSRN*, 2021, doi.org/10.2139/ssrn.3837534.

Wang Ping. *Aching for Beauty*. University of Minnesota Press, 2000.

Wang, Qijun. *Chinese Architecture*. Better Link, 2011.

Wang, Robin R., ed. *Images of Women in Chinese Thought and Culture*. Hackett, 2003.

Wang, Yuan. *Buddhist Monastery South of the Yangtze*. Jiao Tong University Press, 2010.

Watkins, Edward R. "Mindfulness in the Context of Processing Mode Theory." *Handbook of Mindfulness*, edited by Kirk Warren Brown et al., Guilford, 2015, pp. 90–111.

Watts, Fraser. *Psychology, Religion, and Spirituality*. Cambridge University Press, 2017.

Watts, Ian, et al. "Early Evidence for Brilliant Ritualized Display." *Current Anthropology*, vol. 57, no. 3, June 2016, pp. 287–310.

Weisman, Karen, and TM Luhrmann. "What Anthropologists Can Learn from Psychologists and the Other Way Around." *Journal of the Royal Anthropological Institute*, vol. 26, no. S1, Mar. 2020, pp. 131–47.

Welch, Patricia Bjaaland. *Chinese Art*. Tuttle, 2008.

Wellman, James K., Jr. "Religion and Fanaticism (Is Religion Dangerous?)" *Science and the World's Religions*, vol. 3, edited by Patrick McNamara and Wesley J. Wildman, Praeger, 2012, pp. 25–44.

White, L. Michael. *The Social Origins of Christian Architecture*. Volume 1, Trinity Press International, 1990.

Whitehouse, Harvey, and Brian McQuinn. "Divergent Modes of Religiosity and Armed Struggle." *The Oxford Handbook of Religion and Violence*, edited by Mark Juergensmeyer et al., Oxford University Press, 2013, pp. 597–619.

Wildman, Wesley J., et al. "Religion and Biological Evolution." *Science and the World's Religions*, vol. 3, edited by Patrick McNamara and Wesley J. Wildman, Praeger, 2012, pp. 125–64.

Wilkinson, Richard H. *The Complete Temples of Ancient Egypt*. Thames & Hudson, 2000.

Winkelman, Michael J. "The Evolutionary Origins of the Supernatural in Ritual Behaviours." *The Supernatural After the Neuro-turn*, edited by Pieter F. Craffert et al., Routledge, 2019, pp. 48–68.

Winkelman, Michael J. "Shamanic Alterations of Consciousness as Sources of Supernatural Experiences." *The Supernatural After the Neuro-turn*, edited by Pieter F. Craffert et al., Routledge, 2019, pp. 127–47.

Winkelman, Michael J. "Shamanism and the Brain." *Religion: Mental Religion*, edited by Niki Kasumi Clements, Macmillan Reference, 2017, pp. 355–72.
Winkelman, Michael J. "The Supernatural as Innate Cognitive Operators." *The Supernatural After the Neuro-turn*, edited by Pieter F. Craffert et al., Routledge, 2019, pp. 89–106.
Winkelman, Michael, and John R. Baker. *Supernatural as Natural*. Pearson, 2010.
Winnicott, D. W. *Playing and Reality*. Routledge, 1971, 1990.
Winters, Dennis Alan. "Regarding Sacred Landscapes and the Everyday Corollary." *Architecture, Culture, and Spirituality*, edited by Thomas Barrie and Julio Bermudez, Routledge, 2015, pp. 149–63.
Wong, Eva. *The Shambhala Guide to Taoism*. Shambhala, 1997.
Wong, Y. Joel, and Tao Liu. "Dialecticism and Mental Health." *The Psychological and Cultural Foundations of East Asian Cognition*, edited by Julie Spencer-Rodgers and Kaiping Peng, Oxford University Press, 2018, pp. 547–72.
Wright, Robert. *The Evolution of God*. Little, Brown and Company, 2009.
Wu, Guangzheng. "Buddhist-Taoist Rivalry and the Evolution of the Story of Lü Dongbin's Slaying the Yellow Dragon with the Flying Sword." *Frontiers of Literary Studies in China*, vol. 1 no. 4, 2007, pp. 581–609.
Wu, Jiang, and Daoqin Tong. "Spatial Analysis of Buddhist Monasteries in Contemporary China." Working paper 2012, Department of East Asian Studies, The University of Arizona, Tucson, 2015. https://arizona.academia.edu/JiangWu.
Wu, Nelson I. *Chinese and Indian Architecture*. George Braziller, 1963.
Xinian, Fu. *Traditional Chinese Architecture: Twelve Essays*. Princeton University Press, 2017.
Xinjiang, Rong. "Land Road or Sea Route?" *Sino-Platonic Papers*, vol. 144, July 2004, pp. 1–32, www.sino-platonic.org/complete/spp144_han_dynasty_buddhism.pdf.
Xu, Jiang, et al. "Symbolic Gestures and Spoken Language are Processed by a Common Neural System." *PNAS*, vol. 106, no. 49, 8 Dec. 2009, 20664–9.
Yaden, David Bryce, et al. "Neuroscience and Religion." *Religion: Mental Religion*, edited by Niki Kasumi Clements, Macmillan Reference, 2017, pp. 277–99.
Yaden, David Bryce, et al. "The Varieties of Self-Transcendent Experience." *Review of General Psychology*, vol. 21, no. 2, 2017, pp. 143–60.
Yang, Fenggang. *Religion in China*. Oxford University Press, 2012.
Yang, Lihui, and Deming An, with Jessica Anderson Turner. *Handbook of Chinese Mythology*. Oxford University Press, 2008.
Yang, Ying, et al. "Elicited Awe Decreases Aggression." *Journal of Pacific Rim Psychology*, vol. 10, no. e11, pp. 1–13.
Yanxin, Cai. *Chinese Architecture*. Cambridge University Press, 2011.
Yao, Xinzhong, and Paul Badham. *Religious Experience in Contemporary China*. University of Wales Press, 2007.
Yik, Michelle. "How Unique is Chinese Emotion?" *The Oxford Handbook of Chinese Psychology*, edited by Michael Harris Bond, Oxford University Press, 2010, pp. 205–20.
Yu, Luo Rioux. "Pilgrim or Tourist? The Transformation of China's Revolutionary Holy Land." *Faiths on Display*, edited by Tim Oakes and Donald S. Sutton, Rowman and Littlefield, 2010, pp. 79–102.
Yü, Chün-fang. *Kuan-yin*. Columbia University Press, 2001.
Yü, Dan Smyer. *The Spread of Tibetan Buddhism in China*. Routledge, 2012.

Yü, Ying-Shih. "Individualism and the Neo-Taoist Movement in Wei-Chin China." *Individualism and Holism: Studies in Confucian and Taoist Values*, edited by Donald Munro, University of Michigan Press, 1985, pp.121–55.

Yü, Ying-Shih. "'O Soul, Come Back!' A Study in The Changing Conceptions of The Soul and Afterlife in Pre-Buddhist China." *Harvard Journal of Asiatic Studies*, vol. 47, no. 2, Dec. 1987, pp. 363–95.

Yuasa, Yasuo. *The Body, Self-Cultivation, and Ki-Energy*. State University of New York Press, 1993.

Yun, Qiao. *Taoist Buildings*. China Architecture and Building Press, 2012.

Yuqun, Li. "Classification, Layout, and Iconography of Buddhist Cave Temples and Monasteries." *Early Chinese Religion*, part two, vol. 1, edited by John Lagerwey and Mark Kalinowski, Brill, 2009, pp. 575–666.

Zachar, Peter, and Ralph D. Ellis, editors. *Categorical versus Dimensional Models of Affect*. John Benjamins, 2012.

Zacks, Jeffrey M. *Flicker: Your Brain on Movies*. Oxford University Press, 2015.

Zeki, Semir. "Art and the Brain." *Daedalus*, vol. 127, no. 2, March 1998, pp. 71–104.

Zeki, Semir. *Inner Vision*. Oxford University Press, 1999.

Zeki, Semir. *Splendors and Miseries of the Brain*. Wiley-Blackwell, 2009.

Zhe, Ji. "Buddhism in the Reform Era." *Religion in Contemporary China*, edited by Adam Yuet Chau, Routledge Press, 2011, pp. 32–52.

Zhongshu, Zhao. "Round Sky and Square Earth (Tian Yuan Di Fang)." *GeoJournal*, vol. 26, no. 2, 1992, pp. 149–52.

Zi, Yan. *Famous Temples in China*. Huangshan, 2014.

Ziegler, Charles A., and Benson Saler. "Dying for an Idea." *Science and the World's Religions*, vol. 3, edited by Patrick McNamara and Wesley J. Wildman, Praeger, 2012, pp. 45–72.

Ziporyn, Brook, translator. *Zhuangzi: The Complete Writings*. Hackett Publishing, 2022.

Index

Acts of Peter, The 189–90
Abhinavagupta 83–4, 93
abjection 86, 87, 111, 170, 172, 174
abstraction 5, 33, 45, 63, 76, 136, 168, 173–4, 263, 274
abstractive operator 63–4, 66
actor 7, 13–14, 16–17, 51, 54, 58, 80, 85, 91, 94, 182, 190, 204, 261, 264, 265, 275
addiction 8, 40–1, 50, 52, 272
Adolphs, Ralph, 12
Adorno, Theodor W., 259
Agnati, Luigi F., 6, 57
Alcorta, Candace S., 29
alienation 7, 27, 45, 46, 48, 84–6, 87, 91, 96–7, 102, 243, 251
Alimardani, Maryam, 271–2
alloparenting 9, 40
allostasis 6, 58
altered states of consciousness 14–15, 18, 62, 66–7, 103, 245
altruism 40, 49, 77, 263
Ames, Roger T., 219
Ammaniti, Massimo, 7, 86 n.6
amygdala 9, 16–17, 44, 51–2, 61–2, 67, 70, 152
analytical thinking 15, 19, 56–7, 66, 75, 77–9, 82, 91, 176, 204, 245, 248, 267
Anderson, Miranda, 12
angular gyrus 51, 61
anterior cingulate cortex 35, 51, 52 n.8, 53, 62 n.15, 70, 111, 261
anthropocentrism 60
anticipation-reward (*or* expectation) 6, 49–50, 82, 85–6
antisemitism 42
anxiety 40–1, 44, 48, 56, 68, 77, 142, 263
Arbib, Michael, 32
Arian Baptistery (Ravenna) 157–8, 248–9
Aristotle 8, 79, 84–5, 85 n.22, 93–4, 253
Artaud, Antonin, 84, 93

association areas 65–6, 68–70
Atran, Scott, 28

Baars, Bernard J., 6, 13, 19, 35, 51–2, 68, 74
Badgaiyan, Rajendra D., 53
Baiyun Temple (Shanghai) 272
Baldrian-Hussein, Farzeen, 71
Baohua Temple (Shanghai) 162–3, 166, 171, 258
Barrett, Justin, 53
Barrett, Lisa Feldman, 30 n.16, 95
Barrie, Thomas, 15
Barron, Robert, 260
basal ganglia 53, 61, 111
Basilica of Saint John of God (Granada) 111
Basilica of Saint Peter (Vatican City, Rome) 30–1, 119n7, 184–9, 191, 194, 196–7, 204, 225, 240–1, 263, 265–6
Basilica of Saint Stephen in the Round (Rome) 151–2, 254–5
Basilica of Saints Ambrose and Charles (Rome) 111
Basilica of Saints John and Paul (Rome) 109–11, 247
Bassil-Morozow, Helena, 27, 54 n.11
Bastiaansen, J. A. C. J., 243
Bauer, Wolfgang, 26, 83
Beauregard, Mario, 51, 54
Begg, Ean, 181
Bell, Alexander Peter, 4
belonging 1, 27–30, 39–41, 45–6, 48–9, 89, 91, 96, 97, 142, 154, 156, 236, 244, 263
Bellah, Robert N., 48
Belting, Hans, 192
Bendor, Daniel, 30
Benn, James A., 202
Bering, Jesse, 46
Bermudez, Julio, 15–16, 32
Berridge, Kent C., 49
Bharata, 83–84, 93
binary operator 63, 66, 85, 94, 111, 143

Bio-Cultural Study of Religion 2, 26, 27, 29, 34, 41, 50, 52, 57, 62, 72, 84, 89, 95–6, 222, 224, 228, 240
Birch, Robert, 48
Birrell, Anne, 105, 106
Blackmore, Susan, 149
Blake, C. Fred, 73, 161, 163
Blanke, Olaf, 94 n.25
Blattman, Christopher, 94
Bloom, Irene, 83
Blowers, Geoffrey H., 1
Bolton, Brenda M., 192
bonding 44–6, 49–50, 52, 56, 58, 64, 83, 88, 93, 121, 161, 248, 273, 276
Bonnie, Kristin E., 46
bonobos 30, 41, 74, 76
Borup, Jørn, 272
Bosco, Joseph, 232
Bowen, Sarah, 4, 272
brainstem 36, 51, 68
Brattico, Elvira, 6
Bratton, Susan, 108 n.3
Brecht, Bertolt, 84, 91, 93–4
Brennan, Teresa, 34
Brin, David, 29
Broesch, Tanya, 9 n.7
Broeskamp, Bernadette, 213–14
Brook, Timothy, 26
Brookshire, Geoffrey, 35 n.19
Bruntz, Courtney, 23
Buddha-nature 10, 12, 218
Bulbulia, Joseph, 30
Buswell, Robert E., Jr., 71

Calvo-Merino, Beatriz, 64
Candea, Matei, 6, 8, 60
Cannon, Jon, 29, 114, 219
Carmody, James, 271
Caseau, Béatrice Chevallier, 110, 116
Cassaniti, Julia L., 8, 35
Cathedral of Our Lady (Strasbourg) 138–41, 252–3
Catacomb of Saint Callixtus (Rome) 118
Cathedral of Saint George (Ragusa) 111, 169
Cathedral of Saint Gerland (Agrigento) 111
Cathedral of Saint James (Jerusalem) 183, 262
Cathedral of Saint Leontius (Fréjus) 118
Cathedral of Saint Mary's Assumption (Siena) 111
Cathedral of Saint Peter (Cologne) 136–8
Cathedral of Syracuse 145–6, 159, 254
causal operator 63
Cavarero, Adriana, 19, 20–1, 20 n.14, 57
Cenacle (Jerusalem) 67, 181, 262
cerebellum 16, 36, 51, 61, 69, 111
Chaminade, Thierry, 94 n.25
Chandra, Vikram, 17
Chapel of Silence (Kamppi, Helsinki) 238–40
character 7, 13–14, 16, 51, 54, 75, 94, 204
charity 27, 40, 77, 89, 91, 263
Chau, Adam Yuet, 24, 42
Chen Clan Ancestral Hall (Guangzhou) 114, 248
Chiao, Joan Y., 8–9
chimpanzees 29, 41, 76
Ching, Francis D. K., 103, 107
Ching, Julia, 22–5, 113, 115, 202
Chirico, Alice, 18
Chouchou, Florian, 67
Church of Domine Quo Vadis (Rome) 190, 196, 264
Church of Our Savior (Copenhagen) 140–1, 253
Church of Queen Helen (Jerusalem) 181–2, 262
Church of Saint Alexander Nevsky (Jerusalem) 182, 254, 262
Church of Saint Agnes in Agone (Rome) 120–1, 177, 249
Church of Saint Agnes Outside the Walls (Rome) 120–1
Church of Saint Andrew of the Thickets (Rome) 158–9
Church of Saint Anne (Jerusalem) 180–2, 262
Church of Saint Charles at the Four Fountains (Rome) 158
Church of Saint Constantina (Rome) 119–20, 136, 150–1, 153–4, 249, 254
Church of Saint Ildefonsus (Toledo) 169

Church of Saint Laurence in the Palace at the Holy of Holies (Rome) 192
Church of Saint Martin (Canterbury) 167–8, 257
Church of Saints Sylvester and Martin (Rome) 121–2
Church of the Flagellation (Jerusalem) 179–80, 261–2
Church of the Holy Sepulchre (Jerusalem) 152–6, 176, 179, 181–3, 192, 256–7, 261–2
cingulate cortex 35, 51–3, 62, 70, 111, 261
Clark, Andy, 5, 54
Clark, Margaret, 96
Clausen, David Christian, 181
Coburn, Alex, 33, 58
Cochini, Christian, 112, 130, 160, 194, 203
cognitive reappraisal 51
Cohen, Adam B., 22
Cole, Alan, 88
collectivism 8, 60–1
comedy 94
Confucius (Kong) Family Home (Qufu) 115, 248
consolation 3, 76–7
Constantine Basilica (Lutheran Church of the Redeemer, Trier) 136, 252
contempt 30, 86–88, 94
Cook, Amy, 3
Cook, Scott, 177
Corballis, Michael C., 45, 63–4
costly signaling 22, 30, 44, 179
costume-body definer/designer 16, 51, 53, 63, 65, 67, 69, 73, 75, 94, 105, 111, 143, 175, 204, 250, 260–1
Cox, John, 103
Cozolino, Louis J., 64–5
Crosbie, Michael J., 25, 191, 236

Damasio, Antonio, 30 n.16, 52, 58, 68, 72
Dao 22, 90, 105, 108, 170, 220, 228, 231, 274
d'Aquili, Eugene G., 65–6
Davies, J. G., 118, 119, 151, 153, 155, 157, 158
de Bary, William Theodore, 23

debt 15, 46, 73, 87–91, 172, 178, 199 (*see also* duty)
Default Mode Network 16 (*see also* rumination)
De La Torre, Miguel A., 75, 97, 109, 152
De Leersnyder, Jozefien, 12
delusion 88–91, 93, 250
Demaree, Heath A., 36 n.20, 55, 86 n.7
demon 27, 31, 61, 67, 75, 90–2, 131, 139, 141, 143, 145, 151, 160, 171, 196, 204, 205, 231, 253 (*see also* devil)
Dennett, Daniel, 5, 70
devil 11, 14–15, 22, 27–8, 31, 34, 40, 55, 74, 90, 92, 108, 121, 138–9, 141, 143, 145, 156, 162, 169, 171, 176, 252, 268 (*see also* demon)
Devil's Advocate 55–6, 63, 67, 75, 169, 174, 225
de Visser, M. W., 171, 200
de Vries, Hent, 27
de Waal, Frans, 46, 74, 76
Dharma 90, 124–5, 129, 132, 197, 203, 214, 231–2, 250
dialectical thinking 9, 56, 60, 77–80, 94, 98, 101, 142, 175, 177, 204, 206, 219, 234, 240, 245–6, 252, 268–9, 274
director 51, 53–4, 93–4, 129, 152, 190, 204, 250, 255, 261, 265, 275
disgust 6, 30, 40, 55, 61, 75, 83–4, 86–8, 90–1, 95, 111–12, 121, 124, 139, 152, 186, 263, 276
Ditan (*see* Temple of Earth)
Dix, Dom Gregory, 31, 109, 116, 118
Dome of the Rock (Temple Mount, Jerusalem) 155–6, 179, 257
Domínguez, Juan F., 77
Donald, Merlin, 47–8
Donglin Temple (Shanghai) 145, 164–5, 167, 258
dopamine 8, 44, 49–50, 53, 56, 65, 83, 85, 96
dorsolateral prefrontal cortex (DLPFC) 51, 53, 61, 261, 275
dorsomedial prefrontal cortex (DMPFC) 51, 53, 130, 261, 275
Douglas-Klotz, Neil, 80
Downey, Daniel H., 21, 27

Dox, Donnalee, 12
dreams 1, 5, 13–14, 30–1, 43
Dunbar, Robin, 44, 46
Dunlap, Aron, 108
duty 18, 28, 73, 88–91, 162, 170, 240, 245 (*see also* debt *and* filiality)

Eagleman, David, 13
Eberhard, John P., 16, 31
Ebisch, Sjoerd J. H., 7
Edelman, Gerald M., 6, 70
Ejova, Anastasia, 18
elevation 18–19, 86–8, 94, 135, 147
Eller, Cynthia, 104
emotional contagion 6, 34, 52, 66, 76, 176, 243
empathy 7, 17, 40, 51, 53, 57, 59, 61, 64, 75, 76, 77, 86, 93, 152 (*see also* sympathy)
epigenetics 9, 39
epilepsy 62–3, 94 n.25
equanimity 17, 23, 29, 59, 89–90, 127, 162, 171, 255, 260
ethics 17, 20, 47, 82, 87, 89–90, 112, 203 (*see also* morality)
expectation (*see* anticipation-reward)

fairness 40, 43, 47, 76–7, 86–7, 263
Family Extensions Model 31–2, 34, 95–8
Farb, Norman A. S., 272
Farrer, C., 94
Faure, Bernard, 15
Fernández-Cobián, Esteban, 236
Fernyhough, Charles, 13
Fields, R. Douglas, 52 n.7, n.8
filiality 18, 22, 42, 79, 88–90, 104, 162, 170, 172, 180, 229, 245
Fine, Cordelia, 28 n.15
Fink, Bruce, 96
fish 68–9, 108, 158, 164, 165, 167, 211, 218, 258, 268, 274
Fisher, Gareth, 23, 24
Fiske, Allan Page, 8
foot-binding 73
Foucault, Michel, 193
4E cognition 12
Fowler, Jeaneane, 107
Frankfurter, David, 27

Freedberg, David, 53, 64
freedom (*or* liberty), 5, 40, 44, 77, 78, 86–7, 102, 195, 205, 263–4
Fuentes, Augustín, 36, 47

Gallese, Vittorio, 6–7, 64, 86 n.6, 243
Gan, Xianyang, 86 n.2
Gautam, Neeraj, 160, 162
Gazzaniga, Michael S., 54
George, David E. R., 17, 17 n.12, 31, 91
Geva, Anat, 178
ghost money (*see* spirit money)
Giant Maitreya, 133–5
Gibson, James J., 49
Gildow, Douglas M., 205 n.3
Giljov, Andrey, et al., 55
Gilligan, Carol, 20 n.14
Gimbutas, Marija, 104
Gintis, Herbert, 47
Girard, René, 75, 85, 85 n.22, 97
Global Workspace Theory 6, 52
glossolalia (speaking in tongues) 65–7, 70, 143
Goettner-Abendroth, Heide, 20, 72, 104, 105
Goffman, Erving, 6
Goh, J. O., 82
Goodison, Lucy, 104
goodness 46, 94, 145, 157, 161, 193
Goossaert, Vincent, 25, 231
Gordon, Amie M., 18–19
Gottschall, Jonathan, 49
Gough, Michael, 119
Graeber, David, 20, 72–3, 104, 249
Graham, Jesse, 87
gratitude 4, 17, 40, 46, 47, 74, 86–90, 94, 113, 243, 263
Graziano, Michael S. A., 52–3, 53 n.9
Gribble, Father Richard, 180
grief 20, 30, 40, 45, 47–8, 50, 76, 84, 86, 95–6, 114, 121, 161, 164, 179–80, 183, 185–7, 189, 191, 263 (*see also* pity *and* sadness)
Griffith, Brian, 106, 115
Grigg, Richard, 11
grooming/gossip 30, 39–40, 45–9, 75, 88, 161, 170, 241, 245, 270

Guan, Fang, 62
guilt 16, 30, 37, 40, 56, 75, 85–8, 91, 94, 102, 149, 263
Guthrie, Stewart, 52–3

Hagar Qim and Mnajdra temples (Malta), 103–5
Haidt, Jonathan, 18, 85–7
hamartia (error in judgment) 84
Hamilton, J. Paul, 16 n.11
Han, Shihui, 37, 261, 275
Hansen, Chad, 83
happiness 8, 84, 86–7, 92, 125, 132, 210
Harrell, Stevan, 71
Harries, Karsten, 79 n.20
Harvey, Peter, 23, 25–6, 71, 91, 92
hate 4, 50, 84, 93
Hatfield, Elaine, 6
Hayden, Robert M., 245
Hecht, David, 55, 85–6
hindbrain 36, 68
hippocampus 13, 30, 51–2, 61–2, 70, 111
Hoffman, Donald, 11, 11 n.10, 13
holistic operator 63, 66, 94
Hollander, Justin, 31–2
Holtmann, Olga, 86 n.2
Holy Family Basilica (Barcelona) 141–2, 253
Holy Savior Church (Noto) 116
Holy Stairs (Rome) 190–3, 264
homeostasis 6, 47, 58, 245
Homo erectus 46–7
Horkheimer, Max, 259
Howe, David, 98 n.29
Hrdy, Sarah Blaffer, 9 n.7, 18, 45
Hualin Temple (Guangzhou) 145
humility 4, 56, 60, 228
Hureau, Sylvie, 122
hypothalamus 36, 44, 51, 66

Iacoboni, Marco, 64
Iannaccone, Laurence R., 30
Ichiko, Shiga, 229
Imaginary dimension (Lacan) 10, 20, 39, 45, 55–6, 59, 64–5, 74, 93, 97
insula 49, 51–2, 57, 61–2, 67, 139, 152, 261, 272

Irving, Julie Anne, 271
Ishizu, Tomohiro, 111

Jablonka, Eva, 39
James, Craig A., 149 n.9
Jensen, Robin Margaret, 158
Jing'an Temple (Shanghai) 160–2, 258, 272
Johnston, Adrian, 10 n.8
Johnstone, Brick, 12, 22, 50
Jones, Lindsay, 25, 178, 185, 225
Joseph, Rhawn, 62
Juergensmeyer, Mark, 27

Kandel, Eric, 111 n.9
Kawabata, Hideaki, 111
Keltner, Dacher, 18
Kilde, Jeanne Halgren, 15, 92, 109, 117–18, 135, 141, 147, 153, 155, 236, 257
Kim, Hongkyung, 108, 228
Kimball, Charles, 43
King, Karen L., 4
kinship 20, 37, 49, 77, 94, 97, 112–14, 116
Kirkpatrick, Lee A., 49, 68, 98 n.29
Kitts, Margo, 91
Knapp, Keith N., 113, 114
Knight, Chris, 72, 104
Knott, Kim, 55
Ko, Dorothy, 73
Konior, Jan, 90
Krautheimer, 151–2, 153
Kringelbach, Morten L., 95
Kristeva, Julia, 45, 111 n.4, 172 n.14

Lacan, Jacques, 7, 10, 20, 45, 55–6
Lakoff, George, 85–6
Laland, Kevin N., 50
lamb (*or* Lamb of God) 69, 158, 183, 261
Lanteaume, Laura, 67
Laozi, 42, 105 n.1, 108, 123, 170, 228, 230, 232
Larsson, Marcus, 62 n.15
lateral prefrontal cortex (LPFC) 51, 54, 61, 130, 261, 275
Lateran Baptistery (Rome) 158–9, 257
Lau, Hi-Po Bobo, 79
Lavin, Irving, 184–5
Lawtoo, Nidesh, 6, 85 n.22

LeDoux, Joseph, 95
Lehrner, Amy, 9 n.6
Leighton, Taigen Daniel, 71, 160
Lembke, Anna, 8
Leuzinger-Bohleber, Marianne, 44
Levi, Jean, 112–13
Lewis, Mark Edward, 106, 112
Lewis-Williams, David, 103
Li, Peter Ping, 79–80, 204
Li, Wanqing, 16 n.11
liberty (*see* freedom)
Lieberman, Matthew D., 13, 51–4
lighting/sound operator 51, 53–4, 93–4, 105, 169, 204, 250
Lingyin Scenic Area with Feilai Feng caves (Hangzhou) 194–7, 205
Lingyin Temple (Hangzhou) 197–205
Lip, Evelyn, 107, 108, 219
Litian, Fang, 112, 124, 129
Liu, Shi S., 82
Liu, Yanjun, 255 n.1
Lloyd, Michael, 18
Londero, Alain, 61
Lopez, Jr., Donald S., 260
Lower Tianzhu Temple (Hangzhou) 209–10, 268
loyalty 4, 23, 79, 83, 86–7, 89–90, 112, 121, 172
Luhrmann, Tanya Marie, 3, 8, 35, 60, 67, 68, 70–1, 261
lust 30, 40–1, 76, 84, 85, 86, 88, 95, 142, 145, 177, 197, 263
Lutheran Cathedral (Helsinki) 148, 234–6
Lutheran High Church of Saint Michael (Hamburg) 169
Lutheran Rock Church (Temppeliaukion, Helsinki) 236–8, 240

MacKinnon, Ian, 114
Mai, Cuong T., 10, 23
Maison Carrée (Nimes) 149
Malik, Akhtar, 197, 201
Mallgrave, Harry Francis, 32
Malone, Caroline, 104
Marcellinus, Ammanius, 249
Marinkovic, Ksenija, 86 n.6
Mason, David V., 14

Masuda, Takahiko, 57
Mateo, M. Martínez, 60 n.14
Mathews, Thomas F., 117, 158, 189
matriarchy 20, 60, 72, 104–5
Mavelli, Luca, 45
McAvan, Emily, 74
McCormick, Kelly, 96 n.27
McDaniel, June, 83 n.21
McGilchrist, Iain, 35, 51–2, 54 n.10, 54 n.12, 55–57, 59–61, 77, 85, 265
McNamara, Denis R., 135, 138, 144, 147, 184, 260
McNamara, Patrick, 12, 82, 104, 110, 115–16, 130, 143, 253
Meccarelli, Marco, 209
medial prefrontal cortex (MPFC) 16, 51, 53, 54, 58, 80, 130, 261, 275
Mee, Erin B., 17
Melley, Timothy, 3
memory (re)consolidation 13–14, 30, 244
Mesquita, Batja, 12
Meyer, Jeffrey F., 35, 124–5, 162, 167
Michl, Petra, 85
Middle Tianzhu Temple (Hangzhou) 210–13, 258, 268, 269
Mignerot, Vincent, 61
Miles, Margaret R., 150
Miller, Lisa, 272
Min, Hu, 160
mindfulness 2, 16, 19, 51, 54, 57, 80, 84, 95, 121, 178, 193, 216, 271–2
mirror neurons 6–7, 32, 53, 64, 66, 143, 152, 243
misrecognition 7 (*see also* recognition)
Mitchell, Donald W., 10, 250
Mollier, Christine, 42
morality 14, 63, 70, 75, 168, 174, 195, 200, 203 (*see also* ethics)
Morgan, David, 185, 199
mourning 40, 92, 113, 154, 172
Mozina, David J., 24, 90
Munro, Donald, 22, 82–3
mysticism 4, 5, 7, 18, 34, 62, 65–7, 70, 180

Nakatani, Hironori, 86 n.3
Nakul, Estelle, 94 n.25
Nanhai Guanyin (Mt. Putuo Island) 269

Naparstek, Michael E., 231
Naquin, Susan, 220
Narvaez, Darcia, 1 n.1, 54 n.12
Nedostup, Rebecca, 42
Nelson, Kevin, 53, 62 n.15, 111
New Mosque (Istanbul) 156, 257
Newberg, Andrew, 51, 63, 65–7, 69–70, 85, 94 n.25, 95, 143, 191, 260–1
Ng, Emily, 8
Ni, Xueting Christine, 11, 71, 202–03
Nibley, Hugh, 105
Nietzsche, Friedrich, 7, 44, 138
nirvana 10, 23, 71, 89, 129, 167, 193, 201 (*see also* parinirvana)
Nisbett, Richard E., 57, 77–9, 81
noradrenalin 44, 56, 65
Norenzayan, Ara, 18, 44

occipital cortex 19, 68
Old Cathedral (Brescia) 150, 254
O'Malley, John W., 31, 253
Oosterwijk, Suzanne, 95 n.26
opioid (*or* endorphin) 44, 45–46, 49–50, 65, 96
orbital frontal cortex 49 n.6, 53, 111
original sin 88–89, 91, 154, 169–70, 178, 180–1
Oughourlian, Jean-Michel, 97
Out of Body Experience 94 n.25
oxytocin 44, 46, 49–50, 83, 87, 96

Pagani, Catherine, 129
Pallasmaa, Juhani, 32
Palmer, Martin, 104, 105 n.2, 171, 194, 213
panic 30, 40, 45, 47, 48, 50, 67, 76, 84, 86, 96, 243, 263
Panksepp, Jaak, 30 n.16, 35, 49 n.5, 84, 86, 95 n.26
Pantheon (Church of Saint Mary and the Martyrs, Rome) 16, 149–50, 151, 152
Papalexandrou, Amy, 148
Paper, Jordan, 113, 220
parinirvana 125, 131, 250 (*see also* nirvana)
Park, BoKyung, 80
Parker, Suzanne C., 16
Parrinder, Gary, 125

Peiffer-Smadja, Nathan, 96
Pellis, Sergio, 44
Peng, Shengjie, 255 n.2
Pérez-Gómez, Albert, 32 n.17
Persinger, Michael A., 62–3, 65, 70, 94 n.25
Philipchalk, Ron, 67
Piff, Paul K., 16–17
pity 84, 93, 187 (*see also* grief *and* sadness)
plot twist 84, 93
Poceski, Mario, 25, 42,
Pollock, Sheldon, 83
Poo, Mu-chou, 163 n.11
Power, Camilla, 72, 104
Prandi, Adriano, 110
precuneus 51, 58, 61–2
predator 10, 28, 30, 44, 45, 56–7, 228, 245, 255, 256, 275
Preston, Stephanie D., 76
prey 56–7, 152, 245, 255
pride 28, 30, 40–1, 77, 86–7, 89, 172, 249, 263
primates 28–30, 39, 41, 43–7, 49, 55, 69, 76–7, 146
Pringle, Denys, 183
Prinz, Jesse, 82, 85–7
Prochazkova, Eliska, 243
projection 2–3, 6, 20, 21, 28, 32, 34, 56, 72, 74, 76, 87, 91, 93, 94, 102, 147, 173, 178, 181, 193, 243, 244, 271, 273
Prothero, Stephen, 22, 68, 90, 91
Puett, Michael J., 172
puppeteer 68

Qibao Temple (Shanghai) 250–1
qilin 206, 208, 258, 267, 268
Quinter, David, 164

Ramachandran, V. S., 32–3, 55, 61–2, 70, 94 n.25, 96
rats 30, 33, 44
Raz, Gil, 129
Real dimension 10, 45, 55, 75, 96, 172
Reardon, Wendy J., 186
reciprocal altruism (*see* altruism)
recognition 5, 7, 9, 17, 52, 54, 74, 84, 94, 152, 173, 232, 248, 271
Re'em, Amit, 181

Reeves, Gene, 202
Reis-Habito, Maria, 29
Renoult, Julien P., 33
reptile 68, 108, 209
Ricard, Matthieu, 10 n.9
Richie, Cristina, 131–3
Ritzinger, Justin, 92
Roberts, Robert C., 88
Robson, James, 25, 36, 122
Rodríguez, Guillermo, 83
Roepstorff, Andreas, 21, 54
Rolls, Edmund T., 6
Rossano, Matt J., 47
Roth, Leland M., 119, 136, 144, 149–50
Rothman, Naomi, 255 n.1
Roughgarden, Joan, 79 n.18
Ruby, Perrine, 94 n.25
Rudd, Melanie, 18
Rufford, Juliet, 32 n.18
rumination 16, 271–2
Russell, James A., 30 n.16, 95 n.26
Ryff, Carol D., 80

sadness 61, 83–4, 87, 125, 218, 272 (*see also* grief *and* pity)
Sagan, Carl, 68
Sahlins, Marshall, 72
salience 16, 18, 35, 50, 52, 57, 61, 62, 64, 95, 121
salvation 22, 23, 25, 89, 91, 253
sanctity 86–7, 120, 122, 127, 142, 264
Sanyuan Palace (Guangzhou) 229–34, 239, 240, 271
Scarantino, Andrea, 95 n.26
Schaeffer, Kurtis R., 122
Schechner, Richard, 29, 93
Scheff, Thomas J., 94
Schimel, Jeff, 41
Schinz, Alfred, 24–5, 105–6
Schipper, Kristofer, 23, 170, 219–20
Schott, G. D., 152
Schroeder, Timothy, 49 n.6
Scott, Janet Lee, 163, 164 n.12
Scranton, Laird, 107
Seasoltz, Keven, 186
security 16, 40, 41, 67, 76, 97–8, 181, 184, 263, 269, 270, 273

Seghier, Mohamed L., 61
Seigworth, Gregory J., 7
Senft, Nicole, 8
sensorimotor cortex 36, 51, 70, 111
serotonin 9, 62, 65
Shahar, Meir, 24, 194, 204
shame 30, 40, 56, 84–8, 90–1, 94, 150, 263
Shapiro, Yakov, 66
Sharf, Robert H., 22, 220
Sheldrake, Philip, 24
Shiota, Michelle N., 18
Shive, Glenn, 23
Shubin, Neil, 68 n.16
Shults, F. LeRon, 34, 168 n.13
Siegel, Daniel J., 35, 54, 272
Siep, Nicolette, 86 n.1
Simmonds-Moore, Christine, 62 n.15
Siviy, Stephen M., 30
Skeates, Robin, 103, 104
Smith, Eric C., 119
Smith, Peter B., 8, 261
Snodgrass, Adrian, 107
Solms, Mark, 13, 30 n.16, 48, 49, 50, 51, 57
Solomon, Sheldon, 47
Solomon's Temple 147, 179
Sparavigna, Amelia Carolina, 184
Spencer-Rodgers, Julie, 79
spirit (*or* ghost) money 15, 31, 90, 160–63, 167, 172, 218, 247, 258, 272, 274
spirit tablet 35, 113–16, 162, 167, 178, 222, 224–5, 227, 247, 248, 270
stage/film editor 51, 53, 61, 94, 261, 275
stage manager 7, 14, 26, 35, 49, 51–4, 58, 70, 75, 94, 105, 111, 125, 129, 130, 133, 139, 166, 169, 175–6, 190, 204, 231, 247, 250
staging of consciousness 1–2, 6–7, 16–18, 36, 45, 52–4, 59, 63–5, 67, 69, 72, 74, 93, 95–6, 101, 144, 149, 152, 156, 164, 168, 204, 218, 240, 244, 246, 270, 275
Stellar, Jennifer E., 17 n.13
Stemp, Richard, 116, 121, 146
Stevens, Keith G., 106, 108
Stratton, Eric, 107
striatum 44, 51, 80
Strong, John S., 122, 194
Stump, Eleonore, 6 n.4

subconsciousness 6, 17, 50, 61, 96, 213, 243 (*see also* unconscious)
submission 18-19, 55, 86 n.7, 89-90, 91, 157, 176, 193, 241
Sundararajan, Louise, 67
surprise 15, 30, 30 n.16, 40, 84, 86, 111 n.5, 124, 135, 211, 263
Sussman, Ann, 31-2
sutras 10, 81, 90, 92, 125, 129, 193-5, 197, 202, 204, 211, 212, 250, 260, 265
Symbolic dimension 9-10, 11, 20, 30, 31, 32, 39, 41, 45, 46, 55-7, 59, 64, 74, 75, 93, 96-7, 108, 113, 117, 168, 171-2, 175, 177, 205, 222, 226
synesthesia (*or* heuraesthesia) 61, 66

Taoguang Temple (Hangzhou), 207-09, 267-8
Tardif, Twila, 9
Tarocco, Francesca, 15, 25
Taves, Ann, 3, 5, 14
Taylor, Charles, 7
Taylor, Jill Bolte, 85 n.23
Teasdale, John, 19, 45-6
Temple of Apollo (Delphi) 144
Temple of Augustus and Livia (Vienne) 149
Temple of Concord (Agrigento) 145, 254
Temple of Earth (Ditan, Beijing) 227-8
Temple of Heaven (Tiantan, Beijing) 106, 219-27, 228, 239-40, 269-71
temporoparietal junction (TPJ) 51, 53, 53 n.9, 61, 94 n.25, 261
terror 18, 30 n.16
terrorism 9 n.6, 27, 34, 74, 76
Terror Management Theory 7, 41, 111
thalamus 13, 36, 44, 51, 66, 67
Tholos (Delphi) 144
Thousand Buddha Mountain (Jinan) 130-3, 135, 251-2
Thurman, Robert A. F., 92
Tianning Temple (Hangzhou) 123-9, 250, 251
Tiantan (*see* Temple of Heaven)
Tinoca, Carlos A., 62
Tomkins, Silvan S., 7

Topa, Wahinkpe (Four Arrows), 48 n.4, 60, 76 n.17
tragedy 94
Tremlin, Todd, 97
Trimble, Michael R., 54, 55 n.13, 62, 63, 67, 70
Trump, David, 103, 104
trust 22, 30, 40, 46, 49, 75, 86-7, 114, 137, 244, 263, 268
Tsai, Jeanne L., 37, 80-2
Turner, Jonathan H., 28
Turner, Victor, 75

unconscious 6, 10 n.8, 11 n.10, 13-14, 45, 56, 59, 71, 74-5, 80 (*see also* subconscious)
Upper Tianzhu Temple (Hangzhou) 213-18, 268-9
Uspenski Cathedral (Helsinki) 148, 234, 254

Vail, Kenneth E. III, 7
Vanderschulen, Louk J. M. J., 44
Varela, Francisco J., 12
Vartanian, Oshin, 35
ventrolateral prefrontal cortex (VLPFC) 51, 53, 93
ventromedial prefrontal cortex (VMPFC) 49, 51-3, 58, 70, 111, 130, 139, 247, 261, 272
Virtanen, Keijo, 17, 93
Vosko, Richard S., 33

Wakefield Mystery Plays 97 n.28
Walter, Yoshija, 67
Wanfo Dong Cave (Jinan) 130-2, 252
Wang Ping, 73
Wang, Qijun, 114-15
Wang, Robin R., 105
Wang, Yuan, 171
Watkins, Edward R., 16
Watts, Fraser, 3, 6, 65, 67, 71, 95
Watts, Ian, 72
Weisman, Karen, 60
Welch, Patricia Bjaaland, 124, 203, 212
Wellman, James K., Jr., 42
Western Wall (Jerusalem) 155-6, 179, 257

White, L. Michael, 117
Whitehouse, Harvey, 74
Wildman, Wesley J., 12
Wilkinson, Richard H., 147
Winkelman, Michael J., 47 n.2, 65–6, 97
Winnicott, D. W., 95
Winters, Dennis Alan., 178
Wong, Eva, 71, 90, 207
Wong, Y. Joel, 79 n.19
Wright, Robert, 18
Wu, Guangzheng, 207
Wu, Jiang, 26
Wu, Nelson I., 107, 223

Xinian, Fu, 225
Xinjiang, Rong, 194
Xu, Jiang, 64

Yaden, David Bryce, 18, 50
Yang, Fenggang, 24
Yang, Lihui, 35, 105, 106, 115, 224, 227–8
Yang, Ying, 18
Yan Hui Temple (Qufu) 115, 248
Yanxin, Cai, 115, 129, 219

Yao, Xinzhong, 24
Yik, Michelle, 8, 9
Yongfu Temple (Hangzhou) 205–07, 209, 258, 267, 268
Yu, Luo Rioux, 124
Yü, Chün-fang, 213
Yü, Dan Smyer, 24
Yü, Ying-Shih, 71, 83
Yuan Ming Temple (Shanghai) 160
Yuasa, Yasuo, 90 n.24
Yufo Temple (Shanghai) 167, 258
Yun, Qiao, 170
Yunxiang Temple (Shanghai) 166–7, 168, 171, 258
Yuqun, Li, 129–30

Zachar, Peter, 95 n.26
Zacks, Jeffrey M., 51, 52, 53
Zeki, Semir, 33, 111
Zhe, Ji, 61
Zhongshu, Zhao, 219
Zi, Yan, 196, 201
Ziegler, Charles A., 4, 12, 27
Ziporyn, Brook, 219

www.ingramcontent.com/pod-product-compliance
Lightning Source LLC
Chambersburg PA
CBHW070015010526
44117CB00011B/1581